Two Visions of the Way

SUNY Series in Chinese Philosophy and Culture
David L. Hall and Roger T. Ames, Editors

Two Visions of the Way

A Study of the Wang Pi
and the Ho-shang Kung
Commentaries on the *Lao-Tzu*

Alan K. L. Chan

STATE UNIVERSITY OF NEW YORK PRESS

Published by
State University of New York Press, Albany

For information, address State University of New York
Press, State University Plaza, Albany, N.Y., 12246

Library of Congress Cataloging-in-Publication Data

Chan, Alan Kam-leung, 1956–
    Two visions of the way : a study of the Wang Pi and the Ho-Shang
  Kung commentaries on the Lao-Tzu / Alan K. L. Chan.
      p.   cm. — (SUNY series in Chinese philosophy and culture)
    Includes bibliographical references.
    ISBN 0–7914–0455–2 (alk. paper). — ISBN 0–7914–0456–0 (pbk. :
  alk. paper)
    1. Lao-tzu. Tao te ching. 2. Wang, Pi, 226–249. 3. Ho-shang
  -kung, 2nd cent. B.C.   I. Title. II. Series.
  BL1900.L35C48   1990
  299′.51482—dc20   89-78198
                                               CIP

10 9 8 7 6 5 4 3 2 1

To my teachers,
Professors Julia Ching and Klaus Klostermaier

Contents

Preface

What characterizes a "classic," David Tracy writes, is "nothing less than the disclosure of a reality we cannot but name truth."[1] Tracy's "classics" are not limited to written works, but these words apply well to the Chinese classics, foundational texts such as the *I ching* (Book of Changes) and *Lun-yü* (Analects), which are recognized as paradigmatic and normative, and which have exerted a profound influence on the development of Chinese culture and thought. This study initially grew out of a deep fascination with one such classic, the *Lao-tzu* or *Tao-te ching* (Classic of the Way and Virtue).

No doubt, there are other factors that are equally important in the shaping of what has generally been termed the Chinese tradition. Moreover, the kind of domination and ideological control that the classics have been made to justify and support throughout the long course of Chinese history should not be overlooked. Nonetheless, the classics *are* bearers of "truth." They demand attention, and in some instances devotion, because we recognize in them, to use Tracy's words again, "something 'important' . . . which surprises, provokes, challenges, shocks, and eventually transforms us; an experience that upsets conventional opinions and expands the sense of the possible; indeed a realized experience of that which is essential, that which endures."[2] This calls to mind the more succinct comment made by "Master Ch'eng" on the *Lun-yü:* "If having read the *Lun-yü,* you remain the same kind of person you were before, then you have not really read it."[3] To raise this primary experience to the level of reflection, to articulate the content of this hermeneutical encounter, marks a key task of the interpreter of the Chinese classics.

The classic status of the *Lao-tzu* has been recognized for over two thousand years. The wealth of interpretations and translations testifies to the enduring significance of its insights, its "disclosure of reality" centering on the notion of Tao, the "Way." (Like other great classics the *Lao-tzu* seems to contain an inexhaustible fund of meaning that invites interpretation and reinterpretation. With each interpretation, the hermeneutical experience grows richer.) Students of the *Lao-tzu* can stand on the shoulders of abler and more insightful masters in their quest for understanding. Some, to be sure, may feel that the countless interpretations have become a sort of "burden," and that to understand the *Lao-tzu* one must go directly to the text itself. There is room for this approach in *Lao-tzu* scholarship. In my case, however, my initial interest in the *Lao-tzu* has led me to seek help from the acknowledged masters of the field.

The same process can be discerned in the works of traditional Chinese writers as well. They too relied on earlier commentators in their attempts to penetrate into the *Lao-tzu.* A hermeneutical tradition emerges. It informs not only the readers of the *Lao-tzu,* but because of its normative significance, the development of Chinese intellectual history as a whole. The recognition of the "truth" of the *Lao-tzu,* and the consequent explication of its meaning, have come to play a central role in the development of Chinese thought. A number of interpreters themselves have been recognized as "classic" figures, who inspire and give rise to new currents of thought.

The history of interpretations of the *Lao-tzu,* in other words, is itself an important topic worthy of serious attention. As a student of "classic" texts, I was thus drawn to a study of the commentaries on the *Tao-te ching.* This study is not about the *Lao-tzu* itself. It is a study of two commentaries, occasioned by a hermeneutical reflection of the significance of the *Lao-tzu* and the way in which it has shaped the course of Chinese intellectual history.

The commentaries by Wang Pi and Ho-shang Kung, which form the focus of this book, have long been recognized as the two most important commentaries on the *Lao-tzu.* In addition to their understanding of the primary text, I am also interested in the way they operated as interpreters. The process by which they have arrived at their views proves to be as revealing as their interpretations.

This study is not an exercise in hermeneutical theory, but it acknowledges the important concern with basic issues of understanding and interpretation. Recently, in an essay on higher education, Jonathan Z. Smith has argued that the measure of a mature reflection "lies primarily in an attitude towards words and discourse," where:

> words are no longer thought to be expressive of things; in philosophical terms, they are no longer "real"; they are no longer vocabularies to be mastered ("30 minutes a day") or to be judged by the degree to which they correspond to something "out there". . . . Rather than evaluate the relationship of words to things, we evaluate the relationship of words to other words and to other acts of human imagination. It is a process that has many names, but, above all, it is known as argument.[4]

My study of Wang Pi and Ho-shang Kung, in this regard, is also concerned with their attitudes toward "words and discourse," toward meaning. The relationship between words and things is a crucial consideration in my analysis of the two commentaries, especially in the concluding chapter. As we shall see, the kind of "correspondence" model that Smith rejects is precisely what characterizes Ho-shang Kung's hermeneutical universe. Wang Pi's interpretive enterprise, on the other hand, is much more conceptual and resembles what Smith has described here. There is, however, no need to pitch the two models against one another. Both sense and referent, it would appear, are equally significant constituents of meaning.

Taking Smith's emphasis on "argument" into account, I should add that the views to be presented here, despite the considerable attention to historical and technical details, do not claim to be exhaustive, and still less "definitive." The arguments by which they are brought to light, however, are, I hope, made sufficiently clear, if not persuasive. Similarly, little insistence is placed on the particular technical terms to which I have resorted in my discussion. They serve well enough in this context; but I would be the first to change them if more appropriate alternatives come to light.

Many have helped to chart the course of my thinking and research, and it is a pleasant duty to acknowledge their kindness and encouragement here. I remember fondly my first trip to Peking, when I began work on this study, to seek advice from Fung Yu-lan, and my visits to two other masters of Chinese studies, Wing-tsit Chan and D. C. Lau. Short visits though they were, they made a powerful and lasting impression. I also thank Kanaya Osamu for sharing his expert knowledge on early China with me by correspondence, and Roger Ames for his valuable criticism. I am grateful to Elizabeth Moore and her staff at SUNY Press for the work they have done on my manuscript. My colleagues in the department of religion, University of Manitoba, have been most supportive as I try to find my way in academe. The Social Sciences and Humanities Research Council of Canada provided the much appreciated financial support without which the completion of this study would not have been possible.

Kenneth Hamilton and Carl Ridd first directed me to the path of learning, from which I hope I will never stray. Willard Oxtoby did much, and still does, in his warm and charming way, to keep me there. My friend, K. K. Luke of the University of Hong Kong, pushes me along as he walks the same path with more assured steps. At crucial moments, Jan Yün-hua and Yü Ying-shih have given me help and guidance. My sincere thanks go to all of them. Above all, I have the good fortune of having studied under two outstanding teachers, Julia Ching and Klaus Klostermaier, who exemplify the "classic" teacher and scholar, and to whom I owe more than I can ever repay. This imperfect study is offered to them as a small token of my gratitude.

Introduction

The history of interpretation of the *Lao-tzu*, or *Tao-te ching* (The Classic of the Way and Virtue), spans over two thousand years. Few texts in world history, indeed, have commanded as much respect and attention as this Taoist work. The *Lao-tzu* was first recognized as a "classic" *(ching)* in the Han dynasty (202 B.C.– 220 A.D.), and since that time a steady stream of commentators have attempted to lay bare its meaning. A great number of their works have been lost, but over three hundred fifty, according to one count, are still in existence.[1] This study is devoted to two of them: namely, the commentary by Wang Pi (226–249 A.D.) and that ascribed to the second-century B.C legendary figure Ho-shang Kung.

The importance of traditional commentaries goes beyond the interpretation of the *Lao-tzu* itself. They are crucial to our understanding of Chinese intellectual history as a whole, where, as Wolfgang Bauer so aptly puts it, "the most important thoughts emerge in Hermeneutics."[2] In other words, the unfolding of Chinese intellectual history is characterized by a profound recognition of the power of tradition. New ideas take shape and blossom into view only as interpreters discern the words of the ancient sages, as they find new meanings in the older classics.

Beginning with the Han dynasty, commentaries have become the chief medium through which new insights were developed in traditional China. Individual commentators, to be sure, may employ different approaches in their work. Some may focus on grammatical or lexical explanations, while others discourse on the meaning of a text as a whole. The important point, however, remains that, sustained and informed by tradition, commentary is a form of interpretation in which the new arises out of the old, and the two are fused into a unified whole. This study is addressed not only to readers of the *Lao-tzu*, but to the wider community of students of Chinese intellectual history also.

Among the commentaries on the *Lao-tzu*, Wang Pi's and Ho-shang Kung's are undoubtedly the most important. They are the oldest surviving, complete commentaries on the *Tao-te ching*, and in many respects they have set the standard for later commentators. Indeed, the text of the *Lao-tzu* as we have it today is preserved mainly through these two commentaries. It is true that references to the *Lao-tzu* are already found in such early works as the *Chuang-tzu* and the *Huai-nan tzu;* but they remain isolated and are made to lend support to ideas in different contexts.[3] The earliest *Lao-tzu* interpreter is the philosopher Han Fei-tzu (d. 233 B.C.), who is remembered by later historians as a key figure in the "legalist" tradition *(fa-chia)*. Yet even his work is confined to an exposition of selected passages, which are also correlated with concrete "historical" situations to bring out important "legalist" teachings.[4]

The first full commentaries on the *Lao-tzu* did not appear until the Han dynasty. Four such works, in fact, are recorded in the bibliographical section of the *Han-shu* (History of the Former Han Dynasty).[5] Unfortunately, they are no longer extant. There is also a commentary attributed to the first-century B.C. recluse Yen Tsun. But its authenticity remains a problem, and the first part of the commentary has been lost.[6] Similarly, the *Hsiang-erh* commentary, an important work in the institutionalized Taoist religion discovered in Tun-huang and generally dated to around 200 A.D., is incomplete; only the first part has survived.[7] As we shall see, this work is likely indebted to the Ho-shang Kung commentary itself.

Thus, whereas other early commentaries have not withstood the test of time, those by Ho-shang Kung and Wang Pi remain securely anchored at the head of the tradition of *Lao-tzu* studies. Their visions of the *Lao-tzu* have charted the interpretive territories that later commentators were to traverse again. Without exaggeration, subsequent commentaries were as much an encounter with these two works as with the *Lao-tzu* itself. To understand how *Lao-tzu* studies have developed in traditional China, and how that development has shaped Chinese religion and thought, one needs to begin with a careful study of the Wang Pi and the Ho-shang Kung commentaries.

Between the two, despite the popularity of Wang Pi's work in recent times, the Ho-shang Kung commentary was the dominant one in Chinese history up to perhaps the Sung dynasty (960–1279 A.D.). The stele texts of the *Lao-tzu* inscribed during the T'ang dynasty (618–906 A.D.) by imperial command, for example, were mostly based on a Ho-shang Kung version.[8] The authority of the Ho-shang Kung commentary can be traced to its place in the Taoist religion. In Taoist literature, it ranks second only to the text of the *Lao-tzu* itself.[9] Because the commentary speaks of divine beings in its interpretation of the *Lao-tzu,* and because it emphasizes a type of self-cultivation oriented toward personal "immortality," we can easily appreciate why it would be treasured by later Taoists. For this reason also, it has been condemned as "religious propaganda" by some scholars. This is one of the issues that we must carefully examine in subsequent chapters. Although traditionally considered a work of the early Han dynasty, presented to Emperor Wen (r. 179–157 B.C.) by Ho-shang Kung, the commentary may be dated to the Later Han period (25–220 A.D.). It reflects earlier ideas, however. As I shall argue, it was influenced by the Huang-lao tradition, the school of the Yellow Emperor and Lao-tzu, which dominated the intellectual and political scene of the early Han period.

In spite of its importance in Chinese history, the Ho-shang Kung commentary has been somewhat neglected in modern scholarship. Eduard Erkes's 1950 English translation remains the only major study in a Western language, notwithstanding the growing concern with respect to the need for a more critical and updated translation.[10] This state of affairs is by and large true in the domain of modern Chinese scholarship also. Besides the critical edition of Ho-shang Kung's commentary by Cheng Ch'eng-hai, which is invaluable, there are but a handful of articles written on the subject.[11] Fortunately, the provenance of the Ho-shang Kung commentary has received considerable attention in a number of recent Japanese studies, to which I shall refer later in chapter 3.

The commentary by Wang Pi, on the other hand, is today almost taken as the standard work on the *Lao-tzu.* Virtually all the current translations of the *Lao-tzu* are based on the Wang Pi version. In addition to the numerous Chinese and Japanese studies, two English translations of Wang Pi's commentary have appeared in recent years.[12] No doubt, it is favored by most modern scholars because of its keen metaphysical insight. Centered particularly on the notion of *wu*, commonly translated as "non-being" or "nothingness," and associated with the school of "profound learning" *(hsüan-hsüeh)*, Wang Pi's work is often regarded as representative of the revival of Taoist thought—the "Neo-Taoist" movement—during the third and fourth centuries A.D. This general assessment will be scrutinized later in our discussion.

Methodologically, this study is both historical and comparative. The historical component is necessary to bring out the context in which the two commentaries are rooted, and to see how they reflect, as it were, the spirit of their age. As the thirteenth-century commentator Tu Tao-chien observes:

> The coming of the Way to the world takes on different forms each time. Commentators have largely followed the valued norms of their age and sought wholeheartedly to learn from (Tao). Thus what the Han commentaries have is a "Han Lao-tzu"; Chin commentaries, a "Chin Lao-tzu"; T'ang and Sung commentaries, "T'ang Lao-tzu" and "Sung Lao-tzu."[13]

Accordingly, the two commentaries will be examined separately, starting with Wang Pi's simply because it is more familiar to Western readers. Chapter 1 thus explores the historical context of the Wang Pi commentary, focusing especially on a number of questions relating to Wang's political and intellectual orientations. An interpretation of Wang Pi's understanding of the *Lao-tzu* will be offered in chapter 2. In chapters 3 and 4 the same basic strategy is applied to the Ho-shang Kung commentary.

In my translation of the primary texts, I follow no specific "method." Clarity and accuracy are my main concerns. For general references, such as those from the dynastic histories, a more "liberal" approach is adopted to render the original Chinese into current English. To the translation of the *Lao-tzu* and the commentaries, however, a more "literal" approach is applied, so as to convey a sense of the structure of the original as well. Transliterations are also used, especially for key concepts such as *wu* and *ch'i* ("breath"), for they help to avoid possible misunderstandings and ambiguities. But no Chinese term will be left untranslated. A study that seeks to bring the intellectual world of early China to a Western audience cannot be satisfied with transliterations alone. In all cases, an attempt has been made to consult existing translations; but I do not hesitate to depart from or modify them. Translations of key concepts will be discussed individually. Generally, however, priority is given to explaining what these concepts mean, as opposed to inventing and defending novel translations. This statement does not entail a particular theory of translation, but simply suggests what is deemed more appropriate for the present study. Nevertheless, it does reflect my general assumption that a certain openness characterizes all forms of interpretation, including translation. This, essentially, is an insight gained from modern hermeneutics, of which more will be said below. The objective of the historical and textual analysis in the next few chapters is to provide a close reading of the Wang Pi and the Ho-shang Kung commentaries, on the basis of which a comparative study will be undertaken in chapter 5 to highlight the similarities and differences between them.

What accounts for the differences between the two commentaries? The prevalent view in this regard is of course that whereas Wang Pi's commentary exhibits a strong "philosophical" interest, the Ho-shang Kung version is predominantly a "religious" one. In other words, Wang Pi's work is often taken to be concerned solely with the question of being, and with the notion of *wu* in particular. With respect to the Ho-shang Kung commentary, because it addresses the art of self-cultivation oriented toward immortality, it is seen to reflect the interest of the Taoist religion. As one scholar concludes, "The former is strictly philosophical and therefore has appealed to intellectuals while the latter is a religious interpretation and therefore has appealed to the devout Taoist followers."[14] What emerges from our discussion, however, is that there is a need to go beyond this general characterization if we are to do full justice to the two commentaries.

This is not to deny the contribution of Wang Pi to the development of Chinese thought, or the importance of Ho-shang Kung in the Taoist religion. What is suggested here is that to adequately appreciate their work, the assumption that there was a sharp and clear-cut distinction between "religion" and "philosophy" in early Chinese intellectual history should be abandoned. Although the two commentaries may have found different patrons in more recent times, they were not originally intended for different audiences. In the China of the second and third centuries A.D. at least, both "philosophic" and "religious" ideas appealed to the intellectuals;

there was seldom any distinction made between the two. As a literary document, any commentary would have been addressed to the educated elite. It is my contention that the Wang Pi and the Ho-shang Kung commentaries may be better understood in terms of their theoretical and practical concerns. This line of inquiry initially arises out of a consideration of the way in which these two commentaries have been viewed in traditional Chinese sources themselves.

In traditional Chinese sources, there is already a typology of interpretations of the *Lao-tzu*. As early as the seventh century, the famous scholar Lu Te-ming (556–627) has contrasted Wang Pi with Ho-shang Kung in the following way:

> (Ho-shang Kung) composed the *Lao-tzu chang-chü* [*Lao-tzu* Annotated in Sections] in four sections to instruct Emperor Wen (of Han); it sets out the key to self-government and the government of the country. Since then no commentator has not followed his "mysterious words" *(hsüan-yen)*, except Wang Pi who alone attained the essential insight of emptiness and nothingness *(hsü-wu)*.[15]

The context makes it clear that Lu Te-ming favors Wang Pi's work over the Ho-shang Kung commentary. Whereas the former is concerned with the idea of "non-being" or "nothingness" *(wu)*, the latter is said to be a "dark," "mysterious" *(hsüan)* treatise on the art of government. In this instance, it is interesting to note that the word *hsüan* seems to carry with it certain not so favorable connotations, as opposed to the sense of "profundity" and "sublimity" generally associated with the school of "profound learning" *(hsüan-hsüeh)*.[16]

This sentiment, at any rate, in 719 A.D. found its radical expression in a memorial by the historian Liu Chih-chi (661–721):

> The current conventional text of *Lao-tzu* is one with the commentary by Ho-shang Kung. . . . [Concerning the legend of Ho-shang Kung] this is simply a fantastic tale, a vulgar lie. According to the bibliographical section of the *History of Han*, *Lao-tzu* had three commentaries. There was no mention of any commentary by Ho-shang Kung. Is his not the case of a commentator who invented a tale in order to have his work appear miraculous? His language is uncouth and his reasoning distorted. . . . How can Ho-shang Kung be compared with Wang

Pi, whose brilliant talent and superb judgment are well reflected in research and exposition and whose commentary is,
upon examination, indeed superior in interpretation and pur-
port? We must drop the Ho-shang Kung commentary and promote the commentary by Wang Pi. By so doing we shall be
meeting the needs of students.[17]

This bold memorial makes plain that the Ho-shang Kung version of
the *Lao-tzu* was in fact the dominant one at the time. Liu's critique
was prompted by an edict of the Emporer Hsüan-tsung (r. 712–755),
who himself wrote a commentary on the *Lao-tzu*.[18] As the edict has
it, although the Ho-shang Kung version was the better recognized,
"Wang Pi's commentary on *Lao-tzu* is also very brilliant."[19] The
scholars were asked, in effect, to reexamine the existing curriculum
for imperial examinations. The official response came a few weeks
later and suggested an interesting compromise:

The *Tao-te ching* is what is called a "sublime discourse" *(hsüan-
yen)*. Although there have been many commentators, few have
exhausted its meaning. Ho-shang Kung is a fictitious appella-
tion; there was really no such man in Han history. Yet his
commentary is founded upon the idea of nurturing the spirit,
and is rooted in the doctrine of non-action. Its language is
simple, and its reasoning, profound. At the very least, it
is sufficient to guide self-cultivation and to purify sincerity; on
a larger scale, it can bring peace to the people and security to
the nation. Thus Ku Huan said: "Though Ho-shang Kung
was writing a commentary, he was at the same time establishing his teaching. He generally dwells little on abstruse funda-
mentals, but makes clear their immediate application." This
may be accepted as a just characterization of the book. Wang
Pi was skilled in "sublime speech"*(hsüan-t'an)* and had quite
captured the essentials of the Way. Pursuing spiritual illumi-
nation in the bellow-like vacuity (of Tao) and maintaining a
quiet tranquility in the mysterious female, his reasoning is
fluent and his insight subtle. In the realm of "profound learning" *(hsüan-hsüeh)*, he may be said to be an expert. But when it
comes to practical teachings on the cultivation of the self and
the extension of the Way, then Ho-shang Kung is comparatively superior. Now we hope a request may be made to have

students ordered to use both Wang Pi's and Ho-shang Kung's commentaries.[20]

This response was jointly submitted by a group of scholars headed by the noted *Shih-chi* commentator Ssu-ma Chen, who was then a leading official at the imperial academy.[21] Although the legendary character of the figure of Ho-shang Kung was recognized, there is no question that the commentary bearing his name continued to be held in the highest esteem. The importance of Wang Pi's commentary was not denied, but the tone of this memorial shows clearly that Ho-shang Kung's was to be preferred. Whereas for Liu Chih-chi the language of the Ho-shang Kung commentary is "uncouth" and its "reasoning" (*li*) is "distorted," for Ssu-ma Chen it is quite the opposite: "Its language is simple, and its reasoning, profound."

A certain continuity of interpretation can thus be detected, with respect to a comparison of the Wang Pi and the Ho-shang Kung commentaries. Earlier Lu Te-ming has described Wang Pi's commentary as being concerned with abstract ideas, while Ho-shang Kung's is focused on more practical issues. This view is quite clearly maintained by Ssu-ma Chen and his colleagues, although the evaluation is now reversed. Whereas for Lu Te-ming, the strength of Wang Pi's work lies precisely in its concentrated attempt to fathom the meaning of Tao in terms of the notion of "emptiness and nothingness," for Ssu-ma Chen this means that Wang Pi is guilty of neglecting the practical task of self-cultivation and the "extension of the Way."

According to another T'ang commentator, Lu Hsi-sheng (fl. 880), Wang Pi was even guilty of a "crime" as he "had lost the Way of Lao-tzu and became excessively abstruse and wild."[22] But Wang Pi was also accused of a "crime" by the Eastern Chin scholar Fan Ning (339–401) for having followed the *Lao-tzu* and abandoned the Way of Confucius.[23] It is interesting that Wang Pi was thus condemned by both Confucians and Taoists. At this point, suffice it to say that the nature of Wang Pi's thought defies any one-sided categorization.

The continuity of interpretation outlined above is discernible in later sources as well. In the early tenth-century commentary on the *Lao-tzu* by Tu Kuang-t'ing (850–933), we seem to find the same interpretive or hermeneutical tradition at work in assessing the Wang Pi and the Ho-shang Kung commentaries. Tu's commentary, the *Tao-te chen-ching kuang sheng-i* (Preface dated 901), is an ambitious work. In it Tu Kuang-t'ing has listed a total of sixty-one commentaries on the *Tao-te ching*. After discussing the "biography" of Lao-tzu, the "Preface" to Emperor Hsüan-tsung's commentary and other matters, he goes on to classify the various commentaries. According to Tu, the *Tao-te ching* contains an inexhaustible wealth of meaning; commentators have only emphasized different aspects, different levels of meaning:

> Ho-shang Kung and Yen Chün-p'ing both seek to explain the Way of governing the country. The immortal Sung-ling, Sun Teng of the Wei period, the hermit T'ao (Hung-ching) of the Liang dynasty, and Ku Huan of the southern Ch'i all seek to explain the Way of self-government. Kumarajiva in the time of Fu Chien, (Fo) T'u-teng of the Later Chao, Emperor Wu of the Liang dynasty, the Liang Taoist Tou Lüeh—they all explain the Way of the principle of things and of [karmic] cause and effect. The Liang dynasty Taoist Meng Chih-chou, Tsang Hsüan–ching, the Ch'en dynasty Taoist Chu Yu, the Sui dynasty Taoist Liu Chin-hsi, the T'ang dynasty Taoist Ch'eng Hsüan-ying, Tsai Tzu-huang, Huang Hsüan-tse, Li Jung, Chü Hsüan-pi, Chang Hui-ch'ao, Li Yüan-hsing—they all explain the Way of "Double Mystery" *(Ch'ung-hsüan)*. Ho Yen, Chung Hui, Tu Yüan-k'ai, Wang Fu-ssu [i.e., Wang Pi], Chang Ssu, Yang Hu, Mr. Lu, Liu Jen-hui—these explain the Way of ultimate emptiness and nonaction, of governing the family and the country. This goes to show that commentators have a different understanding (of the *Lao-tzu*).[24]

I cannot go into a discussion of all these commentators here; most of their writings are no longer extant. But this is an important document; it remains the most comprehensive attempt in traditional Chinese sources to classify the various commentaries of the *Lao-tzu*. There is no attempt to minimize the differences even among Taoist writers; differences of interpretation should be recognized, for they attest to the richness of the *Lao-tzu*. Few commentators after Tu Kuang-t'ing can claim to equal his effort. The Yüan dynasty commentator, Tu Tao-chien, for example, is content to say simply that "there are some who talk about (the *Lao-tzu*) in terms of emptiness and nonaction; some in terms of the art of breathing and meditation; some in terms of fate and fortune, and military-legalist strategy."[25] The Ming dynasty commentator Chiao Hung (1541–1620), to take but one more example, has simply taken over Tu Kuang-t'ing's classification and added others' comments to it.[26]

Does Tu Kuang-t'ing's interpretation follow the general hermeneutical tradition of Lu Te-ming, Liu Chih-chi, and Ssu-ma Chen, with regard to the assessment of the Wang Pi and Ho-shang Kung commentaries? On the whole, it does seem that the same tradition is maintained, though not without modification. Ho-shang Kung is here described as being concerned with "the Way of governing the country," which fits well with the emphasis on practical teachings. As far as Wang Pi's commentary is concerned, the emphasis on "emptiness" is now qualified by the phrase "governing the family and the country." Is there a discrepancy here?

It may safely be assumed that for Tu Kuang-t'ing, Wang Pi's commentary is not only concerned with the nature of Tao in itself, but with its concrete application as well. The notion of "emptiness" is, in this sense, seen to have practical implications. In addition, Tu Kuang-t'ing's own intellectual preference must also be taken into account. A few lines after his classification of the various commentaries, Tu made it clear that he was in agreement with the Ch'ung-hsüan school, the school of "Double Mystery," which may be regarded as the metaphysical school par excellence in the spectrum of Lao-tzu commentaries.[27] From this perspective, Tu Kuang-t'ing thus sensed a certain inadequacy in Wang Pi's treatment of the Lao-tzu. For him although Wang Pi might have tried to fathom the secret of Tao, in the final analysis he failed to transcend all his worldly preoccupations. As a recognized Taoist master, Tu Kuang-t'ing understandably differs from Ssu-ma Chen and other Confucians in his estimation of the Wang Pi commentary. Keeping in mind the opposite but equally critical assessment of Wang Pi by Lu Hsi-sheng and Fan Ning mentioned above, it seems that whereas for certain Confucians Wang Pi was decidedly too "Taoist," for some Taoists he was perhaps not quite "Taoist" enough.

The interpretation of Tu Kuang-t'ing is both descriptive and normative. Precisely because the Wang Pi commentary is seen to have a practical dimension, it is considered a lesser work when compared with the strictly theoretical or metaphysical Ch'ung-hsüan commentaries. This helps to explain why Tu's analysis seems to diverge from the earlier tradition of Lu Te-ming and Ssu-ma Chen. In their works the distinction between Wang Pi's commentary and the Ch'ung-hsüan school has not yet come into view and is therefore simply not a problem; for Tu Kuang-t'ing, however, it is important that the practical side of Wang Pi's work not escape critical scrutiny.

In sum, there is a fairly consistent reading emerging from these traditional interpretations of the Ho-shang Kung and the Wang Pi commentaries. The case of the former is very clear: all our commentators basically agree that it is concerned with the art of self-cultivation and the government of the country. It is significant that the "religious" aspect is not explicitly identified in the works of Lu Te-ming, Ssu-ma Chen, and Tu Kuang-t'ing. This suggests that the quest for "immortality" was not regarded as the main focus of the Ho-shang Kung commentary. To some scholars at least, the commentary was more concerned with the well-being of the state than with personal salvation or spiritual liberation. Indeed, as we shall see, self-cultivation is inseparably linked with the art of government in the Ho-shang Kung commentary. With respect to Wang Pi, the emphasis on "emptiness and nothingness" is likewise transparent. In addition, I believe that Tu Kuang-t'ing's modification points to an important aspect of Wang Pi's work which has not been adequately dealt with by other commentators.

Derived from traditional sources, this typological guide helps to place the two commentaries in their proper context and offers valuable insight into their understanding of the *Lao-tzu*. Despite the judgment of Liu Chih-chi, the common criticism of the Ho-shang Kung commentary as "religious propaganda" is clearly inadequate. The practical, political interest of the commentary demands our careful attention. Similarly, as I shall argue, Wang Pi's commentary cannot be reduced to a strictly philosophical and politically disinterested inquiry into the meaning of Tao. Both the "theoretical" and "practical" dimensions of the two commentaries, in other words, must be clearly delineated. But it should be emphasized also that these categories serve no more than a heuristic purpose. Although they facilitate a better understanding of the two commentaries, they do not form two separate components in the texts themselves. In the final analysis, Wang Pi's and Ho-shang Kung's commentaries represent two coherent and comprehensive visions of the Way. I propose to describe them as "Tao-ist" visions. Throughout this study, the term "Tao-ist" is used in a restricted, nonsectarian sense, as an adjective of Tao, and not of "Taoism." A common ground can be discerned between these two visions, one characterized by a unity of theory and practice, by a fusion of spirituality and ethics. It is for this reason that the opposition between "philosophy" and "religion" cannot be applied to Wang Pi and Ho-shang Kung. What is "philosophic" or "religious" forms but moments of their comprehensive visions.

By arguing that there is common ground between them, I do not mean to disregard their differences. To adequately explain their differences, however, it is necessary to introduce what may be called a hermeneutical turn, to disclose the interpretive horizon from which they viewed the *Lao-tzu*. In this context, hermeneutics may be defined as the study of interpretations in terms of their presuppositions and frames of reference. This has little to do with the question as to whether Wang Pi and Ho-shang Kung were "faithful" to the original *Lao-tzu*. Both were careful commentators, as they sought to represent the world of the *Lao-tzu* to a new audience. The question, strictly speaking, is also not one of method. What is at issue here is their prior and tacit understanding of meaning itself. For Ho-shang Kung, meaning is always "referential," in the sense that the meaning of the *Lao-tzu* is to be found in the external objects to which it refers. Wang Pi's commentary, on the other hand, is guided by a hermeneutical model that I shall describe as "etiological." For Wang Pi, the meaning of the *Lao-tzu* is ultimately to be found in the text itself, and can be traced to a few fundamental concepts dialectically related to one another.

In this study, I am content to apply a type of hermeneutical analysis to two specific texts, so as to resolve an interpretive problem. This must not be confused with an attempt to reconstruct the "intention" of their authors. From the commentaries themselves, distinctive patterns of interpretation can be discerned, which permits a discussion of their prior understanding of meaning. It is this that shapes their specific readings of the *Lao-tzu*, and for that matter of any text. This is one way in which hermeneutics can be fruitfully applied to the study of Chinese texts, supplementing the task of interpretation by taking into account "metainterpretive" questions.

In a broader context, the importance of hermeneutics is a philosophical one. Its full significance certainly goes beyond the present study. The view I follow is that of Hans-Georg Gadamer and Paul Ricoeur, according to whom hermeneutics is a full-fledged practical philosophy. This view of hermeneutics seeks to transcend the modern concern with method, and to disclose the dynamics of the process of understanding itself. It takes as its point of departure the fundamental historicity of being and understanding. Meaning is always mediated, by language, and more generally by what may be called the paradigm of tradition, in and through which experience is raised into the level of thought.[28] Tradition, in this sense, is an all-encompassing category, into which being is "thrown," to borrow an expression from Heidegger. More simply put, understanding is always finite and on the way; it is shaped by tradition in that the knowing subject "knows" only to the extent that he or she interacts with the world from a specific intellectual horizon.

While recognizing the debate still surrounding the claim to universality of philosophical hermeneutics, this study argues that ancient Chinese writers too operated within their own intellectual horizons, and that their interpretation of classical texts may be described phenomenologically as a "fusion of horizons." The world of the primary text forms the subject. Through the process of interpretation, it becomes a part of the web of meaning—the "woof and warp" of meaningful existence, to use the Chinese expression designating the tradition of the classics and other supporting texts—in which interpreters stand and seek to delineate for their readers. This is the theoretical model, which my concluding analysis presupposes. By identifying the hermeneutical assumptions underlying Wang Pi's and Ho-shang Kung's interpretations, not only would the two commentaries be made better understood, but in future research other commentaries on the *Lao-tzu* may be approached from the same perspective: that is, discussed in terms of their theoretical and practical interests, contained in an etiological or referential reading. Indeed, commentaries on other foundational texts, such as the Confucian *Lun-yü* (Analects) and the *I-ching* (Book of Changes), may also be viewed in this light. In this regard, while the primary aim of this study is to elucidate the "Tao-ist" visions of Wang Pi and Ho-shang Kung, it is also an experiment in a new direction of sinological research.

1 Wang Pi: Life and Thought

One day Wang Pi went to see the prime minister and was granted a private interview. During the meeting, apparently he discussed at length the meaning of Tao and nothing else. The prime minister, according to Wang's biographer, merely laughed at him. Wang Pi was probably not even twenty years old at the time. This story may conjure up images of a young philosopher who has totally dedicated himself to the quest for the Way, and who has no interest in the more mundane affairs of the political world. Why, then, did he bother to see the prime minister at all?

The standard biography of Wang Pi (226–249 A.D.) is found in the *San-kuo chih* (Records of the Three Kingdoms). It is not, however, an "official" biography that forms a part of the *San-kuo chih* original. Rather, it is a separate work attributed to Ho Shao (236–ca. 300) and is preserved by the commentator P'ei Sung-chih (372–451) in a note appended to the biography of Chung Hui (225–264). More precisely, at the end of Chung Hui's biography, there is a passing reference to Wang Pi, to which P'ei Sung-chih added Ho Shao's account.[1] Since this biography is now available in English in Paul J. Lin's translation of the *Lao-tzu* and Wang Pi's commentary, it need not be retranslated here.[2] Instead, selected details from Wang's biography will be discussed later in this chapter. There are a number of references to Wang Pi in other sources, especially in the fifth-century work *Shih-shuo hsin-yü* (New Account of Tales of the

World);[3] but except for a few to be noted later, they do not provide significant new information. In the biography, we find a general account of Wang Pi's life and work, a brief assessment of his character, opinions of his contemporaries, and, most important of all, records of his response to major intellectual issues of the day. An examination of the relevant biographical and historical data reveals a puzzling ambiguity. On the one hand, we see that the common assessment of Wang Pi as a "pure" philosopher leaves much room for doubt. On the other hand, his connection with the movement of "profound learning" suggests that his philosophic interest is not to be underestimated. According to some, Wang Pi was a leader of the "Neo-Taoist" movement; according to others, he was a staunch defender of the Confucian tradition. This raises the question of Wang Pi's intellectual stance, which has an important bearing on our understanding of his *Lao-tzu* commentary.

To help to resolve this issue, aspects of Wang Pi's life and thought, including his interpretation of the *I-ching* and of the ideal sage, will be examined in what follows. These are selected not only because they provide insight into Wang's intellectual orientation; they also signal in anticipation major themes in the commentary on the *Lao-tzu*. By themselves, as we shall see, these background considerations cannot resolve the question posed here; but they do serve to establish a framework in which Wang Pi's understanding of the *Lao-tzu* can be properly appreciated.

Wang Pi: Pure Philosopher or Political Activist?

Defining the Two Points of View

According to his biographer, Wang Pi, styled Fu-ssu, was a precocious child; in his teens he was attracted to the *Lao-tzu* and was already fluent in the art of disputation. Ho Yen (ca. 190–249), a leading political and intellectual figure at the time, was certainly very much impressed by the young Wang Pi. He said of him, "Confucius said that 'the young are to be held in awe.' Is he not a person with whom one can discuss the boundaries of heaven and man?"[4] The *Shih-shuo hsin-yü* provides further details:

> Ho Yen was the head of the Personnel Ministry, and enjoyed both status and acclaim. At that time his house was always filled by guests who came for debates or conversations. Wang

Pi, who was then not yet twenty, also went to visit him. Since Yen had heard of Pi's reputation, he culled some of the best arguments from past conversations and said to Pi, "These arguments I consider to be final. Could you perhaps refute them?" Pi then proceeded to refute them, and all those present agreed that Ho Yen had been humbled. Pi then went on to act as both "guest" and "host" [i.e., assuming both sides of a debate] several times, and in every case he was unequalled by anyone in the entire company.[5]

This was no small accomplishment, for Ho Yen himself was known to be an expert in disputation. At that time, most of the literati skilled in the art of disputation "looked up to Ho Yen as their ideal."[6] Well conversant with both the Confucian and Taoist traditions, Wang Pi was evidently a young man of great learning and of refined taste. There is little question that Wang Pi was highly regarded by his friends and contemporaries, especially with respect to his philosophic and literary talents.

Nevertheless, despite his close friendship with Ho Yen, Wang Pi never gained prominence in office. This is often explained in terms of his youth and inexperience, and his preoccupation with abstract philosophic thought. Indeed, Wang Pi's talent did not appear to have impressed Ts'ao Shuang (178–249), who then controlled the political machinery of the Wei (220–265) court prior to the "regency" of the Ssu-ma clan. Ts'ao was the prime minister who laughed at Wang Pi.

Wang did hold a minor official post for a short time, but he seems not to have taken much interest in it. Moreover, his biography relates how he liked to make fun of others who were not his equal in ability and talent, and this certainly did not contribute to his career in officialdom. He was not interested in "fame and high office."[7] Wang Pi died of an "illness" in the same year when Ts'ao Shuang and Ho Yen were "executed" by Ssu-ma I (179–251), at the age of twenty-four.[8]

What is the personality that emerges from this traditional account? On the whole, it seems clear that the biographer was not entirely uncritical of Wang Pi, and as we shall see there are good historical reasons for this. Although Wang Pi's achievement is not denied, at one point Ho Shao also describes him as "shallow and ignorant of the ways of the world."[9] The Wang Pi that seems to emerge from this biography appears to be a young, bright, and somewhat proud intellectual who, though very much gifted philosophically and artistically, was perhaps not quite at home in the political world of his day. This view, for example, is reflected in Mou Tsung-san's assessment of Wang Pi as a rather naive young man who because of his "ignorance of the ways of the world" was able to deal with fundamental philosophic concepts in a fresh, concentrated, and "uncontaminated" way.[10] The picture of Wang Pi as a "pure," politically disinterested thinker has thus come to be widely accepted by students of Chinese intellectual history. The reason for this, as we shall see later in this chapter, has also to do with Wang Pi's connection with the movement of "pure conversation" (ch'ing-t'an).

There is a second view, however. For example, the Soviet scholar A. A. Petrov has argued that Wang Pi "as a member of the ruling class, discarded quietism and found in philosophic Taoism the justification for a strong central government."[11] According to Petrov, what Wang found in "philosophic Taoism" was a kind of "monism," which underlies the plurality of phenomena.[12]

In a study by Jen Chi-yü and T'ang Yung-t'ung this emphasis on Wang Pi's political involvement is spelled out even more specifically, although it reaches a very different conclusion in terms of Wang Pi's central philosophy.[13] According to this study, Wang Pi was indeed very much a part of the ruling establishment. However, as Wang Pi himself did not have any real political power, he was dependent on his friend and patron Ho Yen for his own security and comfort. Because Ho Yen was opposed to the rising Ssu-ma faction, Wang Pi "therefore" proposed a theory of "individualism," based on the Taoist notions of "nonaction" (wu-wei) and "spontaneity" (tzu-jan), to counteract the threat generated by the Ssu-ma clan's attempt to centralize power.[14] The historical context and the meaning of these concepts will be discussed later; at this point, it is enough to see that Wang Pi did not appear to some scholars as "disinterested," still less uninterested in politics, as others might have supposed.

It seems to me that this emphasis on Wang Pi's possible political involvement raises a legitimate question. I am not convinced that these views can be rejected offhand, because of their apparent "Marxist" perspective. Their conclusions are of course open to debate, but they deserve a fair hearing. In particular, a few episodes in Wang Pi's biography may be interpreted in the direction of political involvement. In the biography, we are told that Wang Pi sought out a number of high officials in the Wei government. First of all, he went on his own initiative to see P'ei Hui, who was then secretary or deputy under Ho Yen in the important Ministry of Personnel, overseeing the appointment of officials.[15] The biography then goes on to describe the meeting between Wang Pi and Ho Yen cited earlier, which according to the account in the *Shih-shuo hsin-yü* was again initiated by Wang Pi himself. And as soon as Wang Pi was awarded a post, though not the one he had hoped for, he requested a private interview with the prime minister Ts'ao Shuang. This sequence of events merits special attention. It suggests not only that Wang Pi had actively pursued a political career, but that he had done so carefully and in the proper order, beginning with the deputy minister. Incidentally, the biography also tells us that Wang Pi broke off his friendship with Wang Li, after the latter was appointed to the position for which Ho Yen had recommended Wang Pi. If we take the narrative at face value, it would appear that Wang Pi had gone through the proper channels, as one might expect of an ambitious young man. His death, indeed, might have even been caused by an "illness" of a political nature.[16]

More recently, Noma Kazunori has likewise argued that Wang Pi should be viewed primarily as a political theorist, who was concerned with limiting the control of the powerful families of the aristocracy in favor of a strong, centralized government.[17] This resembles closely the view of Petrov, and there is no reason to read any "Marxist" agenda into Noma's analysis.

Noma's study, published in 1982, draws especially from Wang Pi's commentary on the *Lao-tzu*. In another Japanese study published in the same year, however, it is argued that Wang Pi's commentary has in fact turned whatever possible political implications in the *Lao-tzu* into moments of a metaphysical theory centered on the notion of "non-being."[18] This conflict of interpretations shows well why we need to examine Wang Pi's life and thought before we turn to the commentary on the *Lao-tzu* itself. To further explore the question of Wang Pi's political orientation, a brief discussion of the historical and intellectual context is in order.

The Cheng-shih Political Scene

The Cheng-shih era (240–249) of the Wei dynasty is what concerns us most. When Ts'ao Fang (Wei Fei-Ti) inherited the Wei empire in 240 A.D., he was merely a young boy. The responsibility of guiding and supporting the young emperor was entrusted to Ts'ao Shuang and Ssu-ma I. Conflict soon arose between the two. The Ts'ao faction took control early; but it was Ssu-ma I who secured the final victory. In 249 A.D. the latter engineered a coup that led to the death of Ts'ao Shuang, Ho Yen, their families, and scores of others. The Cheng-shih period represents a turning point in the history of the Wei dynasty; from then on, it was the Ssu-ma family who dominated the political scene and eventually established the Chin dynasty in 265 A.D.

A major consideration in this regard is the power of the important families or clans of the nobility in the politics of the day. In particular, key government positions were then basically monopolized by members of these families; their power and the power struggle among them posed a serious threat to a stable, centralized government. This, to be sure, can be traced back to the latter part of the Han dynasty when clashes between the aristocracy and the eunuchs especially had significantly weakened the control of the Han house. When Ts'ao Ts'ao (155–220), the real founder of the Wei empire, rose to power after the Yellow Turban Rebellion (184 A.D.), he certainly saw the problem and attempted to reverse it. Ts'ao Ts'ao himself came from a eunuch family which, though powerful, could not compare with other major clans—for example, the family of his archrival Yüan Shao—in terms of "distinction" and "legitimacy." It is thus not surprising that the ambitious Ts'ao Ts'ao repeatedly spoke against the system of appointing officials from among the nobility.[19]

Despite his effort, the Wei dynasty actually saw an increase of this monopoly of power by the influential families. The question of the lineage of the Ts'ao family was no longer a serious problem when Ts'ao Ts'ao established himself as the unquestionable leader of the dying Han court. Moreover, when his son Ts'ao P'ei (r. 220–226) formally ended the rule of Han and became emperor of Wei, he needed the support of the leading families for his claim to the throne. Ssu-ma I was among those who supported this new regime, and he became a prominent figure during the reign of Ts'ao P'ei. This sets the stage for the later struggle between the party of Ts'ao Shuang and the Ssu-ma clan. By the Cheng-shih period the conflict among the major families has crystallized into a struggle between these two camps.

Most of the leading intellectuals of the period can be shown to have a close connection with either one of these two camps.[20] The case of Ho Yen, for example, is very clear. From a distinguished family, he was related to the Ts'ao family by marriage. From this perspective, it is not difficult to see why the biography of Ho Yen, and Wang Pi's also, are not properly included in the *San-kuo chih*, which is after all a Chin document. Ho Shao, the author of Wang Pi's "unofficial" biography, was himself a childhood friend of Ssu-ma Yen (Chin Wu-ti, r. 265–290), the first emperor of the Chin dynasty. Although there is no need to suspect unduly the accuracy of Ho's biography of Wang Pi, the turbulent political situation does not seem to warrant a hasty conclusion with respect to Wang's political noninvolvement.

Was Wang Pi, then, a pure philosopher or political activist? By "political activist" I mean a person who is motivated by political concerns, and actively engaged in political pursuits. A "pure philosopher," on the other hand, is dedicated to the world of philosophic ideas and totally unconcerned with political affairs. These are extreme positions, but they serve to bring the question into sharper focus. In Wang Pi's case, this question has deeper implications, since the view that he was a pure philosopher is generally understood in a "Neo-Taoist" context, which often implies a kind of "anti-Confucian escapism."

Names and Principles (*Ming-li*)

From traditional Chinese sources, we can piece together the intellectual context of the Cheng-shih period. According to the *Shih-shuo hsin-yü*, Yüan Hung (328–376) in his work *Ming-shih chuan* (Lives of Famous Men of Letters) has singled out Hsia-hou Hsüan (209–254), Ho Yen, and Wang Pi as the representative "famous men of letters" (*ming-shih*) of the Cheng-shih period.[21] What characterizes a "famous man of letters"? Another entry in the *Shih-shuo hsin-yü* reads:

> During the Cheng-shih era, Wang Pi and Ho Yen had favored the profound and abstruse discourse of the *Chuang-tzu* and the *Lao-tzu*, and after that the world set great store by them.[22]

In the *Chin-shu* (History of the Chin Dynasty), there is another reference to this same topic: "In the Cheng-shih period of the Wei dynasty, Ho Yen, Wang Pi, and others had expounded on the *Lao-*

tzu and *Chuang-tzu;* they established the view that heaven and earth and everything in the world all have their roots in 'non-being' *(wu)."*[23] In the early sixth-century work *Wen-hsin tiao-lung* (The Literary Mind and the Carving of Dragons), we also read:

> When the Wei house first established supremacy, it followed the methods of the "logicians" *(ming)* and the "legalists" *(fa)*. Fu Chia [ca. 209–255] and Wang Ts'an [177–217] emphasized the teaching of "names and principles" *(ming-li)*. By the Cheng-shih era, the focus was on the preservation of culture. It was then that Ho Yen and his followers had put the (genre of) "profound discourse" *(hsüan-lun)* into wide currency. Thus Lao-tzu and Chuang-tzu came to occupy the main road, and competed with Confucius for the right of way.[24]

According to these accounts, there was a Taoist revival during the Cheng-shih era. It was centered on the *Lao-tzu* and the *Chuang-tzu*, and was represented especially by Wang Pi and Ho Yen. Moreover, according to the *Wen-hsin tiao-lung*, Wang Pi and Ho Yen did not only spark new interests in the Taoist classics, but had in fact charted a new course in the intellectual landscape of third-century China. This is described in terms of a shift from the doctrine of "names and principles" *(ming-li)* to that of "profound discourse" *(hsüan-lun)*, which was perceived as a challenge to the Confucian orthodoxy long established since the Han dynasty. This is clearly confirmed by another reference from the *Chin-shu*, in which Fan Ning (339–401) is said to have lamented on what he took to be the sad state of the Chin intellectual scene: "(Fan) Ning thought that its origin could be traced to Wang Pi and Ho Yen; (he argued that) their crime was worse than that of Chieh and Chou."[25] Chieh and Chou are of course the legendary diabolic tyrants of the Hsia and Shang dynasties respectively whose "crime" led to the downfall of their empires. Wang Pi's "crime," as the passage continues, is precisely that he abandoned the teaching of the Confucian sages. I shall return to this serious charge later.

What do "names and principles" and "profound discourse" mean in this context? The early Wei dynasty is, first of all, said to have been dominated by the teaching of *ming* and *fa*. These two terms hark back to the so-called School of Names *(Ming-chia)* and the Legalist School *(Fa-chia)*, which first arose during the Warring

States period (480–221 B.C.). It may be said that whereas the former is concerned with the nature of names and their relation to reality, the latter seeks to establish a strict rule of law.[26] Although Confucianism was made the official state ideology during the Han dynasty, the School of Names and the School of Law remained active and were integrated into the Confucian orthodoxy.

The dominant interpretation of Confucianism in the Han dynasty, as is well known, was based on a cosmological theory that emphasized a direct correspondence between heavenly and human phenomena.[27] For example, on the basis of an analysis of the word *wang*, "king," the great systematizer of Han Confucianism, Tung Chung-shu (ca. 179–104 B.C.) explained that the figure of the king assumes the key role of interrelating the three realms of heaven, earth, and humankind.[28] When translated into a political ideal, this means that the way of government should mirror the "Way of heaven"—that is, the perceived structure of the cosmos itself. In terms of political office, this means that appointed positions must not be determined arbitrarily, for they hold the key to a harmonious empire. As Wang Fu (ca. 76–157 A.D.) remarks in his work *Ch'ien-fu lun* (Discourse of a Recluse):

> When there is a title, it must be recorded in legislative documents. What is of "names and principles" *(ming-li)* must be verified in actuality. Then indeed no office would abandon its duty, and no position would be filled by the wrong person.[29]

In this context, *ming-li* may be defined as a type of inquiry that aims at discerning the "names and principles" of the cosmos, so as to institute a perfect political system. There are, in other words, two aspects to the term *ming-li*. In the Wei-Chin period, as Robert Henricks has pointed out, the art of disputation enjoyed a strong revival. "Famous men of letters" *(ming-shih)*, including Ho Yen and Wang Pi, engaged in debates and intellectual conversations that probably involved the kind of logical tools associated especially with the School of Names.[30] *Ming-li*, in a technical sense, thus refers to the methods of argumentation and more generally to a type of theoretical discourse that seeks to identify the meaning of "names and principles." Yet these methods were not used for the sake of winning debates alone; they were engaged in the political arena to ensure that "names and principles" are matched in "reality," especially in terms of political appointment and performance. This is indicated by the fact that in the Wei period, *ming-li* was extended to include the methods of judging and evaluating human character. In other words, *ming-li* served to identify the best candidates for political office, so that no office would be "filled by the wrong person."

Ideally, of course, only those who were "worthy" of the position would be appointed. And in the traditional Confucian understanding, what made a person worthy of office was largely a matter of learning and individual virtues; integrity and filial piety were especially important in this regard. In practice, however, this often meant that only members of the wealthy and well-connected families were considered "virtuous"—that is, having been brought up in the proper way, taught the classics, groomed for office, acquired a good reputation, and judged to be outstanding individuals.

When Ts'ao Ts'ao took control of the political stage, he attempted to reverse this trend by emphasizing the ability of an individual as opposed to "virtue." Indeed, he went as far as to say that even those "who lack benevolence and filial piety but are skilled in the art of government and military strategy" should not be left out of office.[31] This direct challenge to the old Confucian model means that the measure of a good official cannot be determined by empty "reputation," but by actual performance. This was essentially a "legalist" view, which together with a system of reward and punishment sought to ensure the effective operation of government.

The question of "names and principles" was hotly debated during the Cheng-shih period, usually in the context of a discussion of the notion of "talent" *(ts'ai)* and its relation to human nature *(hsing)*. Again, this should not be limited to the kind of semantic and logical analysis of names and concepts associated with the School of Names in the Warring States period. Although the analytic tools may be traced there, they were made to serve the political process. Once "talent" and "nature" were understood, a system of official appointment could be implemented, which would ideally lead to a strong government.[32] It is in this sense that the early Wei ethos is said to be characterized by the teachings of both *ming* and *fa*.

Although there is no historical record of Wang Pi's having participated in this debate, he was undoubtedly aware of it. Indeed, as we shall see in the next chapter, Wang Pi's concern with the problem of appointing officials is reflected in his *Lao-tzu* commentary. The importance of this question indicates that literati of the Cheng-shih period were not interested only in the kind of abstract speculation known as "profound discourse" *(hsüan-lun)*.

Pure Conversation (Ch'ing-t'an)

From Ch'ing-i to Ch'ing-t'an

The movement of "profound discourse" is more commonly known as "profound learning" (hsüan-hsüeh). The term hsüan, originally a color word signifying a shade of dark red, is often translated by the word "mystery." Although hsüan does signify the "dark," "mysterious," "secret," it is not entirely satisfactory to render hsüan-lun as "mysterious discourse" or hsüan-hsüeh as "mysterious learning." The subject under investigation may verge on the "mysterious," but the discourse itself does not. Of course, if a pejorative meaning is intended, then "mysterious" or "abstruse" would be appropriate. Otherwise, as an adjective modifying a type of learning or discourse, the term hsüan is better served by such words as "profound" or "sublime."Hsüan-lun, in this sense, is a type of discourse that addresses fundamental concepts not easily intelligible to the common people; it is a "profound" discourse in that it seeks to lay bare the meaning of what is beyond common understanding.

While "profound learning" first arose during the Cheng-shih period, it was a major characteristic of the more general movement known as "pure conversation" (ch'ing-t'an). This latter is usually discussed from a historical point of view; that is, ch'ing-t'an is generally explained in terms of a reaction to the socio-political realities at the time. The phenomenon of ch'ing-i, "pure criticism," "unspotted, purifying critique," or "righteous protest," which arose during the Later Han dynasty, is often cited as the immediate predecessor of ch'ing-t'an in this connection.[33]

According to this view, ch'ing-i is primarily a political movement organized by the scholar-officials who collectively came to criticize the politics of the Later Han court. However, because these attempts were met with harsh reprisals and because the Wei dynasty later was torn by power struggles among factions of the ruling elite, the ch'ing-i movement is thus said to have been transformed into an essentially nonpolitical phenomenon, ch'ing-t'an. Instead of criticizing the questionable political practices of the day, the Wei literati turned their attention to, as it were, "purer" pursuits. Instead of engaging in political criticism that might easily invite personal danger, "pure conversationists" diverted their creative energy to music, poetry, witty repartee, and—most important for our purposes—discussion of abstract philosophical concepts. The Cheng-shih era is thus taken as the turning point after which active political involvement gave way to a more politically disinterested, "pure" and "free" way of life, on the part of the literati.

The Decline of Han Confucianism

This view seems to find further support in a consideration of the decline of Han Confucianism, especially with regard to the interpretation of the classics. As indicated above, a key feature of Han Confucianism was the emphasis on the correspondence between the human and the heavenly realms. This is reflected in the interpretations of the classics as well, in that individual concepts were seen to refer to many other related phenomena in the framework of a cosmology based especially on the notions of *yin-yang* and *wu-hsing* (five phases or elements).[34] The five phases themselves—metal, wood, water, fire, and earth—were correlated with the five Confucian virtues, the five musical notes, the five cardinal points, the five mythical emperors, and so forth. The potential for further elaboration of this kind is virtually endless; even the four seasons were split into five in order to accommodate this five-faced cosmological scheme. The task of the interpreter, in this context, has thus become one of identifying this "referential" dimension in the classics. In other words, when a text speaks about "x," it is "in fact" also referring to "y," "z," and so on. In practical terms, however, this often led to inordinately long and cumbersome discussions on the multiple meanings of a particular word or phrase. Indeed, it is not difficult to see why Pan Ku (32–92 A.D.) complained in the *Han-shu* that the study of the classics had greatly deteriorated; often, he says, "a discussion of a text of five words can take up to twenty or thirty thousand words."[35]

The importance of this consideration will become more apparent when we compare Wang Pi's *Lao-tzu* commentary with that of Ho-shang Kung. Here, what merits special attention is that the *ch'ing-t'an* movement is seen to be a reaction against the "corrupt" political and intellectual conditions at the time. Because the literati were disillusioned by the political reality, concerned with their own safety, dissatisfied with the prevalent thought and scholarship, they "therefore" turned to wine, music, and speculative discourse. The movement of "pure conversation" is, as a result, often regarded as essentially a form of escapism.[36]

To supplement this historical interpretation of *ch'ing-t'an*, Yü Ying-shih has argued that it may also be understood in terms of the individual and collective self-consciousness of the literati that peaked especially during the Cheng-shih period.[37] That is to say, it was when the literati acquired a sense of group identity that they emerged as a united front to form the *ch'ing-i* movement. Similarly, it was when the literati developed a sense of individual identity that *ch'ing-i* was transformed into *ch'ing-t'an*. In other words, the movement of "pure conversation" seems to presuppose a strong sense of individualism, a deep awareness that the intellectual is standing apart from the socio-political whole. Although the historical context is important, according to Yü Ying-shih, the phenomenon of *ch'ing-t'an* cannot be properly understood if this self-awareness of the literati is not recognized.

Thus, the political background, the decline of Han Confucianism, and the self-awareness of the literati all contributed to the rise of "pure conversation." The phenomenon of "profound learning" is to be placed in this context. In terms of content, the importance of the *Lao-tzu* and *Chuang-tzu* has already been mentioned. In addition, the *I-ching* was central to the *hsüan-hsüeh* movement as well. Indeed, these three texts were then together known as *san-hsüan*, the "three profound treatises," to which most "famous men of letters" of the Cheng-shih era were drawn.[38] Ho Yen, for example, is known to have "favored the words of Lao-tzu and Chuang-tzu, and written a 'Discourse on the Way and Virtue' (*Tao-te lun*)."[39] Chung Hui, another major figure of the Wei period, is known for his discourse on the *I-ching*; in a gloss to his biography, it is further said that he "especially favored the *I-ching* and the *Lao-tzu*."[40] Wang Pi himself has commented on both the *I-ching* and the *Lao-tzu*.[41] In general, it can be said that the early *hsüan-hsüeh* of the Cheng-shih era has primarily focused on the *Lao-tzu* and the *I-ching*; the special emphasis on the *Chuang-tzu* belonged to a slightly later period.

As far as the *Lao-tzu* is concerned, the notion of *wu* is particularly important. It is often singled out as the one major concept that characterizes the *hsüan-hsüeh* movement as a whole. More specifically, it is *wu* as the underlying principle of being, as the ultimate source of everything in the world, that is at issue here. Although a more detailed discussion of this concept will not be presented until the next chapter, *wu* is essentially employed in this context to describe the nature of Tao. As far as the *I-ching* is concerned, a new interpretation based on this understanding of Tao came into wide currency and challenged the traditional Confucian interpretations. We shall have occasion to see an example of this in the next section.

The historical background of the "pure conversation" movement is clear enough. It is also clear why Wang Pi has been understood as a "pure" philosopher. But the generally negative assessment of *hsüan-hsüeh* as "escapist" and "anti-Confucian" remains a debatable interpretation. Whether this is a valid assessment of *ch'ing-t'an* and *hsüan-hsüeh* as a whole need not concern us. Our task is to see if this general understanding of *hsüan-hsüeh* may be applied to Wang Pi's thought.

Wang Pi: "Taoist" or "Confucian"?

The Reinterpretation of Confucianism

According to Ho Shao's account, when Wang Pi was not yet twenty he went to see P'ei Hui. The latter was "immediately amazed" by the appearance of the young Wang Pi, and asked:

> *Wu* is indeed that on which all things rest. But the sage did not venture a word on it. Why is it then that Lao-tzu found it necessary to keep explaining it?

To this, Wang Pi replied:

> The sage embodied *wu*, and since *wu* cannot be taught, he therefore did not discuss it. Lao-tzu, however, remained on the level of "being" *(yu)*; thus he constantly addressed the inadequacies (of being).[42]

This reply may seem a little surprising in view of the fact that Wang Pi is so often seen as the leading spokesman of "Neo-Taoism." The "sage" in question here is of course Confucius. In fact, according to the fifth-century scholar Chou Yung, "The old views of Wang (Pi) and Ho (Yen) all regarded Lao-tzu as inferior to Confucius."[43]

This reference is important because it points to the complexity involved in an assessment of Wang Pi's intellectual stance. As we may recall, the Chin scholar Fan Ning has precisely accused Wang Pi of abandoning the way of Confucius. Here we have an opposite assessment suggesting that Wang Pi was a supporter of the sage.

In the *Lun-yü* (Analects), there is an interesting story relating how Tzu-lu, one of Confucius's chief disciples, was displeased with the Master after the latter's visit to Nan-tzu, the wife of Duke Ling of Wei, whose character and reputation apparently left much to be desired. The Master, in response, exclaimed: "If I have done anything improper, may Heaven's curse be on me, may Heaven's curse be on me!"[44] Despite Confucius's vehement protest, the incident has proved to be a source of embarrassment to later Confucians. For one thing, the visit to an "unworthy" woman itself seems to have compromised the sage's integrity. Worse still, from the account in the biography of Confucius in the *Shih-chi* (Records of the Historian), one may even surmise that the sage visited Nan-tzu because of the latter's influence on her husband.[45]

Regardless of the real motive or even the historicity of the incident, one can easily see how critics of Confucianism might react to this story. Wang Ch'ung (27–97 A.D.), the famous "skeptical" philosopher of the Later Han period, for example, has found both the visit and Confucius's reply problematic.[46] Wang Pi, however, has argued that Confucius was unable to avoid the meeting with Nan-tzu because it was a matter of "heaven's ordinance" (*t'ien-ming*). Indeed, according to Wang Pi, Confucius's declaration has little to do with his conduct during the meeting with Nan-tzu; rather, it was a solemn admission that his unsuccessful political career then was part of heaven's ordinance.[47] It is significant that Wang Pi found it necessary to defend the behavior of the sage. In fact, in the T'ang dynasty, Wang Pi was officially recognized as one of the twenty-eight "worthies" (*hsien*), to whom sacrifices were to be made in Confucian temples.[48]

If Wang Pi did not criticize Confucius, his adherence to Confucian teachings was nevertheless not a naive or unquestioning one. The reply to P'ei Hui's question above, for example, is a good indication of how Wang Pi has reinterpreted the Confucian tradition in a new and profound way. Although Lao-tzu is said to be inferior to Confucius, the sage is now described as the champion of the doctrine of *wu*, the key doctrine in the *hsüan-hsüeh* movement. To further explore this radical reinterpretation of the Confucian tradition, we may turn briefly to Wang's understanding of a controversial passage in the *I-ching*.

The Number of the Great Expansion

Since the T'ang dynasty, Wang Pi's commentary on the *I-ching* was recognized officially by the imperial government.[49] Before that, the commentary was not without its critics. For example, Wang

Chi (ca. 240–285 A.D.), a high official and Confucian scholar who "criticized the *Lao-tzu* and *Chuang-tzu*," described it as largely "mistaken."[50] The noted historian Sun Sheng (302–373 A.D.), to take but one more example, found it strong on "flowery expression" but feared that it might leave the great Way blemished in the end.[51] These comments are suggestive especially because they were made by well-known Confucians; in other words, the commentary on the *I-ching* will provide us with excellent clues with respect to Wang Pi's departure from the traditional understanding of Confucian teachings.

Needless to say, a detailed study of Wang Pi's commentary on the *I-ching* is beyond the scope of the present work. The particular passage that concerns us is from the first part of the *Hsi-tz'u* (Appended Remarks) and has to do with the meaning of the so-called number of the Great Expansion. The text reads: "The number of the Great Expansion *(ta-yen)* is fifty, but use is made only of forty-nine."[52] On this, Wang Pi comments:

> In the amplification of the numbers of heaven and earth, fifty form the basis. Forty-nine are used, but "One" is not used. Because it is not used, use (of the others) is made possible; because it is not a number, numbers are made complete. This indeed is the Great Ultimate *(t'ai-chi)* of Change. Forty and nine, these mark the end of the numbers. As *wu* cannot be made manifest by *wu* itself, it must be mediated by *yu*. Thus, focus on the ultimate of things, then one will understand the root from which they spring.[53]

Before I examine Wang Pi's remarks more closely, a brief excursion to a few of the Han interpretations of this passage of the *I-ching* will prove illuminating. For instance, Ching Fang (ca. 77-37 B.C.) has read this passage in a radically different way: "The number 50 here refers to the 10 days [of the traditional Chinese ten-day 'week'], the 12 hours [of the day], and the 28 stellar constellations [*hsiu*, or 'lunar mansions']. The total amounts to 50. The reason why 'one' is not used is because heaven produces the breath of life *(ch'i)*, so as to fill (the universe) by what is empty *(hsü)*. Thus only 49 are used."[54]

Ma Jung (79–166 A.D.), the master commentator of the classics during the Later Han dynasty, is even more elaborate. On the "number of the Great Expansion" he comments:

Change has the Great Ultimate, and that is the North Star. The Great Ultimate gives birth to the Two Forms; the Two Forms give birth to the Sun and the Moon; the Sun and the Moon give birth to the Four Seasons; the Four Seasons give birth to the Five Phases or Elements; the Five Phases give birth to the 12 Months; the 12 Months give birth to the 24 calendrical periods. The North Star resides in the middle and does not move, while the remaining 49 revolve around it and are used.[55]

One + 2 + 2 + 4 + 5 + 12 + 24 = 50; it is quite an ingenious scheme indeed.

These examples reflect well the emphasis on cosmology, on the direct correspondence between the natural and the cosmic, to which attention has already been drawn. They reflect also the kind of "referential" reading that I have ascribed to Han interpretations of the classics in general. Even Cheng Hsüan (127–200 A.D.), arguably the greatest Han commentator of the classics, was not untouched by this mode of understanding. With regard to this passage of the *I-ching*, Cheng Hsüan attempted to combine it with another passage of the *Hsi-tz'u* that reckons the numbers of the universe to be fifty-five.[56] Although the number of the "Great Expansion" is fifty, according to Cheng, it does not include the five phases or elements. After explaining the genesis of these numbers by correlating heaven, earth, the numbers one to ten, the five cardinal points, and the five phases, Cheng Hsüan then goes on to say quite simply that "one" is not used in the "Great Expansion," because it does not serve the purpose of divination. That is to say, when the divining stalks are divided into two sets, fifty would yield two even or two odd numbers; forty-nine, on the other hand, would give one even and one odd, which can then be correlated with the *yin* (broken) and *yang* (unbroken) lines of the hexagrams.[57]

What is important here is that Wang Pi's interpretation of the *I-ching* has abandoned this "referential" mode of understanding typical of the Han period. As the Sung poet Chao Shih-hsiu (fl. 1190) writes, "In (Wang) Fu-Ssu's command of the *I-ching* there is no Han learning."[58] Instead of concentrating on what the numbers stand for, Wang Pi is concerned with unveiling the deeper significance of the "One," which seems to stand apart from the other numbers. The "One," as we have seen, is described as the "Great Ultimate of Change" (*I-chih t'ai-chi*). Although it is not used and is not a number, the "One" makes possible and complete the process of change. Moreover, according to Wang Pi, "One" is also related to "non-being" (*wu*). This becomes a very important point when we come to Wang Pi's commentary on the *Lao-tzu*.

Words and Meaning

The traditional Confucian understanding of the *I-ching* is thus transformed into an explication of the fundamental ground of change. This has important hermeneutical implications. How did Wang Pi arrive at his interpretation? On what basis could he justify his departure from the older hermeneutical model? The answer to this may be gathered from Wang Pi's understanding of the relationship between "words" (*yen*) and "meaning" (*yi*), or as Tu Wei-ming puts it, between "expressed form" and "implied meaning."[59]

The whole issue of *yen* and *yi*, words and meaning, has its root in the *I-ching* as well. In the *Hsi-tz'u* we read: "The Master said, 'What is written does not completely express what is said, and what is said does not completely express the intended meaning.' "[60] Obviously this raises a key hermeneutical question as to the possibility of fully understanding the meaning of an author or a text. Indeed, as the passage goes on to ask, "If so, does it mean that the thoughts of the sages cannot then be seen?" To this, the "Master" (Confucius) replied:

> The sages established the "images" (*hsiang*) to fully bring out what they mean; the "hexagrams" (*kua*) were designed to fully express the true and the false; and the "Appended Remarks" (*Hsi-tz'u*) to give full expression to their words.[61]

This explanation serves to outline the place of the "images," the "hexagrams," and the "Appended Remarks" in an understanding of the *I-ching*. It has a modern ring to it, in that the question of meaning is here brought to the forefront of intellectual inquiry. Are the "images," then, enough to bring across the meaning of change? Wang Pi could hardly avoid this question, for he was concerned with the underlying principle of change. For Wang, the problem goes beyond the "images" and the "hexagrams." In section four of his *Brief Discourse on the I-ching* (*Chou-i lüeh-li*), entitled *Ming-hsiang* (Elucidation of the Images), he writes:

> An "image" (*hsiang*) is that which yields "meaning" (*yi*). And "word" (*yen*) is that through which the image can be un-

derstood. To fully bring out the meaning there is nothing better than the images; to fully express the image there is nothing better than words. Words are born of the image; thus one can untangle the words to view the image. Images are born of meaning; thus one can untangle the images to view the meaning. Meaning is reached by the images, and the image is expressed by words. *Therefore* while the image is made understood by words, the words themselves are forgotten when the image is attained. And while images preserve the meaning, they are forgotten when meaning is comprehended.[62]

Although this is not a direct commentary on the passage in question, Wang Pi is clearly addressing the same issue raised by the author(s) of the *Hsi-tz'u*. At first glance, Wang Pi appears to be following the basic argument of the *Hsi-tz'u*; that is, the fundamental relationship between *yen, hsiang,* and *yi* is preserved. The "expressed form," epitomized by the *Hsi-tz'u* itself, serves to explain the "images," which in turn bring out the deeper meaning. Yet Wang Pi has also introduced a new element here, which in effect takes away the ultimate importance invested in the "words" and "images," including the hexagrams, by the *Hsi-tz'u*. From the above passage, it is clear that the "therefore" with which Wang Pi introduces his own view does not quite follow from the preceding argument taken basically from the *Hsi-tz'u*. When meaning is understood, as Wang Pi now argues, words and images can then be forgotten. In other words, the emphasis is shifted from the *means* of interpretation to the *end* itself.

How can this be justified, especially when the *Hsi-tz'u*, and indeed the *I-ching* as a whole, does not seem to support it? It is interesting to note that Wang Pi sought help from the *Chuang-tzu* to push his argument one step further. As Wang sees it, "words" and "images" are like the tools of the hunter or fisherman:

They are like the trap or net which catches the hare; when the hare is caught, the trap is forgotten. Or (they are like) the container that catches the fish; when the fish is caught, it too is forgotten. In this sense, words are the "traps" of the image; and the images are the "containers" of meaning. For this reason, those who cherish the words have not attained the image; those who cherish the images have not attained the meaning.[63]

This metaphor may not carry the kind of necessity that Wang Pi's argument claims to demonstrate, but it brings out clearly the logic of the argument. It is not only that words and images may be forgotten when meaning is comprehended; rather, it is *necessary* to "forget" these tools of interpretation before meaning can be truly understood. According to Wang Pi, "The attainment of meaning lies in the forgetting of the images; the attainment of the image lies in the forgetting of the words."[64] In the concluding lines of this section of his *Brief Discourse on the I-ching*, Wang Pi speaks very forcefully against the Han method of reading the *I-ching* in terms of external referents. In the end, as Wang concludes, "it misses the original meaning (of the *I-ching*)."[65]

The whole issue of the relationship between *yen* and *yi* was evidently a much debated topic in the Wei-Chin period. Ou-yang Chien (ca. 265–300), for example, has written a treatise entitled "Words Fully Express Meaning" *(Yen-chin-i lun)*.[66] Hsün Ts'an (ca. 212–240), on the other hand, is a well-known supporter of the opposite view—that "words do not fully express meaning" *(yen pu chin-i)*.[67] For our purposes, the importance of this debate lies in the fact that it points to the interpretive framework in which Wang Pi stands. Meaning, in this framework, is above all "nonreferential," in the sense that it is not to be found in external objects to which the author or text may be seen to refer. On the contrary, meaning is identified with the essence or ground of the ideas themselves. Although meaning is mediated by words and images, understanding itself transcends the tools, the media through which meaning is brought to light. In this respect, interpretation is primarily a process of "reduction," though in the descriptive, nonpejorative sense of the word. Instead of extending a concept or "image" to include other phenomena, Wang Pi is arguing for a return to the essential ground of what lies behind the "words" and "images." The importance of the intermediate steps is not denied; what Wang Pi is arguing against is a kind of "idolatry" that attaches ultimate significance to "words" and "images." This insight, as I shall argue in the next chapter, can ultimately be traced to Wang's understanding of the Tao as what is "nameless" and "formless."

Sagehood and Feelings

Wang Pi is thus somewhat of an iconoclast. There is little doubt that he found the traditional interpretations of the classics lacking in insight and understanding. He did not simply replace the old interpretations by a new one, however. Wang Pi's reading of the *I-ching* is based on a radical reformulation of the process of interpretation itself. In order to overcome what I have called the referential mode of interpretation, Wang Pi did not hesitate to draw from Taoist sources to bring his point across. Does this make him a "Neo-Taoist" or "anti-Confucian"?

It may be suggested that Wang Pi was merely "using" Confucius to legitimize his "Neo-Taoist" philosophy. In the *Chuang-tzu*, for example, Confucius is made into a student of Taoism. The *Shih-chi* also reports that "presently those who study the *Lao-tzu* all spurn the teaching of Confucius, and Confucian scholars also spurn the *Lao-tzu*."[68] But as far as Wang Pi is concerned, there is no evidence to suggest that he was involved in this kind of sectarian dispute. While historical considerations alone may not be able to determine the question of Wang Pi's intellectual leanings, on the basis of the above analysis it seems fair to say that neither "anti-Confucian" nor "Neo-Taoist" can adequately describe Wang Pi's thought. Indeed, the difficulty of understanding Wang Pi's work is precisely that it has so often been interpreted from the point of view of Neo-Taoism. Although Wang Pi was at the center of the "profound learning" movement, he did not adhere to all its tenets. To conclude this preliminary discussion, I may point to Wang's view on the "feelings" *(ch'ing)* of the sage. On this question, which is important to my analysis in the next chapter as well, Wang Pi again shows himself to be an independent thinker.

According to Ho Shao's biography of Wang Pi, "Ho Yen believed that the sage does not experience joy, anger, sorrow, and pleasure. His view was most penetrating, and Chung Hui and others all elaborated on it."[69] This was the dominant view at the time; the *Shih-shuo hsin-yü*, for example, also records other exponents of it.[70] Wang Pi, however, took exception to this. As the biography continues:

> (Wang) Pi disagreed and argued that the sage differs from the ordinary people in spirituality and wisdom *(shen-ming)*, but is the same in terms of the five feelings. Because the level of spirituality and wisdom is different, the sage is therefore able to embody emptiness and harmony so as to become one with *wu*. Because the five feelings are the same, the sage therefore cannot be without sorrow and pleasure to respond to things.

Nevertheless, while the feelings of the sage respond to things, they are not bound by things. Now, if one thinks that because the sage is not bound by things, he therefore does not respond to them, he indeed far misses the mark.[71]

This debate on the sage's emotive nature calls into question the possibility of attaining sagehood itself. According to T'ang Yung-t'ung, the prevalent view at the time, current since the Han dynasty, was that sagehood is impossible to achieve.[72] If the sage were without emotions, as Ho Yen and others had suggested, then sagehood would become a "superhuman" phenomenon, and hence beyond human ability to achieve. Yet Wang Pi has argued to the contrary; the sage does have feelings and differs from the ordinary people only in terms of wisdom and spirituality. It seems to me that the possibility of attaining sagehood is left open in Wang Pi's interpretation.

The question of sagehood is very important for our understanding of Wang Pi, and indeed of Wei-Chin intellectual history as a whole. For Wang Pi, the concrete expression of the sage's wisdom lies in his ability to embody "emptiness and harmony" (ch'ung-ho), and ultimately wu. The sage's feelings allow him to respond (ying) to things, and thus he is able to truly affect change in the socio-political world. Otherwise, the sage would remain absolutely transcendent and could not bring in the reign of "great peace" (t'ai-p'ing), the ideal state or utopia in traditional Chinese thought. As T'ang Yung-t'ung also points out, the Wei literati in general adhered to the view that only the sage could bring about genuine peace and harmony in the world.[73]

The sage is able to respond to things, but he is never bound or fettered (lei) by them. Here, Wang Pi may be alluding to a passage in the Chuang-tzu, which states that "hatred, desire, joy, anger, sorrow, and pleasure, these six are what bind (lei) virtue."[74] According to the Chuang-tzu, human feelings are what bind men to the world of artificiality, and prevent them from attaining genuine virtue. Wang Pi is probably arguing against this view, at least as it is applied to the sage. It should be recognized that just as Wang Pi has reinterpreted the Confucian tradition, he was never a naive or uncritical reader of the Taoist classics as well. The question of Wang Pi's intellectual orientation is to be approached from this perspective. In the next chapter, it will be shown that Wang's understanding of the Lao-tzu transcends any sectarian considerations.

At this point, however, I wish to turn attention to a number of textual issues concerning the history and structure of Wang Pi's *Lao-tzu* commentary.

Wang Pi's *Lao-tzu* Commentary and Other Writings

Wang Pi was a prolific writer; but there is some confusion as to what he wrote during his short life. There are varying accounts in Wang's biography by Ho Shao and in the bibliographical records of the dynastic histories. Moreover, most of his writings have not been preserved.

Most records indicate that there was a collection of Wang Pi's works in five *chüan*, which is now lost but was probably still in existence in the eleventh century.[75] Wang's work on the *Lun-yü*, entitled *Lun-yü shih-i* (Explanation of Doubtful Points in the Analects), is also well attested in traditional sources. Unfortunately it, too, has not survived, except for a small number of quotations preserved in other commentaries.[76] Wang Pi's major work on the *I-ching*, which consists of a commentary on the sixty-four hexagrams, is still extant, thanks to the effort of the fourth-century scholar Han K'ang-po (fl. ca. 365). He completed Wang Pi's work by commenting on the remaining chapters, beginning with the *Hsi-tz'u*. There is also the shorter work, *Brief Discourse on the I-ching*, to which I have already referred.[77]

According to Wang's biography, he also wrote a treatise on the "Meaning of the Great Expansion," which as we have seen is focused on a specific passage of the *I-ching*. Except for a few sentences quoted by Han K'ang-po in his commentary on the *Hsi-tz'u*, we have no further record of it today.[78] Wang Pi's commentary on the *Lao-tzu* is of course still extant. Finally, Wang has also written at least one shorter work on the *Tao-te ching*. For a long time believed to have been lost, it is identified by many scholars today with the anonymous treatise entitled *Lao-tzu wei-chih li-lüeh* found in the *Tao-tsang* (Taoist Canon).[79]

Transmission of the Lao-tzu Commentary

The textual history of Wang Pi's commentary on the *Lao-tzu* is difficult to trace. It was not widely recognized prior to the Sung dynasty. As a result numerous textual problems confront students of the commentary. As Takeuchi Yoshio observes, "Today it is almost impossible to find a good text of the Wang Pi commentary."[80]

The problem is a long-standing one. In the bibliographical section of the *Sui-shu* (History of the Sui Dynasty), Wang's work is clearly identified as the "*Lao-tzu tao-te ching* in two *chüan* with Wang Pi's commentary."[81] In the *Chiu T'ang-shu* (Old History of the T'ang Dynasty), however, Wang Pi's work is recorded as *Hsüan-yen hsin-chi tao-te* (Profound Words on the Way and Virtue Newly Recorded) in two *chüan*.[82] To further complicate the issue, the *Hsin T'ang-shu* (New History of the T'ang Dynasty) assigns this title to the well-known scholar Wang Su (195–256 A.D.). Wang Pi's own work is now listed under a slightly different title, *Hsin-chi hsüan-yen tao-te* (New Account of the Profound Words on the Way and Virtue).[83] It is only in the *Sung-shih* (History of the Sung Dynasty) that the more familiar title *Lao-tzu chu* is restored to the Wang Pi commentary, whereas the work of Wang Su disappears altogether from the scene.[84]

There is no reason not to believe that all these titles refer to the same work. The editors of the *Ssu-k'u ch'üan-shu* (Complete Four Libraries Collection) in the Ch'ing dynasty (1644–1911) have long suspected that these titles were variants of one single commentary.[85] More recently, and more convincingly, Takeuchi has shown that the title *Hsüan-yen hsin-chi* (Profound Words Newly Recorded) was a generic term applied to Taoist works in general during the T'ang dynasty.[86] There is a Tun-huang manuscript (P 2462), for example, that applies this title to other works on the *Tao-te ching*.[87] Moreover, there is also a *Hsüan-yen hsin-chi ming-Chuang pu* (Profound Words Elucidating the *Chuang-tzu* Newly Recorded) listed in the *Sui-shu*.[88]

The important point here is that confusion easily arose as a result of these different listings; or more precisely, these different entries reflect the state of uncertainty surrounding the work of Wang Pi from an early time. According to the Sung Taoist work, *Hun-yüan sheng-chi* (Sacred Annals of the Undifferentiated Ultimate) by Hsieh Shou-hao (fl. 1194), there were then two versions of Wang Pi's *Lao-tzu;* one with 5,683 characters, and the other with 5,610.[89] This is repeated in the commentary by P'eng Ssu (fl. 1229), and likewise in Chiao Hung's (1541–1620) *Lao-tzu i* (Guide to the *Lao-tzu*).[90] In another Sung commentary by Tung Ssu-ching (fl. 1246), the number of versions is even increased to four, although it is almost certainly an error on Tung's part, for the two "new" versions are ascribed to Ho-shang Kung in the other works.[91] Nevertheless, the error itself is indicative of the difficulty involved in tracing the textual transmission of Wang Pi's commentary.

By the Sung dynasty, it seems that Wang Pi's commentary on the *Lao-tzu* was no longer widely known or readily available. According to Hung I-hsüan (1765–1833), "The current text of the Wang Pi commentary did not appear until the Ming dynasty; perhaps it was reconstructed by later scholars."[92] And if we were to believe the early Ch'ing scholar Ch'ien Tseng (1629–1701), Wang Pi's work was apparently not even extant by the seventeenth century.[93] This may appear surprising, given the wide currency of Wang Pi's commentary today; but, as we have seen, it was Ho-shang Kung's commentary on the *Lao-tzu* that remained the dominant one in traditional China.

The standard text of the Wang Pi commentary today is that of the *Ssu-pu pei-yao* (Essential Works of the Four Libraries Collection) edition, on which my analysis in the next chapter is based. This edition contains, besides the text of the *Lao-tzu* with Wang Pi's commentary, a colophon or book note by the Sung scholar Ch'ao Yüeh-chih (1059–1129), a second note by Hsiung K'o (ca. 1111–1184), and Lu Te-ming's (556–627) *Lao-tzu yin-i* (The *Lao-tzu* Phonologically Explained), which claims to be based on Wang Pi's text and is taken from Lu's larger work, the *Ching-tien shih-wen* (Explanation of the Classics).[94]

The *Ssu-pu pei-yao* edition is a reproduction of the Ch'ing "Collected Treasures" (*Chü-chen*) edition. The term *Chü-chen* refers to a movable block type instituted in 1773 by imperial command when the collection of the monumental *Ssu-k'u ch'üan-shu* began (completed 1782). The term "Wu-ying palace edition," incidentally, is also often used in this context, because it was under the auspices of the Wu-ying palace that the type was cut. The *Chü-chen* edition itself is based on the Ming edition of Chang Chih-hsiang (1496–1557), which includes the two book notes mentioned above and is taken from Chang's *San-ching Chin-chu* (Chin Commentaries on Three Classics). The *Ssu-k'u* editors, however, collated Chang's edition with Lu Te-ming's *Lao-tzu yin-i* and the Ming *Yung-lo ta-tien* (The Great Collection of the Yung-lo Era) (1403–1428) edition.[95]

In other words, although the *Ssu-pu pei-yao* edition can be traced to the edition of Chang Chih-hsiang via the *Chü-chen* edition, it cannot be said that we have here the original of Chang's edition, first published sometime during the Wan-li era (1573–1619) in the latter part of the Ming dynasty. Indeed, according to the *Ssu-k'u* editors, although the text they have "can still be made out on the whole," it is not without errors.[96] However, it remains true that the edition of Chang Chih-hsiang, or at least that "family" of texts, forms the basis of almost all current editions of Wang Pi's commentary on the *Lao-tzu*. For example, the *Tao-tsang* edition is clearly from the same textual family as Chang's version, for it also contains the book notes by Ch'ao Yüeh-chih and Hsiung K'o.[97] The same may be said for the Japanese edition (Preface dated 1769) revised by Usami Shinsui (1710–1776), to take but one more example. Incidentally, he also states that "the current texts of the Wang Pi commentary contain a great many mistakes, and there is no good text to serve as a standard."[98]

The text of Chang Chih-hsiang itself can be traced to that of Ch'ao Yüeh-chih (styled I-tao), a distinguished Sung scholar who was especially well versed in the *I-ching*.[99] Ch'ao appended a note, dated the tenth month of 1115, to his edition of Wang Pi's commentary on the *Lao-tzu*. In it, Ch'ao observes that Wang Pi is very good on the *Lao-tzu*, but not quite as proficient with respect to the *I-ching*. Ch'ao also indicates that the text he has seems rather corrupt: "The writings or characters are full of mistakes, and sometimes they cannot even be deciphered."[100] But it appears to be an old one because it is not divided into a *Tao* section and a *Te* section. Finally, as Ch'ao concludes, since Wang Pi's commentary is accomplished and surpasses those of later commentators, he therefore made a copy despite the unsatisfactory condition of the text at his disposal.

This version eventually found its way into the hands of Hsiung K'o, who was a younger contemporary of Ch'ao and is now chiefly remembered for his historical works.[101] Hsiung writes in his book note on Ch'ao's version that since he learned from other sources that Wang Pi's commentary has captured the essence of the *Lao-tzu*, he had been looking for a copy of it for quite some time. However, according to Hsiung, the Wang Pi commentary was by then no longer easily available, and it was only after an extended search that he managed to obtain a copy, which he soon published. Shortly after, Hsiung came across Ch'ao's version. As he himself relates:

> Then I obtained the copy with Master Ch'ao I-tao's note, which is not divided into a first *Tao* section and a second *Te* section, and also does not have section titles *(p'ien-mu)*. As I like its old style, I therefore carefully copied it for my collection, and in 1170 . . . I had the blocks engraved for its trans-

mission. As to possible textual errors, since even former scholars could not correct them, how could I dare to make any rash changes?[102]

This 1170 edition, then, forms the prototype of a line of texts, from the Ming edition of Chang Chih-hsiang, through the Ch'ing *Chü-chen* edition to the present *Ssu-pu pei-yao* edition; it is to the work of Ch'ao Yüeh-chih and Hsiung K'o that we owe our gratitude for the preservation of Wang Pi's commentary on the *Lao-tzu*.

Structure of the Lao-tzu Commentary

Hsiung's remarks point to a discrepancy in the current editions of the Wang Pi commentary, which claim to go back to the first edition of 1170. This concerns the original form of Wang Pi's commentary. Most current editions of the *Lao-tzu* are divided into two sections and eighty-one chapters; but the Ch'ao-Hsiung edition of 1170, as the two book notes make clear, does not divide the text into a *Tao* section and a *Te* section. Does this mean that Wang Pi's commentary was originally without chapter and section divisions? Does this mean that the current versions, the *Ssu-pu pei-yao* and the Usami edition, for example, no longer reflect the original form of Wang Pi's commentary?

According to Ch'en Chen-sun (fl. 1235), who is arguably one of the most knowledgeable bibliophiles of the Sung dynasty, Ch'ao's version is indeed a rare treasure. As he explains, "The current versions of the *Lao-tzu* all divide the *Tao-te ching* into two separate sections [i.e., a *Tao-ching* and a *Te-ching*]. This copy [Ch'ao's version] of the *Tao-te ching*, however, does not even have chapter titles *(chang-mu)*; it should certainly be an ancient version."[103] Ch'en is thus of the opinion that Wang Pi's version of the *Lao-tzu* originally did not have section and chapter divisions; but by the Sung dynasty most versions were already divided into sections and chapters, and some probably have chapter titles as well. The same is already implied by Hsiung K'o who, as may be recalled, was pleasantly surprised when he saw the "old style" of Ch'ao's text after he had just published another version, which presumably has section and chapter divisions.[104]

However, Lu Te-ming's *Lao-tzu yin-i*, which is based on Wang Pi's text, does divide the *Lao-tzu* into two sections, a *Tao-ching* and a *Te-ching*. Since Lu's work dates back to the beginning of the T'ang dynasty at the latest, this would seem to contradict the view that Wang Pi's text was "originally" undivided. This interesting puzzle has led the *Ssu-k'u* editors, for example, to suspect that the work of Lu Te-ming was tampered with by subsequent scholars so that it conforms to the format of the later editions of the *Tao-te ching*.[105] The view that the text of Wang Pi's *Lao-tzu* was originally not divided into a *Tao-ching* and a *Te-ching*, or into chapters, has found many able supporters since the Sung dynasty.[106]

Critics of this view, whose prominence has been on the rise since the nineteenth century, will no doubt point out that the *Lao-tzu* is known to have been divided into two sections since the Han dynasty. Moreover, there seems to be internal evidence to suggest that the Wang Pi text was originally divided into sections and chapters. According to Ch'ien Ta-hsi (1728–1804), the version of Ch'ao Yüeh-chih itself may well be a product of the Sung dynasty trying to imitate the style of more ancient works.[107] In other words, there is no reason not to believe that the work of Lu Te-ming has in fact preserved the original form of the Wang Pi commentary.[108]

The "internal evidence" mentioned above refers to chapters 20, 23, 28, and 57 in the current 81-chapter version of Wang Pi's commentary, in which passages from other chapters (48, 35, 40, and 48) are quoted. The chapter numbers are of course not identified, but such phrases as "section below" (*hsia-p'ien*), "chapter below" (*hsia-chang*), and "chapter above" (*shang-chang*) are used. According to Hatano Tarō, the terms *p'ien* and *chang* are used interchangeably in this context, and the vagueness of these references would indicate that Wang Pi's text was originally undivided.[109] According to Wing-tsit Chan, however, these references form "the strongest proof that the original edition of the Wang Pi commentary had two parts and many chapters."[110] In this respect, we may add that the recent discovery of the two Ma-wang-tui *Lao-tzu* silk manuscripts appears to lend further support to the latter view. In one of the manuscripts (Text B), dated 194–180 B.C., the text of the *Lao-tzu* is explicitly divided into a *Te* part and a *Tao* part, marked by the editorial notations "*Te* 3,041" characters and "*Tao* 2,426" respectively.[111]

Given these considerations, I am inclined to believe that the Wang Pi commentary was originally divided into two sections. However, it seems that the division into eighty-one chapters remains a later addition, perhaps to conform to the popular Ho-shang Kung version. The references to a "chapter above" or "chapter below" cannot by themselves be taken as proof of the contrary, for they may simply be general spatial indicators. If there were chapter divisions, they would have been reflected in such a work as Lu Te-ming's *Lao-tzu yin-i*. In his *Chuang-tzu yin-i* (The *Chuang-tzu* Phonologically Explained), for example, all chapter divisions and titles are clearly indicated. Since the division into eighty-one chapters can be traced to Liu Hsiang (79–8 B.C.) and is associated with the Ho-shang Kung commentary, there is little reason why later redactors might want to suppress it. This whole issue is best summed up by the Ming scholar Chu Te-chih:

> The origin of the chapter divisions can now no longer be discerned. They were standardized by the Emperor Hsüan-tsung [r. 712–755] in the T'ang dynasty. Older versions have different chapter divisions: some have 55 chapters (Han Fei-tzu), some have 64 (K'ung Ying-ta), 68 (Wu Ch'eng), 72 (Yen Tsun), or 81 (Liu Hsiang et al, or some say Ho-shang Kung), and some are not divided into chapters (for example, Wang Pi and Ssu-ma Kuang).[112]

The claim that Wang Pi's commentary was originally divided into two sections does not necessarily contradict the testimony of Ch'ao Yüeh-chih and Hsiung K'o. Their notes indicate that the Wang Pi text was not divided into a *Tao-ching* and a second *Te-ching*. It is possible that the Wang Pi text in their possession was divided into two untitled sections. This distinction is not unimportant. As Tōjō Ichitō (1778–1857) pointed out long ago, the division into two sections may be compared with the structure of the *Hsi-tz'u* in the *I-ching*, which though divided forms a unified whole with regard to its content.[113] In other words, the notion that the first thirty-seven chapters of the *Lao-tzu* are focused on *Tao*, while the remaining forty-four are focused on *Te*, reflects an interpretive stance, but is not intrinsic to the text itself. Takeuchi Yoshio, even more specifically, has also argued that the division into a *Tao* section and a *Te* section in the version of Lu Te-ming is both extraneous and late; it does not reflect the original form of the Wang Pi commentary.[114]

Admittedly, this does not agree with the evidence of the Ma-wang-tui *Lao-tzu* manuscripts. Nevertheless, I do not see why it is necessary to assume that a uniform *Lao-tzu* text had existed from such an early date. The fact that the Ma-wang-tui manuscripts begin with the *Te* section—that is, chapter 38 of the modern text—is itself a telling indication of the fluid state of the text of the *Lao-tzu* at the time. There is no reason why the Wang Pi text must conform to any one particular format. Indeed, the *Tao-tsang* edition of the Wang Pi commentary is even divided into four *chüan*.[115] And it is also not divided into chapters.

The original format of Wang Pi's commentary is ultimately a matter of conjecture, and it should not distract us from the main task of interpretation itself. In conclusion, Wang Pi's commentary was no longer widely recognized by the Sung dynasty. Copies were then rare, mostly in poor conditions, and there were significant differences among them.[116] In part, this neglect may be due to the prestige and influence that the Ho-shang Kung commentary enjoyed from the Six Dynasties period onward, as Taoism gradually developed into a major religious institution.

Toward the end of the twelfth century, we begin to see a renewed interest in the Wang Pi commentary, no doubt owing to the rise of Neo-Confucianism. To what extent this latter movement was indebted to Wang Pi is difficult to determine, though it is clear that they both share a same deep interest in a number of fundamental concepts, especially that of *li*, "principle." At any rate, from the thirteenth century on, Wang Pi's commentary on the *Lao-tzu* began to reemerge as a major intellectual force, and by the Ch'ing dynasty it began to acquire its present status as one of the most important, if not the most important, commentary on the *Lao-tzu* ever written.

2   Wang Pi: Non-being, Principle, and the Ideal Sage

It is difficult to apply the terms "Neo-Taoist" or "anti-Confucian" without qualification to Wang Pi, as I have argued in the last chapter. This serves as the point of departure for the following analysis. The task of chapter 2 is to show that Wang's understanding of the *Lao-tzu* cannot be taken as exclusively concerned with abstract metaphysics. The argument here is focused on a dialectical interpretation of the concepts of "non-being" (*wu*) and "principle" (*li*). This reading takes into account the importance of practical concerns, centering on the figure of the ideal sage, which permeate Wang Pi's commentary on the *Lao-tzu*. On the basis of this analysis, the question raised in the last chapter can then be more fully considered.

The Question of Non-being (*Wu*)

From biographical records and other commentaries, we have seen that the notion of "non-being" (*wu*) is central to Wang Pi. He was remembered by later historians as having brought this concept to the forefront of Chinese thought, and was in fact accused of a serious "crime" on that account. In Wang Pi's commentary on the

Lao-tzu, the term *wu* is used to describe the nature of Tao. What does *wu* mean in this context?

There is little disagreement as to what *wu* does *not* mean. It is not "being" (*yu*); Tao as *wu* cannot be identified with any "thing" of this world. In this sense, *wu* can be translated as "non-being" or "no-thing," with the emphasis on the negative prefix. The problem arises, however, when one tries to describe it in a positive way.

The negative meaning of *wu* is emphasized especially by philologists and linguists. The most radical expression of this is the view of Peter Boodberg, who states that in classical Chinese *yu* and *wu* "remained securely within the semantic and philosophical category of habit or possession, being both essentially transitive verbs: 'to have (something)' and 'not to have (something)'."[1] This view has been criticized for not recognizing cases in pre-Han literature where these terms are used as nouns.[2] While this is a just criticism, it does not solve the problem. As A. C. Graham points out, "When *yu* and *wu* are used as nouns, a serious ambiguity arises; they may mean either '(there-)being' and '(there-)not-being' or 'something' and 'nothing'."[3] The question, in other words, is whether *wu* can be taken as an *abstract* noun when it is applied to Tao. Again, as Graham writes, "Those who identify the Tao with *wu* mean primarily that it lacks form and other qualities, and . . . that it is not a thing which exists in the world."[4] Wang Pi, according to Graham, is precisely one of those who exemplified this interpretation.

This casts a doubt on the use of "non-being"—or better, "Nonbeing"—to translate *wu* as an abstract noun signifying the presence of a transcendental subject. Although it is clear that *wu* means "not having" any determination or limitation, the problem remains whether it does not mean *more*. Indeed, as Graham also recognizes, as a "positive complement" of *yu*, *wu* does not mean a "mere absence."[5] Nevertheless, as a "complement" one cannot strictly speaking ascribe any sort of ontological independence to it. As such, Tao defined as *wu* would mean quite simply that it is the opposite of being, or as Wang Pi puts it, of what has "form" and "names."

In what regards Wang Pi's commentary on the *Lao-tzu*, this view has so far made little impact. The dominant interpretation of the notion of *wu* in Wang Pi's commentary is precisely that it means more; that is, Tao is designated by "Nonbeing" because it is that "original stuff" from which all beings originate. Wang Pi's understanding of *wu* as applied to Tao is not only a negative one, in other words, but implies the existence of a fundamental "substance," which is ontologically distinct from and prior to "being."[6] It is in this technical sense that the term "Nonbeing" will be used throughout this study, as distinguished from the more general "non-being."

This metaphysical interpretation is clearly reflected in the two English translations of the Wang Pi commentary. Paul J. Lin has, for example, quite explicitly identified *wu* with "substance" in his general discussion of Wang Pi's thought.[7] Among French scholars, Isabelle Robinet has similarly argued that the term *wu* has acquired a significant "philosophical extension" in the work of Wang Pi. More precisely, according to Robinet, the philosophy of Wang Pi is focused on the "ontological plane," and to deny the metaphysical nature of *wu* would reduce it to a "moral" level, associated especially with the idea of "not having any desire" (*wu-yü*).[8] This insight is a telling one, as it shows how the interpretation of *wu* will affect our understanding of Wang Pi's commentary as a whole. Turning to the text itself, the meaning of the concept of *wu* must now be examined. Both "non-being" and the transliterated form, *wu*, will be used in what follows. While the term "non-being" is admittedly rather awkward and may not be acceptable to all translators, it is nonetheless familiar to students of Chinese thought and forces us to focus on the question of being, which is central to this discussion. In this context, "non-being" is preferable to such alternatives as "nothingness" or "vacuity," which do not immediately address the issue of a possible ontological dimension in Wang Pi's thought. The crucial question, again, is what does "non-being" mean in the Wang Pi commentary? Using Wang Pi's own cross-references as a guide, individual chapters of the commentary will be grouped together and discussed thematically.

From Non-being to Principle (*Li*)

The Nature of Tao

The opening chapter of the *Lao-tzu* is arguably one of the most important statements of classical Taoism. In Wang Pi's commentary on this chapter, one sees the notion of "non-being" emerging as a dominant theme of his work. Commenting on the line, "The nameless is the origin of heaven and earth; the named is the mother of all things," Wang Pi says: "All beings (*yu*) originated from nonbeing (*wu*)."[9] In chapter 42, the priority of *wu* is brought out more fully. Here the *Lao-tzu* reads, "Tao begets One. One begets Two. Two begets Three. Three begets all things." Wang Pi comments:

> The ten thousand creatures have myriad forms; but they are ultimately one. How can they become one? Because of *wu*. From *wu* comes "One"; "One" may be called *wu*. Since it is called "One," how can it be without words? With words and with the "One," how can there not be "Two"? With "One" and "Two," "Three" is thus born. From *wu* and *yu*, all numbers end here.[10]

On chapter 40, where the *Lao-tzu* itself states that "All things in the world come from *yu*; *yu* comes from *wu*," Wang Pi remarks: "The things of this world have life by virtue of being; the origin of being is rooted in *wu*. If fullness of being is to be attained, one must return to *wu*."[11]

These passages need to be examined more closely. They are chosen because they exhibit a common concern with the relationship between being and "non-being." The claim that *wu* is the origin of being may seem to suggest the idea of an "original substance." When viewed more closely, however, *wu* remains primarily a negative concept.

Chapter 1 of the *Lao-tzu* begins with the well-known statement that "The Way that can be told of is not the constant Way; the name that can be named is not the constant name." In what sense can *wu* be said to describe the Way, if the latter is beyond description? On this line, Wang Pi comments:

> The Way that can be told of and the name that can be named: these have to do with things and forms, which are not constant. Hence (the constant) cannot be told of and cannot be named.[12]

The notion of "constancy" (*ch'ang*) will be explained in greater detail later; here, it is equated with the "nameless," which as we have seen is also the "beginning of heaven and earth." It is in this context that we find Wang Pi's statement that "all beings originated from *wu*." Thus, *wu* cannot be identified with anything that can be named or pointed to, anything that has form. What can be named "have to do with things and forms" (*chih-shih tsao-hsing*). This phrase is revealing for it suggests what may be called the "linguistic" character of the world of things. Literally meaning the "pointing to things" and the "making of forms," it calls to mind the work of the Han scholar Hsü Shen (fl. 100 A.D.), who defined the Chinese language in terms of six general categories, the first two of which are "pointing to things" (*chih-shih*) and the "symbolization of form" (*hsiang-hsing*).[13]

This allusion to a linguistic theory addresses well the concern with language that is evident in the opening words of the *Lao-tzu*. The Way is beyond description, beyond language. Yet it is also the "beginning," from which all things originated. In this regard, I take Wang Pi's comments to mean that Tao can be expressed as *wu* in the sense that it does not have an objective referent. Tao as *wu*, in other words, transcends the phenomenal world that is always mediated by language, in the broadest sense of the term.

The metaphysical basis is thus related to a theory of language, in terms of which the apparent paradox in chapter 1 is explained. On the next line of chapter 1, "The nameless is the beginning of heaven and earth; the named is the mother of the ten thousand things," Wang Pi writes:

> All beings originated from *wu*. Thus before there were form and names, (Tao) then is the "beginning of the ten thousand things." When there are form and names, (Tao) then "brings them up, nourishes them, makes them secure and stable"; it is their "mother." This means that Tao in its formlessness and namelessness originates and completes the ten thousand things. They are thus originated and completed, but without knowing why—this is what is "more profound than the deepest profundity."[14]

The myriad creatures are not only produced by Tao, but are in fact dependent on it in every aspect of their existence. But Tao is here described as *wu* only in the sense of what is "formless" and "nameless"; there is no direct ontological discussion of the nature of *wu* as "Nonbeing."

The description of Tao as *wu* is further found in a number of related chapters. The commentary on chapter 1, first of all, is partly repeated in chapter 21. Here the *Lao-tzu* describes the Way as "elusive and vague," which according to Wang Pi means that Tao appears "formless and without ties." The *Lao-tzu* goes on to say, "Vague and elusive, within it are images; elusive and vague, within it are things." Does this not suggest that there is "something" within the Tao? Wang Pi explains:

> In formlessness things are originated; without ties things are completed. The ten thousand things are thus originated and completed, but without knowing why it is so.[15]

What is "within" the Way is thus simply related to its creative and sustaining power.

However, chapter 21 continues with the statement that "dim and dark, within it is an essence." What is this "essence" (ching)? According to Wang Pi, "dim and dark" describes what is "deep and far," and what is "deep and far cannot be obtained and seen; but the ten thousand things are all derived from it. It cannot be obtained or seen; but their true nature is determined by it."[16] In this regard, the "essence" of Tao does not appear to be "something" that can be positively identified. It is true that the *Lao-tzu* then describes this "essence" as "very real" and that "from ancient times to the present its name has not been abandoned, by which the beginning of all things can be discerned." Does this not imply that the Tao not only has an essence, but that this essence has a "name" as well? Wang Pi's understanding of this passage is very clear:

> If things return to the "dim and dark," then the ultimate of true essence can be attained, and the nature of the ten thousand things can be determined. . . . The ultimate of the truly real cannot be named. "Nameless" is indeed its name. From ancient times to the present, never has anything become complete except through it. . . . This is to describe the beginning of the ten thousand things in terms of the nameless.[17]

Concluding his commentary on chapter 21, Wang Pi emphasizes again that the "ten thousand things"—that is, all beings— "originated from *wu*"; but the notion of *wu* must be taken in its proper context. Throughout the entire chapter, and in chapter 1 also, Tao is described essentially in terms of its namelessness and its generative force. There is no clear ground to extend the concept of *wu* to mean "Nonbeing" in the sense of "substance." Although the concept of *wu* is central, for Wang Pi the important point is precisely to eliminate any idea of "thingness" or "substance" from one's contemplation of the meaning of the Way.

As in chapter 21, the Tao is also said to be "vague and elusive" in chapter 14. Wang Pi's understanding of the latter further reinforces my interpretation. Moreover, the commentary on chapter 1 quotes directly from the text of chapter 51. And Wang Pi's analysis of this latter likewise adds to my conviction. Both chapters 14 and 51 are important, though for different reasons. The former is important because the *Lao-tzu* original is somewhat ambiguous. While it seems to emphasize the "negative" nature of the Way, the paradoxical expression employed here may also suggest the idea of a transcendental substance. Chapter 51, on the other hand, is important because it sets out the fundamental relationship between the Way and "virtue" (*te*), or the "power" of Tao, and provides a more detailed analysis of the process of creation.

Chapter 14 begins with a description of Tao as what cannot be "seen," "heard," or "touched." Tao is beyond the world of sensory experience; it is "nameless" and it "returns" to the realm of "nothing" (*wu-wu*): "This is called the shape that has no shape, the image that has no objects."[18] Wang Pi is certainly sensitive to this use of paradox in describing the Way. As he explains, "One may want to speak of *wu*, but things become complete through it; one may want to speak of *yu*, but its form cannot be seen. Hence it is said, 'The shape that has no shape, the image that has no objects.' "[19] It is interesting that Wang Pi again alludes to the theme of language here. More will be said on this point later in the discussion.

According to Wang Pi, in this same chapter, "What is formless and nameless (*wu-hsing wu-ming che*) is the source of the ten thousand things." It is true that the phrase *wu-hsing wu-ming che* grammatically involves a nominal construction, which may therefore seem to imply the existence of a "substantivized" subject, but my contention remains that *logically* the idea of substance is not intrinsic to Wang Pi's analysis. The ubiquitous presence of Tao is of course not denied, but it does appear that Wang Pi has taken pains to differentiate it from other concepts that can be grasped by reason and language. If we consider Wang Pi's understanding of chapter 14 as a whole, the central insight that emerges with respect to the nature of Tao remains that of its ineffability and its claim to be the "source" of all things. The question is how these two aspects of Tao can be maintained philosophically at the same time.

Chapter 51 is especially concerned with the latter aspect of Tao as the source of all beings. The *Lao-tzu* reads:

> The Way gives them life.
> Virtue nurtures them.
> Matter gives them form.
> The environment completes them.[20]

Wang Pi comments:

> Things are born and then nurtured; nurtured and then en-
> dowed with form; endowed with form and then made com-
> plete. What causes them to be born? It is Tao. What nurtures
> them? It is virtue. What gives them form? It is matter. What
> makes them complete? It is the environment. . . . For things
> which are born, and for efforts which are made complete,
> there are always causes. As there are causes, then none is not
> caused by Tao. Thus when (the argument is) pushed to the
> limit, we again find the ultimate Tao. On account of their (im-
> mediate) causes, they are therefore accorded different titles.[21]

Although a sequential order is provided by Wang Pi to explain the
process of creation, the more important insight is that the cause of
all creation is said to be ultimately one. In this sense, Wang Pi's
understanding of Tao as the source of all beings can be expressed in
terms of a principle of causation and a principle of unity.

Tao as Principle

The very idea that the Way may be described as a "principle"
(*li*), first of all, must be carefully examined. The concept of *li*, as is
well known, is especially associated with the Neo-Confucian movement of the Sung dynasty. But as Ch'ien Mu has shown, the concept of *li* was already developed by Wang Pi.[22] Following Ch'ien's
lead, Wing-tsit Chan has similarly argued that the concept of *li* is a
key characteristic of Wang Pi's thought. In Wang's commentary on
the *Lao-tzu*, as Chan points out, the word *li* appears some eight
times even though it is not used in the *Lao-tzu* itself. In some instances, the word *li* is used as a verb in the sense of "to organize"
or "to put into order"; but in other places it seems to have taken on
a deeper philosophical meaning, as the fundamental principle of
the cosmos itself.[23]

According to the *Lao-tzu*, the sage "knows the world without having to set foot outside his door; sees the Way of heaven without having to look through his window" (chap. 47). How is this possible? Wang Pi is especially concerned to bring out the underlying reason for this remarkable achievement:

> Every occurrence has its source; everything has its master. [To borrow from the *I-ching*:] The paths may be different, but they reach the same end; considerations may be many, but they all lead to one. The *Way* has its great constancy and *Principle* (*li*) has its general structure. By holding fast to the way of old, one can master the present; though living in the present, one can know the beginning of antiquity. This is why (the sage) knows without having to set foot outside his door or to look through his window.[24]

In this instance, there is no doubt that the notion of "principle" is made to parallel that of Tao.

It is also interesting that the commentary here refers back to chapter 14, where the idea of "holding fast to the way of old" is first introduced. As the *Lao-tzu* has it, "The ability to know the beginning of antiquity is called the thread running through the Way."[25] The reason for this, according to Wang Pi, is that even though "high antiquity is far, its Tao remains." And the reason for that is because "what is formless and nameless is the source of the ten thousand things." The Way is constant, as we have seen, transcending the limitation of space and time, and its constancy can be interpreted in terms of a "principle," structured, intelligible, the understanding of which would give one the ability to "know the beginning" and to "master the present." Chapters 14 and 47, in this regard, mutually interpret and support one another.

"Thus the sage," as chapter 47 of the *Lao-tzu* concludes, "knows without having to move, identifies without having to look, and accomplishes without having to act."[26] Wang Pi's commentary here may serve to sum up our discussion of his understanding of Tao and *li* so far:

> (The sage) grasps the structure of things; therefore though he does not move, through contemplation, he is able to know. He

recognizes the source of things; therefore though he does not look, he is able to grasp and identify the principles of right and wrong. He understands the nature of things by simply following it; therefore though he does not take any action, he is able to bring about all his accomplishments.[27]

The knowledge of the sage, in other words, has nothing to do with outward appearances or trivial details; rather it has to do with the inner structure, with the "nature" of things. And what makes this kind of knowledge possible is precisely the idea of a "principle" that characterizes the workings of the Way. In itself the Way is indeed beyond description, but its "constancy" reveals a meaningful pattern which can be captured by our "following" it. The nature of this mode of knowing will be examined later; at this point, suffice it to say that the concept of *li* serves to describe the ordered and ordering manifestation of Tao in the world.

In this sense, it seems to me that Wang Pi's understanding of *li* cannot be equated with that of the Neo-Confucians. The idea of principle in Wang Pi's commentary on the *Lao-tzu*, like the notion of *wu*, lacks the sense of ontological independence that is apparent in the later development of the concept. It is not my intention, however, to reduce the richness of Neo-Confucian philosophy into any single formulation. My point is simply that in the Wang Pi commentary, *li* is understood primarily as a *heuristic* concept, which seeks to articulate the way in which Tao is related to the world, and its implications for the task of self-cultivation. In this case, it may be permissible to abandon the standard translation of *li* as "principle," and to render it by "pattern" or "paradigm." "Principle" is retained mainly because it is important not to lose sight of Wang Pi's contribution to Neo-Confucianism.

Limiting my discussion to the theoretical level of Wang Pi's interpretation here, the idea of *li* is seen particularly as a principle of causation and as a principle of unity. The former should be clear from my earlier discussion of the emphasis on the creative power of Tao. Events and things of this world have their causes, which can be traced ultimately to Tao itself (chaps. 21, 51). This is the "principle" evident in the "Tao-ist" universe, in the proper, non-sectarian sense of the word. As a principle of causation, the Tao may indeed be described as the "beginning" and the "mother" of the world (chaps. 1, 14, 21, 51).

Moreover, as we have also seen, chapter 42 of the *Tao-te ching* depicts the "Tao-ist" cosmogony in terms of the generation of the primary numbers (see p. 48, above). For Wang Pi, this signifies that the "ten thousand things," despite their myriad forms, all stem from "One." In this sense, the principle of causation is also a principle of unity. However, for Wang Pi, "One" may be identified with the notion of *wu* as well: " 'One' may be called *wu*. Since it is called 'One,' how can it be without words? With words and with the 'One,' how can there not be 'Two'? With 'One' and 'Two,' 'Three' is thus born. From *wu* to *yu*, all numbers end here." What does this mean?

Wang Pi's commentary, as Hatano Tarō has shown, is here partly adapted from a passage in the *Chuang-tzu*, which is chiefly concerned with the inadequacy of language and of the calculating mind in reaching the truth of the Way:

> Heaven and earth were born the same time I was, and the ten thousand things are one with me. We have already become one, so how can I say anything? But I have just *said* that we are one, so how can I not be saying something? The one and what I said about it make two, and two and the original one make three. If we go on this way, then even the cleverest mathematician can't tell where we'll end, much less an ordinary man. If by moving from *wu* to *yu* we get to three, how far will we get if we move from being to being? Better not to move, but to let things be.[28]

Although the irony and playfulness of the *Chuang-tzu* original is not reproduced, this explains the reference to language in Wang Pi's analysis of the movement from "one" to "three" and the ten thousand things. The concern with language points to the fact that Wang Pi's interest here is essentially a logical one. After indicating the "oneness" of all creation and the movement from *wu* to *yu*, Wang Pi continues:

> Thus with respect to the production of the ten thousand things, I know its master. Although there are myriad forms, the blending of the generative force (*ch'i*) makes them one. The people have their own minds and different states have different customs; but kings and rulers who have obtained the

"One" become their master. Since "One" is the master, how can it be abandoned?[29]

The Way, in this instance, is taken to be the "master," because it is the source and the principle of unity—symbolized by "the blending of *ch'i*," generative force or the primordial "breath" of life, as Wang Pi repeats Lao-tzu's phrase here—which reconciles external differences. Later in the chapter, this is described by Wang Pi as the "ultimate principle," which brings "fortune" to those who follow it, and "misfortune" to those who decide to run contrary to it.

The political parallel suggested in this passage is significant, for it shows that Wang Pi's concern is not an exclusively metaphysical one. The reason why *wu* may be identified with "One" is quite clearly that they both point to the Way. Whereas the former describes its formlessness and namelessness, the latter explains the principle of unity that is inherent in the "Tao-ist" world. When the *Lao-tzu* (chap. 47) exclaims that "the further one goes, the less one knows," Wang Pi adds that it is because "*wu* lies in 'One,' but (the people) seek it in the multiplicity of things."[30] Neither *wu* nor "One," however, may therefore be elevated to the level of an absolute; they remain servants of the mind in its attempt to disclose the wonder of the Way. Nowhere in the Wang Pi commentary are they made into a godlike substance which exists independently of the realm of experience.

The commentary on chapter 42 again refers to another chapter. The idea of "kings and rulers" who represent the unity of the political world is one of the main topics of chapter 39 of the *Lao-tzu*. On the opening line of chapter 39, "Of old, those who obtained the One," Wang Pi comments:

"Of old" means the beginning. "One" is the beginning of numbers and the ultimate of things. As things are produced by "One," it is thus their master.[31]

By extending the meaning of "One" as the source of all numbers to signify the "ultimate of things," the centrality of unity is driven home with unmistakable clarity. It describes the power of Tao as the source of unity that safeguards order and harmony in the world. As the remainder of chapter 39 makes clear, the crux of the matter is that one must not lose sight of the "mother," of the fundamental principle through which the genesis of beings and the unity at the root of multiplicity may be understood.

The Dialectic of *Wu* and *Li*

The Inadequacy of Language

So far I have looked at a number of related chapters with the view of identifying the theoretical basis of Wang Pi's commentary on the *Lao-tzu*. These chapters are thematically similar; they all focus on the nature of Tao as *wu*, as *li*, and as the source of all beings. Wang Pi's understanding of these chapters is, in my view, remarkably consistent. Tao in itself is characterized by its transcendence, and that means it is sui generis, without determination or limitation, and cannot be "named" by language. This insight is crucial to Wang Pi's understanding of the *Lao-tzu* as a whole. The Tao is known only in the sense that its "constancy" is manifested in the world. Ostensibly the manifestation of Tao is seen in the plenitude of nature, in the multiplicity of things. But on a deeper level, according to Wang Pi, the manifested Tao may be understood negatively as *wu* and positively as *li*.

Although in itself beyond language and thought, the Way may be understood as *wu*, which conceptually sets it apart from the domain of beings. The use of "non-being" to explain the concept of *wu* in Wang Pi's commentary is thus justified, if the negativity is properly recognized. The notion of principle serves to explain the manifestation of Tao in nature. It can be defined as the underlying reason or structure of the cosmos. The "constancy" of the Way is such that seemingly diverse phenomena can be traced to a fundamental unity and a common source. Philosophically, then, Tao as "principle" points to the nonduality and creative power of the Way; politically it is paralleled by a system of government led by an enlightened king—that is, a "Tao-ist" ruler. Together "non-being" and "principle," properly understood, form a dialectic in which the ineffable Tao and the "Tao-ist" world find their balance.

Chapter 25 brings out this balance very well:

Text	*Commentary*
There was something undifferentiated and complete, which existed before heaven and earth.	Undifferentiated, it cannot be known; but through it all things are made complete. Thus, it is said,

"undifferentiated and complete." "It is not known whose son it is."[32] Thus (it is said), "existed before heaven and earth."

Silent and void, it stands alone and does not change.

"Silent and void" means without form or body; nothing can stand up to it. Thus it is said, "it stands alone." Returning and transforming, ending and beginning, it does not lose its constancy. Thus it is said, "It does not change."

It goes round but is without danger; it can be considered the mother of the world.

"Goes round" means that there is nowhere it does not reach; but it is free from danger and is able to produce and preserve the great form [i.e., the world]. Thus, it can be considered the mother of the world.[33]

I do not know its name.

Names serve to determine form. Completely undifferentiated and without form, it cannot be pinned down and determined. Thus it is said, "do not know its name."

I style it Tao.

Names serve to determine form; style-names serve to designate what can be expressed. "Tao" is chosen because there is nothing which does not follow (its "Way"). This means that of the "undifferentiated and complete," "Tao" is the greatest of all designations for what can be expressed.

If forced to give it a name, call it great.

The reason I style it "Tao" is that I chose the greatest of all designations for what can be expressed. When we examine the ground for the choice of this word, we therefore see that it is tied to (the idea of) greatness. But, what has ties is sure to have divisions.[34] With divisions, then the sense of the ultimate is lost. Thus it is said, "If forced to give it a name, call it great."[35]

This detailed commentary on chapter 25 is important because it shows that Wang Pi was keenly aware of the radical transcendence of the Way *in itself*. Even the word "Tao" is to be used with caution, and with understanding; otherwise the sense of the "ultimate" would have been lost. Moreover, as suggested earlier, Wang Pi has a strong interest in the phenomenon of language. And the limitation of language is certainly brought out very clearly in this instance. The world of human understanding is mediated by language; but the nature of the transcendent Tao, "undifferentiated and complete," cannot be "tied" to the way of rational discourse or measured by words. Chapter 1 of the *Lao-tzu* has already stated that "the Way that can be told of is not the constant Way." Why? The mediation of language "determines" (*ting*), "names" (*ming*), and "divides" (*fen*); it objectivizes. For Wang Pi, to put it bluntly, the Way can never be made into an object; one must not ascribe "form" and "names" to what is beyond the realm of phenomena. After all, although the Tao is described here as "great," it is also said to be "small" in the *Lao-tzu* (chap. 34).

Yet the Way *can* be expressed if one is careful not to turn what is heuristic into a literal representation. Such words as "Tao" and "great" can be used if we do not mistake "what can be expressed" for the Way in itself. The Way is the source of all things, the "mother," and this should be recognized. The constancy of the Way, which can be communicated and understood, may indeed be called "great." In chapter 25, the *Lao-tzu* further states that "great is called proceeding (*shih*). Proceeding is called far-reaching. Far-reaching is called returning." According to Wang Pi, this cryptic description characterizes the movement of the Way:

> "Proceeding" means movement, and not holding to any one form of greatness. (The Way) goes round, and there is nowhere it does not reach. Thus it is said, "proceeding." "Far-reaching" means reaching the ultimate. (The Way) goes round, and there is no limit it does not exhaust. It does not confine (its movement) to any one direction. Thus it is said, "far-reaching." Not resting in where it goes, it stands alone by itself. Thus it is said, "returning."[36]

The Way gave rise to all beings, but it does not "rest" with them or become a part of the world of phenomena. It "stands alone," as Wang Pi's repeats Lao-tzu's expression, in the sense that in itself the Way remains "undifferentiated and complete." The movement of

Tao may therefore be visualized as a process of the Way's going out of itself in its creative activity, and its returning to itself in its unfathomable sublimity. This signifies a pattern that can be discerned in the world. As our text continues:

Text	Commentary
Thus Tao is great, heaven is great, earth is great, and the king is also great.	The nature of heaven and earth is such that man is most valued. And the king is the master of men. . . . Thus it is said, "The king is also great."
Within the realm, there are four great ones.	The four great ones are Tao, heaven, earth, and the king. Things all have designations and names, and as such they are not the ultimate. To speak of "Tao" is to have recourse to reason. Based on reason, it is then called the Tao. This means that Tao is great among what can be designated. It is not as great as what cannot be designated. Without designation, it cannot be named; (thus) it is called the "realm." Tao, heaven, earth, and the king are all within that which cannot be designated. Thus it is said, "Within the realm there are four great ones."

Again, the theme of the inadequacy of language is emphasized. This indeed seems to rule out the possibility that Wang Pi had defined the unnameable Tao in terms of an identifiable "substance." However, what we can say about the Way is also more clearly spelled out. Within the "realm" of the Way in itself, "undifferentiated and complete," four "great" manifestations can be discerned. Their relationship is explained in Wang Pi's concluding commentary on chapter 25 of the *Lao-tzu*. The *Lao-tzu* reads:

> Man models himself on earth;
> earth models itself on heaven;
> heaven models itself on Tao;
> Tao models itself on the naturally so (*tzu-jan*).

Wang Pi comments:

> "To model" means to follow specific rules. Man does not act contrary to (the rules of the) earth, and thus he obtains safety and comfort: this is what is meant by "model himself on earth." Earth does not act contrary to (the rules of) heaven, and thus it can support (all things): this is what is meant by "model itself on heaven." Heaven does not act contrary to (the rules of) Tao, and thus it can shelter (all things): this is what is meant by "model itself on Tao." Tao does not act contrary to what is naturally so, and thus it realizes its nature. To model on what is naturally so means to follow the rules of the square while inside the square, or to follow the rules of the circle while inside the circle; that is, to adhere without exception to what is naturally so. "Naturally so" is a term for what cannot be designated, an expression for the ultimate. . . . Thus, they model after one another.

This is the "model," the hierarchical structure of the "Tao-ist" world. This is the principle through which the Way manifests itself in nature. Ultimately, for Wang Pi, the Way can be expressed in terms of what is "naturally so" (*tzu-jan*). In this regard, the dialectic of "non-being" and "principle" finds its balance in the concept of *tzu-jan*.

Spontaneity and Naturalness (tzu-jan)

The concept of *tzu-jan* is indeed central to Wang Pi's commentary on the *Lao-tzu*. Literally meaning what is "self-so," *tzu-jan* suggests spontaneity and naturalness; in modern Chinese it is used to translate the English "nature." The concept of *tzu-jan* is one of the most often used concepts in the commentary.[37] On the theoretical level, it is a concept that seeks to describe "what cannot be designated," and to bring into view the nature of the "ultimate." As we shall see, on the practical level *tzu-jan* characterizes the way of the sage himself.

When applied to Tao, *tzu-jan* does not suggest anything specific. It simply indicates that Tao always follows its own "way"; that is, it affirms again that the Way cannot be tied to any specific mode of operation. But the concept of *tzu-jan* is applicable to the world of nature also, for it is perceived to be "modeled" on the Way. In other words, *tzu-jan* serves to capture the sense of an inherent order in a "Tao-ist" universe. According to the *Lao-tzu*, "Heaven and earth are not benevolent; they regard all things as straw dogs" (chap. 5). The "straw dogs" here were most probably used in sacrifices of ancient times; as the *Chuang-tzu* observes, before the sacrifice they are much valued and revered: "But after they have once been presented, then all that remains for them is to be trampled on . . . to be swept up by the grass-cutters and burned."[38] Wang Pi, however, understands this quite differently:

> Heaven and earth abide by *tzu-jan*. Without their doing or making anything, the ten thousand things themselves govern one another and put their affairs into order. Thus (heaven and earth) "are not benevolent." To be benevolent is to make, to institute, to endow, and to change things; it involves favors and action. If one undertakes to make, institute, endow, and change things, then things will lose their true nature. With favors and action, then things will not be equally pre-served. . . . (Heaven and) earth do not produce straw for animals, but animals eat it; they do not produce dogs for men, but men eat them. Do nothing (artificial) to the ten thousand things, and they will be at ease in their own functions; then indeed nothing will not be self-sufficient.[39]

It is interesting that Ho-shang Kung too seems to have taken the phrase "straw dogs" as referring to two separate entities.[40] Perhaps sacrifices involving token animals were no longer understood by the latter part of the Han dynasty.

At any rate, Wang Pi's point is quite clear. What may be called the principle of heaven and earth follows the course of nature, ef-fortlessly and without artificial action. What is "naturally so" has nothing to do with human virtues, which involve "favors" and seek to "improve" nature. The way of *tzu-jan* is simple and constant; ag-gressive intervention merely leads one away from one's "roots." As Wang Pi puts it, "The way of *tzu-jan* is like a tree. The more it turns, the farther it strays from its roots; the less it turns, the closer it gets to its ground. Having more, it then distances itself from its true (source) . . . less, it then reaches its roots."[41]

Wang Pi is saying that one should return to the "roots." He identifies the "root" with the notion of the "mother" (chap. 52), both of which point to the centrality of the Way as the ground and source of all beings. But leaving aside for the moment the practical import, the important insight here remains that the world is ultimately "modeled" on the "naturally so," which expresses the positive presence of Tao in nature.

Two Objections

It may be objected that by denying the "substance-nature" of Tao, the philosophical or more precisely ontological import of Wang Pi's thought would have been undermined. There is no question that the Wang Pi commentary has a strong philosophical interest. By emphasizing the negative nature of Tao in itself, nothing is taken from the philosophical side of Wang Pi's analysis; it merely seeks to clarify it.

Instead of turning the Way into an abstract substance, the notion of *wu* seeks to preserve its mystery and transcendence. Instead of yielding to a mystical silence, the idea of *li* brings out the pervasive presence of the Way in nature. The Way is *wu*, but because of it all things come into being. This is what Wang Pi calls the Way of *tzu-jan*. Surely Wang Pi's analysis is *ontological*, for it is concerned with the question of being, its nature and source. But to borrow a Heideggerian distinction, this does not necessarily mean that Tao is therefore *ontic*. Wang Pi's emphasis on the limitation of language suggests clearly that *wu* cannot be "ontically" understood. What gives rise to being itself does not "have" being. The dialectic of *wu* and *li* is precisely able to maintain both the depth and the clarity of the Way.

It may also be suggested that our understanding of Wang Pi's thought cannot be limited to his commentary on the *Lao-tzu* alone. Fung Yu-lan, for example, has argued that Wang Pi's treatment of the *Lao-tzu* and the *I-ching* reveals a certain inconsistency in that, while the former takes the idea of the "One" as a "product of Tao," the latter identifies it with Tao itself. This would mean that, as Fung concludes, while commenting on the *Lao-tzu* "Wang is trying to explain Lao Tzu's original meaning, whereas in his *Book of Changes* commentary he is developing his own idea."[42] Similarly, according to W. T. Chan, Wang Pi's work on the *I-ching* remains crucial to our understanding of the idea of *li*, and consequently of the nature of Tao as well.[43]

Wang Pi's work on the *I-ching* is undeniably important; but my contention remains that as far as the Wang Pi commentary on the

Lao-tzu is concerned, the ideas of *wu* and *li*, dialectically understood, serve best to capture its theoretical orientation. In addition, this interpretation is also supported by a reading of Wang Pi's shorter work on the *Lao-tzu*, in which the inadequacy of language is especially emphasized.[44] For example, we read that "if one speaks of Tao, one loses its constancy; if one were to name it, one misses its truth." Indeed, "while such words as 'Tao,' 'profundity,' 'deep,' 'great,' 'subtle,' and 'far-reaching' do have their specific meanings, they do not exhaust (the meaning of) the ultimate."[45] "Thus," as the text concludes, "to name (Tao) is to greatly miss its meaning; to designate it means that one does not completely understand its depth."[46] In this work, the negativity of the Way and its practical implications are both heavily underlined.

With respect to the *I-ching*, though it lies outside the scope of this study, I would venture to suggest that Wang Pi's interpretation appears quite consistent also. In the *Chou-i lüeh-li*, for example, the idea of *li*, especially as the principle of unity, is indeed emphasized; but there is no mention of Tao "being" any "substance."[47] As we have seen in the study of Wang Pi's life and thought in chapter 1 above, the idea of *wu* and the principle of unity certainly dominate his reading of the *I-ching*. The "number of the Great Expansion," for instance, is taken to be rooted in the "One," which is also linked to the idea of *wu*. But Wang Pi also writes, "As *wu* cannot be made manifest by *wu* itself, it must be mediated by *yu*. Thus focus on the ultimate of things, then one will understand the root from which they spring."[48] I should think that this rather explicitly brings out the negative nature of *wu*, forming one end of a dialectic.

Thus even in the commentary on the *I-ching*, there is no indication that Wang Pi's interpretation is different from that of his *Lao-tzu* commentary. If we view such concepts as "One" and "root" in the context of a dialectic of *wu* and *li*, they do not signify the Tao in itself but rather articulate the meaning of Tao as it is manifested in the domain of beings. *Wu* is opposed to *yu*: but when *wu* is seen in the light of the principle or pattern governing all beings, then it points to the "sublimity" (*hsüan*) of the Way. We must remember that for Wang Pi true understanding is attained only when "words" and "images" are forgotten. To ascribe a "substance-nature" to the idea of *wu* would, it seems to me, verge on the kind of "idolatry" from which Wang Pi was careful to dissociate himself (see pp. 32-34, above).

Substance and Function

The dialectical interpretation of *wu* and *li* is thus quite in keeping with the findings of our background study of Wang Pi. Turning back to the *Lao-tzu* commentary itself, we may briefly look at chapter 38 before concluding this discussion. The long commentary on chapter 38 sums up in many respects Wang Pi's understanding of the *Lao-tzu*. The emphasis here is predominantly on the practical application of the Way, but the centrality of *wu* is also highlighted.

Chapter 38 of the *Lao-tzu* is especially concerned with the idea of virtue (*te*). According to Wang Pi, virtue means to "obtain" or "attain" (*te*), playing on the homonymic relation of the two words. How can one "obtain virtue"? Through Tao, and more specifically by taking *wu* as "function" (*yung*), which is to say to follow the Way. As Wang Pi explains:

> Virtue means to obtain. It means constant attainment without loss, and benefit without harm. Therefore it is called "virtue." How can virtue be obtained? It is to follow Tao. How can virtue be fully utilized? It is by using *wu*. With *wu* functioning, then nothing will be left unsupported. . . . Thus though heaven and earth are vast, they take *wu* as their heart. Though sages and kings are great, they take emptiness (*hsü*) as their master.[49]

Wu, in this instance, is clearly paralleled with the idea of *hsü*, "emptiness" or "vacuity"; and the implication is that sages and kings are "great" because they have followed the way of emptiness. The concept of *hsü* is in fact used interchangeably with *wu* in Wang Pi's commentary (e.g., chaps. 5, 16, 48). The Way is "empty" because in itself it does not "have" any "substance." But *hsü* is also a positive concept. According to Wang Pi, when one embodies the Way one attains "vacuity and nothingness" (*hsü-wu*).[50] I shall return to this point later.

The idea of "function" (*yung*) in the above passage is also important, especially because it may call to mind the Neo-Confucian understanding of "substance" (*t'i*) and "function." However, in the Wang Pi commentary, the term *yung* seems to have retained the concrete meaning of "use." Chapter 11, where the idea of "function" as grounded in *wu* is brought out most clearly, is a good example in this regard. The reason why a "window," for instance, is "use-ful" is because of the empty space that forms its "heart." The "function" of an object is no doubt dependent on *wu*; but, the identification of *wu* with "substance" appears to be a later development. In Wang Pi's commentary on the *Lao-tzu*, the idea of *yung* is mostly paralleled with that of *li*, "benefit" or "profit," which together describe the unlimited resourcefulness of the Way (chaps. 4, 6, 11, 38).

Similarly, though the term *t'i* is found some ten times in five chapters of the Wang Pi commentary (chaps. 4, 6, 23, 25, 38), it need not be equated with the Neo-Confucian understanding of the concept of substance. The word *t'i*, which does not appear in the *Lao-tzu* itself, is generally used in the Wang Pi commentary as a counterpart to "form" and verbally to denote the "embodiment" of the Way. This is recognized by our two translators of the Wang Pi commentary, despite the fact that they favor the identification of *wu* with "substance." Paul J. Lin, for example, has not used the term "substance" even once to render *t'i*; when a nominal expression is required, Lin chooses the more concrete equivalent, "body." Ariane Rump also senses the concrete meaning of *t'i* and translates it as "body" on three occasions (chaps. 4, 6, 25).

In chapter 23 Wang Pi describes the follower of the Way as "one *t'i* with Tao" (*yü Tao t'ung-t'i*). This may indeed seem to justify the use of "substance" in rendering *t'i* in this context. But Wang Pi goes on to say, one who seeks to "attain" (*te*) virtue is also "one *t'i* with attainment," and one who "loses" it is "one *t'i* with loss." If one does not wish to extend the same metaphysical meaning of "substance" to "attainment" and "loss," which I do not, it is better to render the *literary* expression of the type *yü x t'ung-t'i* in a verbal sense as "embodying x" or metaphorically as "one body with x," or simply "one with x." The word "literary" is emphasized here because Wang Pi's fine skill as a writer, though generally recognized, does not appear to have been taken much into account in current interpretations of his work.

In other words, while later Confucians may have found a source of inspiration in the Wang Pi commentary, it cannot be said that Wang Pi had the same sort of Neo-Confucian ideas. The commentary on chapter 38, to take but one more example, states that one must not "leave *wu* as one's *t'i*" (*pu-neng she-wu i wei-t'i*). If we look at Paul Lin's and Rump's translations of this phrase, the latter's emphasis on "substance" stands out very clearly: "cannot cease to embody non-being" (Lin); "there cannot be substance without non-being" (Rump). The former, I submit, is much more appropriate in this instance, since the context makes it clear that Wang Pi is not discussing the abstract nature of "substance," but rather what one must do in the quest for the Way.

I propose, then, to describe Wang Pi's understanding of the *Lao-tzu* in terms of a dialectic of *wu* and *li*. *Wu*, "non-being," depicts heuristically the nature of Tao as "empty" and transcending the domain of ordinary understanding mediated by language. *Li*, on the other hand, describes the world of beings as it is related to Tao. "Principle" suggests order and harmony, which ideally underlie the phenomenal world. This sense of a "Tao-ist" cosmos is fundamentally expressed by the concept of *tzu-jan*, the "naturally so" that mediates between the two ends of the dialectic. The Way as *wu* is "modeled" (*fa*) on what is "naturally so," and this is reflected in the natural and spontaneous functioning of the universe. It is in this sense that the dialectic is not just between "non-being" and "being," but more precisely between "non-being" and "principle."

Other related concepts such as "root" (*pen*), "mother" (*mu*) and "function" (*yung*) can then be placed within the framework of this dialectic. Tao is the "mother" and "root" of all things in the sense that it is the principle of unity to which the world of beings can ultimately be traced. And it is "use-ful" because the "emptiness" of Tao has practical implications and can never be exhausted. Similarly, in Wang Pi's commentary *wu* is also applied metaphorically to the notion of the "uncarved block" (*p'u*). For example, Wang Pi writes:

> The Way is formless and without ties, constant and cannot be named. . . . The "uncarved block" is something with *wu* as its heart; it is also nameless. Thus if one wishes to reach the Way, there is nothing better than to keep the "uncarved block."[51]

The emphasis of this passage, as the remainder of the commentary on this chapter even more clearly indicates, is on how to obtain the Way. It also explains why the "uncarved block" is an appropriate symbol for Tao, for it is untouched by what is not "naturally so." The notion of *p'u*, in other words, signifies a kind of utter simplicity that transcends the world of human action and desires. If the concept of *wu* is not properly understood, what is metaphoric in Wang Pi's commentary would have been turned into the literal.

I have argued in some detail that the notion of *wu*, when applied to Tao, cannot be regarded as "substance" for essentially two reasons. First, it is important to see Wang Pi's own philosophical horizon in his interpretation of the *Lao-tzu*. I contend that what may be called a metaphysics of substance remains quite foreign to Wang Pi's thought. If *wu* is ontologically prior to *yu*, and if *wu* is identical to "substance," then " substance" should be on a higher level than "function." This is clearly not the case in Wang Pi's thought, where "substance" and "function" are viewed as equal.[52] Although chapter 40 of the *Lao-tzu* states that "*yu* comes from *wu*," we must not forget that chapter 2 also says: "*yu* and *wu* give rise to each other." This ambiguity calls for a clear formulation of Wang Pi's understanding of the *Lao-tzu*.

Secondly, the reading proposed here enables us to assess better the practical import of Wang Pi's thought. The identification of *wu* with "substance" tends to undermine Wang Pi's contribution to the world of ethics and politics, for it subsumes other aspects of his interpretation of the *Lao-tzu* to the "ontological" level. Wang Pi's recognition of the transcendence of Tao signals a dual emphasis on the nature of Tao and its concrete applications. Even in the discussion above, it is evident that the practical aspect is at least equally important and closely related to the more abstract inquiry into the depth of the Way. In this regard, I am taking seriously Tu Kuang-t'ing's suggestion that the Wang Pi commentary is focused on "the way of ultimate emptiness and nonaction, of governing the family and the country" (see p. 9, above).

The Ideal Sage

Critique of Legalism

When the focus of attention is shifted from the ineffable Tao to its constant manifestation, it implies that one must respond to the Way. This "response" (*ying*) is expressed concretely in the realm of politics. When the *Lao-tzu* says, "Hold fast to the great image and the world will come (to you)," Wang Pi draws out the political implication: "If the ruler holds fast to it, then the world will come to him" (chap. 35). In chapter 36, the *Lao-tzu* states:

> The yielding and weak will overcome the
> hard and strong.

> Fish cannot leave the deep;
> Sharp weapons of the state must not be
>   shown to anyone.

Playing on the word *li*, which means both "sharp" and "profit," and the opposite "loss," Wang Pi explains:

> "Sharp weapons" (*li ch'i*) means instruments that profit the state. Follow only the nature of things; do not resort to punishment to put things in order. The instruments cannot be seen, but all things acquire their proper place. Then these are indeed "sharp weapons" of the state. To show them to the people is to use punishment. To use punishment to profit the state will only lead to loss. If the fish leaves the deep, it will certainly be lost. If the instruments that profit the state are turned into the establishment of punishment in order to show the people, then they too will certainly lead to loss.[53]

Wang Pi is concerned with politics. In this instance, he is reacting to what may be regarded as a "legalist" teaching, which emphasizes reward and punishment. Support for this interpretation can be gathered from Han Fei-tzu's reading of the same passage, in terms of the concept of "power" (*shih*):

> Strong central power is the "deep" of the ruler of men. Ministers are the "fish" of this power. When the fish is lost to the deep, it cannot be regained. When the ruler of men loses his power to the ministers, he will never get it back. Ancient people could not speak of this explicitly; they therefore made use of the metaphor of the fish.[54]

With respect to the "sharp weapons" of the state, Han Fei-tzu writes:

> Reward and punishment are the sharp weapons of the state. On the side of the king, they keep the ministers in check. On the side of the ministers, they overpower the king. If the king is the first to show the reward, then the ministers would diminish it by claiming it to be their own virtuous action. If the ruler is the first to show punishment, the ministers would add to it by claiming it to be their own forceful action. The king

shows reward and the ministers make use of its power; the king shows punishment and the ministers ride on its force. Thus it is said, "Sharp weapons of the state must not be shown to anyone."[55]

Although both Han Fei-tzu and Wang Pi agree that what will benefit the state must not be revealed, they differ on the use of punishment. For the former, punishment is to be carried out by the ministers; for Wang Pi, it is not to be used at all. If Wang Pi is critical of the "legalist" doctrine, what is his own understanding of the way of government? The answer to this lies in Wang Pi's understanding of the sage.

The sage represents the ideal ruler in Wang Pi's commentary. There are two aspects to this statement. First, the sovereignty of the king must be recognized. As we have seen, the king is one of the "four great ones" in the realm of Tao (chap. 25). Secondly, the figure of the sage provides a model for all rulers to emulate. The king is great, as we have also seen, only because he adheres to the way of "emptiness" (chap. 38). In other words, Wang Pi's interpretation of the *Lao-tzu* did not aim at challenging the existing political structure, but at improving it.

From chapter 36 we see that the ideal ruler governs by not revealing the "sharp weapons" of the state. In so doing, these tools will become "instruments that profit the state." If these "instruments" (*ch'i*) are not reward and punishment, what are they and why must they not be shown? The word *ch'i* literally means a vessel, and by extension any useful object. In addition to its political meaning, according to Wang Pi, the term "sharp weapons" also means "all instruments that profit the self" (chap. 57). As such, they serve an important function; even the sage makes use of them, albeit for a different purpose. But, they remain means to an end, and the two must not be confused. In terms of government, the ideal ruler must precisely recognize these instruments as they are, and stand above them. If these instruments are self-oriented, "it is only when one becomes uninvolved with the self, when all things return to him, then one can establish the instruments that will profit the world and become the master of all things" (chap. 67).[56]

When this is accomplished, then these instruments can be made to serve the political process. The ultimate goal, leaving aside the ethical implications for the moment, is to reestablish the true nature of things, to return to the "One" (chap. 28):

Text	*Commentary*
When the uncarved block is shattered (*san*), it becomes vessels. The sage makes use of them and becomes the leader of officials.	The "uncarved block" means the true. When what is true is shattered, many ways and types (of being) are born. They are like vessels. The sage, in view of the fact that they are scattered (*fen-san*), therefore appoints officers for them. He takes the good as teachers, and the bad as material (to learn from); he changes their ways and transforms their customs, so as to enable them to return to the "One."[57]

In this instance, "instruments" are extended to mean in effect all beings and their ways of life. "Instruments," though useful, are ultimately not to be confused with the "true."

The reason why "instruments that profit the state" must not be revealed is that the "uncarved block" will be shattered even further. The sage does "teach" and "transform" the people, as the above passage indicates; but this is to be interpreted in light of what the *Lao-tzu* calls the "teaching that uses no words" and the "action that takes no action" (chaps. 2, 17, 43, 63). The sage knows that the reason why "instruments" are useful is because of *wu*, for all "functions" are derived from it. The ideal ruler therefore governs by modeling on the negativity of the Way.

The Way of Nonaction (Wu-wei)

The sage governs, above all, by means of "nonaction" (*wu-wei*). This is an important concept. While *wu-wei* may be rendered "nonaction," "doing nothing," "nonassertive action" or "nonaggressive action," it is best understood in the Wang Pi commentary as a mode of being. That is to say, "nonaction" is neither total inaction nor any type of action; it is rather an expression signifying the "Tao-ist" way of life. In chapter 18, for example, the term "great Tao" is simply equated with *wu-wei* by Wang Pi. While the *Lao-tzu* states that "those who follow the Way" are "the same as the Way," Wang Pi brings out the importance of "nonaction":

The Way, in its formlessness and with nonaction, completes and sustains all things. Therefore those who follow the Way take nonaction as their master, and teach with no words. . . . Then, things will obtain their true (nature) and become one with Tao. Thus it is said, "the same as Tao."[58]

Wu-wei, in other words, is another way of describing the manner in which Tao is manifested in nature. Like the discourse on Tao, *wu-wei* can be expressed both negatively and positively. Negatively, it is especially characterized by the sage's having no thought of self (*wu-ssu*) and having no desires (*wu-yü*). Positively, *wu-wei* is equated with emptiness (*hsü*) and tranquility (*ching*), and most importantly with *tzu-jan*.

The sage is not selfish. The term *wu-ssu* means generally impartiality but in this context suggests the sage's being unattached to personal concerns. This does not imply self-denial, however. The *Lao-tzu* says, "The sage puts his person last and it comes first, treats it as extraneous to himself and it is preserved. Is it not because he is without thought of self that he is able to fulfill it?"[59] Wang Pi's commentary here is very brief: "Without thought of self (*wu-ssu*) means not doing (*wu-wei*) anything for oneself. (Yet) the self comes first and is preserved. Thus it is said, 'the self is fulfilled.'" It should be noted that Wang Pi is not concerned with any "technique," which by placing personal considerations last aims at achieving specific ends. The "fulfillment" in question points rather to the mode of being exemplified by the figure of the ideal sage. This same idea is brought out more fully in the commentary on chapter 13, where it is said that one who regards "favors and disgrace" as equally worrisome knows the true meaning of valuing oneself. This person, indeed, may be entrusted with the government of the world. On the other hand, if "deluded by favors and disgrace," the self will become one's biggest enemy.[60]

"Favors and disgrace" (*ch'ung-ju*) point to the perilousness of the political world, which is particularly important given the political instability of the Cheng-shih period. To have no thought of self, one must have no self-oriented desires, the presence of which would lead inevitably to conflict. As Wang Pi puts it, commenting on Lao-tzu's idea that the sage does not value "rare treasures": "Desires, however small, give rise to striving and conflict. Rare treasures may be small, but they lead to greed and thievery" (chap. 64). This theme is repeated in chapter 3, where "desirelessness" is applied to actual political practice:

Text	Commentary
Do not exalt the worthy, so that the people will not contend. Do not value rare treasures, so that the people will not become thieves. Do not display what is desirable, so that the people's minds will not be unsettled.	"Worthiness" means ability. "Exalt" is the name for praise. "Value" designates high esteem. Only the able should be appointed: why praise them? Only the useful should be employed: why value them? Exalting the worthy and glorifying their names, then fame exceeds their appointment and they will always compete with one another. Valuing goods more than their usefulness, the greedy will rush to . . . steal, heedless of their lives. Thus, what is desirable should not be displayed; then, the mind will have no cause to be unsettled.[61]

The sage having no desires himself will try to keep the minds or hearts of the people from becoming greedy and contentious. The emphasis on "ability" certainly recalls our earlier discussion of "names and principles." If Wang Pi did not participate in the debate on "talent and nature" (ts'ai-hsing), he nevertheless shared with his contemporaries the same concern for a system of official appointment based on ability and performance alone. This is why I have discussed this general concern at some length in the last chapter.

The fact that this is a "Tao-ist" model is emphasized by Wang Pi. All beings originate from *wu*; and it is by "constantly having no desires and being empty" that one is able to "perceive the wonder of the origin of things" (chap. 1). On a larger scale, Wang Pi writes:

> The ten thousand things all came into being from Tao. But having been born in this way, they do not know the reason. Therefore, when the world is always without desires, all things will (naturally) have their proper place—as if the Way has done nothing for them.[62]

Ultimately, in such terms as *wu-ssu* and *wu-yü* the emphasis is always on *wu*.

Having no desire is further identified with being "empty" (*hsü*). The desire for emptiness is perhaps the one desire that is exempted from the call to limiting one's desires. For instance, explaining Lao-tzu's paradox that, while learning involves an accumulation of knowledge, the pursuit of Tao "decreases" everyday (chap. 48), Wang Pi simply states: "It is to desire to return to emptiness and non-being" (cf. chap. 30). Although later thinkers, especially under Buddhist influence, might question the logical validity of this claim, Wang Pi's concern is chiefly to bring out the way of *wu-wei*.

To be empty is a positive way of describing *wu-wei* because it signifies a mode of being characterized by tranquility or quietude (*ching*). The commentary on chapter 16 is very clear on this score:

Text	Commentary
Attain utmost emptiness; maintain complete tranquility.	This means that "attain emptiness" is the ultimate (nature) of things; "maintain tranquility" is the true (nature) of things.[63]
The ten thousand things rise together.	They are active and grow.
And I watch their return.	With emptiness and tranquility, one watches their return. All being arises from emptiness; movement arises from tranquility. Therefore, although the ten thousand things rise together, in the end they return to emptiness and tranquility. This is the ultimate (nature) of things.[64]

In Wang Pi's commentary, *hsü* and *ching* are thus synonymous. They are described as the basis of being and movement, and they form the source to which all things return. The notion of "return" will be discussed shortly. At this point, the question is how *wu-wei* as tranquility and emptiness can be applied to political affairs. The *Lao-tzu* says, "When the people do not fear (the use of) force, great force will erupt. Do not restrict their residence. Do not repress their ways of life" (chap. 72). Wang Pi's commentary here is very interesting, taking the "force" (*wei*) in question in two senses and the word *chü*, "residence" or "dwelling," to be more than a place to live:

Tranquility and nonaction are what is meant by "residence." Humility and not being full (of oneself) are what is meant by "way of life." If one forsakes tranquility, acts on impetuous desires, abandons humility and abuses one's authority, then things will be disturbed and the people will become perverse. Force can no longer control the people, and the people will no longer tolerate the use of force. Then above and below will both be in great disorder, and destruction by heaven will be near at hand. . . . This teaches that one must not rely on the strength of force.[65]

Politically, oppressive force stems from abandoning the way of tranquility. This will give rise to an even greater destructive force, the inescapability of which is brought out by the reference to "heaven," and under which both the ruler "above" and the people "below" will suffer. Although Han Fei-tzu did not comment on this chapter, one can see how a "legalist" might disagree with Wang Pi's interpretation: because trouble arises when the people are not afraid of the law and other types of force, the government should instill fear by imposing stiff punishment.

For Wang Pi, government by force is only slightly better than a lawless state; but it ranks below two other types of government. These four types of government are distinguished in Wang's commentary on chapter 17:

Text	*Commentary*
The highest is (merely) known by those below.[66]	"The highest" means the great man. The great man (rules) above; thus, it is said, "the highest." The great man "dwells in the affairs of nonaction, and practises the teaching that uses no words. The ten thousand things stir, but (the stirrings do) not (appear to have been) initiated (by him)."[67] Therefore, those below merely know of his existence. This means that one should follow the (ruler) above.[68]
Next comes the one who is loved and praised.	Unable to do things by nonaction and to teach with no words, he institutes kindness and governs with generosity. He thus endears himself to the people below, who love and praise him.

Next comes the one who is feared.	No longer able to command things by favors and benevolence, he relies on force and authority.
Next comes the one who is despised.	Unable to regulate the people by law,[69] (he) resorts to cunning manipulation to govern the country; he is avoided by the people and his command will not be followed. Thus it is said, "he is despised."

The ideal ruler is thus barely known to the people, because he does not impose his power on them. By being tranquil, he accomplishes the task of government. According to Han Fei-tzu, however, the reason why the ruler is not visible lies elsewhere. It is because the system of reward and punishment is so firmly established that the people believe they themselves are the cause of all political measures.[70]

For Wang Pi, the way of *wu-wei* is ultimately a matter of following what is "naturally so" (*tzu-jan*). When the *Lao-tzu* declares that the sage "practises the way of nonaction," Wang Pi explains: "To be naturally so is sufficient. To act, one will end in defeat" (chap. 2; cf. chap. 48). When the *Lao-tzu* says, "The Way never acts," Wang Pi comments: "This means to follow what is naturally so" (chap. 37).

Tao itself is characterized by *tzu-jan*, and the government of the sage is based on this insight. To listen to Wang Pi's own words again, we see how *wu-wei* is related to *tzu-jan* (chap. 29):

Text	Commentary
(The empire) must not be acted upon. To act upon it is to destroy it; to hold it by force is to lose it.	The nature of the ten thousand things is (characterized by) *tzu-jan*. Therefore it can be followed (*yin*), but not acted upon; one can go along with it, but not hold it by force. Things have their constant nature. If one artificially acts upon it, one will surely fail. . . .
Thus things may lead or follow, breathe hot or breathe cold, strong or weak, destroy or be destroyed. Thus the sage avoids extremes, extravagance, and excess.	. . . the sage realizes the (nature) of *tzu-jan*, and penetrates into the feelings of all things. Thus he follows (*yin*) and not acts, flows along and not interferes. He eliminates

what deludes, and rids of what se-
duces. The mind is therefore not
confused and things naturally attain their true nature.[71]

Wang Pi's elaboration certainly brings out his emphasis on the concept of *tzu-jan*. The ability to recognize the true nature of things is
elsewhere called the "virtue of heaven and earth." And according
to Wang Pi, it is only when one has no thought of self and follows
tzu-jan that one can "become one in virtue with heaven and earth"
(chaps. 77, 5, 16).

Following, Honoring, and Returning to Tao

Enough has already been said on the concept of *tzu-jan* in the
preceding section; but the idea of "following" *tzu-jan* deserves attention. The common word *shun*, which suggests the sense of flowing along with the current, is sometimes used by Wang Pi (chaps.
27, 37, 65). But the word that Wang uses most often in this context
is *yin* (chaps. 2, 27, 29, 36, 41, 45, 47, 48, 49, 51, 56).[72] In addition to
the primary meaning of "to follow," *yin* also has a cognitive dimension, which the word *shun* does not have. As noun, *yin* means reason or cause, and this meaning is carried over to the verbal usage.
To follow *tzu-jan*, in this sense, involves a mode of knowing and
being; it is a realization—in both senses of the word—of *tzu-jan*.

In Wang Pi's commentary, *wu-wei* and *tzu-jan* are most concretely described by the word *yin*. This allows us to pinpoint further
the way of the sage, to supplement the passivity that is at the heart
of his being. To follow *tzu-jan* is contrasted with *wei*, "action"; but
this latter is interpreted in a special sense by Wang Pi, in terms of
the cognate *wei*, which means what is false and artificial (chap. 2).
In other words, as a mode of being, *wu-wei* stems from a prior dis-
cernment of the true from the false. In order to "return" to the true,
the sage follows, realizes the way of "honoring the root, and putting to rest the branches" (*ch'ung-pen hsi-mo*).

The notion of "return" or "reversal" (*fan*) is used in the *Lao-tzu*
to describe the movement of the Way (chap. 40). Literally the word
fan means "opposite," but is used interchangeably with the cognate
fan, "to return." Wang Pi's commentary on chapter 40, quoting and
adapting from chapters 39 and 11, respectively, focuses on the sense
of "opposite" that is inherent in the Way's reversal:

"The foundation of the high lies in the low; the root of honor lies in the humble" [chap. 39]; the function of being lies in non-being [chap. 11]. This is its reversal. . . . Thus, it is said, "Reversal is the movement of Tao."

In chapter 28, however, the sense of "returning" is brought out more clearly. The *Lao-tzu* is again concerned with reversing the normally accepted mode of value, by describing the importance of "know the male but keep to the female," "know the white but keep to the black," and "know honor but keep to the disgraced." Wang Pi explains:

These three mean constant returning. When that is accomplished, then one is able to complete one's dwelling [being]. A later chapter says, "Reversal is the movement of Tao." Success should not be claimed; (rather) remain constantly with the mother.[73]

The symbol of the "mother," as we have seen, is also called the "root"; both describe Tao as the source of creation. Returning to the root is identified in the *Lao-tzu* with tranquility; but Wang Pi's interpretation is highly interesting:

Text	*Commentary*
To return to the root is called tranquility.	Returning to the root, *then* one becomes tranquil; thus it is called "tranquility."
This is what is meant by returning to destiny.	Being tranquil, *then* one returns to one's destiny; thus it is called "returning to destiny."
Returning to destiny is called the constant.	Returning to one's destiny, *then* one obtains the constant in one's nature and destiny; thus it is called "the constant" [chap. 16; my italics].

The identity of these terms now becomes a series of steps leading to the attainment of the "constant." To follow (*yin*) *tzu-jan* is to realize these steps, so that the "virtue of heaven and earth" may be obtained. As we recall, "virtue" (*te*) is defined in chapter 38 as "obtaining" (*te*) the Way.

The first step, then, is to return to the root. The ideal ruler realizes the importance of "honoring the root and putting to rest the branches" (chap. 57):

Text	Commentary
Govern the country with rectitude. Use the army with expedient tactics. Win the world with nonactivity.	Govern the country with Tao, then the country will be at peace. Govern the country with rectitude, then military expedience[74] will arise. With nonactivity, then one can win the world. . . . To govern the country with Tao, one honors the root so as to put the branches to rest. To govern the country with rectitude, one institutes punishment to tackle the branches. If the root is not established, the branches will be sparse. If the people are not taken care of, it will as a result lead to the use of military expedience.

The people must be supported; this is one meaning of "putting to rest the branches" (hsi-mo). However, as the commentary goes on to say, "when the people are strong, the state will be weak." That is, according to Wang Pi, when the people are concerned with "profit" and use "sharp instruments" to achieve self-oriented goals, they will be "strong"; the country, as a result, will be weakened by conflict. In other words, desires of the people, which characterize the "branches," must be "put to rest," put to an end. As chapter 57 concludes:

Text	Commentary
Thus the sage says: I take no action and the people are of themselves transformed. I love tranquility and the people are of themselves rectified. I do not engage in affairs and the people of themselves become rich. I have no desire and the people of themselves become simple.	What the ruler above desires, the people will follow quickly. If what I desire is only to have no desires, then the people also will have no desires and become simple of their own accord. These four [nonaction, tranquility, nonactivity, no desire] indicate honoring the root so as to put to rest the branches.

These comments describe well the ideal state of the *Lao-tzu*, as represented by Wang Pi. By *wu-wei*, "honoring the root," the sage will lead the people away from falsehood and return to the true. The assumption is that the people will follow the example of the sage as a matter of course. They will have few desires; they will not "avoid" the ruler, as Wang Pi puts it in a number of places (e.g., chaps. 17, 33, 49). At the same time, however, they will hardly know that the sage is governing at all. Specific policies or techniques of government are not the issue here. The political vision of Wang Pi is centered on the claim that the transforming power of Tao, exemplified by the ideal ruler, would permeate "naturally" the minds and hearts of the people. When Wang Pi went to see the prime minister Ts'ao Shuang, he probably talked about this, as opposed to the abstract meaning of Tao in itself. This, I suspect, is also why Ts'ao Shuang laughed at him.

The "Tao-ist" Vision

The Concept of Response (Ying)

Although we have focused our discussion on the political level, it is clear that politics and ethics, in the broad sense, cannot be separated in Wang Pi's thought. The sage governs by *being* without desires. The way of government, in other words, ultimately rests on self-cultivation. In a passage reminiscent of the *Great Learning*, the *Lao-tzu* (chap. 54) says:

> Cultivate (Tao) in the person,
> and one's virtue will be genuine.
> Cultivate it in the family,
> and its virtue will be overflowing.
> Cultivate it in the village,
> and its virtue will be lasting.
> Cultivate it in the country,
> and its virtue will be abundant.
> Cultivate it in the world,
> and its virtue will be all-pervading.

Wang Pi's commentary basically repeats this and adds, "Start with oneself so as to reach the others."

The response (*ying*) to Tao thus begins with the self. Modeled on the movement of Tao, it is essentially a process of "self-emptying." Besides such concepts as *wu-ssu* and *wu-yü*, Wang Pi also emphasizes the sage's being not "bound" or "fettered" (*lei*) by things. The word *lei* is equated with "loss" (chap. 23). The sage is one who "embraces simplicity and *wu-wei*, whose true nature is not fettered by things, and whose spirit is not injured by desires" (chap. 32). The concept of *lei* thus explains in a more concrete way the meaning of *wu-ssu* and *wu-yü*. But it is for another reason that the concept of *lei* is discussed here.

We have already met this concept in the last chapter, in the context of a discussion of the sage's emotive nature. The sage, according to Wang Pi, is the same as the people in that he too has feelings, which allow him to respond to things; the difference is that he is not "fettered" by them. This is important because it concerns the very possibility of attaining sagehood. Although human feelings may become a source of evil, they are necessary conditions without which response to Tao would not be possible.

The concept of "response," with which I have begun discussion of the ideal sage, underlies much of Wang Pi's understanding of the *Lao-tzu*. The word *ying* appears only twice in the *Lao-tzu*. In one of these instances, it is used to describe the "Way of heaven," which "does not speak but is good in responding."[75] Wang Pi's comment presupposes a total acceptance of this concept: "To follow it will bring fortune; to act contrary to it will bring harm" (chap. 73). In other places, Wang Pi extends this concept to describe the way of *tzu-jan* (chaps. 10, 17, 23, 38, 49, 62). When the Way is practised, a response will come regardless of distance (chap. 62); when the sage speaks, there will "always" be a response (chap. 17); when the name "goodness" arises, its opposite will arise also in response (chap. 38). There is almost a karmic ring to this, for the concept of *ying* is pervasive and is determined by the constant "principle" of Tao itself.

This is not to say that Wang Pi was influenced by Buddhism. The concept of *ying* is already found in the *I-ching*. On the meaning of the first hexagram, the *I-ching* has Confucius saying that "similar sounds respond to one another; similar breaths seek out one another. . . . The sage operates and the ten thousand things watch on. He who is rooted in heaven is akin to the above; he who is rooted in the earth is akin to the below. This means that each will follow its own kind."[76] Although Wang Pi did not elaborate on this passage, he explained in the *Chou-i lüeh-li* that all the hexagrams can be understood in terms of their inherent "movement" or "quietude." This would allow one to make use of them "in response":

> Response signifies the image of an identity of intention. . . . Thus, though far, things can be moved: this is due to one's obtaining the appropriate response. Although dangerous, situations can be managed: this is due to one's obtaining the proper timing. . . . Although being last, one can venture to be first: this is responding to the beginning. Although things compete, one can remain tranquil: this is grasping the end.[77]

The concept of response, in other words, is another expression of the dialectic of "non-being" and "principle," especially as it is applied to the world of human living. It serves to explain the reason why Wang Pi believes that the transforming power of Tao will have an effect on the people. In the "Tao-ist" world, there is a response to every action.

Beyond Sectarianism and Polemics

The universality of this claim affirms the possibility of becoming a sage. The sage is able to respond to Tao, and by extension to the needs of the people. The Way and the sage have "identical intentions" (*t'ung-chih*). As such, the emotive nature of the sage must be maintained. At one point, Wang Pi does describe the Way as "empty and without feeling" (chap. 5). But this is to be interpreted in light of the dialectic of "non-being" and "principle." Thus, Wang Pi also says that the feelings of the sage are not visible (chap. 20). Philosophically, the dialectic of Tao permits the possibility of sagehood. Politically the task of government, the establishment of the "Tao-ist" utopia, demands it.

Wang Pi was never an "escapist." He was never "disinterested" in politics. On the contrary, he was concerned with tradition and with government. Indeed, the model of the sage itself is rooted in tradition. In chapter 80, the *Lao-tzu* describes the ideal state as a "small country with few people," where the people are simple and content. According to Wang Pi, however, this does not describe any particular type of country; rather, the expression "small country" serves as an example urging all rulers to return to the ways of old.

On the long description of this "small country" in chapter 80, Wang Pi simply states: "Without desires."[78]

As we shall see in chapter 5 of this study, this brief comment is important to an understanding of Wang Pi's interpretive framework. At this point, the place of tradition in Wang Pi's vision of the ideal state must be underlined. Elsewhere in his commentary, Wang Pi speaks of the significance of "holding fast to the Way of old so as to master present situations" (chaps. 14, 47). Inasmuch as Tao is constant, its manifestation can be discerned in nature and in history. This is why I have said earlier that Wang Pi's aim is not to change the existing political structure. The emphasis is not on innovation, but on reestablishing order and harmony. To return to the "root," in this regard, is also to return to tradition. Does this make Wang Pi a supporter of "Confucianism"? Or was he just making use of Confucius as a mouthpiece to propagate the teaching of "Taoism"?

As we have seen, literati of the Cheng-shih period regarded Confucius as the ideal sage. On the same level with Yao and Shun, the legendary sage kings at the dawn of Chinese history, Confucius served as the model for all to emulate. He was able to "embody *wu*," as Wang Pi is quoted to have said, while Lao-tzu remained on the level of "being." This alone, however, cannot determine Wang Pi's intellectual stance, as there are other evidence which render the whole issue more complex. In the *Lun-yü*, for example, Confucius says, "I transmit but do not innovate. I believe in and devote myself to antiquity. I venture to compare myself to Lao P'eng."[79] Wang Pi, in agreement with Cheng Hsüan, has taken "Lao P'eng" to mean Lao-tzu and P'eng-tsu; thus placing Lao-tzu above Confucius.[80]

More puzzling still, commenting on Confucius's remark that he has set his mind (*chih*) on Tao, Wang Pi is quoted to have said:

Tao is the designation of *wu*. There is nowhere it does not penetrate; there is nothing which does not follow from it. Metaphorically it is called Tao. Quiet and without shape (*wu-t'i*), it cannot be made into an image. This is why Tao cannot be embodied (*t'i*). Thus it can only be intended (*chih*) and emulated.[81]

The first part of this passage adds nothing new, though it serves an important function here. The conclusion, however, seems to challenge the very possibility of sagehood.

Here, I believe that Wang Pi is most concerned with the meaning of the word *chih*, "intention" or "will," which Confucius has specifically chosen to describe his own work. The reason why Confucius speaks of *chih* instead of "embodiment" (*t'i*) is because the negativity of Tao must be emphasized. We should not forget that the word *chih* is also used by Wang Pi to explain the concept of "response." The embodiment of *wu*, in other words, is no more than a way of depicting the sage's not being deluded and bound by human feelings. The Way in itself cannot be embodied; there is no "thing" to become one with. What is important is that Confucius is "mindful" of and "responsive" to the Way.

This interpretation is further supported by two considerations. Another version of this text, first of all, has "This is why Tao cannot be a body/substance" (*Shih Tao pu-k'o wei t'i*), with the extra particle *wei*, which nominalizes the final word *t'i*.[82] More importantly, Wang Pi's remarks are appended to Ho Yen's commentary on this passage, which simply states that *wu* cannot be embodied.[83] Wang Pi's initial explanation is thus important, for it establishes the context in which the conclusion is to be understood. Taking into account Wang Pi's disagreement with Ho Yen on the question of the emotive nature of the sage, it seems that Wang was careful to explain and to distinguish his own view from the latter's.

At any rate, this is an isolated case. The answer to Wang Pi's intellectual leanings must be sought in his commentary on the *Lao-tzu* itself. Although the *Lao-tzu* often refers to the ideal sage, it also says that "sageliness" (*sheng*) should be abandoned (chap. 19). Wang Pi's understanding of this passage shows well his own contribution to the development of Chinese thought.

As a human virtue, according to Wang Pi, "sageliness" is inferior to the ideal of nonaction (*wu-wei*). Indeed, all virtues, championed especially by Confucians, are secondary when viewed from a "Tao-ist" light. This, however, does not suggest that Wang Pi is then engaged in an "anti-Confucian" polemic. As he comments on chapter 19 of the *Lao-tzu*:

Text	Commentary
Eliminate sageliness and discard wisdom; the people will benefit a hundredfold. Eliminate benevolence and discard	Sageliness and wisdom are the finest of human talents. Benevolence and righteousness are the finest of human virtues. Skill and profit

righteousness; the people will again be filial and kind. Eliminate skill and discard profit; there will be no more thieves and robbers. These three are artificial *ornaments* (*wen*), and not adequate. Therefore let the people abide by these: Discern simplicity; Embrace the uncarved block; Reduce selfishness; Have few desires.

are the finest of human resources. But it is plainly said that these should be "eliminated." As *expressions* (*wen*), these are indeed greatly inadequate. If they are not made adequate, their meaning cannot be seen. Thus it is said, "These three are artificial ornaments and are not adequate." Therefore let the people abide by something: abide by simplicity and having few desires.[84]

Sageliness as such is therefore not an "ornament" (*wen*) to be discarded, as the *Lao-tzu* seems to imply; rather, as "expressions" (*wen*) such words as "sageliness" and "benevolence" are inadequate and should be improved. The key word *wen*, which Wang Pi uses in two senses here, is difficult to translate, for it has a wide range of meaning. Generally it means "culture," "letters," or "words"; but it also has the connotation of what is superficial and artificial. I am suggesting that Wang Pi is taking advantage of the openness of the word *wen* to alleviate the attack on Confucian virtues in the *Lao-tzu*.

This is not to say that Wang Pi does not take the words of the *Lao-tzu* seriously. Common Confucian virtues *are* inferior to the way of *wu-wei* and *tzu-jan*. In chapter 10 the idea of "eliminating sageliness" is again mentioned by Wang Pi:

Text	*Commentary*
Purifying the profound vision, can it be without blemish? Loving the people and governing the country, can one be without knowledge?	To use artful means to achieve one's goal and to manipulate things to unveil the hidden, this is (cunning) wisdom. The (expression) "profound vision without blemish" is like (saying) "eliminate sageliness." The (expression) "to govern the country without knowledge" is like (saying) "discard wisdom." Can one be without wisdom? (If so,) then the people will not avoid you and the country will be governed.[85]

Wang Pi's answer to Lao-tzu's questions is clearly in the affirmative. Although the idea of abandoning sageliness is not mentioned again in other chapters, it can be inferred from Wang Pi's understanding of "wisdom" (*chih*). The word *chih* is defined in the commentary on chapter 3 as "knowing-action" (*chih-wei*), as a type of knowledge oriented toward finite goals. In this context, it may be called "instrumental knowledge," keeping in mind the discussion on "instruments" (*ch'i*) above, to distinguish it from the true wisdom of the sage. "If one relies on instrumental knowledge and does not follow the nature of things," Wang Pi writes, "one will surely lose the Way" (chap. 27). Self-knowledge is also said to be "above" instrumental knowledge (chap. 33); and the sage precisely "does not use instrumental knowledge," for he "embodies the wisdom of *tzu-jan*" (chap. 28).

Although "sageliness" and "wisdom" are the "finest of human talents," these *expressions* are ultimately human constructs and cannot be idolized. The idea of eliminating sageliness is likened to a "profound vision." What is this vision? On chapter 60, Wang Pi comments:

Text	*Commentary*
Governing a big country is like cooking a small fish.	This means not to disturb it. Agitation will bring much harm; tranquility will preserve one's true nature. Thus the larger the country, the more tranquil the ruler should be. Then he can win the hearts of the people completely.
If Tao prevails in the government of the world, ghosts will not have any spirit.	Governing a big country, then, is like cooking a small fish. If Tao prevails in the government of the world, then ghosts will not have any spirit.
Not only will they have no spirit, but the spirits themselves will not harm the people.	Spirits do not harm what is naturally so. If things remain naturally so, then spirits could not do anything to them. If spirits could not do anything to them, then one would not know the spirits as spirits.
Not only will the spirits not harm the people, but the sage will also not harm the people.	If the Way is in harmony, then spirits will not harm the people. If spirits do not harm the people,

then people will not know them as spirits. If the Way is in harmony, then the sage will also not harm the people, then they will not know the sage to be a sage as well. That is, not only will the people not know the spirits to be spirits, but they will also not know the sage to be a sage. Thus if the ruler relies on force and regulation to control things, government will be doomed. To bring about the state of not knowing the spirits and the sage to be spirits and sage, this is the ultimate of Tao.

As both do not harm one another, virtue will merge and return.

If spirits do not harm the people, the sage will also not harm the people. If the sage does not harm the people, then spirits will also not harm the people. Thus it is said, "both do not harm one another." When spirits and sage accord with Tao, all will converge and return to them.

When sagehood is realized, it is abandoned at the same time. When meaning is understood, words and images must be forgotten. This is not a "mystical" vision, however. Wang Pi's laborious commentary explains clearly that sagehood is abandoned only in the sense of not being known to the people. When the sage embodies Tao—responds to it by being *wu-wei*—the resulting "harmony" may then be expressed *poetically* as a merging of the human and the divine. But just as it is not a mystical vision, Wang Pi's ideal is also not a form of "naturalism." Tao in itself remains utterly transcendent. The "vision" of Wang Pi recognizes both the profound spirituality of Tao and its practical significance. To avoid the Scylla of mysticism and the Charybdis of naturalism is to recognize the dialectical thinking that dominates Wang Pi's thought. Wang Pi's "profound vision," I suggest, is ultimately a *Tao-ist* vision.

In a sense, Fan Ning was right when he accused Wang Pi for abandoning the teaching of Confucius. By the same token, later Taoists such as Lu Hsi-sheng were also right when they condemned

Wang Pi for deserting the teaching of Lao-tzu. This is because Wang Pi was neither a "Confucian" nor a "Taoist."

Such terms as "Confucian" and "Taoist" are historical categories, abstractions, and they should be recognized as such. When used properly, they serve to simplify in a meaningful and systematic way complex historical phenomena; when misused, they merely reduce, if not distort, the rich and diverse data to a superficial mode. In the case of Wang Pi, the difficulty is that he does not fit into any one of these categories. Although Wang Pi is chiefly remembered for his commentary on the *Lao-tzu*, we should not forget that he has written a work on the *Lun-yü* as well. From the passage on Confucius's self-understanding cited above, it is clear that he is interpreting these two texts from the same perspective.

There is no reason to suspect that Wang Pi was insincere when he defended Confucius. If he had not shown himself to be interested in political affairs, and if he had not interpreted the Tao dialectically, this view might seem appealing. There is also no need to see Wang Pi as attempting a "synthesis" of Lao-tzu and Confucius. In my estimation, the genius of Wang Pi lies precisely in his ability to go beyond a fragmented sense of tradition dominated by individual schools of thought. For Wang Pi, there is only one "Taoist" tradition, exemplified and transmitted by the ancient sages. Responsive to Tao and responsible for the people, the sage represents the focus of an ideal vision.

3 Ho-shang Kung: Legend and Commentary

Despite its importance in traditional China, the Ho-shang Kung commentary has its critics. The T'ang historian Liu Chih-chi, as noted earlier, has described it as a "vulgar lie" and a "fantastic tale" (see p. 6, above). Ch'ao Kung-wu, writing in the twelfth century, extended this line of thought by emphasizing the commentary's concern with breathing techniques and other physical exercises: "It is close to the Immortalist school. Liu Chih-chi has called it a forgery; could it be because of this?"[1] In the Ch'ing dynasty, to take but one more example, Nao Yai (1731–1815), brought this critical tradition to a conclusion:

> There were many commentators on the work of Lao-tzu before the Six Dynasties, but their writings are now all lost. The only exception is the so-called *Ho-shang Kung chang-chü*, which is really the work of an uneducated man claiming to be the words of an immortal. Its chapter division is especially unreasonable. But since the T'ang and Sung dynasties, none has dared to challenge it, except Liu Chih-chi who alone realized that it was false.[2]

Consequently, the Ho-shang Kung commentary is today often viewed as a kind of "religious propaganda," and deemed not worthy of serious scholarly attention.

Although the concern with immortality is important, it should be understood in its own context, in relation to other equally important aspects. The Ho-shang Kung commentary, like that of Wang Pi, contains a unified vision. This is the claim which I shall explicate in what follows. Before an analysis of the commentary is undertaken in the next chapter, two questions must first of all be addressed. They concern the legend of Ho-shang Kung and the date of the commentary.

The figure of Ho-shang Kung is known to us only through a legend, or more precisely a complex of legends, in which his "authorship" of a *Lao-tzu* commentary is asserted. It is unlikely that Ho-shang Kung, the "Old Man by the River," was a historical individual. At least, the legendary web surrounding this figure has by now become so dense that the historical core, if any, can no longer be penetrated. Yet the legend itself is important because it serves as an introduction, and sets the tone as to how the commentary is to be read. For our purposes, the historicity of the figure of Ho-shang Kung is a secondary issue; what is primary is the context and the kind of fundamental presuppositions reflected in the legend. Accordingly, the origins of the Ho-shang Kung story and the key ideas contained in it will be considered, before we turn to the question of the date of the commentary. It will be shown that a strong political emphasis, centering on the figure of the ideal sage, permeates the Ho-shang Kung legend. Like our background study of Wang Pi, the following discussion is also intended to isolate major themes that are important to an understanding of the commentary itself.

The Formation of the Ho-shang Kung Legend

The "biography" of Ho-shang Kung is today most readily available in the Preface to the current *Ssu-pu ts'ung-k'an* (Four Libraries Series) edition of the Ho-shang Kung commentary, which is based on a Sung version.[3] This Preface is traditionally ascribed to the famous Taoist Ko Hsüan (ca. 164–244 A.D.), as one of his honorary titles, "The Great Ultimate Immortal Master of the Left" (T'ai-chi tso-hsien-kung), is found at the beginning of the text. The first half of this Preface is concerned with the deified Lao-tzu and the genesis of the *Tao-te ching;* the second is devoted to the legend of Ho-shang Kung.

According to the mature version of the legend, Ho-shang Kung "appeared" during the reign of Emperor Wen of Han (r. 179–157 B.C.). As he made his home by the "river"—presumably the Yellow River—he was therefore called the "Old Man by the River." Emperor Wen was apparently a keen student of the *Tao-te ching,* and since he heard that Ho-shang Kung was an expert on the words of Lao-tzu, he therefore sent messengers to ask him to explain certain difficult passages to him. Emperor Wen "decreed" that the *Lao-tzu* be studied by all at court; later sources report that his son, Emperor Ching (r. 156–141 B.C.), then established the *Lao-tzu* officially as a "classic".[4]

The interesting point here is that Ho-shang Kung refused Emperor Wen's request, claiming that the *Lao-tzu* is too important to be answered "from a distance." More interesting still, Emperor Wen himself then went to see the master. While he planned to chastise Ho-shang Kung at first, quoting in fact from the *Shih-ching* (Book of Poetry) and even alluding to the *Lao-tzu* to assert his sovereign power, the emperor was brought to his knees when Ho-shang Kung soared "high into midair like a rising cloud" and revealed his true identity as a deity sent by the "Supreme Lord of the Way" (T'ai-shang Tao-chün) specifically to teach him. The commentary on the *Lao-tzu* was thus finally transmitted to Emperor Wen after he was shown the power of the Way and submitted to its teaching:

> Ho-shang Kung bestowed to him the unadorned text (*su-shu*) of the *Tao-te ching chang-chü* in two *chüan,* and said to the Emperor: "If you study this thoroughly, then your doubts will be explained. It has been over 1,700 years since I commented on this classic; I have transmitted it to only three people, and now four including you. Do not show it to those who do not deserve it." Emperor Wen thus knelt and received the classic. And after these words, Ho-shang Kung was nowhere to be found.

Historically, the importance of this legend can be traced to the rise of Taoism as an institutionalized religion. As is well known, the T'ang emperors have traced their ancestry back to Lao-tzu himself. In the Sung dynasty, Lao-tzu was formally endowed with the all-embracing title of "Emperor on High of the Undifferentiated Ulti-

mate" (T'ai-shang hun-yüan huang-ti).[5] The Ho-shang Kung
legend, with its emphasis on the divine task of the "Old Man by the
River" commissioned by the Supreme Lord of the Way, has thus enjoyed great prestige and imperial support. Undoubtedly the legend
was well established by the seventh century. The question is, When
was it first formed?

The Authorship of Ko Hsüan

If the authorship of Ko Hsüan can be confirmed, the mature
legend would date to around 200 A.D. According to one Buddhist
source, Ko Hsüan had fabricated the story of Ho-shang Kung to
"confuse" the people.[6] Although opponents may criticize the legend, the authorship of Ko Hsüan is seldom denied in traditional
China. In modern scholarship, Takeuchi Yoshio has shown that the
Sung version of the Ho-shang Kung legend can be traced to an earlier work, the Lao-tzu Tao-te ching hsü-chüeh (Lao-tzu's Tao-te ching:
Introduction and Instruction), which is also ascribed to Ko Hsüan.[7]
However, following Takeuchi's lead, Ōfuchi Ninji has published an
exhaustive study of this work in which Ko Hsüan's authorship is
seriously called into question.[8]

The Lao-tzu Tao-te ching hsü-chüeh (hereon abbreviated as
Hsü-chüeh) is a composite work, and its precise date is difficult to
determine. It is found, mainly in fragments, in a number of sources,
including several Tun-huang manuscripts.[9] The text of the Hsü-
chüeh may be divided into five sections, again with Ko Hsüan
clearly identified as the author.[10] The first two sections, which deal
with the legends of Lao-tzu and Ho-shang Kung, are essentially
the same as the Preface to the Sung edition of the Ho-shang
Kung commentary.[11] The last three sections are concerned with
events leading to the writing of the Tao-te ching and instructions in
the area of what has come to be known as "internal alchemy" in the
Taoist religion.

A reading of the Hsü-chüeh shows that Ko Hsüan's authorship
cannot be maintained, especially since quotations from one of Ko's
disciples are also found in the text, although the tradition or school
of Ko Hsüan seems to have played an important role in its compo-
sition. As far as the legend of Ho-shang Kung is concerned,
the Hsü-chüeh account can also be traced to another work connected with the Ko family: Ko Hung's Shen-hsien chuan (Lives
of Immortals).[12]

According to Ko Hung's (ca. 284–364) own account, he wrote the *Shen-hsien chuan* when he was in his thirties, which would place it at the beginning of the Eastern Chin dynasty (317–420).[13] The Ho-shang Kung legend contained here is generally more concise, when compared with the *Hsü-chüeh* account. In the *Shen-hsien chuan* Ho-shang Kung is said to have presented Emperor Wen with an "unadorned text" (*su-shu*), literally a text written on a type of raw silk but which in this context connotes a "book of simplicity"; the *Hsü-chüeh*, however, clearly identifies it as the Ho-shang Kung commentary. Whereas in the former it is simply said that a deity (*shen-jen*) came to teach Emperor Wen, the latter explains that it was the "Supreme Lord of the Way" who sent a special deity to earth. On the basis of Ōfuchi's careful analysis especially, it seems certain that the *Hsü-chüeh* account of the Ho-shang Kung legend represents a later elaboration of the *Shen-hsien chuan* original.[14]

Thus, the Sung version of the Ho-shang Kung legend can be traced, via the *Hsü-chüeh*, to the *Shen-hsien chuan*. Can Ko Hung, then, be regarded as the author of the legend of Ho-shang Kung? It may also be that Ko Hung was putting into words a tradition of long standing. Perhaps the Ho-shang Kung legend in the *Shen-hsien chuan* may itself be a later interpolation. Since able exponents can be found for all these views, the formation of the Ho-shang Kung legend remains indeed a thorny issue in contemporary sinological research.[15] It is my contention that the time of Ko Hung may be taken as the terminus ad quem, when the Ho-shang Kung legend was committed to writing.[16] There is reason to believe that the core of the Ho-shang Kung legend was already formed toward the end of the Former or Western Han dynasty.

Ho-shang Kung and Ho-shang Chang-jen

According to the *Shih-chi*, in the Warring States period (480–221 B.C.) there was a certain Ho-shang Chang-jen who was also well versed in the *Lao-tzu*.[17] The title "Ho-shang Chang-jen" of course also means an "Old Man by the River," and by the third century A.D. this figure was commonly identified with Ho-shang Kung.[18] Traditionally this identification served to establish the antiquity and historicity of Ho-shang Kung; today this opens interesting possibilities with respect to a critical study of the Ho-shang Kung legend.

As I have elaborated elsewhere, the Ho-shang Chang-jen tradition originated in the eastern state of Ch'i toward the end of the

Warring States period. The transmission of this school clearly indicates that it was rooted in the Huang-lao tradition, the tradition of the Yellow Emperor and Lao-tzu. Without going into any detail here, it can be said that the figure of Ho-shang Kung was modeled on that of Ho-shang Chang-jen. But it is not so much a case of "mistaken identification," as it has been suggested, as a conscious attempt to represent the older tradition in a new context.[19]

This hypothesis hinges on another figure known as Master An-ch'iu, who was according to tradition a disciple of Ho-shang Kung. Master An-ch'iu, like Ho-shang Kung, was also sought by an emperor, Han Ch'eng-ti (r. 32–7 B.C.), for his expert knowledge on the *Lao-tzu*. Like Ho-shang Kung again, Master An-ch'iu is said to have refused the request of the emperor. Furthermore, in the sixth-century work *Tao-hsüeh chuan* (Lives of Taoist Masters), Master An-ch'iu was identified with Yüeh Chü-kung, who was a key figure in the Huang-lao tradition and closely associated with the school of Ho-shang Chang-jen.[20] This identification may be accepted because the name "An-ch'iu" refers to a small fief reestablished by Emperor Ch'eng, precisely in the same area where the Ho-shang Chang-jen school first originated. When all the relevant data are taken into account, what emerges is that the core of the Ho-shang Kung legend was formed quite early, probably during the reign of Emperor Ch'eng or shortly after. Most likely it was a product of the school of Master An-ch'iu, and was aimed at propagating the teaching of the Huang-lao tradition. It was then transmitted and elaborated in Ko Hung's *Shen-hsien chuan* and in the *Hsü-chüeh*, until it reached its final form in the Sung dynasty as the Preface to the Ho-shang Kung commentary.[21]

It has been suggested, however, that the legend of Ho-shang Kung itself seems to contain certain ideas that bear the imprint of a later date. In particular, Kusuyama Haruki has argued that on the basis of internal evidence the legend should be placed toward the end of the Six Dynasties period, around the sixth century A.D.[22] Although the conclusion reached in this study differs from Kusuyama's, it is instructive to review his argument especially since it is concerned with the political dimension of the legend also.

As indicated earlier, the mature version of the legend describes the encounter between Emperor Wen and Ho-shang Kung. The fact that Ho-shang Kung refused to answer the emperor at once—and the same is true for Master An-ch'iu's refusal to see Emperor Ch'eng—is itself significant. According to Kusuyama, this may reflect Buddhist influence, given the importance of the early controversy as to whether monks should "bow" to the emperor—whether Buddhist monks should not be exempted from imperial rule—which was in full debate during the Eastern Chin dynasty (317–420 A.D.).[23] This later became a Taoist concern as well, for in T'ang sources we find the Ho-shang Kung legend being used as a test case, as it were, for Taoist superiority. This, then, has led Kusuyama to conclude that the Ho-shang Kung legend was probably formed sometime during the sixth century A.D., after the Buddhist case was established and extended to the Taoist arena.[24]

The sources cited by Kusuyama clearly attest to the importance of the Ho-shang Kung tradition in the T'ang dynasty. But whether Buddhist influence played a major role in the formation of the Ho-shang Kung legend remains, in my view, open to debate. The political dimension of the legend, which Kusuyama has emphasized, should be recognized, but it may well be indigenous to the Chinese imagination itself.

What, then, is the political emphasis in the Ho-shang Kung legend? This brings us to a consideration of the difficult topic of Huang-lao thought, to which the Ho-shang Kung tradition is closely related. My discussion, however, is not meant to be exhaustive; it seeks only to highlight certain aspects of the legend.

Huang-lao Thought

Historical sources indicate that the Huang-lao tradition dominated the early Han political and intellectual scene. Yet little is certain about its precise nature; the early texts of this school are virtually all lost. Often the teaching of the Huang-lao school is described in terms of the ideas of "quietude," "nonaction", and "resting with the people"; but it is not always clear what they mean in this context. This situation is slightly improved by the discovery in 1973 of two *Lao-tzu* silk manuscripts at Ma-wang-tui, Ch'ang-sha. Appended to the so-called B text of the *Lao-tzu* are four lost texts, which may be traced to the school of Huang-ti and Lao-tzu. Other early references to the Huang-lao tradition are few and largely unexplained, and some of the most important ones are especially connected with the Ho-shang Chang-jen tradition. Key figures in the latter such as T'ien Shu, Ts'ao Ts'an, and the Empress Dowager Tou are all instrumental in establishing the Huang-lao tradition as the dominant ideology in the early Han dynasty.[25]

In the *Shih-chi* some early philosophers are also identified as belonging to the Huang-lao tradition, and this forms the basis of the commonly accepted view that the Huang-lao school can be traced to the Warring States period.[26] Because many of these figures were active in the famous Chi-hsia "academy," which flourished under King Hsüan of Ch'i (r. ca. 319–301 B.C.), Kuo Mo-jo has proposed that the Huang-lao tradition originated from this school.[27] According to Kanaya Osamu, however, the key to the origin of the Huang-lao tradition may be found in the figure of Yüeh Chü-kung himself, in which case the Ho-shang Chang-jen tradition and the Huang-lao school would have come from the same source.[28] The larger question of the origins of the Huang-lao tradition cannot be resolved here. It is enough to recognize that the Huang-lao tradition flourished during the early Han dynasty. What remains to be further explored is the teaching of the Huang-lao tradition, especially as it relates to the legend of Ho-shang Kung.

The Theory and Practice of Hsing-ming

Chief among the philosophers identified by Ssu-ma Ch'ien in the *Shih-chi* as members of the Huang-lao tradition are Han Fei-tzu, Shen Pu-hai, and Shen Tao—all of whom are connected with the "legalist" school.[29] According to Ssu-ma Ch'ien, "Shen Tao . . . [and others] all studied the art of Huang-lao and *Tao-te*."[30] Concerning Shen Pu-hai, the *Shih-chi* states that "the thought of Shen-tzu is rooted in Huang-lao and focused on *hsing-ming*."[31] And Han Fei-tzu is said to have "favored the thought of *hsing-ming* and the legalist art; but it is ultimately rooted in Huang-lao."[32]

These brief statements indicate well the dearth of information concerning the nature of Huang-lao thought. The *Shih-chi* seems to have assumed that its readers were all familiar with the term "Huang-lao." And indeed they probably were, for the *Han-shu* has included a number of works attributed to the Yellow Emperor in its bibliographical section.[33] Unfortunately these are no longer extant, perhaps with one exception besides certain medical texts—namely, the *Huang-ti ssu-ching* (The Four Classics of the Yellow Emperor), with which the Ma-wang-tui find has been identified. I shall turn to the Ma-wang-tui manuscripts shortly.

On the basis of Ssu-ma Ch'ien's testimony, the term "Huang-lao" appears to be linked to both the *Lao-tzu* and the "legalist" school. First of all, "Huang-lao" is often paralleled with the term

"The Way and Virtue" (*Tao-te*), as in the case of Shen Tao, which suggests a close relation with the *Tao-te ching*. The term *hsing-ming* also appears in this context as an expression of Huang-lao thought. The art of *hsing-ming*, "form and names," is concerned with the understanding of "names" and their corresponding "reality." In Wang Pi's time, forming a part of the discussion on "names and principles" (*ming-li*), it was primarily concerned with such issues as the assessment of human character and the appointment of officials. But in the Han period and earlier, it was a key feature in both "legalism" and the Huang-lao school. Numerous questions, to be sure, still surround the nature of Huang-lao teaching as a whole, but an examination of the concept of *hsing-ming* will help to clarify the Huang-lao dimension of the Ho-shang Kung legend.

Prior to the Wei-Chin period, the precise meaning of *hsing-ming* is not easy to define. Traditionally it has often been equated with a system of law and punishment, which is designed especially to keep state officials in check.[34] Nevertheless, it is now widely recognized that the concept of *hsing-ming* extends beyond strictly political and practical measures, to include a philosophical and theoretical dimension. Indeed, according to Léon Vandermeersch, the notion of *hsing-ming* may even be taken as an expression of a kind of "Legalist epistemology."[35] In other words, the early theory of *hsing-ming* is not only concerned with reward and punishment, management and control, but with the grounds on which a system of government may be built as well.

The practical side of the notion of *hsing-ming* is clear enough, as H. G. Creel has admirably demonstrated.[36] According to the *Han Fei-tzu*, for example, "if *hsing* and *ming* are harmonized, the people will keep to their proper functions."[37] According to Liu Hsiang, "the doctrine of Shen-tzu is called *hsing-ming*. *Hsing-ming* is to demand actual performance (*shih*) on the basis of the title (*ming*) held, thus honoring the ruler and humbling the minister, exalting superiors and curbing inferiors."[38] In this sense, as Creel also points out, the notion of *hsing-ming* is essentially identified with that of "names and actuality" (*ming-shih*).[39] During the reign of Emperor Hsüan (r. 73–49 B.C.), according to the *Han-shu*, *hsing-ming* was employed to keep officials in order.[40] This would suggest that the art of *hsing-ming* was very much in force during the second half of the Former Han dynasty.

The theoretical side of the notion of *hsing-ming*, on the other hand, is less well documented. But it is this which provides the ultimate justification for any practical political measures. The *Han Fei-tzu* has no doubt emphasized that the harmony of "form" and "names" would act to maintain order and balance among officials, if not the populace as a whole. What should not be overlooked is that prior to this passage, the *Han Fei-tzu* also explains that it is the nature of the Way itself that gives rise to this consequent "function."

Just as the Way is not the same as the "ten thousand things," the ruler is different from his ministers: "The Way is nondual; it is therefore called 'One.' This is why the enlightened ruler treasures the solitary figure of the Way. As the ruler and the minister differ from the point of view of the Way . . . the ruler holds to his 'name,' and the ministers imitate his 'form.' Form and name merge into one; this then is the harmony between the superior and the inferior."[41] This, in short, is the ground of the "legalist" measure that emphasizes just rewards, severe punishment, and generally a close monitoring of the performance of officials. This, I suggest, is true for the Huang-lao school as well, as the Ma-wang-tui silk texts demonstrate. Indeed, in the Huang-lao tradition, this theoretical dimension figures much more prominently in the foreground.

The Ma-wang-tui Evidence

The Four Classics of the Yellow Emperor

As already mentioned, among the Ma-wang-tui corpus are four hitherto lost texts attached to the front of the so-called B text of the *Lao-tzu*. This manuscript as a whole is written in a "clerical" script (*li-shu*) and avoids the use of the word *pang*, the personal name of Han Kao-tsu (r. 206–195 B.C.); in over twenty instances the semantically equivalent word *kuo* is used in place of *pang*. However, the word *ying*, name of Emperor Hui (r. 194–188 B.C.), is not "tabooed" or avoided. As a result, this manuscript is usually dated between 194 and 180 B.C.[42] And the tomb itself in which the manuscript is found can be dated to 168 B.C., during the reign of Han Wen-ti (r. 179–157 B.C.).

The four texts in question are on the whole well preserved, and their length and titles are indicated in the manuscript itself. They are: *Ching-fa* (Invariable Law), *Shih-liu ching* (Sixteen Scriptures), *Ch'eng* (Balancing), and *Tao-yüan* (Origin of the Way), in a total of over eleven thousand characters.[43] The last of these, *Tao-yüan*, has since been translated into English by Jan Yün-hua.[44]

In 1974 T'ang Lan first proposed that these four texts might be iden-
tified with the *Huang-ti ssu-ching* (The Four Classics of the Yellow
Emperor), long lost but listed in the bibliographical section of the
Han-shu.[45]

The late Professor T'ang has persuasively argued that these
four texts constitute a coherent whole. As the Yellow Emperor is
figured prominently in the *Shih-liu ching*, it is safe to say that these
treatises are at least associated with the school of Huang-ti. Moreover, since the manuscript can be dated to the early Han dynasty
when the Huang-lao tradition flourished, the fact that these four
texts are placed *before* the *Lao-tzu* may not be entirely accidental. In
the bibliographical section of the *Sui-shu*, as T'ang points out, the
Huang-ti in four sections (*p'ien*) and the *Lao-tzu* in two are singled
out as the most important among all known Han Taoist works.[46]
And of all the titles attributed to the Yellow Emperor in the *Han-
shu*, only the *Huang-ti ssu-ching* is said to have four sections.[47]

This identification is today widely respected, though it remains a hypothesis and scholars may disagree on specific details.[48]
Regardless of whether these four texts are in fact the *Huang-ti ssu-
ching*, they are important to our understanding of Huang-lao
thought.[49] On the whole, they are often interpreted in terms of
their affinity to both the *Lao-tzu* and the "legalist" school. The *Shih-
liu ching*, for example, is basically structured in dialogue form, involving a series of exchanges between the Yellow Emperor and his
ministers, notably Li Mu. According to Jan Yün-hua, this text is generally "closer to legalism than to *Lao-tzu*," and more specifically it
"substitutes the political philosophy of *Lao-tzu* with that of
legalism."[50] The fourth treatise, *Tao-yüan*, however, is very different
in tone. It is extremely short, consisting of only 464 characters, and
as its title suggests, it is concerned with the "Tao-ist" cosmogony.
In this sense, it is perhaps closer to the thought of *Lao-tzu* than to
"legalist" doctrines. What concerns us most is the notion of *hsing-
ming* in these four texts, which forms a principal feature of Huang-
lao teaching. The *Ching-fa* is especially important in this regard, for
it describes in detail the meaning and application of *hsing-ming*,
though the other three also make references to this concept.

The Soteriological Significance of Hsing-ming

The *Tao-yüan* describes the primordial Tao as "vacuous" and
"identical with the One": "It had no form (*hsing*) since ancient

times, / it was undifferentiated and nameless (*wu-ming*)."[51] The third treatise, *Ch'eng* (Balancing), slightly damaged and also very short, again describes the notion of *hsing-ming* in terms of the nature of the Way:

> Tao has no beginning, though it is responsive. When it has not come, there is nothing. When it has come, (everything) follows. When a thing is about to come into being, its form (*hsing*) appears first. It is formed by its form, and named by its name (*ming*).[52]

Here the notion of *hsing-ming* has acquired a metaphysical status in that it is made to describe the ontological constitution of beings. The Tao or Way is precisely beyond the realm of beings; it is without form or name. These two passages together serve to bring out the general theoretical foundation of the notion of *hsing-ming*. In the *Shih-liu ching* the practical nature of this concept is spelled out more clearly.

In the section known as "Complete Law" (*Ch'eng-fa*), the *Shih-liu ching* has the Yellow Emperor questioning his minister Li Mu whether there was a perfect law that would completely rectify the people. The minister affirms this and remarks that "in ancient times when heaven and earth were made, to be rectified was to have (the proper) name, and to be in harmony was to have (the proper) form."[53] To establish the "Complete Law" then, according to Li Mu, is to "follow the name and return to the One," which is also equated in this context with the Way.[54] If practised within the "four seas," extended to all aspects of government, this would bring perfect order and harmony. This is why the Yellow Emperor in a different passage states that "I carefully guard the correct name, and I do not lose my constant form: this I will show posterity."[55] This is also why the concluding section of the *Shih-liu ching* observes that "if one wishes to know the advantages and disadvantages, one must examine the names and scrutinize the form."[56] In this last instance, the notion of *hsing-ming* is further related to those of "quietude" (*ch'ing-ching*) and "nonaction" (*wu-wei*).

This, in sum, is the practical dimension of the notion of *hsing-ming*. Rooted in the Way and expressed in terms of quietude and nonaction, *hsing-ming* is not a "detached" discussion of the relationship between "form" and "names"; rather it has what may be called a "soteriological" concern, in the sense that proper application of *hsing-ming* would lead to a utopian type of government and collective existence. A brief examination of the *Ching-fa* will further clarify this.

The *Ching-fa* (Invariable Law) is perhaps the most important of the four Ma-wang-tui lost texts that precede the B version of the *Lao-tzu*. It is also the longest, consisting of nine sections in five thousand characters. Again, my discussion here does not claim to address the text as a whole; it is the notion of *hsing-ming* that forms my point of focus. In this regard, the first section, entitled *Tao-fa* (Law of the Way) is particularly important, since it sets out the basic tenets to be amplified in the other sections.

Our text begins with the fundamental claim that it is the Way that produced law (*Tao sheng fa*).[57] And law is defined in this context as what "measures the advantages and disadvantages, and illuminates the crooked and the straight."[58] This general definition works very well to explain the theoretical foundation of law in itself, as opposed to the various individual applications of it. The foundation of law is traced to the beginning of the cosmos. The undifferentiated Tao is "empty" (*hsü*); but with the appearance of even the smallest creatures, "form and names" arrived on the scene: "When form and names (*hsing-ming*) are established, black and white are already distinguished."[59] In this sense, the basis of law is rooted generally in Tao but more specifically in a theory of *hsing-ming* as "cosmic paradigms"—as constitutive and regulative principles of the cosmos.

With the initial theoretical basis established, the text goes on to say that "therefore he who holds the Way" does not stubbornly hold to his own views (*wu-chih*), and does not stay ahead of others or rashly rush to conclusions (*wu-ch'u*). He does not act in an aggressive way (*wu-wei*); and he is not partial, does not rely solely on his private standards (*wu-ssu*).[60] When troubles arise, they will be identified by their "form and names." When the form and names are established, nothing will escape justice and the rule of law.[61] When applied to the art of rulership, this means that the ruler can manage the task of government by "nonaction"; there is no need to intervene at all. So long as the "law of the Way" is firmly in place, the ruler needs only to "examine the form and scrutinize the names," to borrow a phrase from the *Shih-liu ching* quoted earlier, and order will prevail. The ideal ruler is thus to imitate the Way, to attain that state of "formlessness" (*wu-hsing*) that characterizes the Tao, and be a model to the world. No doubt, this entire edifice pre-

supposes a constant and perfectly harmonious universe with an
"Invariable Law." Ultimately this view presupposes that "since
the names and form are already fixed, things will (naturally) rectify themselves."[62]

For our purposes, the crucial point is that the "Invariable
Law" is here seen to be rooted in Tao, and is expressed chiefly in
terms of *hsing-ming*. The notion of *hsing-ming* is, in other words,
considered a characteristic of the phenomenal world, and it serves
as a guide to ideal rulership in the form of quietude and nonaction.
As the *Ching-fa* elsewhere concludes, because "the Way of heaven
and earth" is constant, the man of Tao must act accordingly:

> (He) must carefully observe the origins of things and events,
> and scrutinize their form and names. The form and names are
> already fixed (which means that) adversity and ease have their
> places; death and life are distinguished; survival and destruc-
> tion, success and ruin have their stations. He then combines
> (these insights) with the constant Way of heaven and earth,
> and determines the place of misfortune and fortune, death and
> life, survival and destruction, success and ruin. Thus, he does
> not lose the Principle (*li*) in his dealings with all things; he
> does not leave out a single detail in his understanding of
> heaven and earth. . . . This is called possessing the Way.[63]

This passage sums up nicely both the theoretical basis and the
practical implications of the notion of *hsing-ming* in the Huang-lao
tradition. It may be tempting to enter into a debate as to whether
this formulation of *hsing-ming* is more "legalist" or "Taoist." Suffice
it to say that the Huang-lao school may be described in terms of
both these traditions, that it is concerned with both the "law" and
the "Way."[64] Indeed, if we were to follow Ssu-ma Ch'ien's assessment of Han Fei-tzu, Shen Pu-hai, and Shen Tao discussed above,
"legalism" may even be regarded as a development of the Huang-
lao tradition.

Earlier we have seen that, according to Kusuyama, the legend
of Ho-shang Kung was a product of the sixth century A.D. and
heavily indebted to Buddhist influence. We may now say that
although Buddhist influence remains a possibility, there is no
reason why the Ho-shang Kung legend could not have grown out
of an indigenous tradition. The political insights reflected in the

Ho-shang Kung legend have a long history, dating back to the Warring States period and coming into full bloom during the early Han dynasty.

The Ma-wang-tui evidence is important because it provides a detailed description of the key concept of *hsing-ming*. This in turn helps us to understand the meaning of "quietude" and "nonaction," which are often used to depict the teaching of the Huang-lao school. These ideas are all rooted in a "Tao-ist" cosmology and expressed politically in terms of a highly structured government with a sharp distinction between ruler and ministers. The ruler "does nothing" and remains "quiet," for the political machinery modeled on Tao itself is already in place. The ideal ruler needs only to ensure that "form" and "names" do not run contrary to one another, to watch the smooth functioning of the political system. In this framework, the figure of the sage has a special role to play.

The "Saving" Knowledge of the Sage

The Ho-shang Kung legend, it seems to me, reflects an attempt to reinforce the view that the Huang-lao sage occupies a special place in the political world. The encounter with Emperor Wen, in particular, seeks to bring out this idea in a forceful and unambiguous way.

The visit is itself extraordinary, given the sovereign power of the emperor. Indeed, Emperor Wen's initial admonition is precisely focused on this question. As we may recall, the emperor quotes from the *Shih-ching* and alludes to the *Lao-tzu* to assert his sovereignty. In other words, the text here is certainly aware of possible charges of what may be called a kind of Huang-lao "arrogance," if not insubordination itself. It is resorting to traditional sources so as to set up a Huang-lao response or critique. The sage is above even imperial rule because his point of reference and source of authority is not this world, but rather that on which this world is said to depend.

In the earlier Ho-shang Chang-jen tradition, the ideal sage is depicted as a true hermit who refused office, fame, and wealth. Yet the sage is always sought by those in power. Master An-ch'i, a disciple of Ho-shang Chang-jen, is a good example of this, for he was repeatedly approached by Ch'in Shih-huang-ti (259–210 B.C.), the first emperor of the Ch'in dynasty.[65] Ko Kung, another key figure in the same tradition, is also said to have refused office, though he was "persuaded" to teach the prime minister Ts'ao Ts'an the art of Huang-lao, the theory and practice of quietude and nonaction.[66] There is thus a sense of involvement from the beginning, despite the apparent emphasis on detachment from the political stage. It is not as if the sage were totally divorced from the political world; ideally, rather, he deliberately decides to stay away from it. In the Huang-lao tradition at least, the sage is distinguished from ordinary men not so much in the degree of involvement as in the attitude and insight that he bears on things of this world. Because of his dedication to the cultivation of the Way, which distinguishes him from people motivated by self-interests, he is best suited to be a teacher of rulers. Indeed, as the *Ching-fa* pushes the argument one step further, the ideal sage can even "establish the son of heaven."[67] In other words, only the sage can be entrusted with the supreme responsibility of choosing the right occupant for the throne.

The sage is sought for his superiority of knowledge and insight. This insight is first of all esoteric. This is indicated in the Ho-shang Kung legend by the special transmission of the Ho-shang Kung commentary on the *Lao-tzu*. Emperor Wen was only the fourth to receive the text in a course of seventeen hundred years, according to the legend, and he was instructed not to show it to anyone not worthy of it. The *Sui-shu*, in this connection, has an interesting passage that well describes this esoteric side of the knowledge of the sage in the early stages of the Huang-lao tradition. After outlining the meaning of Tao, it states:

> But beginning with the Yellow Emperor, saintly thinkers have transmitted their doctrine of the Way only to special individuals, and the world did not speak of any "school" (of Huang-lao thought). During the Han dynasty, Ts'ao Ts'an was the first to recommend Ko Kung for his expert interpretation of Huang-lao, to which Emperor Wen adhered. Since then the line of transmission was established, and many thus studied the doctrine of the Way.[68]

Moreover, the content of this special knowledge can be divided into three component parts. First, there is the knowledge of the texts of the Huang-lao school. Secondly, the knowledge of the art of self-cultivation and government is definitely also stressed. Third, there is the much coveted knowledge of the secret to immortality itself. All these are important to our understanding of the Ho-shang Kung legend and, as I shall argue in the next chapter, to our understanding of the Ho-shang Kung commentary on the *Lao-tzu* as well.

The second of these is expressed in terms of the concepts of *hsing-ming*, quietude, and nonaction, which I have already discussed. The ideal ruler is to imitate the Tao and, as it were, the world would be at peace of its own accord. And it is to the sage that the ruler must look for help and instruction. This ethical and political dimension of the knowledge of the sage is perhaps best represented by the figure of Ko Kung, for he is both a true hermit and an astute political thinker.

The third component is more difficult to define, but it is quite unmistakably an important element in the Ho-shang Chang-jen tradition, and as such in the Huang-lao school as a whole. Master An-ch'i, for example, is clearly identified as an adept in the tradition of "immortals." Master An-ch'iu, Ho-shang Kung's disciple, is also said to have preferred practising his divining and medical magic to serving Emperor Ch'eng.[69] This aspect of the special knowledge of the Huang-lao sage can be traced to the influence of the *fang-shih* tradition.

The *fang-shih* were diviners, doctors, magicians, and "immortals"; they grew out of the land of Ch'i, out of which the Ho-shang Chang-jen tradition also developed. The quest for immortality is of course a major distinguishing characteristic of the *fang-shih* tradition, or the "school of immortals" (*Shen-hsien chia*) as it is later called; but it is difficult to assess the precise relationship between the *fang-shih* and the Huang-lao school. Ostensibly the quest for immortality does not appear to be a central concern in the Huang-lao tradition, since the emphasis is mostly placed on a political utopia modeled on the Way. According to T'ang Lan, these two traditions had really little in common prior to the Later Han dynasty, when with the rise of Taoism as an institutionalized religion they were amalgamated.[70] Yet the connection of such major figures of the Huang-lao school as Master An-ch'i with the *fang-shih* tradition cannot be denied. Ho-shang Chang-jen himself is described as "old but not deficient or weak," which may reflect a certain interest in a productive and indefinitely prolonged life on earth, if not immortality itself.[71]

On this question, the Ma-wang-tui discovery is again helpful. In addition to the silk manuscripts, there is also an exercise manual now entitled *Tao-yin t'u* (Diagrams of Guidance)—that is, diagrams of exercises modeled on animal movements designed to "guide" the circulation of "breath" (*ch'i*) within an individual in his or her quest for immortality. Moreover, a burial shroud or banner was also found in the third tomb of the Ma-wang-tui site, in which the journey of the deceased to the "other world" is vividly depicted.[72] This indicates concretely that the concern with immortality and the afterlife was very much a part of the early Han ethos, and that it flourished in the same environment as the Huang-lao school.[73] In this context, it would be difficult to argue that the quest for immortality, characteristic of the *fang-shih* tradition, was not a constituent of the Huang-lao tradition also.

As far as the Ho-shang Kung legend is concerned, the idea of immortality is admittedly not explicitly present. But the *divinity* of Ho-shang Kung performs a similar role. Furthermore, as is well known, the reign of Emperor Wu (r. 140–87 B.C.) marks the high point of the *fang-shih* tradition in Han China; it would be surprising if the Ho-shang Kung legend, which appeared shortly after, was not aware of it. At any rate, the Ho-shang Kung legend was certainly understood to be related to the *fang-shih* tradition. The three recipients of the Ho-shang Kung commentary before Emperor Wen has traditionally been identified with Wu Kuang, Hsien-men Tzu-kao, and Ch'iu-tzu, two of whom at least were major figures of the *fang-shih* tradition.[74]

This should suffice to show that the "saving" knowledge of the sage involves a religious dimension associated with the idea of immortality. Finally, the special knowledge of the sage is also concerned with the texts of the Huang-lao school itself. The texts of *Huang-ti* and *Lao-tzu* are specified, for example, in the biography of the Empress Dowager Tou in the *Shih-chi*.[75] This indeed is to be expected; after all, the school must be recognized if the sage were to make his mark in the political world. Yüeh Chü-kung, to take another example, was renowned throughout the state of Ch'i especially for his expert interpretation of Huang-lao thought.[76] The Huang-lao school, like other contending schools at the time, aspired to imperial favor by emphasizing the superiority of its own writings.

In sum, the Ho-shang Kung legend was probably formed originally to enhance the teaching of the Huang-lao school, especially in terms of the superior status of the sage. The sage can sharply articulate the difference between the ruler and the minister because he stands apart from the ministers and claims a special place in the political system. The divinity of Ho-shang Kung suggests to me that the figure of the sage cannot be regarded as ordinary advisor; rather, he has a "mission" to see that the political utopia modeled on Tao be attained. As Anna Seidel has suggested, concern with immortality and concern with ideal government are merged into one in the Huang-lao tradition. Yet Seidel is careful to point out that despite this overarching interest, the figures of Huang-ti and Lao-tzu have their unique roles to play. Whereas the Yellow Emperor is particularly associated with the quest for immortality, Lao-tzu is portrayed as the sage par excellence, whose teaching is to be obeyed by all rulers.[77] Even the Yellow Emperor himself is seen as a disciple of Lao-tzu. The ideal ruler is above all presented in the Huang-lao tradition as the dedicated student of the Way, mediated by the sage. As Seidel puts it, "Houang-ti est, aux yeux des maîtres Houang-lao, l'empereur *converti* à l'art taoiste de gouverner."[78] Just as the Yellow Emperor submits to the teaching of the sage, Emperor Wen must bow to the words of Ho-shang Kung. It is in this sense that the eremitic heritage of the Huang-lao tradition displays an important political dimension.

When Confucianism finally triumphed over the other schools in the Han dynasty, references to the Huang-lao school gradually started to fade out of official records. However, the Huang-lao tradition continued to flourish. According to Kimura Eiichi, Han Confucianism itself seems to have absorbed certain Huang-lao elements into its own framework.[79] More specifically, Seidel has shown that despite the rise of Han Confucianism, the Huang-lao tradition was able to survive and to exert its influence, "thanks to its teaching of the practice of longevity."[80] Furthermore, the teachings of the Huang-lao school were then widely disseminated among the people, especially with regard to the idea of immortality and the kind of self-cultivation that would lead to it. As Yü Ying-shih has pointed out, in the Later Han dynasty the Ho-shang Kung tradition may have become a part of the "small tradition" also, reflecting the popular imagination as distinguished from the official ideology of the cultured elite.[81] From these references, we also see why the emphasis on the quest for immortality has often been identified as the key to the Ho-shang Kung commentary.

The Date of the Ho-shang Kung Commentary

Because of the legend, the Ho-shang Kung commentary has traditionally been dated to the time of Emperor Wen in the Former

Han dynasty. This view is largely rejected today, although no new consensus on the date of the commentary has yet emerged. Scholarly opinions on this question range from the first century B.C. to the end of the Six Dynasties period, around 500 A.D.

Those who favor a late date have especially emphasized the concern with immortality. Naitō Motoharu, for example, has argued that the Ho-shang Kung commentary cannot be a Han product, precisely because of its teaching on immortality.[82] In other words, the emphasis on methods of self-cultivation in the pursuit of immortality has convinced some scholars that the Ho-shang Kung commentary was closely related to the established Taoist religion. And the Taoist religion was not fully developed until the Six Dynasties period. Because this has an important bearing on the argument that the Ho-shang Kung tradition originated from the Huang-lao school, with its dual emphasis on self-cultivation and government, the date of the commentary demands careful investigation.

The earliest extant reference to the Ho-shang Kung commentary is attributed to Hsüeh Tsung (d. 243), who cited Ho-shang Kung while commenting on the Han poem *Tung-ching fu* (Eastern Metropolis Rhapsody) by Chang Heng (78–139).[83] The quotation is taken from chapter 46 of the Ho-shang Kung commentary, and it agrees well with the modern text.[84] If the authenticity of this reference is acceptable, it would indicate that the Ho-shang Kung commentary was current in the early third century A.D. at the latest.

There is a second early reference to the Ho-shang Kung commentary, which involves the famous calligrapher Wang Hsi-chih (321–379). This reference is recorded in a number of places, the earliest of which seems to be a sixth-century essay on calligraphy by Yü Ho.[85] The story has it that Wang Hsi-chih was fond of geese. When he heard that a certain village Taoist had kept some fine specimens of that gourmet item, he went to see him. The Taoist then confided that "for a long time" he had wished a written copy of the "Ho-shang Kung *Lao-tzu*," and would gladly exchange his whole collection of fine geese for it.[86] The deal, we are told, was happily concluded to the delight of both parties. This charming story is also attested in the biography of Wang Hsi-chih in the *Chin-shu*.[87] However, the difficulty here is that in the *Chin-shu* account the Ho-shang Kung version is not specified; Wang is simply said to have written a copy of the *Tao-te ching* for his Taoist host.

While it is possible that the Ho-shang Kung commentary was current in the third and fourth centuries, these references alone cannot determine its date. Incontestable references to the commentary did not appear until the sixth century.[88] The lack of solid evidence had led to a lively debate on the subject especially among Japanese scholars.

This debate can be traced to the works of Ma Hsü-lun and Takeuchi Yoshio, who have both argued that the Ho-shang Kung commentary postdated that of Wang Pi.[89] Until 1956, when Jao Tsung-i published his seminal study of the *Hsiang-erh* commentary, this view had dominated the sinological scene. The appearance of Jao's work, however, altered the entire situation, for it shows that the *Hsiang-erh* might be dependent on the Ho-shang Kung commentary.[90] Since then Jao's hypothesis has gained the approval of many scholars, though there are some important critics.

According to Jao Tsung-i and others, the *Hsiang-erh* commentary discovered in Tun-huang (S 6825) may be attributed to Chang Lu (fl. 195 A.D.), one of the founders of the "Celestial Master" sect (*T'ien-shih tao*) of the Taoist religion.[91] If the *Hsiang-erh* is dependent on the Ho-shang Kung commentary, and given the unlikelihood of an early Former Han date, then the latter should be dated to the Later Han period (25–220 A.D.). This forms the central claim around which the debate on the date of the Ho-shang Kung commentary revolves. Among Jao's supporters we may include Ōfuchi Ninji, Yoshioka Yoshitoyo, Anna Seidel, and Yü Ying-shih; among Jao's critics we may name Shima Kunio, Kusuyama Haruki, Naitō Motoharu, and Kobayashi Masayoshi.[92]

Critics of Jao would readily date the Ho-shang Kung commentary to a later period, usually around the late fifth or early sixth century A.D. Shima Kunio, for example, has argued that the Ho-shang Kung commentary had borrowed from the *Hsiang-erh*, and not the other way round.[93] He believes that the Ho-shang Kung commentary may be traced to the Taoist master Ch'iu Yüeh of the Southern Ch'i dynasty (479–502).[94] The work of Shima Kunio has occasioned a sharp critique by Yoshioka Yoshitoyo, who has carefully reviewed every one of Shima's arguments.[95] We need not rehearse the controversy here; but it shows well that the relationship between the *Hsiang-erh* and the Ho-shang Kung commentary remains a crucial point of contention in this debate.

Jao has singled out six passages from the *Hsiang-erh* to demonstrate his thesis; they correspond in their order of presentation to chapters 19, 28, 34, 6, 8, and 15 of the modern *Lao-tzu*.[96] By themselves, it cannot be said that they make a very strong case. Chapter

6, in which the *Lao-tzu* equates the "spirit of the valley" with the "mysterious female," is a good case in point. On the term "mysterious female" or more literally "dark female" (*hsüan-p'in*), the Ho-shang Kung commentary remarks that "the 'mysterious' is heaven, in man it is the nose; the 'female' is earth, in man it is the mouth." According to Jao, because the *Hsiang-erh* also "follows" this rather unique interpretation by identifying the "mysterious female" with "heaven and earth," it betrays its indebtedness to the Ho-shang Kung commentary.[97] Interestingly, E. Erkes has also employed a similar argument to show the antiquity of the Ho-shang Kung commentary. The Han commentator Kao Yu (fl. 205–212) has taken the word *hsüan* to mean "heaven" in his work on the *Huai-nan tzu*, and Erkes concludes that Kao must have "borrowed" it from Ho-shang Kung.[98] There is, of course, no sure way of determining who has borrowed from whom, or if it was a case of "borrowing" at all. Jao's discussion of chapters 8 and 15 may also be included in this category.

The treatment of chapters 28 and 34 in the *Hsiang-erh*, according to Jao, shows an interesting pattern. In both instances, it seems to have taken key terms from the Ho-shang Kung commentary, but out of their original context. In chapter 28 the *Lao-tzu* likens the perfect man of Tao to the "valley of the world," and Ho-shang Kung has taken this to mean that "the world returns to him, like water flowing into a deep valley." The *Hsiang-erh*, however, focuses on the man of Tao's own resolve to follow the Way, and compares it to "the water of the valley which desires to flow eastward and return to the sea." Although the *Hsiang-erh*, argues Jao, has "borrowed" the water imagery, it has in fact reversed the meaning of Ho-shang Kung's interpretation. Instead of taking the *valley* to which all things return as the key symbol, the *Hsiang-erh* has "mistaken" the *water* that flows away from the valley as the point of focus. This reflects the *Hsiang-erh's* tendency to "copy the words" from the Ho-shang Kung commentary but "forgetting their meaning."[99]

The case of chapter 34 is also interesting, though more difficult. The difficulty lies very much with the *Lao-tzu* itself. It concerns the verse in the current Ho-shang Kung text, *Wan-wu shih-chih erh sheng, erh pu-tz'u*. Because the *Hsiang-erh* version, and for that matter the Wang Pi text also, are substantially the same, textual emendation need not be considered as far as a comparison of these commentaries is concerned. The first half of this passage is straightforward enough, and may be translated as "The ten thousand things depend on (Tao) for their existence." The second half, however, is highly problematic. Not only is the verb *tz'u* difficult to interpret, but the subject of the action is also not entirely clear.[100] Ho-shang Kung understands this to mean that everything is indeed dependent on Tao, and "the Way does not decline (them) and becomes alienated" (*Tao pu tz'u-hsieh erh ni-chih yeh*); or as E. Erkes puts it, "Tao rejects nobody and is opposed to nothing."[101] The *Hsiang-erh*, on the other hand, explains that even if the ten thousand things "do not voice their gratitude, the Way will not reprove them" (*Pu tz'u-hsieh en, Tao pu tse yeh*).[102]

Without insisting on my translation of these passages, the difference between Ho-shang Kung and the *Hsiang-erh* is at least clear. As Jao sees it, the latter has "borrowed" the term *tz'u-hsieh*, "to decline," from Ho-shang Kung; but by taking the surface meaning of the term in the sense of "giving thanks" and ascribing it to the myriad creatures, the *Hsiang-erh* has committed an "error." Both the meaning and the subject of the verbal phrase *tz'u-hsieh* are thus altered in this exchange, which according to Jao suggests the *Hsiang-erh's* indebtedness to Ho-shang Kung.

The Ho-shang Kung commentary, we may add, is consistent, for the same interpretation is given in chapter 2 where the term *tz'u-hsieh* also appears. Unfortunately this chapter is missing in the *Hsiang-erh* manuscript, which precludes a more thorough comparison. It is also noteworthy that in the commentary by Ku Huan (fl. 480), both of these interpretations are preserved.[103] Although the authenticity of the Ku Huan commentary itself is not beyond dispute, this should serve to caution us from accepting too hastily the claim that the Ho-shang Kung commentary is to be dated to the sixth century.

Chapters 28 and 34 may seem to work in Jao's favor, but other possibilities should not be discounted. The metaphor of "water returning to the sea" in the *Hsiang-erh* commentary is not only found in chapter 28, but also in chapters 15 and 32. This may suggest that the *Hsiang-erh* is not dependent on Ho-shang Kung, but is simply repeating a favorite theme of its own. In the case of chapter 34, the use of the term *tz'u-hsieh* may be entirely coincidental. Indeed, while a detailed discussion of the *Hsiang-erh* lies outside the confines of the present work, even a cursory reading would confirm that it often takes the Tao as the subject of Lao-tzu's sayings. Its interpretation here, in other words, may be guided by this basic assumption, as opposed to any borrowing from Ho-shang Kung.

Besides, there are other instances where the two commentaries employ identical expressions, especially compound terms used to explain individual words in the *Lao-tzu*. No firm conclusions, however, can be drawn from them, in regard to the question of possible influence.[104] In both chapters 28 and 34 one may perhaps argue that the Ho-shang Kung commentary offers a stronger interpretation; but it does not quite follow that the *Hsiang-erh* is therefore "erroneous," or that it has "borrowed" from the Ho-shang Kung commentary.

Chapter 19 is also singled out by Jao. This case is more complex because the *Lao-tzu* text itself is different in the two commentaries. In the Ho-shang Kung version, the *Lao-tzu* reads, "These three (*tz'u san che*) are inadequate as they remain external ornaments." In the *Hsiang-erh*, the phrase *tz'u san che* is replaced by *tz'u san yen*, "these three sayings." The "three" in question refer to the ideas of eliminating "sagehood," "wisdom," etc., with which chapter 19 of the *Lao-tzu* begins. The important point, however, is that in both commentaries the phrase "three things/matters" (*san shih*) is used to explain the text. Given the variant reading in the *Hsiang-erh* text, the use of *san-shih* seems inappropriate. According to Jao, the *Hsiang-erh* may have intentionally altered the text so that the latter agrees better with its general interpretation. But without realizing the resulting awkwardness, it has "retained" the words *san-shih* from Ho-shang Kung. From this, as Jao concludes, it is "obvious" that the *Hsiang-erh* is dependent on the Ho-shang Kung commentary.[105]

The claim that the *Hsiang-erh* has changed the *Lao-tzu* text is difficult to maintain, especially because, as William Boltz has pointed out, the Ma-wang-tui *Lao-tzu* manuscripts have *tz'u san yen* also.[106] Indeed, according to Boltz, this would suggest that "textual priority" lies on the side of the *Hsiang-erh*, contrary to what Jao has proposed.[107] While I am not convinced that there is sufficient evidence to determine the question of textual priority, Jao's argument here is evidently not without difficulties.[108] One may insist that regardless of the wording of the *Lao-tzu* original, the agreement of the commentaries is not accidental. Nevertheless, even if this were the case, the question of "borrowing" remains unresolved. The evidence presented so far, in other words, remains inconclusive. On the basis of a comparison of the two commentaries alone, it is not possible to say with any degree of certainty whether the *Hsiang-erh* is "dependent" on the Ho-shang Kung commentary or vice versa.[109] But, in addition to the textual analysis, Jao is also able to provide external evidence that makes his thesis highly attractive.

First, there is the testimony of the early T'ang Taoist Ch'eng Hsüan-ying (fl. 630), according to whom the Ho-shang Kung text was edited by Ko Hsüan.[110] This would certainly place Ho-shang Kung's version of the *Lao-tzu* before the Six Dynasties period. More precisely, Ko Hsüan is said to have shortened the text mainly by eliminating the particles in the original to fit the magical number "five thousand characters." According to Ch'eng Hsüan-ying, this edited version was in fact the dominant version of the Ho-shang Kung text at the time.[111]

Second, a Tun-huang fragment of the *Tao-te ching* dated 751 A.D. bears the signature of *Hsi-shih ting Ho-shang chen-jen chang-chü*— that is, the Ho-shang Kung version of the *Lao-tzu* as established by the *Hsi-shih*, the rightful "Master Successor." Because in Taoist literature the title *Hsi-shih* is ascribed to Chang Lu or his father Chang Heng (not to be confused, however, with the author of the *Tung-ching fu*), both of whom are of course founding figures of the *T'ien-shih tao*, this would indicate that the Ho-shang Kung commentary was edited and transmitted by the "Celestial Master" sect of the Taoist religion, which is precisely Professor Jao's main contention.[112]

Moreover, an early Taoist text provides an interesting discussion of the "order" of basic Taoist education. The *Ch'uan-shou ching-chieh i-chu-chüeh* (The Transmission of Scriptures, Rules, Customs, Commentaries, and Instructions), dated by Ōfuchi Ninji to the sixth century, specifically instructs that students of Taoist teaching should begin with the *Tao-te ching* itself in "large characters," then followed by the Ho-shang Kung commentary, and third by the *Hsiang-erh* commentary.[113] As Jao suggests, this would seem to give textual priority to the Ho-shang Kung commentary, vis-à-vis the *Hsiang-erh*. Indeed, according to Yoshioka Yoshitoyo, on the basis of another document preserved in the *Tao-tsang*, this order of instruction was perhaps established even before the Liang dynasty (502–557).[114]

Finally, one must also mention Jao's discussion of the so-called *Su Tan* fragment of the *Tao-te ching*.[115] This manuscript, also discovered in Tun-huang and now in the possession of a private collector, contains the last thirty-one chapters of the *Lao-tzu* beginning with chapter 51 of the modern text. It is signed at the end by the third-century scholar and diviner Su Tan and dated to 270 A.D. This date, if accepted, would certainly put it among the oldest extant

Lao-tzu manuscripts. Most important, according to Jao, the *Su Tan* manuscript also shows indebtedness to the Ho-shang Kung text, though not the "five thousand characters" version allegedly edited by Ko Hsüan. As Jao himself puts it, the *Su Tan* is derived from "the *Ho-shang* text that was current at the end of the Eastern Han (A.D. 220)."[116]

Much more can be said on these arguments, but my point is simply that together they offer a good case in support of an early date for the Ho-shang Kung commentary. Critics of Jao may perhaps have focused too exclusively on the comparison between the Ho-shang Kung commentary and the *Hsiang-erh* itself; the context in which the comparison is made and the supporting evidence that stands behind the comparison are equally important. To be sure, critics may argue that the supporting evidence outlined above is itself a matter of debate, especially as far as date and authenticity are concerned. Yen Ling-feng, for example, has argued that the *Su Tan* manuscript is probably a later forgery.[117] However, the point remains that although certain early references may be corrupt, to reject them *all* would seem difficult and, indeed, unwarranted.

Thus, from early references ascribed to Hsüeh Tsung and Wang Hsi-chih, the *Hsiang-erh* fragment and other supporting evidence, the Later or Eastern Han period proves to be the most likely date for the Ho-shang Kung commentary. Nevertheless there is another alternative that should be mentioned. This has to do with Kusuyama Haruki's suggestion that there were *two* Ho-shang Kung commentaries, which must be clearly distinguished.[118] First, according to Kusuyama, the "original" version appeared sometime during the Later Han dynasty. This text was lost, and a second, "expanded," version came into being toward the end of the Six Dynasties period, together with the mature Ho-shang Kung legend.[119]

One major factor in this consideration is that besides Ho-shang Kung, traditional sources also ascribe a *Lao-tzu* commentary to Ho-shang Chang-jen of the Warring States period. In the third century work *Kao-shih chuan* (Lives of Exemplary Men) by Huang-fu Mi, for example, Ho-shang Chang-jen is said to have written a *Lao-tzu chang-chü*, the exact same title as Ho-shang Kung's commentary.[120] A "Commentary on the *Lao-tzu Classic*" by Ho-shang Chang-jen is also recorded in the bibliographical section of the *Sui-shu*, right next to the Ho-shang Kung commentary. The *Sui-shu* adds that this work has been lost since the Liang dynasty.[121]

If the figure of Ho-shang Kung is modeled on Ho-shang Chang-jen, do these titles refer to the same work? Yet the *Sui-shu* lists them as two separate commentaries. This, in part, has thus led to the view that the work attributed to Ho-shang Chang-jen may be identified as the "original" Ho-shang Kung commentary. In terms of content, according to Kusuyama, this "original" version is characterized by a strong political interest. When the second version appeared, it incorporated the tenets of religious Taoism, especially the practice of self-cultivation aimed at spiritual realization and everlasting life.[122]

This hypothesis, at first glance, may seem attractive, but it is not without difficulties. It too has to reject the early references to the Ho-shang Kung commentary, as distinguished from the work attributed to Ho-shang Chang-jen. Hsüeh Tsung's quotation from the Ho-shang Kung commentary, for example, would have to be regarded as a later interpolation.[123] The *Hsiang-erh* commentary is similarly seen to be a late product of the Six Dynasties period.[124] In this respect, it seems to me that the burden of the critic then becomes unnecessarily heavy; at any rate, there is yet no solid evidence to reject the authenticity of all the early references. On the contrary, there is much to be said for an Eastern Han date. In particular, it would tie in with the Huang-lao tradition, which as I have argued was closely related to the Ho-shang Kung legend. More importantly, Kusuyama's hypothesis divides the content of the Ho-shang Kung commentary into two separate parts. The political component is viewed as "older" and distinct from the "religious" concerns of the commentary. What I shall argue in the next chapter is precisely that no such distinction can be made. The Ho-shang Kung commentary reflects a unified vision, characterized by both self-cultivation and the art of government.

The reference to a commentary by Ho-shang Chang-jen, however, requires further comment. Indeed, besides the two "Ho-shang" figures, there is yet a third individual to whom a *Lao-tzu chang-chü* is credited. A number of sources report that Master An-ch'iu, the disciple of Ho-shang Kung, also wrote a *Lao-tzu* commentary with that title.[125] Lu Te-ming, for example, refers to it in his *Ching-tien shih-wen*.[126] The *Sui-shu* mentions it also, together with the Ho-shang Chang-jen and the Ho-shang Kung commentaries.[127] Indeed, the noted *Lao-tzu* scholar Fu I (555–629) is even said to have examined these texts himself.[128] Does this not indicate that there was more than one commentary with the title *Lao-tzu chang-chü?* Even if we regard the two "Ho-shang" commentaries to be variants of the same text, the work attributed to Master An-ch'iu remains to be explained. According to Anna Seidel, it may be that the work of the disciple was later ascribed to his more famous teacher; that is, the An-ch'iu commentary forms the "original" to which the others may be traced.[129] This view is not without merit; but more likely these titles refer to the same work. There is no need to identify here any historical author for the commentary. What needs to be emphasized again is that all these figures are connected with the Huang-lao tradition.

More specifically, the following hypothesis may be suggested. The commentary entitled *Lao-tzu chang-chü* appeared in the Later Han dynasty. Since there is no mention of a *Lao-tzu* commentary by Ho-shang Chang-jen, Ho-shang Kung, or Master An-ch'iu in the *Shih-chi* and the *Han-shu*, it may be dated to after 100 A.D. At first, it was variously ascribed to key figures in the Huang-lao tradition. Thus, while the *Shih-chi* does not mention any writing by Ho-shang Chang-jen, Huang-fu Mi's *Kao-shih chuan* names him as the author of a *Lao-tzu chang-chü*. Similarly, whereas the *Hou Han-shu* (History of the Later Han Dynasty) identifies Master An-ch'iu only as a teacher of the Huang-lao school, the *Kao-shih chuan* reports that he wrote a *Lao-tzu* commentary.[130] When the "Celestial Master" tradition was established toward the end of the Later Han dynasty, it adopted the commentary as one of its scriptures and attributed it to Ho-shang Kung.[131] When the legend of Ho-shang Kung gained prominence in the Six Dynasties period, the authorship of the commentary was finally settled in his favor. By the sixth century, we thus begin to find clear references to the Ho-shang Kung commentary in diverse sources, while the other two candidates gradually faded into oblivion.

The confusion in the bibliographic records may be traced to the sources on which these records themselves are based. First of all, the *Sui-shu* reports that the Ho-shang Chang-jen and the An-ch'iu commentaries were lost since the Liang dynasty. This means that the *Sui-shu* was relying on earlier bibliographic sources, and did not have firsthand knowledge of these works. Four bibliographic catalogues are in fact singled out in the *Sui-shu* as particularly important. They are Liu Hsiang's (79–8 B.C.) *Pieh-lu*, Liu Hsin's (d. 23 A.D.) *Ch'i-lüeh*, Wang Chien's (452–489) *Ch'i-chih*, and Juan Hsiao-hsü's (479–536) *Ch'i-lu*.[132] As is well known, the work of Liu Hsin was based on his father Liu Hsiang's *Pieh-lu*, and together these two were extensively consulted by Pan Ku (32–92 A.D.) when compiling the bibliographical section of the *Han-shu*.[133] Since no mention of the commentaries in question is made in the *Han-shu*, it may be surmised that the *Sui-shu* is mainly indebted to the works of Wang Chien and Juan Hsiao-hsü in this instance.

These works are no longer extant, but they are singled out by Lu Te-ming as well.[134] Lu was aware of the Ho-shang Kung legend, and did not mention any commentary by Ho-shang Chang-jen. He did name a commentary by Master An-ch'iu. But this reference is found only in the general "Preface"; Lu did not actually cite it in his "phonological" commentary on the *Lao-tzu*.[135] This too suggests that Lu Te-ming did not know this work himself, but had taken the title from the catalogues by Wang Chien and Juan Hsiao-hsü. In this way, even when Ho-shang Kung's authorship of the *Lao-tzu chang-chü* was firmly established, references to Ho-shang Chang-jen and Master An-ch'iu survived in T'ang and later sources.

The testimony of Fu I, however, may seem to pose a real problem. This reference is found in a number of Taoist works, the earliest of which appears to be Hsieh Shou-hao's (fl. 1194) *Hun-yüan sheng-chi*. According to Hsieh, Fu I examined a number of versions of the *Lao-tzu*, including an An-ch'iu version "obtained" by the Northern Wei dynasty Taoist patriarch K'ou Ch'ien-chih during the reign of T'ai-ho (477–499), and a Ho-shang Chang-jen version "transmitted" by the Taoist Ch'iu Yüeh in the second half of the fifth century.[136] Does this not suggest that these texts were still current in the early T'ang dynasty? This is why Shima Kunio, as mentioned earlier, concluded that the Ho-shang Kung commentary is to be traced to the Taoist master Ch'iu Yüeh of the Southern Ch'i dynasty.

Three points may be made in this connection. First, the famous Taoist K'ou Ch'ien-chih flourished in the court of Emperor T'ai-wu (r. 424–451) and died in the year 448; he could not have "obtained" a commentary during the reign of T'ai-ho.[137] This immediately calls into question the trustworthiness of Hsieh Shou-hao's report. Furthermore, even if we accept Hsieh's report, what Fu I has seen are different versions of the *Lao-tzu* text. It does not necessarily imply that they were followed by different commentaries. Indeed, the Ho-shang Kung text is known to have different versions. It may be recalled, according to Ch'eng Hsüan-ying, the dominant version of the Ho-shang Kung text in the T'ang dynasty was the "five thousand-character" version supposedly edited by Ko Hsüan. In the work of Lu Te-ming, references are also made to an "old version" (*ku-pen*) of the Ho-shang Kung *Lao-tzu* text.[138] There is no reason not to believe that these different versions were accompanied by the same commentary.

Finally, the fact that the An-ch'iu and the Ho-shang Chang-jen versions are linked to specific Taoist masters may be significant. Perhaps they were especially valued by certain Taoist sects that sought to reform the "Way of the Celestial Masters," and to distinguish themselves from the particular group with which the Ho-shang Kung version was closely associated. While nothing is known of Ch'iu Yüeh, K'ou Ch'ien-chih is well remembered by later historians as the great reformer of the Taoist religion in north China.[139] In the south, there were also important changes, as diverse Taoist traditions were consolidated by such figures as Lu Hsiu-ching (406–477) and T'ao Hung-ching (456–536).[140] Could the name Ch'iu Yüeh be a corruption of Sun Yu-yüeh, the student of Lu Hsiu-ching and teacher of T'ao Hung-ching? The words *yu* and *ch'iu* are phonetically similar and, in one Buddhist source at least, the name Sun Yu-yüeh is contracted to Sun Yüeh.[141]

These speculations, admittedly, do not resolve the issue at hand. The origin and transmission of the Ho-shang Kung commentary will no doubt continue to attract diverse opinions. Nevertheless, on the whole, I believe that the commentary is best placed in a Later Han context, and more specifically in a Huang-lao setting. Whether or not the commentary was made with the legend in mind remains a question. Inasmuch as the commentary does not allude to the legend in any way, it does not seem likely that the former was made with the latter in view. What may be suggested is that because of their similar background and because of the fame of the legend, the commentary was ascribed to Ho-shang Kung after its appearance in the Later Han dynasty. When the legend itself was committed to writing in the fourth century, or shortly after when the *Hsü-chüeh* version of the legend was compiled, it was made to complement the commentary. In other words, when the later version of the legend identified the "unadorned text" or "book of simplicity" with the *Lao-tzu chang-chü*, the relationship between the legend and the commentary was firmly established. In the next chapter, it will be shown how the Huang-lao dimension, which is so important in the legend, is also reflected in the commentary.

4   Ho-shang Kung: Cosmology, Government, and the Ideal Sage

The Ho-shang Kung commentary, as Lu Te-ming has stated, "sets out the key to self-government and the government of the country" (see p. 6, above). This assessment captures well the general tenor of the work. More specifically, the political and ethical aspects are merged into one in Ho-shang Kung's commentary. They are grounded in a vision of the past and in a cosmological framework. Moreover, there is also a religious side to this, oriented toward immortality and centered on the figure of the ideal sage. The special knowledge of the sage, so important in the Ho-shang Kung legend, is again crucial to an understanding of the commentary. As I shall argue, these themes are woven into a unified vision. With this analysis, we can then bring the Wang Pi and the Ho-shang Kung commentaries together in the next chapter.

History and Polemics

As in my analysis of Wang Pi, this discussion will begin with chapter 1 of the *Lao-tzu*. Ho-shang Kung's commentary is very precise. On the opening phrase of the *Lao-tzu*, "The Way that can be told of," which differs from the constant and ineffable Tao, Ho-shang Kung comments: "This means the Way of the art of the classics and the teaching of government." There is a clear polemical tone to the Ho-shang Kung commentary.

Unlike Wang Pi's commentary, there is little attempt to mediate the attack of the *Lao-tzu* on Confucian teaching. When the *Lao-tzu* states, "Eliminate sageliness," Ho-shang Kung does not hesitate to say: "Eliminate the work of the sages; return to the beginning and keep to the origin."[1] The work of the sages is here specifically identified with that of the "Five Emperors" and Ts'ang Chieh. The former is said to have observed the "heavenly images"—that is, the constellations that gave rise to the speculation of the *I-ching*—while the latter created the written Chinese language.[2] This is contrasted with the work of the "Three Sovereigns," who "tied cords" together to record events without the use of language.[3] In this instance, it appears that Ho-shang Kung is simply contrasting the Confucian model of sagehood with a "higher" one. But the situation is more complex.

Traditions vary with respect to the identity of the "Three Sovereigns" and the "Five Emperors." According to the *Shih-chi*, the "Five Emperors" include the Yellow Emperor, Yao, and Shun.[4] The "Three Sovereigns," on the other hand, were commonly identified in the Han dynasty with Fu-hsi, Shen-nung, and Nü-kua, especially because Cheng Hsüan accepted this view.[5] The difficulty lies in the fact that the "Three Sovereigns" and "Five Emperors" were revered by practically all schools of Chinese thought. Moreover, commenting on the line in chapter 39, "The valuable has its root in the despised," Ho-shang Kung writes: "This states that if one desires to be honored, one ought to take what is despised as one's root. This is like Yü and (Hou) Chi who worked on the crops, like Shun who made potteries by the riverside, and like the duke of Chou who humbled himself to stay in a lowly house."[6] Shun, Yü, Hou Chi, and the duke of Chou are of course key figures in the Confucian imagination as well. For example, the *Lun-yü* also says, "Yü and (Hou) Chi worked on the crops and thereby won the empire" (14.6). Is there an inconsistency in the Ho-shang Kung commentary?

The "Three Sovereigns" are mentioned again in chapter 62. The *Lao-tzu* here suggests that the Way does not abandon "even those who are not good." Ho-shang Kung explains, "Although they are not good, they should be transformed by Tao. Thus *before* the Three Sovereigns, there was no one abandoned. The people were transformed by virtue and became simple and sincere."[7]

The word "before" is important. It suggests the standard by which Ho-shang Kung's attack on Confucian doctrines is to be measured. The "Five Emperors" cannot compare with the "Three Sovereigns"; but even the latter pale by comparison with the "golden age" of the "beginning" when Tao prevailed. Chapter 18 continues the polemics against Confucian virtues in this light:

Text	*Commentary*
When the great Way declined, benevolence and righteousness arose.[8]	In the age of the great Way, there were filial children at home, and there were loyalty and trust in the household.[9] Benevolence and righteousness were not to be seen. When the great Way was abandoned, hatred and disobedience came into being. Then there were benevolence and righteousness to preach the Way.
When knowledge and wisdom appeared, there was great hypocrisy.	The ruler of "knowledge and wisdom" despises virtue and values words, despises substance and values external ornaments. The people below thus respond to this with great hypocrisy and deceit.
When the six relations are not in harmony, there will be filial kindness.	When the six threads are destroyed, family relations will fall into disharmony.[10] Then there will be filial kindness to reconcile them.
When the country is in disorder, there will be loyal ministers.	When government commands are not in force, the (ruler) above and the (people) below will blame each other, and employ evil ways to compete for power. Then there will be loyal ministers to rectify the ruler. This means that when the world is in great peace, benevolence will not be known. When the people are completely without desires, (the doctrine of) integrity will not be known. When the people have all purified themselves,

chastity will not be known. In the
world of the great Way, benevolence and righteousness disappear,
and filial kindness is eliminated.[11]
This is like when the multitude of
stars lose their brightness against
the splendor of the midday sun.

Confucian virtues, in this sense, are but remedies that arose
after the world "fell" from the paradisaic condition of the
"beginning."[12] They reflect symptoms of the disease, as it were, but
are unable to cure it. Although the Three Sovereigns and Five Emperors are virtuous, they remain bound by the "fallenness" of the
world. The polemics against Confucian teaching thus reveals an understanding of history characterized by an increasing deterioration
of the human condition. Commenting on Lao-tzu's remarks that
"When the Way is lost, virtue then arises," Ho-shang Kung writes:
"This means when the Way declined, then virtue came into being"
(chap. 38). It is interesting that Ho-shang Kung replaces the word
"loss" (*shih*) with "decline" (*shuai*). Not only is the "historical" development brought out more clearly, but the possibility of reviving
the rule of Tao is left open also.

This is the significance of the commentary on chapter 1 quoted
above. There is no need to see in this a reflection of ancient mythological traditions, however. There is no evidence in the Ho-shang
Kung commentary to suggest that it is working from a mythological
core. What is evident is that the Confucian understanding of history
is taken to be ultimately inadequate. Although the cause of this
"fall" from Tao is not explained, it is clear that Ho-shang Kung is
most concerned with the way in which the original reign of "great
peace," the ideal utopian state, can be reestablished. To achieve
this, the nature of Tao must be understood before one can return to
the "beginning."

The "One": Cosmological Speculation in the Ho-shang Kung Commentary

The Emptiness of Tao

The nature of Tao, as we have seen, is the major theme of
chapter 1 of the *Lao-tzu*. The "nameless" is said to be the "beginning of heaven and earth." Ho-shang Kung explains, "The 'name-

less' means the Way. The Way is without form. Therefore it cannot be named. The 'beginning' means the root of the Way. (Tao) emits the breath (ch'i) and gives rise to change. Originating from emptiness and nothingness (hsü-wu), it forms the beginning of heaven and earth." Furthermore, on the next line, "The named is the mother of all things," the commentary reads:

> The "named" means heaven and earth. Heaven and earth have form and place, yin and yang, softness and hardness. This is why they have names. The "mother of all things" means that heaven and earth retain the breath and give birth to the ten thousand things. They let them grow and mature, like a mother bringing up her children.[13]

The Way is thus formless and originates from emptiness (hsü) or nothingness (wu). The terms hsü and wu are identified by Ho-shang Kung in chapter 11, where he explicitly defines wu as what is empty (k'ung-hsü). In this sense, there is little metaphysical or ontological significance attached to wu; as such, "nothing" or "nothingness" may serve better to capture the meaning of wu than "nonbeing" in the Ho-shang Kung commentary. In chapter 11 the Lao-tzu concludes that because of wu, "function" is made possible. Ho-shang Kung explains:

> This means what is empty can be used because it is able to hold and to receive all things. Thus it is said that emptiness and nothingness can fashion what has form. Tao means what is empty.[14]

The idea of wu, in other words, is important in the Ho-shang Kung commentary only as a way of describing the unlimited resourcefulness of the Way. Indeed, beyond the definition of Tao as what is empty, there is little discussion of the nature of Tao as such in the commentary as a whole. Rather, the emphasis is shifted to the creative power of Tao, especially as it is mediated by "heaven and earth." This is clear from Ho-shang Kung's interpretation of the famous statement in chapter 40 of the Lao-tzu, "All things in the world come from yu, yu comes from wu":

> Heaven and earth, spirits and enlightened beings, insects that fly and worms that crawl—all these are produced by Tao. The

Way is formless, and thus (being) is said to be born of *wu*. This means that the root is superior to the branches; the weak is superior to the strong; the humble and empty, to the proud and full.[15]

In this instance, the emphasis is clearly not on the concept of *wu*. The *Lao-tzu* original is explained in terms of something much more concrete and closer at hand. As we shall see in the next chapter, this sense of concreteness is closely associated with Ho-shang Kung's hermeneutical presuppositions.

The nature of Tao is thus to be viewed primarily in terms of its relation to the world. Tao is the source from which all things spring, and this plays an important role in the Ho-shang Kung commentary. The metaphor of the "mother bringing up her children" in chapter 1 is repeated in chapter 25. Here, the *Lao-tzu* describes the Way as "something undifferentiated and complete," and "born before heaven and earth." Ho-shang Kung's commentary especially highlights the theme of creation: "This means that Tao is formless; undifferentiated, it completes all things. Thus it preceded heaven and earth." Moreover, when the *Lao-tzu* describes the Way as "standing alone and does not change," Ho-shang Kung takes the unchanging nature of Tao to mean that its transforming power is constant (*hua yu ch'ang*). Chapter 25 continues:

Text	Commentary
(Tao) can be considered the mother of the world.	Tao nurtures the essential breath (*ching-ch'i*) of all things, like a mother bringing up her children.
I do not know its name. I style it Tao.	I do not see the form and shape of Tao, and do not know how to name it. I see that the ten thousand things are all produced by Tao; thus I style it Tao.

The apparent logical difficulty involved in the last comment above need not trouble us. What is important is that the word "Tao" itself is explicitly linked to the process of creation, which is also said to be "constant." From chapters 1 and 25 we see that the notion of "breath" (*ch'i*) is central to Ho-shang Kung's understanding of this process.

The Fullness of Ch'i

The word *ch'i* is difficult to translate. The earliest definition in the *Shuo-wen* dictionary is "mist," literally *"ch'i* of the clouds," and by extension any type of vapor: "breath," "air," or "gas." But it also signifies a more fundamental substance, a creative force, energy, or "life-breath." It is the basic "stuff" of life that constitutes all beings and pervades the universe. It is in this sense that some scholars render the term *ch'i* as "material force." The difficulty, however, is that *ch'i* cannot be reduced to the "material" level alone. As B. Schwartz has pointed out, *"ch'i* comes to embrace properties which we would call psychic, emotional, spiritual, numinous, and even 'mystical.' "[16] In this discussion, "breath" or "life-breath" may be adopted, for the simple reason that the Ho-shang Kung commentary itself makes use of the imagery of breathing (e.g., chap. 1). What we should bear in mind is that *ch'i* encompasses both the "material" and the "spiritual" in a unified understanding of the constitution of the cosmos. The world's coming into being is most vividly depicted in the commentary on chapter 42:

Text	Commentary
Tao begets one.	What the Way produced in the beginning was (the One).[17]
One begets two.	The One gave birth to *yin* and *yang*.
Two begets three.	*Yin* and *yang* gave birth to the harmonious, (the clear) and the turbid.[18] These three breaths were differentiated and became heaven, earth, and man.
Three begets all things.	Heaven, earth (and man) together gave birth to the ten thousand things.[19] That is, heaven gives, earth transforms, and man nurtures them.

The *Lao-tzu* original is difficult; there is no clear indication that the generation of things is to be taken in the past tense, for example, or that the "two" and "three" be taken in the plural. In Ho-shang Kung's commentary, however, the ambiguity is clarified by interpreting the *Lao-tzu* as referring to the coming to be of the constituent forces of the world.

The notion of *ch'i* is thus divided threefold into the "turbid"/ *yin*, "clear"/*yang*, and the "harmonious" (*ho*) blending of the two. These three are then correlated with earth, heaven, and human beings respectively. The cosmogony presented here is not unique to Ho-shang Kung. On the contrary, it is commonly found in Han literature. For example, the *Huai-nan tzu* says:

> Before heaven and earth took shape, there was only undifferentiated formlessness. Therefore it is called the great beginning. Tao originated in emptiness, and from emptiness the universe was born. The universe produced the breath of life [*ch'i*]. . . . The clear and light drifted upward and became heaven. The heavy and turbid solidified and became earth.[20]

The *Shuo-wen* dictionary, under the word "earth" (*ti*), also says: "When the original breath began to differentiate, the light, clear, and *yang* became heaven, while the heavy, turbid, and *yin* became earth."[21] And the *Lieh-tzu*, to take but one more example, states: "'One' signifies that form is beginning to change. The clear and light rises to become heaven. The turbid and heavy descends to become earth. The breaths blend and harmonize to become man."[22]

These references point to the fact that Ho-shang Kung's understanding of the *Lao-tzu* is rooted in a cosmological theory prevalent in the Han dynasty. The formation of the universe is portrayed in terms of the differentiating and mixing—or more graphically as the commentary on chapter 1 has it, the "spitting out"/"emitting" (*t'u*) and "holding"/"retaining" (*han*)—of the "breath" of Tao. Originally the words *yin* and *yang* probably denoted the sun's being hidden by clouds and its being unobstructed, respectively.[23] It is possible that *yin* ("cloudy sky"), *yang* ("clear sky"), and *ch'i* ("mist") were originally "weather" words, and later acquired deeper cosmological meanings. The connection with the sun is still preserved in the Ho-shang Kung commentary. Chapter 42 states:

Text	*Commentary*
The ten thousand things carry the *yin* on their backs and embrace the *yang*.	Without exception the ten thousand things all carry the *yin* on their backs and face the *yang*, turning their hearts to the sun.

Incidentally, this comment is repeated in chapter 73 as well, to describe the "Way of heaven."

The pervasiveness of the idea of *ch'i* is further attested in the commentary on the next line of chapter 42. The concreteness of Ho-shang Kung's interpretation is also very clear in this instance:

Text	*Commentary*
Through the blending of the breaths, (all things) become harmonious.	Within the ten thousand things, all have the original breath, through which they attain harmony. This is like within the chest there are internal organs, within each bone there is marrow, within grass and trees there are empty spaces, where *ch'i* flows through them. Thus they are able to attain longevity.[24]

The rather unexpected conclusion is important, and will be examined more closely later in this chapter. At this point, it should be noted that the free circulation of *ch'i* is ultimately the reason why "emptiness" or "nothingness" is important to an understanding of Tao. The definition of Tao as what is empty, in this regard, also means the fullness of *ch'i*.

The "One"

The view of an original generative force permeating the universe is inseparably tied to the idea of the "One." This latter is certainly one of the most important concepts in Ho-shang Kung's commentary, appearing in some twenty chapters and closely related to the task of self-cultivation and government. The concept of the "One" is ambiguous in the *Lao-tzu*. While chapter 42 speaks of the "One" as being produced by Tao, in other instances the two appear to be identified (e.g., chaps. 14, 39). At first glance, this ambiguity seems to be found in the Ho-shang Kung commentary as well.

In some cases, Ho-shang Kung clearly distinguishes the Way from the "One." For example, the commentary on chapter 52 describes the two in this way:

Text	*Commentary*
The world has a beginning, which may be regarded as the mother of the world.	The "beginning" is the Way.[25] The Way is the mother of all things in the world.

Having known the mother, one then knows the son.[26]	The "son" is the One. Having known the Way already, one then ought to know the One.
Having known the son, one then keeps to the mother.	Having known the One, one then ought to keep to the Way and return to nonaction.

The "One" is further identified with "virtue" (*te*) in the commentary on chapter 51:

Text	*Commentary*
The Way gives birth to them.	The Way gives birth to the ten thousand things.
Virtue rears them.	Virtue is the One. The One takes charge of dispensing the *ch'i* and nurtures them.

However, the distinction between Tao and "One" does not seem to agree with the opening lines of chapter 14:

Text	*Commentary*
Look at it and it cannot be seen; its name is "invisible" (*i*).	Without color is called *i*. This means that the One is without hue and color, and cannot be seen by looking.
Listen to it and it cannot be heard; its name is "inaudible" (*hsi*).	Without sound is called *hsi*. This means that the One is without noise and sound, and cannot be heard by listening.
Touch it and it cannot be found; its name is "subtle" (*wei*).	Without form is called *wei*. This means that the One is without form and body, and cannot be found by touching.
The three cannot be fathomed; they merge into one.	The "three" means *i*, *hsi*, and *wei*. . . . "Merge" means unified. Thus the three are unified and called the One.[27]

What is "it," if not the Way itself? Later in this chapter the *Lao-tzu* calls it "the form without form." Ho-shang Kung explains: "This means that the One is without form and shape; but it can create form and shape for the ten thousand things." Would it not appear that the "One" is here equated with Tao?

It is significant that up to this point the word "Tao" does not appear at all in chapter 14. It is mentioned in the concluding commentary; but again as distinct from the "One":

Text	Commentary
Hold fast to the Way of old, so as to master present situations. With this, one knows the beginning of antiquity. This is called the thread running through the Way.	The sage holds fast to the Way of old, which produced the One to master all things. He knows that the present must have the One. If one can come to know that the primordial beginning of high antiquity has the One, this then is called knowing the structure and pattern of the Way.

Without the "One," in this sense, a person would not be able to realize the Way in the present and to return to the "beginning." The "One," in Ho-shang Kung's commentary, means the *essence* of Tao. As the commentary itself puts it, the "One" is the "key" or "kernel" (*yao*) of the Way (chap. 1).

The ambiguity of the *Lao-tzu* is thus resolved by positing an essence that renders intelligible the formlessness of Tao. In this respect, Ho-shang Kung's commentary on chapter 39 is most revealing:

Text	Commentary
Of old, these obtained the One:	"Of old" means the past. The One means nonaction, the son of the Way.
Heaven obtained the One and became clear. Earth obtained the One and became tranquil.	This means that heaven obtained the One, and is therefore able to administer the constellations (*ch'ui-hsiang*) and to shine clearly. Earth obtained the One, and is therefore able to be quiet and still.

Following the same literary pattern, the analysis is applied to the "spirits" and the "valley," which because of the "One" are able to realize their potential. The text then continues:

| The ten thousand things obtained the One and came into being. | This means that the ten thousand things all need the *Way* in order to be born and made complete. |
| Princes and kings obtained the One and became rulers of the world. | This means that princes and kings obtained the One, and is therefore able to bring peace and order to the world. |

The sudden shift of terminology from the "One" to Tao should not escape our attention. There is no reason to suspect that the text is corrupt;[28] indeed the entire sentence structure is changed when the discussion shifts from heaven, earth, and the like, to the generation of beings.

Ho-shang Kung is consistent; the "One" is always subordinated to Tao, the "mother," when the theme of creation is in question. "Having known the mother," if we recall, one "ought to" understand the "One," through which one can return to the "beginning" (chap. 52). The reason for the careful distinction between Tao and "One" ultimately lies in Ho-shang Kung's strong practical emphasis. Responding to Lao-tzu's question whether one can always "embrace the One" (Chap. 10), Ho-shang Kung writes:

> This means that if one could embrace the One, so that it does not leave the body, then one would live long. The One is what the Way produced in the beginning; it is the essential breath of the great harmony. Thus it is called the One, and its name is made known to the world. "Heaven obtained the One and became clear. Earth obtained the One and became tranquil." Princes and kings obtained the One and realized justice and peace. Inwardly it is the heart; outwardly it is (expressed in) action; in dispensing favors it is virtue. Collectively it is called One. Expressed in words, the One means single-mindedness.

Various themes are thus combined and synthesized to form one key concept. The reading that the "One" forms the essence of Tao is also supported by Ho-shang Kung's treatment of chapter 21. Here the *Lao-tzu* original employs a parallel construction to depict the Way as "elusive"/"deep" and "vague"/"dark"; but within it is a "thing" (*wu*)/"essence" (*ching*). Ho-shang Kung's commentary retains the word "essence," but replaces "thing" with "One." They are then related to the original breath and the union of *yin* and *yang*.

The importance of the concept of the "One," the "son" of Tao, goes beyond the resolving of a difficulty in the *Lao-tzu*. Mediating between the formless Tao and the cosmos, it forms the basis of Ho-shang Kung's entire intellectual enterprise. In itself, the Way transcends the realm of human experience. Because of its "essence" and "virtue," however, the creative and sustaining power of Tao is made manifest in the world. As the "breath" of Tao, the "One" is at the same time materially conceived. It gives rise to "heaven and earth," which mark the boundaries of the physical universe. Because of the "One," heaven is "clear," as indicated by the splendor of the stars. Indeed, at one point, Ho-shang Kung identifies the rather obscure expression "door of heaven" in the *Lao-tzu* explicitly with the polar star (chap. 10). Because of the "One," earth is "tranquil," as indicated for example by the abundance of the "five grains" (chaps. 25, 30) and the regularity of the "four seasons" (chaps. 27, 59). The "five phases," which correspond to the five visible planets and the five basic materials (metal, wood, water, fire, and earth), likewise figure in the Ho-shang Kung commentary (chaps. 28, 39). Together these form the basic elements of a cosmological vision, based ultimately on the idea of the "One." Conversely, without the "One," heaven will "crack" and earth will "tremble" (chap. 39). It is in this sense that the created order is said to be "constant."

The cosmos, however, is more than the physical universe in the modern sense. It includes a world of spiritual beings, themselves produced by the "essential breath" of Tao. More importantly, the cosmos is also correlated with a microcosm in the human body itself. For example, according to Ho-shang Kung, while heaven corresponds to the nose, earth becomes the mouth in the human body (chap. 6). Similarly, there are indwelling spirits within each individual being.

According to Yü Ying-shih, the traditional understanding that there are two "souls," *hun* and *p'o*, within each human being was formed around the sixth century B.C., when two originally separate views of the soul were amalgamated.[29] The *hun* and *p'o* souls were identified with *yang* and *yin*, respectively. The former is "light" and will ascend to heaven at death; the latter is "heavy" and is bound to earth.

In the Ho-shang Kung commentary, and perhaps more generally in Han thought as a whole, the *yin-yang* theory is combined with that of the "five phases" to yield five major indwelling spirits.[30] They are "located" in the five viscera. Commenting on the enigmatic expression, "the spirit of the valley never dies," Ho-shang Kung explains:

> The "valley" means to nourish. If one could nourish one's spirits, then one would not die. "Spirit" means the spirits of the five viscera. The liver contains the *hun*; the lungs contain the *p'o*; the heart contains the spirit (*shen*); the kidneys contain the essence (*ching*); the spleen contains the will (*chih*). If the five viscera are all damaged, then the five spirits will be gone.[31]

The interpretation of "valley" (*ku*) as "to nourish," incidentally, is not as farfetched as it may sound. Ho-shang Kung is taking the word *ku* as a loan for *ku*, which means "grain" and "to nourish."[32] Interestingly, although the "five grains" are valued highly by Ho-shang Kung, they are considered harmful to the five spirits by later Taoist writers. More will be said on this subject later; at this point, we may consider this as yet another indication of the antiquity of the commentary.

This is the full significance of the cosmological theory of Ho-shang Kung. The physical and spiritual merge into one. This is the "great harmony" in which the "One" dwells. This is the "naturally so" (*tzu-jan*), as Ho-shang Kung understands the term (chaps. 1, 5, 25). In this respect, to return to the "primordial beginning" does not mean going back to the undifferentiated formlessness of the Way. The "One" represents ideal *order*, as opposed to an ideal "chaos" usually associated with creation myths of the "cosmic egg" type.[33] The symbolism of the "newborn babe" is often used in the Ho-shang Kung commentary (chaps. 1, 10, 20, 49, 55, 67), but never the fetus or the return to the womb.

Without the "One," heaven will "crack," nations will fall and human beings will die a premature death. In this cosmological framework, every outward action has its internal counterpart. It is in this sense that "self-government" (*chih-shen*) and "government of the country" (*chih-kuo*) are equated in the Ho-shang Kung commentary. Indeed, as Kristofer Schipper has suggested:

> It even may be said that for the Ho-shang-kung commentator the correspondence between the administration of the country and that of the human body is the cornerstone of his interpretation of the *Tao te ching*.[34]

The following discussion will show that this is in fact the case.

Government and Self-government: The Huang-lao Dimension

Chapter 3 of the Ho-shang Kung commentary remarks, "This states that the sage governs the country in the same way as governing the body." Equally explicit statements on this subject can be found in about twenty-five of the eighty-one chapters. There is no question that the emphasis on the dual nature of government is central and highly unique to the Ho-shang Kung commentary.

The commentary on chapter 3 contains in fact a concise summary of the ethical and political program of Ho-shang Kung, and deserves close attention. It also shows how the commentator interacts with the original text, and brings out new insights in the process:

Text	*Commentary*
Do not exalt the worthy,	"The worthy" means able men of the mundane world. They indulge in debates and flowery words, abandon the Way, and tread the road of power, desert what is substantial for artificial ornaments. "Do not exalt" means not honoring them with titles and riches, and not honoring them with official appointment.
so that the people will not contend.	Not competing for success and fame, and returning to the naturally so.
Do not value rare treasures,	This means that the ruler does not value priceless jewels. Precious metal is left in the mountain; pearls and jade are cast into the deep.
so that the people will not become thieves.	The (ruler) above transforms with quietude, and the (people) below will not be greedy.

Do not display what is desirable,	Banish the songs of Cheng; keep away from attractive people [beautiful women].
so that the (people's) minds or hearts will not be unsettled.	Not giving in to the evil of sexual indulgence, and not being confused by delusion.

In this first half of chapter 3 Ho-shang Kung is staying quite close to the *Lao-tzu* original. The theme of "having no desires" is portrayed as a key to good government, as the *Lao-tzu* itself suggests. The political implication is now brought out more fully. For example, a personal attitude toward "worthiness" is related directly to the appointment of officials. Traditional insights are also made use of in explaining the text. For example, the early Han work *Hsin-yü* (New Discourse) by Lu Chia (216–176 B.C.) records that the legendary sage-kings Shun and Yü have precisely left the precious metal and pearls in the mountains and lakes, where they naturally belong.[35]

The commentary on the fifth line, moreover, is probably a quotation from the *Lun-yü*. It reads, "Banish the songs of Cheng and keep away from hypocritical people" (15.10). While songs from the state of Cheng are "wanton," as the *Lun-yü* explains, hypocrites (*ning-jen*)—literally those who flatter and slander others to serve their own interests—are "dangerous." Most scholars would emend the commentary to agree with the *Lun-yü*, especially because some versions have precisely that reading. I have retained the standard SPTK version because the danger of sexual indulgence is a recurring theme in the Ho-shang Kung commentary.

These traditional sayings were likely common literary expressions. But it is possible that they served to legitimize the teaching of Ho-shang Kung. The legend of Ho-shang Kung also deliberately quotes from the *Shih-ching* (Book of Poetry) to bring out its claim to teaching the emperor. This does not in any way contradict Ho-shang Kung's understanding of history. Legendary sages and even Confucius himself were exceptional individuals: they would agree with Lao-tzu on the importance of governing the country and the body in the same way.

The commentary on the sixth line is even more interesting, and marks a new point of departure. The context and the language both make it clear that the *Lao-tzu* is speaking of the minds or hearts (*hsin*) of the people (*min*), and in fact Wang Pi's text has the extra word *min*. While the *Lao-tzu* seems to be concerned with the well-being of the people, Ho-shang Kung places the emphasis on the self-government of the ruler. This is not to suggest that Ho-shang Kung alters the text to fit his purpose; on the contrary, most scholars would prefer the Ho-shang Kung reading.[36] My only point is that the commentator saw the opening to bring out what he considers to be the full meaning of Lao-tzu's teaching.

The commentary on chapter 3 continues:

Text	Commentary
Therefore in the government of the sage:	This states that the sage governs the country in the same way as governing the body.
he empties their (*ch'i*) minds [his mind],	Eliminate desires and get rid of unsettling troubles.
(but) fills their bellies [his belly];	That is, carry the Way and embrace the One; securing the five spirits.
weakens their wills [his will],	That is, being harmonious and gentle, humble and yielding, and not relying on power.
(but) strengthens their [his] bones.	Value the essence and use it sparingly, then the marrow will be full and the bones will be strong.
Always keep the people without knowledge and without desires,	Return to the simple and keep to the innocent.
so that the clever will not dare to act.	Deep in thinking, and never take words lightly.
Act with no action,	Not to act with artificiality, but follow the natural course of things.
then nothing is not governed.	If the transforming power of virtue is full, the people will be at peace.

Although the subject is not specified, there is little question that the possessive *ch'i* in the first few lines is taken by Ho-shang Kung as referring to the sage, not to the people. Each line taken separately, Ho-shang Kung's commentary seems plausible enough; but as a whole, the emphasis is clearly shifted to the person of the sage. More precisely, the "government of the sage" is here translated into a lesson on self-cultivation for the ruler. When the *Lao-tzu* again explicitly toward the end refers to the people, the commentary becomes very brief. Still, "will not dare to act" is interpreted to mean that the ruler should not take his words lightly; the "clever" refers to the ruler who is "deep" in his planning and thinking. Ho-shang Kung's interpretation *is* cogent, however, if one shares the cosmological framework in which the commentary is rooted.

The various themes invoked in the commentary on chapter 3 need to be examined more closely. First, it should be made clear that the Ho-shang Kung commentary is primarily addressed to the ruler. Besides the general emphasis on the art of government, this is also shown in small but revealing details, which often escape attention. For example, when the *Lao-tzu* states, "When the Way prevails in the world," Ho-shang Kung explains: "This means when the ruler possesses the Way" (chap. 46). Similarly, such terms as "the highest" (chap. 17) and the "man of superior virtue" (chap. 38) are interpreted to mean "the anonymous ruler of the primordial past." The "great man" (chap. 38) and the "able officers of old" (chap. 15) both refer to "the ruler who has obtained the Way." Even more explicitly, "the adepts of Tao in ancient times" is carefully identified with "those who were adept in using the Way to govern the body and the country in ancient times" (chap. 65). Finally, to take but one more example, chapter 64 of the *Lao-tzu* begins with the rather abrupt statement that "what is stable (*an*) is easy to maintain (*ch'ih*)." Ho-shang Kung's commentary builds on the two key words: "He who is stable and quiet in governing the body and the country, secures and maintains (himself) with ease."

Taken together, these references point to the underlying political interest of the Ho-shang Kung commentary. The teaching is aimed at the ruler, and the ruler alone. Chapter 32 describes the Way as an "uncarved block," which "though small, no one in the world dare to lord over (*ch'en*) it." In the Ho-shang Kung commentary, I would argue, the author is taking the word *ch'en* as a noun to mean "minister" or "official":

> Although the simple Tao is small, it is subtle and without form. There is no minister in the world who dares to use the Way (*T'ien-hsia pu-kan yu ch'en shih Tao che yeh*).[37]

Admittedly this reading is not without difficulty; the last sentence may also be translated as "There is no one in the world who dares to treat the Way like a minister (servant)." What is suggested here, however, is supported by other considerations, and is intended to highlight a major theme in the Ho-shang Kung commentary.

The commentary on chapter 32 goes on to say that if the ruler is able to "secure" (*shou*) the Way, everything will be transformed naturally by the power of virtue. In light of the preceding sentence, this indicates to me that a distinction is made between the ruler and the ministers, a distinction found in the commentary on chapter 70 as well. Chapter 30 of the *Lao-tzu*, however, begins with the remark that "he who assists the ruler with Tao" (*i Tao tso jen-chu che*) does not rely on military might. This would seem to contradict the assertion that the ruler alone is able to secure the Way. Recognizing this problem, Ho-shang Kung writes, "This means that the ruler is able to support and assist himself with Tao," and therefore shuns the use of force. The *Lao-tzu* elsewhere advises the ruler, "Sharp weapons of the state must not be shown to anyone" (chap. 36). According to Ho-shang Kung, by "anyone" the *Lao-tzu* has specific people in mind:

> "Sharp weapons" means the way of power (*ch'üan*). The power of government must not be shown to the officials (*ch'en*) who administer the daily affairs of the empire. The way of self-government must not be shown to those who do not deserve it.

This is what I would call the Huang-lao dimension of the Ho-shang Kung commentary. The word *ch'üan*, translated generally as "power," is essentially a "legalist" concept signifying the ruler's authority and right to rule. In the discussion of Wang Pi we have already seen how Han Fei-tzu has interpreted Lao-tzu's "sharp weapons" to mean a system of reward and punishment, and why the ruler must conceal them from his ministers. It is in this same sense that I understand the expression "way of power" (*ch'üan-tao*) in the Ho-shang Kung commentary. The added emphasis on self-government, however, distinguishes Ho-shang Kung from the "legalist" school. The concluding sentence in the passage quoted above is also found in the Ho-shang Kung legend. When Ho-shang Kung gave his commentary to Emperor Wen, he specified that it "must not be shown to those who do not deserve it."

Securing the One (*Shou-i*)

In this light, such concepts as "nonaction," quietude, and returning to *tzu-jan* mentioned in the commentary on chapter 3 acquire a more concrete meaning. In the Ho-shang Kung commentary, these concepts are subsumed under the rubric of "securing the One" (*shou-i*). In the *Lao-tzu* itself, the expression "embrace the One" (*pao-i*) is used twice (chaps. 10 and 22); but Ho-shang Kung prefers the word *shou* to emphasize the importance of "securing" what has been "embraced." In other words, ideal government, both politically and with respect to the interior life, depends on the ruler's ability to acquire and to maintain the "One," and to guard against harmful influences.

"The Way is constantly without action" (*Tao ch'ang wu-wei*), chapter 37 of the *Lao-tzu* begins. Ho-shang Kung's commentary seems like a close paraphrase: "The Way takes/with (*i*) *wu-wei* as/is (*wei*) constant (*ch'ang*)." The juxtaposition of *wei* and the opposite, *wu-wei*, is interesting, and suggests a course of action to be followed. The rest of the chapter provides a general picture of the art of "nonaction." Although the term *shou-i* is not mentioned, the Way is qualified by the power of virtue:

Text	Commentary
. . . but nothing is left undone. If princes and kings could secure it, all things would be transformed of their own accord.	This states that if princes and kings could secure the Way, all things would be transformed of their own accord, and model themselves (after them).[38]
If, after they are transformed, desires should surface, I shall subdue them with the nameless uncarved block.	"I" means the self [i.e., the ruler himself]. The "nameless uncarved block" is the Way. If, having been transformed and having modeled themselves (after the ruler), the ten thousand things again desire to be clever and become false, princes and kings should personally subdue and calm them with the virtue of the Way.
The nameless uncarved block is without desires. Being without desires, it is tranquil.	This states that if princes and kings subdue and calm them with the virtue of the Way, the people

will also become free of desires. Thus the ruler should guide and transform them with quietude and tranquility.

The world will then be at peace of its own accord.

If this can be done, the world will then be rectified and at peace of its own accord.

The "I" is here equated with the ruler, and more literally with the "self," or even the "body" (*shen*). The problem of government is seen to be rooted in desires. The solution to the problem, moreover, lies in the ruler's being tranquil and transforming the people with the virtue of Tao. The notion of "virtue" (*te*), as noted earlier, is identified with the "One," the essence of Tao, the attainment of which is measured by the fullness of *ch'i*. Beneath the close paraphrase a strong practical concern emerges: the question in the Ho-shang Kung commentary is not so much what is the case, as what the ruler should do in order to realize the reign of "great harmony," and indeed the way of immortality itself.

The Spiritual Body

The body is a microcosm, mirroring heaven and earth. This concept must now be examined more carefully. Ho-shang Kung's understanding of the human "body" is brought out most clearly in the commentary on chapter 6, the first part of which I have already cited. This is arguably the most difficult chapter in the entire commentary:

Text	Commentary
The spirit of the valley never dies.	"Valley" means to nourish. If one could nourish one's spirits, one would not die. "Spirit" means the spirits of the five viscera. . . . If the five viscera are all damaged, then the five spirits will be gone.
It is called the mysterious female.	This means that the way[39] of immortality lies in the mysterious female. "Mysterious" refers to heaven; in man it is the nose. "Fe-

male" refers to earth; in man it is the mouth. Heaven nourishes man with the five breaths (of the five viscera),[40] which come through the nose and are stored in the heart. The five breaths are clear and rarefied. They form the spirit and essence, hearing and sight, voice and sound, and the five natures (of the five viscera).[41] Their soul (*kuei*) is called *hun*.[42] *Hun* is male. It is in charge of what leaves and enters (the body) through the nose, which is connected with heaven. Thus, the nose is the "mysterious."

Earth nourishes man with the five tastes,[43] which come through the mouth and are stored in the stomach. The five tastes[44] are turbid and dense. They form the frame and skeleton, bones and flesh, blood and pulse, and the six feelings.[45] Their soul is called *p'o*. *P'o* is female. It is in charge of what leaves and enters (the body) through the mouth, which is connected with earth.[46] Thus, the mouth is the "female."

The door of the mysterious female is called the root of heaven and earth.

"Root" means the origin. This refers to the door of the nose and of the mouth, through which the original breath that penetrates heaven and earth comes and goes.

Flimsy and continuous, as if barely existing;

The exhaling and inhaling, the successive breaths of the nose and mouth, should be continuous and subtle, as if one could preserve them, and yet (in such a way that) as if one is not doing anything.[47]

yet use will never exhaust it.

One's breathing should always be leisurely and at ease, and not rushed and exhausting.

I do not pretend to know what the *Lao-tzu* is aiming at here; Ho-shang Kung's commentary is able to make sense of it by identifying key terms in the chapter with elements of the "spiritual" body. The "spirit," the "mysterious" or "dark" (*hsüan*) "female," the "door," and the "root" all have a place in the universe and its internal counterpart. For our purposes, the exact correspondence of the "five natures" and the "six feelings" is less important than the direct *passage* that bridges the macrocosmic and microcosmic world. If the passage is not guarded, the spirits will leave the body and cause death. On the other hand, if the passage is well guarded and the spirits properly nourished, the harmonious functioning of all the faculties will be assured. As a result, as chapter 6 puts it, "one would not die." It is in this sense that the term "body" is used in the Ho-shang Kung commentary. Moreover, when this is accomplished, the power of the indwelling spirits will express itself in the form of virtue and thereby transform the multitude. It is in this sense that the commentary on chapter 3 equates "embrace the One" with "securing the five spirits." This is what is meant by such terms as "securing the One" (chaps. 20, 22, 27, 81), "like the One" (chaps. 32, 45) or "concentrating on the One" (chap. 55).

To achieve this, one must make sure that the indwelling spirits have a nice home in which they would want to dwell. The concreteness of Ho-shang Kung's imagination is very clear in this regard. Explaining the phrase "between heaven and earth" (chap. 5), Ho-shang Kung writes:

> Between heaven and earth, it is empty. Everywhere the harmonious breath flows, and therefore the ten thousand things are born spontaneously. If one can eliminate feelings and desires, restrain rich tastes, purify the five viscera, then the spirits will dwell in them.

The well-being of the five viscera is thus dependent on the curbing of desires. What kind of desires? Chapter 12 is most explicit on this score:

Text	Commentary
The five colors cause man's eyes to be blind.	Desirous of lust and beautiful sight, one injures one's essence and loses one's vision.

The five tones cause man's ears to be deaf.	Desirous of hearing the five tones, then the harmonious breath departs from the heart, and one cannot listen to the soundless sound.
The five tastes cause man's palate to be ruined.	"Ruined" means lost. If one indulges in the five tastes, the mouth is lost. This means that one loses the Way.

The "five colors" are now related to lust, especially sexual craving. The ruler, as Ho-shang Kung even more concretely advises, should stay away from the alluring quarters of his royal consorts (chap. 26). Sexual indulgence is harmful because it causes the emission of "essence" (*ching*), which as we have seen a moment ago is defined in chapter 6 in terms of the male/*hun* soul, and the "breaths of the five viscera." Generally "essence" denotes *ch'i* in its purest and most refined state, but in this context because of its potent power it refers also, more specifically, to semen. In order to retain the "harmonious breath," then, one ought to abstain from excesses of any kind. This is the meaning of *wu-wei*, which according to Ho-shang Kung is the same as "diminishing one's desires" (chap. 48).

Among the various desires that are said to be harmful to the body, sexual indulgence and greed for wealth are especially singled out by Ho-shang Kung (chaps. 9, 10, 22, 26, 29, 36, 41, 44, 46, 59, 72). Ultimately, the emphasis on abstinence is modeled on the emptiness of the Way. Chapter 11 of the *Lao-tzu* begins with the factual claim that "thirty spokes together make one hub." Ho-shang Kung's commentary is equally concrete at first, explaining that because of the lunar calendar, wheels had thirty spokes in ancient times. Then the commentary shifts to the main theme:

> He who governs the body should eliminate feelings and get rid of desires, so as to make the five viscera empty. The spirits will then return to him. He who governs the country, though alone, can gather the multitude; though weak, he can master the strong.

The empty space surrounded by the wheel turns out to be a message to the ruler.

Methods of Self-cultivation

Beyond the general emphasis on abstinence, it is difficult to be more precise as to how the "One" can be secured. Some form of breathing exercise is probably involved, as the last two sections of chapter 6 seem to suggest. The commentary on chapter 10 also points to this conclusion. The *Lao-tzu* here is structured in the form of a series of questions. "Can one carry the soul and embrace the One without departing from them?" The commentary on this first question elaborates on the *hun* and *p'o* souls, how alcohol and tasty food will damage the liver and lungs where they reside, and how longevity is reached when the souls are tranquil. Next comes the long definition of the "One," which we have already quoted (see p. 130, above). The text continues:

Text	*Commentary*
Can one concentrate the breath,	Concentrate on securing the essential breath so that it is not confused, then the body can respond to it and become supple.
and become as supple as an infant?	If one can be like an infant, inwardly without worrisome thought and outwardly without political action, then the essence and spirit will not go away.
Can one purify the profound vision,	One should cleanse the heart (or mind) so that it is clear and tranquil. The heart dwells in the profound and silent, gazes and knows all things. Thus it is called the profound vision.
so that it is without blemish?	This means without lust and evil thought. Being tranquil, can one not become without blemish and disease?[48]
In loving the people and governing the country,	If in governing the body, one loves the breath, then the body will be preserved. If in governing the country, one loves the people, then the country will be at peace.

can one be without knowledge?

Self-government means the exhaling and inhaling of the essential breath, without letting the ear hearing it. Government of the country means the dispensing and distributing of beneficent virtue, without letting the people below knowing it.

This detailed description of both forms of government captures well the ethical and political ideals of Ho-shang Kung. The rest of the commentary on this chapter repeats the importance of the human nose in communicating with heaven. The opening and closing of the "door of heaven," identified with the polar star, is interpreted in terms of breathing and the succession of breaths. What kind of meditative technique is intended in this instance?

This calls to mind the famous passage in chapter 15 of the *Chuang-tzu:*

Blowing out and sucking in, exhaling and inhaling, emitting the old (breath) and drawing in the new, imitating the bear's stretching its body and the bird's extending its wings, all these are only aimed at longevity. This is what is favored by the adept in leading and guiding the breath, by the man who nourishes his body, or by those who hope to live to be as old as P'eng-tsu.[49]

From the Ma-wang-tui finds, as indicated earlier, we know that exercises modeled on the movement of animals were common in the Han dynasty. The purpose of these exercises is to "lead and guide" (*tao-yin*) the "essential breath," so that it circulates freely throughout the body. This may be part of Ho-shang Kung's meditative regimen, although the commentary does not mention any form of physical exercise. The same may be said with respect to dietary practices, given the importance of keeping the five viscera clean and empty. But it should be noted that total avoidance of the "five grains" or cereals is not prescribed by Ho-shang Kung. While this method was current in the Han dynasty and has become an important aspect of later Taoist formulations of *shou-i*, it stands contrary to Ho-shang Kung's appreciation for the gifts of nature. It is true that the commentary does speak of abstinence and the elimination of one's desires, but generally what is under attack are harmful indulgences and excessive cravings. In this respect, if dietary practices form a part of Ho-shang Kung's program, they may be closer to those presented in the *T'ai-p'ing ching* (Scripture of Great Peace). As M. Kaltenmark points out, generally "the book [*T'ai-p'ing ching*] recommends that one eat moderately," which in actual practice may perhaps be translated to mean "a single meal a day."[50] Since the theoretic justification for dietary control is to keep the five viscera pure, it is not difficult to see how later proponents of *shou-i* would take the extra step to identify the "five grains" as among the harmful influences against which the adept must vigilantly guard.[51] This development, however, is not what concerns us here. Coming back to the *Chuang-tzu* passage quoted above, it seems that the reference to breathing exercises does not add much to what we have already gathered from the commentary itself. What it does suggest is that the Ho-shang Kung commentary is closely connected with the *fang-shih* tradition, which specialized in these techniques and formed an important component of the Huang-lao school.

The commentary on chapter 12, as we have seen, speaks of the danger of indulging in the five musical tones, which will apparently lead to the departure of the "harmonious breath" and consequently the "soundless sound" cannot be heard. This latter is to be interpreted from the perspective of breathing exercises. The commentary on chapter 10, also translated above, indicates that the art of breathing lies in not letting the ears hear it. This is the closest the Ho-shang Kung commentary comes to explaining the technique of meditation. In chapters 15, 33, and 52 it is more generally described as the art of "reverse hearing" (*fan-t'ing*) and "inward vision" (*nei-shih*). The first of these passages reads:

Text	*Commentary*
Of old the able officers were subtle and wondrous, profound and penetrating,	This refers to the ruler who has obtained the Way. "Profound" means heaven. This states that his will or mind is profound and subtle; his essence is connected directly with heaven.
deep and cannot be identified.	The virtue of the Way is deep and far-reaching; it cannot be identified and known. Inward vision is like

blindness; reverse hearing is like deafness. No one knows how this is so.[52]

The sudden introduction of "inward vision" and "reverse hearing" is puzzling. Perhaps they were common practices, or they may simply function as general terms referring to meditation, as distinguished from other "outward" activities. They reappear in the commentary on the second verse of chapter 33, in the context of a discussion of "self-knowledge":

Text	Commentary
He who knows others is wise;	The ability to know what others like and dislike is what is meant by wisdom.
he who knows himself is enlightened.	The ability to know one's own worthiness and unworthiness means that one is able to hear in reverse the soundless, and to see inwardly the formless. Thus he is enlightened.

In both chapters 15 and 33 the expressions "inward vision" and "reverse hearing" are consistently related to the importance of curbing one's desires, being empty and tranquil, and to the possibility of attaining longevity. Chapter 33 of the *Lao-tzu*, for example, ends with the baffling statement that "he who dies but does not perish has longevity." Focusing on the ethical side of self-cultivation, Ho-shang Kung explains: "The eyes do not perversely see; the ears do not perversely hear; the mouth does not perversely speak: then one will not be blamed and hated by the world. Therefore one lives long." In the next chapter, I shall contrast this with Wang Pi's interpretation.

Finally, "inward vision" is also mentioned in the commentary on chapter 52, which begins with a description of the "One." "Having known the One," as we have seen, "one then ought to keep to the Way and return to nonaction." The *Lao-tzu* continues to describe what it calls the practice of the "constant," including: "Use the light, revert to enlightenment, and thereby avoid personal danger." On this, Ho-shang Kung comments:

This means to use one's vision externally to see the good and bad fortune of the present situation. (Having done this,) then one ought to revert one's vision inwardly, so as not to allow the essence and spirit to be discharged. Inward vision preserves the spirit.[53]

The external counterpart of this "inward vision" is thus quite important as well; it allows the ruler to discern and to evaluate the pros and cons of any given situation.

The precise nature of the art of "inward vision" and "reverse hearing" cannot be reconstructed. These expressions are rare in the early literature. They are found in the *Shih-chi* once, and are explained merely as "clear hearing" (*ch'ung*) and "bright vision" (*ming*).[54] The basic technique seems to involve deep and even breathing, concentrating on the succession of breaths, during which one visualizes the interior cosmos and listens to the movement of the spirits. This resembles what the *Chuang-tzu* has called the "fasting of the mind/heart" (*hsin-chai*):

Do not listen with the ear, but rather listen with the mind/heart. Do not listen with the mind/heart, but rather listen with the breath. . . . Emptiness is the fasting of the mind/heart.[55]

Ho-shang Kung would no doubt agree that ultimately the "One" can be secured only when the mind/heart is empty of desires.

The Politics of Wu-wei

Up to this point, attention has been focused on the personal quest for the "One." But just as the well-being of the individual hinges on emptiness and tranquility, the government of the country is no different. As the *Lao-tzu* rather playfully puts it, "Governing a large country is like cooking a small fish" (chap. 60). Characteristically, Ho-shang Kung's commentary begins by explaining concretely why one must not take away the intestines or remove the scales if one wants to preserve the whole fish, and then goes on to the main point: "If government of the country is troublesome, then the people below will be confused (*luan*). If government of the body is troublesome, then the essence will be scattered (*san*)."

This really sums up the practical advice to the ruler in the Ho-shang Kung commentary. The word *luan* means confusion, disorder, and rebellion; it signifies the greatest political evil in the world of Ho-shang Kung. The pairing of *luan* with the word *san* is also interesting. As I understand it, the imagery that lies behind the parallelism pictures the "scattering" of the people in times of war and famine, both of which were rampant toward the end of the Later Han dynasty.[56]

That government must not be "troublesome" (*fan*) is a recurrent theme in the Ho-shang Kung commentary. It describes specifically the politics of *wu-wei*. For example, the *Lao-tzu* states, "To take the world, always be without activity. To have activity is not sufficient to take the world" (chap. 48). Ho-shang Kung translates the sense of conquest into a theory of government:

> "To take" means to govern. To govern the world, one should always rely on nonactivity and not be troublesome and demanding. If one is given to engaging actively in affairs, his policies and teachings will be troublesome, and the people will not be at peace. Thus it is not sufficient to govern the world.[57]

If the body is not given to excesses, it will attain longevity. Similarly, if the people are not troubled, the implication is that the government will last long (chaps. 44, 59).

The phrase "nonactivity" or "without engaging in affairs" (*wu-shih*), a phrase used interchangeably with *wu-wei* in the *Lao-tzu*, is found in chapter 63 as well. This time Ho-shang Kung's commentary introduces an important but easily missed qualification. "To engage in no activity" is taken to mean "be prepared in advance; eliminate what is troublesome and avoid meddling in affairs." What does this "preparation" involve? What are the policies that will "trouble" the people?

To answer the second question first, according to Ho-shang Kung, warfare is above all to be avoided (chaps. 30, 31, 46, 50, 57, 68, 69). Generally the *Lao-tzu* does not advocate the use of arms; but it does discuss the art of warfare on occasions. The most telling example is chapter 69, which begins with a quotation from military strategists. On Lao-tzu's very reference to the strategists, Ho-shang Kung explains: "This sets out the way of military strategy. Lao-tzu was disgusted with the use of military force at the time. Thus he took upon himself to explain its principles." With this disclaimer, implying that Lao-tzu's discussion is aimed at explaining the art of warfare only to defeat it, the commentary is thus able to elucidate the rest of the chapter without fear of contradiction.

War disrupts the harmony symbolized by the unity of the "One." It is not only a human problem, but involves a direct "response" from the cosmos as well. As far as war is concerned, Ho-shang Kung writes, "heaven will respond with a foul breath which harms the five grains. If the five grains are destroyed, the people will be hurt" (chap. 30). The same logic applies to other "troublesome" political measures. What is important is that it is the ruler who is directly responsible for the suffering of the people. For example, chapter 75 explains why the people suffer from hunger:

Text	Commentary
The reason why the people are hungry is that those above eat too much tax-grain.	The reason why people are hungry and cold is that their ruler above taxes the people below too much.[58]
This is why there is starvation.	The people are all changed by the ruler above and become greedy. They rebel against the Way and oppose virtue, and are therefore hungry.[59]

In addition to identifying clearly the "above" with the ruler himself, the second half brings out the kind of "response" that is presupposed in the commentary as a whole. The choice of the verbs "rebel" (*pan*) and "oppose" (*wei*) in this instance points to the disastrous consequences of bad government. As the commentary goes on to say, the reason why the people are difficult to govern is because they have become hypocritical as a result of the ruler's indulging in his desires.

Excessive punishment, too, will disturb the balance of the cosmos. The *Lao-tzu* asks, "If the people are not afraid of death, why frighten them with death?" Ho-shang Kung again relates this to both the personal and political aspects of government (chap. 74):

If the ruler of the country imposes cruel and severe measures and punishment, the people have nothing to live for. Therefore they are not afraid of death. If the ruler of the body indulges in desires which harm the spirits, and craves for wealth which harms the body, the people will not be afraid of him. Why does the ruler not ease the strict measures and punishment, and teach the people to eliminate their desires; why does he establish punishment and laws to frighten them with death?

This is the best example of what Ho-shang Kung means by "troublesome" policies. Notice, however, that the commentary does not advocate eliminating the system of punishment altogether. Excessive punishment is opposed to the harmony of the "One"; but the ruler must be "prepared." Chapter 74 of the *Lao-tzu* continues:

Suppose the people are always afraid of death and we can seize those who are vicious and kill them, who would dare to do so? There is always the master executioner (Heaven) who kills. To undertake executions for the master executioner is like hewing wood for the master carpenter. Whoever undertakes to hew wood for the master carpenter rarely escapes injuring his own hands.[60]

The first sentence is ambiguous; it can also be rendered in the sense of "who would then dare to violate the law?[61] Although the chapter as a whole tends to support the translation adopted above, it is the second interpretation that Ho-shang Kung has followed:

One ought to eliminate what harms the self and to teach the people to discard their greed and desires. If in applying the Way to teach and to transform, the people do not follow and turn to deceit and hypocrisy instead, then the ruler should respond with his imperial laws to seize and kill them. No one would then dare to commit violations. Lao-tzu was lamenting that the king at the time did not first use the Way and virtue to transform the people, but started with punishment.

The ideal ruler is thus firm and inspires awe, although he governs by means of *wu-wei*. This state of "preparedness," I suggest, is essentially the same as the notion of *hsing-ming* discussed in the last chapter.

The remainder of the commentary on chapter 74 further describes the cosmic root of this model of government. The "master executioner" is explicitly identified with the "Tao of heaven," which is constant, "just as spring gives life, summer grows, autumn reaps, and winter stores; the Dipper turns and moves to regulate them."

Modeling himself on the cosmos, knowing that all things are regulated and have their proper place, the ruler can truly rest with the people. The ideal ruler is prepared because he realizes that "when disorder and rebellion have not yet grown from their seeds," they are weak and can be stopped quickly. Thus "he who governs the body and the country should shut the door before any disorder arises" (chap. 64). When the "door" is shut, the "One" is secured.

The Family of Tao

The art of rulership is never haphazard. Such concepts as *wu-wei* and *tzu-jan* presuppose a definite program of government, which can best be described as a form of "parenting." The Way itself is like a "mother," as we have seen, generating all things through its essence and seeing to their well-being (chaps. 1, 25, 51). The ethical and political implication did not escape Ho-shang Kung: "In relation to the ten thousand things, the Way does not only produce them; it also nurtures them, brings them into maturity, protects them, and preserves their lives. The ruler in governing the country and the body *ought* to be like this also" (chap. 51; emphasis added). The ideal parent, in the Ho-shang Kung commentary, is represented by the figure of the sage. We shall soon see why the "ought to" is significant in this context.

The importance of the theme of parental love can be seen from Ho-shang Kung's interpretation of the famous "three jewels" of the *Lao-tzu*. The text reads, "I have three jewels; keep and treasure them. The first is called deep love (*tz'u*)" (chap. 67). Although the term *tz'u* is often used in the context of a parent's love for his or her children, most translators of this passage prefer to take it in a more general sense.[62] Ho-shang Kung, however, clearly identifies *tz'u* as "loving the people as if they are newborn babies." The sage, because of his understanding of Tao, is precisely able to love his "children" and be loved in return.

The sage, as the *Lao-tzu* itself puts it, is able to lead the people without fear that they may harm him (chap. 66). The reason for this, according to Ho-shang Kung, is that "although the sage is ahead of the people, he does not conceal from view those after him with his own splendor. Therefore the people love him as their father and mother, and have no thought of harming him."[63] The love of the sage is deep, as the commentary goes on to complete the parallelism, "and he regards the people as newborn babes." This is why the *Lao-tzu* states that "the world rejoices in supporting him without ever getting tired of it."

This provides a model for the ruler to emulate. The sage teaches by means of personal examples; this is how Ho-shang Kung has interpreted Lao-tzu's idea of a "teaching without words" throughout the commentary (chaps. 2, 34, 43). This teaching is what we have already described as the way of "securing the One." The commentary on chapter 35, for example, summarizes it in this way:

Text	*Commentary*
Hold fast to the great image, and the world will come to you.	"Hold fast to" means to secure. The image is the Way. When the sage secures the great Way, all the people in the world will be reformed and return to him. In governing the body, spirits will then descend from heaven and dwell in him.
Coming to you without being harmed, it will be safe and enjoy peace.	When all things return to him without being harmed, the country will be safe and families will be settled. Great peace is thus attained. In governing the body, if the spirits are not harmed, then the body is safe and will attain great longevity.

"Longevity" and "great peace" are two gifts, or more precisely two aspects of the same gift, which the sage can bring to the world. The sage is able to accomplish this for two reasons. First, he knows all things; second, he is blessed.

Precisely because of his profound knowledge, the sage is able to serve as a model. The *Lao-tzu* states, "Thus the sage embraces the One and becomes the model of the world" (chap. 22). Ho-shang Kung brings out the importance of the sage's knowing power: " 'Embrace' means to secure. 'Model' means standard. The sage secures the One and thus knows all things. Therefore he can become the model of the world." How does the sage know all things? The same chapter continues, commenting on the verse, "He does not hold to his own views,[64] and is therefore comprehending":

The sage does not use his own eyes to see things at a great distance. Instead, because he uses the eyes of the world to see, he therefore comprehends and penetrates into all things.

Does this mean that the knowledge of the sage is dependent on others? On the contrary, the knowledge of the sage is based on a self-knowledge, generated by a fundamental recognition of the identity of the "Tao of heaven" and the "Tao of man." The reason the sage "knows the world without having to set foot outside his door" is that he is able to extend his self-knowledge to other phenomena. How can the sage "see the Way of heaven without having to look through his window"? Ho-shang Kung explains (chap. 47):

The Way of heaven is the same as the Way of man. Heaven and man[65] penetrate one another; the essence and breath permeate one another. If the ruler is pure and tranquil, the breath of heaven will be in order of its own accord. If the ruler has many desires, the breath of heaven will be troublesome and turbid. Fortune and misfortune, benefit and harm, they all stem from the self.

This, too, sums up nicely the interrelatedness of self-government and government of the country discussed earlier.

This knowledge is not to be confused with the kind of cunning know-how and conventional wisdom, denounced repeatedly in the Ho-shang Kung commentary (e.g., chaps. 19, 20, 48, 64). Conventional wisdom, typified by the emphasis on propriety and other traditional virtues, is in fact one of the contributing factors to a "troublesome" government. The commentary on chapter 65 is important in this regard:

Text	*Commentary*
The adepts of Tao in ancient times	This refers to those who were adept in using the Way to govern the body and the country in ancient times.
did not try to enlighten the people;	They did not use the Way to teach the people to be intelligent and wise, clever and deceitful.

but to make them ignorant.	They would instead teach the people with the Way and virtue, to make them simple and honest.
The reason why the people are difficult to govern is that they have too much knowledge.	Because they have too much knowledge, therefore they become clever and deceitful.
He who uses knowledge to govern the country is an enemy of the country.	If one allows knowledgeable and clever men to manage the political affairs of the country, they will always forsake the Way and virtue, abuse their power, and become the enemy of the country.
Not to use knowledge to govern the country is the good fortune of the country.	If one does not allow knowledgeable and clever men to manage the political affairs of the country, then the people will remain fair and honest, and will not become perverse and hypocritical. Then the ruler above and the people below will love one another; the ruler and his ministers will work together. Thus this is the good fortune of the country.[66]

The contrast is clear. The special knowledge of the sage is later in this chapter simply called "ignorance," and is identified with the "model of self-government and government of the country." To have *this* knowledge is what Ho-shang Kung means by "having the same virtue as heaven" (chap. 65).

The commentary on chapter 65 also points to the interesting relation between the ruler and his ministers. The subtle change of subject in the last two sections is revealing. The ruler, as the sage advises, must not allow his ministers to abuse their power. Without the context, indeed, one might mistake this for a "legalist" saying. If the ruler is to be the parent of the people, the ministers of state are but servants of the house. More appropriately, taking into account the traditional Chinese family setting, the ministers or officials are but "nurses," who must not be allowed to impose their ways on the "children" and take the place of the real parents. Although loving and not troubling the household, as we have seen, the master of the house will be prepared if occasions demand a swift and firm response.

The special knowledge of the sage can be summed up in one word: "correspondence." The sage realizes the exact correspondence between "heaven and earth" that governs the cosmos, and is therefore able to follow the way of the "One." Any technique with respect to self-cultivation and government fades into secondary importance when compared with this foundational insight. "Heaven lasts and earth endures," chapter 7 of the *Lao-tzu* says. Ho-shang Kung's comment is straightforward and unquestioning: "This states that heaven and earth will last forever; it is used to teach the people." This is what is presupposed. If the Way of heaven is realized, longevity and the reign of great peace will naturally follow. Underlying the Ho-shang Kung commentary is a profound idealism, mediated by the special knowledge of the sage.

Paradoxically, the reason why heaven and earth are everlasting is that they never seek to be everlasting; their constant operation is never motivated by any thought of self-preservation. Chapter 7 continues:

Text	*Commentary*
The reason heaven and earth can last and endure is that they do not exist for themselves.	The reason heaven and earth alone can last and endure is that they are tranquil; they give and do not seek to be repayed.[67]

This introduces an important element into the discussion of the teaching of the sage. Responding to the Way, even in the quest for longevity, the sage is never motivated by self-interest. It is in this sense, according to Ho-shang Kung, that the *Lao-tzu* says, "He who loves the world as his body can be entrusted with the world."[68] The commentary reads:

> This means that the ruler is able to love his body, without doing it for his own (benefit). Thus he desires to become the father and mother of all the people, and through this is able to become the ruler of the world.

Like the "ought to" mentioned in the commentary on chapter 51, the language employed here is interesting and will be explained shortly. The idea of not expecting any reward in return is a recurring theme in the Ho-shang Kung commentary, applied to both the action of Tao (chaps. 2, 10, 51) and to that of the sage (chaps. 49, 77). In chapter 49, for example, Ho-shang Kung writes: "The sage loves and thinks of the people as infants and newborn babes. He brings them up and nurtures them, but does not expect or hope for any reward from them."

The commentary on chapter 7 of course goes on to explain why the sage is able to perfect his being without self-interest. The theme of the family of Tao again figures in the foreground of Ho-shang Kung's discussion:

Text	*Commentary*
(The sage) treats his body as extraneous to himself, and his body is preserved.	This means to give little to oneself, but much to others. The people love him as their father and mother. The spirits protect him as if he were a newborn babe. Thus his body is always preserved.

The family of Tao is growing. Just as the people are like the children of the sage, the latter is, so to speak, blessed by his parents in heaven. The microcosmic and macrocosmic correspondence that characterizes the world of Ho-shang Kung is essentially hierarchical.

There are two issues to be further discussed here. In what sense is the sage "blessed" by heaven? Secondly, what is the relationship between the ruler and the sage? To put it bluntly, according to Ho-shang Kung, the sage is even above the ruler and he is destined to be blessed.

All beings are produced by Tao, as we have seen on a number of occasions. In chapter 1, the *Lao-tzu* calls this the profound, "dark" mystery (*hsüan*). We have also seen how Ho-shang Kung has understood the word *hsüan* to mean "heaven," and how the generation of all things is mediated by the "One," the "son" of Tao, and the blending of the "essential breath." Yet the *Lao-tzu* goes one step further to suggest that there is something even darker than the "dark," more profound than the deepest profundity. On this famous line, *hsüan chih yu hsüan*, Ho-shang Kung comments:

This means that there is yet another heaven within heaven. The received breath may be full or thin. If it obtains the harmony and is enriched, it gives birth to great men and sages. If it is in a state of confusion and is deprived, it gives rise to greed and perversity.

A person is, in other words, either born a sage or not a sage at all. In this regard, as Isabelle Robinet has pointed out, Ho-shang Kung was simply affirming a common belief established early in the Han dynasty.[69]

This sets the sage apart from the rest of the people, including the emperor. The sage alone can "return to the infinite," as the *Lao-tzu* puts it (chap. 28). In Ho-shang Kung's rendition, this means that the sage is everlasting, whose "body" returns to the infinite. Even more boldly, taking off from Lao-tzu's observation that the root cause of human peril lies in the self, Ho-shang Kung exclaims: "If I have no physical body, if I have obtained the Way and become naturally so, I shall lightly lift myself and rise into the clouds. Coming and going between the empty space, I become one in spirit with the Way. What trouble could I have?" (chap. 13). How literally this is to be interpreted is difficult to decide; the specification of the "physical body" may suggest an element of belief beyond poetic flight. What is clear, nevertheless, is that the sage transcends even the royal "household." We should not forget that the legend of Ho-shang Kung also describes how the sage soars into the sky and reveals his true identity to the emperor.

Elsewhere, the *Lao-tzu* intimates that the sage is valued by the whole world (chap. 56). Just as the legendary Ho-shang Kung reproved Emperor Wen for his initial self-aggrandizement, and just as Master An-ch'iu refused to serve Emperor Ch'eng, the commentator explains: "His virtue is like this! The ruler cannot make him a minister; the princes cannot make him submit to them." The sage is an honored guest of the family, to complete our metaphor, whose special knowledge on "parenting" is indispensable to the ruler.

This is why Ho-shang Kung is careful to say that the ruler "ought to" (chap. 51) and "desires" to be (chap. 13) the father and mother of the people. Without the sage, the ruler is but a taskmaster. This does not mean, however, that the ruler is like the people. It is a question of degree; in Ho-shang Kung's universe, nothing does not conform to the order of the "One." The commentary on chapter 57 is very clear on this:

Text	*Commentary*
Govern the country with rectitude.	. . . Heaven causes the person who is rectified to come into possession of a country.
Use the army with expedient tactics.	. . .Heaven causes the person who is deceitful to use the army.
Win the world with nonactivity.	(Heaven causes) the person who is without activity and without action to win the world, and to become its master.

It is important to find out where one stands in the family of Tao, and the sage is precisely able to reveal even the darkest mystery. If the ruler submits himself to the teaching of the sage, the latter's blessing may even pass on to him. According to the *Lao-tzu*, "He who possesses virtue in abundance can be compared to a newborn babe" (chap. 55). Ho-shang Kung brings this back to the fold of the family of the Way: "The spirits will bless him who possesses virtue, just as the father and mother will do also to their newborn babe." Possessing virtue, of course, is but another way of saying that the "One," the essence of Tao, is secured. In the final analysis, the teaching of Ho-shang Kung, like that of Wang Pi, is rooted in a "Tao-ist" vision.

5 Wang Pi and Ho-shang Kung Compared

By describing both Wang Pi's and Ho-shang Kung's representation of the *Lao-tzu* as "Tao-ist" visions, I am suggesting that despite important differences, there is common ground between them. This renders a comparison of these two commentaries more complex, and raises the question as to how the differences are to be explained. It is my contention that a comparison of Wang Pi and Ho-shang Kung must take into account not only their interpretations of the *Lao-tzu*, but also their different hermeneutical orientations.

Points of Divergence: "Philosophy" vs. "Religion"?

Initially, specific differences ought to be identified, which point to the distinctiveness of the two commentaries. For example, toward the end of chapter 1, the *Lao-tzu* concludes by saying that "these two issue from the same source, but have different names." Which "two" is the question:

Wang Pi	*Ho-shang Kung*
The "two" are the "beginning" and the "mother." "Issue from the same source" means that they both issue from the "dark." Having different names, they apply to different things.[1]	The "two" refer to having desires and not having desires. "Issue from the same source" means that they both issue from the human heart. "But have different names" means that they are named differently. One whose name is "not having desires" lives long; one whose name is "having desires" loses his body.

For Ho-shang Kung, as we have seen, the "dark" or "mysterious" (*hsüan*) refers to heaven. For Wang Pi, however, the word *hsüan* means "dim, silent, and void; it is the source of the 'beginning' and 'mother.'"

While the "spirit of the valley" in chapter 6 gives rise to a long discussion of nourishing the indwelling spirits in Ho-shang Kung's commentary, Wang Pi takes the expression to mean the "middle of the valley" and expounds on the idea of *wu*, which the imagery suggests. The word *k'ung* in chapter 21 is identified by Wang Pi with the phonetically equivalent *k'ung*, which means "empty." Ho-shang Kung, on the other hand, takes it to mean "great" (*ta*). Both interpretations are possible, as any good dictionary will confirm. In chapter 29 the *Lao-tzu* describes the world or empire as a "sacred vessel" (*shen-ch'i*), which therefore should not be interfered with:

Wang Pi	*Ho-shang Kung*
"Sacred" means without form and without limit. "Vessel" is made by unifying different things. Without form yet unified, it is therefore called a "sacred vessel." The nature of the ten thousand things conforms to *tzu-jan*. Therefore it can only be followed, but not acted upon.	Vessels are things. Human beings are the sacred things of the world. Sacred things prefer to be tranquil; they cannot be governed by active intervention.

In chapter 59, the *Lao-tzu* states that "in governing the people and serving heaven, nothing is better than frugality (*se*)." The word *se* may also mean a farmer, as Wang Pi interprets it to suggest a parallel between government and the farmer's following the way of *tzu-*

jan in his work. Ho-shang Kung, however, understands the word *se* in the sense of "coveting" or "loving" something, and thus using it only sparingly: "He who governs the country should love the people and not be given to excesses; he who governs the body should love the essential breath and not let it run wild."

Examples of this kind can easily be multiplied. These are selected because they clearly attest to the different emphases of the two commentaries. Equally important, they show that both Wang Pi and Ho-shang Kung are careful commentators. The interpretation of individual words is especially revealing, as there is not one instance too outlandish or completely unjustified. It cannot be said that they are merely using the *Lao-tzu*, because of its authority, as a springboard to promote their own ideas.[2] In these two commentaries, as we shall see more clearly later in this chapter, new ideas are formed only on the basis of the old.

The visions of Wang Pi and Ho-shang Kung *are* different. Wang Pi's emphasis on the key concept of *wu* is without question lacking in Ho-shang Kung. This difference is especially marked in their commentaries on chapters 1 and 6. In both instances, Ho-shang Kung speaks mainly of the spiritual body and the way to attain everlasting life. Similarly, the example of chapter 21 cited above testifies succinctly to Wang Pi's central insight.

The same difference extends to the account of the generation of beings from Tao. While Wang Pi focuses on what may be called the logic of production, in terms of the generation of the primary numbers from *wu*, Ho-shang Kung recounts the way in which the universe was formed by the blending of the "breath" of Tao (chap. 42). In this instance, indeed, the word *wu* is not even mentioned in the Ho-shang Kung commentary. On the concluding line of chapter 40, "All things in the world come from being; beings come from non-being," our commentators have written:

Wang Pi	*Ho-shang Kung*
The things of this world have life by virtue of being; the origin of being is rooted in non-being. If fullness of being is to be attained, one must return to non-being.	Heaven and earth, spirits and enlightened beings, insects that fly and worms that crawl—all these are produced by Tao. The Way is formless, and thus (being) is said to be born of *wu*. This means that the root is superior to the branches; the weak is superior to the strong.

Viewed side by side, compared to the ease with which Wang Pi discusses the notion of "non-being," one gets the impression that Ho-shang Kung is laboring to explain how being can be "said" to have come from *wu*.

The same is true for the idea of "principle" (*li*), the positive correlate of *wu*, which is hardly mentioned in Ho-shang Kung's commentary. To take but one example, in chapter 47 the *Lao-tzu* states that the sage "knows the world without having to set foot outside his door; sees the Way of heaven without having to look through his window." While Wang Pi is concerned with explaining why this is the case, Ho-shang Kung seems more interested in how this is accomplished:

Wang Pi	*Ho-shang Kung*
Every occurrence has its source; everything has its master. . . . The Way has its great constancy, and Principle has its general structure. By holding fast to the way of old, one can master the present.	The sage "knows the world without having to set foot outside his door" means that on the basis of his own self, he knows those of others; on the basis of his own family, he knows the families of others. In this way, he sees the world. The Way of heaven is the same as the Way of man. . . . If the ruler is pure and tranquil, the breath of heaven will be in order of its own accord. . . . Fortune and misfortune, benefit and harm, they all stem from the self.

Instead of a general principle paralleling the Way and depicting the presence of Tao in the cosmos, Ho-shang Kung's emphasis is in this instance placed on the self.

Conversely, the quest for immortality is simply not an issue in Wang Pi's commentary. The importance of the self is certainly not denied; *wu-wei* is ultimately a mode of being, as we have seen, and "not having desires" (*wu-yü*) and "without thought of self" (*wu-ssu*) are major themes in the Wang Pi commentary. But the interior cosmos that figures so prominently in the Ho-shang Kung commentary remains foreign to Wang Pi's thought.

According to the *Lao-tzu*, by returning to the root one becomes tranquil and returns to "destiny" (*ming*), which is also called the "constant" (chap. 16). While Ho-shang Kung's analysis is built around the view that "returning to destiny" means "deathlessness," Wang Pi identifies the former with "obtaining the constant in one's nature and destiny." When the "constant" is realized, as the *Lao-tzu* continues, one is in accord with Tao and becomes "everlasting." According to Wang Pi, this means that one attains the utmost of emptiness and is therefore "without limit." When one is everlasting, as the *Lao-tzu* concludes, one will "meet with no danger throughout life." Wang Pi's explanation is carefully prefaced with the words, "*Wu* as applied to things." What is everlasting and free from danger is thus not the person, as the *Lao-tzu* seems to imply and as Ho-shang Kung has clearly understood it; what is important to Wang Pi is that the reason why anything can be enduring lies in the concept of "non-being."

Yet the *Lao-tzu* also says, "He who dies but does not perish has longevity" (chap. 33).[3] Does this not suggest that the *Lao-tzu* is at least concerned with the quest for longevity? There is no question that Ho-shang Kung would answer in the affirmative; but Wang Pi's answer is quite different:

Wang Pi	*Ho-shang Kung*
Although one dies, the Way by which life is made possible does not perish; one's life is then preserved. The Way remains even if the body ceases to exist. How much more if the body is preserved and the Way does not perish?	The eyes do not perversely see; the ears do not perversely hear; the mouth does not perversely speak; then one will not be blamed and hated by the world. Therefore one lives long.

The concluding question in Wang Pi's commentary is interesting, for it shows that he was aware of the implication of Lao-tzu's words. Nevertheless, perpetual existence is a predicate attributed only to Tao; the possibility of an everlasting human life is lightly left aside by way of a rhetorical question. When the *Lao-tzu* again refers to the theme of longevity (chaps. 44, 59), and to the opposite that one will perish "early" if the Way is abandoned (chap. 55), Wang Pi is silent.[4]

On this level, then, the dialectical understanding of Tao that characterizes Wang Pi's commentary does not address the precise hierarchical correspondence between the microcosmic and macrocosmic world, which is so important to Ho-shang Kung. This affects their political visions as well. The example of chapter 29 cited above is especially instructive in this regard. Because the reason why the world or empire (*t'ien-hsia*) is a "sacred vessel" is understood differently, the interpretation of the politics of *wu-wei* is also different. For Wang Pi, *wu-wei* is essentially to follow (*yin*) the course of *tzu-jan*; for Ho-shang Kung, however, it involves a definite program designed with both the internal and external aspects of government in view. Wang Pi's analogy of the ruler's governing the country and the farmer's tending his field in chapter 59, also cited above, is again focused on the idea of "bringing the natural course of things into completion." For Ho-shang Kung, on the other hand, loving the people is an art modeled on loving one's "essential breath."

In the commentary on chapter 74, as we have seen in the last chapter, Ho-shang Kung embarks on a lengthy discussion of the danger of "troubling" the people with excessive punishment. At the same time, however, the ruler must be "prepared" to deal with disorder quickly and in a forceful way. In chapter 75 the commentary turns to a long critique of heavy taxation. Although length is normally not a reliable measure when applied to literary analysis, in this case it suggests the different degree of emphasis in Wang Pi's and Ho-shang Kung's treatment of Lao-tzu's political insight. Chapters 74 and 75 total some 110 characters. When compared with Ho-shang Kung's 350 or so characters, Wang Pi's 55 is telling.[5] This is not to say that Wang Pi is not interested in politics; I have in fact argued to the contrary. What it does show is that, when compared with Ho-shang Kung, Wang Pi is less concerned with specific policies or techniques of government.

Because the art of rulership is for Wang Pi ultimately a matter of being *wu-wei* and *tzu-jan*, the figure of the sage is presented as a model of the ideal ruler. The sage embodies the Way in the sense that he responds to it by emptying his heart or mind of self-oriented desires; he "values the root and putting to rest the branches." Without thought of self (*wu-ssu*), the sage "teaches with no words" (chaps. 2, 17, 23, 63). If the ruler realizes this, he then does not only have the right to rule, but truly deserves to be the master of the world.

While Wang Pi sees the term *wu-ssu* to mean "without thought of self" (chaps. 7, 77, 81), Ho-shang Kung always takes the more general meaning of impartiality or being a just ruler (chaps. 7, 16, 19). While Wang Pi simply uses the expression "teaching with no words" without explaining it, Ho-shang Kung is concerned with emphasizing the sense of "teaching by personal example" (chaps. 2, 34, 43). In the world of Ho-shang Kung, the sage is not only a model to be emulated; he is also a teacher of rulers whose mission, to use our metaphor again, is to establish the family of Tao on earth. In this sense, because of his special knowledge, the sage rules the empire *through* the ruler. While the possibility of attaining sagehood is left open in Wang Pi's commentary, Ho-shang Kung sees the sage as having been "blessed" by Tao. The figure of the sage is important to Wang Pi, but the view that the sage occupies a special place in the cosmos, because of his being endowed with the fullness of *ch'i*, is largely unique to the latter.

Chapter 27 of the *Lao-tzu* describes the sage as a man of many talents, and ultimately as a savior figure:

1. One who is good at traveling leaves no track or trace.
2. One who is good at speaking leaves no flaw or cause for blame.
3. One who is good at reckoning uses no counting sticks.
4. One who is good at shutting doors uses no bolts, and yet they cannot be opened.
5. One who is good at tying knots uses no cords, and yet they cannot be untied.
6. Therefore the sage is always good at saving people;
7. thus no one is abandoned.[6]

While Wang Pi's commentary is focused on one central idea, Ho-shang Kung takes pains to explain what each of these marvelous feats means:

Wang Pi	*Ho-shang Kung*
1) Walk along the course of *tzu-jan*, without making or instituting things; then things reach their end, leaving no track or trace.	1) One who is good at walking with the Way, looks for it in one's body. He does not go down to the outer chamber or go out of doors; thus he leaves no track or trace.
2) Follow the nature of things, without discriminating or separating them; thus no flaw or blame can reach him.	2) One who is good at speaking means that one chooses his words before he speaks. Then his words will have no flaw or fault, and will not be blamed or reproved by the world.

3) This means to follow the numerical figure (*shu*) of the things themselves, without relying on external forms.

3) One who is good at using the Way to calculate his affairs secures the One and does not change. He does not calculate much; thus without having to use counting sticks, he is able to know.

4–5) To follow what is *tzu-jan* in things, without establishing or doing anything; this is why, without using bolts or cords, they cannot be opened or untied. These five all speak of not making or doing anything, of following the nature of things, and not restraining them with external forms.

4) One who is good at shutting one's desires and feelings, and securing the essence and spirits with Tao, is not like a door with bolts which can be opened.

5) One who is good at tying things with Tao, is able to tie their cores together. This is not like using cords which can be untied.

6–7) The sage does not establish forms and names so as to keep check of things; he does not create standards so as to distinguish and to abandon the unworthy. Rather, he assists what is *tzu-jan* in all things, and does not claim to have originated anything. Thus it is said, "no one is abandoned."[7]

6) The reason why the sage always teaches the people to be loyal and filial is that he wants to save their lives.

7) This means that he causes the honored and the despised each to attain its proper place.

The centrality of the concept of *tzu-jan* in Wang Pi's understanding of the "saving" work of the sage is very clear. For Ho-shang Kung, however, it is important to bring out what the sage can do and teach. From the point of view of the sage, loyalty and filial piety are no doubt inferior virtues when compared with the primacy of the "One"; but they serve a useful function in managing the people, on the way to reestablishing that utopian society of the primordial past. The example of chapter 27, as we shall see, also testifies to the difference in hermeneutical outlook, which guides our two commentaries.

Because of Wang Pi's emphasis on the concept of "non-being," which pervades his understanding of the *Lao-tzu* as a whole, his interpretation is often labeled "philosophical." Because of Ho-shang Kung's emphasis on the interior cosmos and the way to secure the "One," his commentary is thus described as "religious." This is not necessarily an unfair assessment, for the differences detailed above are real and important. What is equally important, however, is the common ground between them. Viewed in this light, the "philosophic" does not stand in *opposition* to the "religious"; a comparison of Wang Pi with Ho-shang Kung must take into account that both the "philosophic" and "religious" stem from a vision grounded in the Way.

Common Ground

There is no question in my mind that both Wang Pi and Ho-shang Kung are motivated by a fundamental practical concern for the well-being of the country. This, indeed, is true not only for the two commentaries, but characterizes much of traditional Chinese thought as a whole. Neither work is engaged in a kind of "pure," speculative discourse on the nature of Tao as such, untouched by the moral and political issues of their days. In the end, it is a "Tao-ist" utopia that lies at the heart of their visions.

The "Tao-ist" utopia is rooted not only in an understanding of Tao, but also in a vision of the past. Both Wang Pi and Ho-shang Kung have drawn from traditional sources, regardless of any possible polemical intention, to represent the *Lao-tzu* to their audience. To be sure, their understanding of history is not the same. Whereas Ho-shang Kung has a definite chronological scheme in mind, Wang Pi is content to say that Tao is present from the "beginning." Wang Pi's emphasis, as we have seen, is on the importance of discerning the constant principle of Tao in history so as to "master present situations" (chaps. 14, 47). For Ho-shang Kung, however, the goal is to reestablish the paradisaic condition of the time even before the "Five Emperors" and the "Three Sovereigns" (chap. 62). Yet, the fact remains that both Wang Pi and Ho-shang Kung recognize the relevance and authority of the past, to which the figure of the sage is also traced (e.g., chap. 65). This has important implications for the kind of utopian society to be realized.

Chapter 80 of the *Lao-tzu* describes the ideal state as small and sparsely populated. On the first two lines, Wang Pi comments:

Text	*Wang Pi*
The country is small, and the people are few.	Even a small country with few people can be made to return to antiquity. How much more so for a

	large country with many people? Thus, the example of a small country is used.
Let there be tens and hundreds of utensils (*shih-po chih ch'i*); but they are not used.	This means to make it so that although the people have tens and hundreds of utensils, they have no use for them. Why worry about not having enough?

The logic of the first half of Wang Pi's commentary seems somewhat difficult, but it is at least clear that he sees in Lao-tzu's words a general indication of the importance to return to "antiquity."[8] The second half is more problematic. The phrase *shih-po chih ch'i* literally means "ten hundreds of utensils." Since the term *shih-po* was used in ancient China as a military expression signifying the division of soldiers into equal units of "tens and hundreds," some scholars have suggested that the *Lao-tzu* original refers to military equipment in general. The concluding question in Wang Pi's commentary, however, suggests that he is taking the term *shih-po* as an expression of quantity, as opposed to a specific type of utensils or instruments.[9] What is of even greater interest is that Ho-shang Kung has punctuated the second line differently:

Text	*Ho-shang Kung*
The country is small, and the people are few.	Although the sage may be ruling a large country, he treats it like a small one: being frugal and not given to excesses. Although the people may be many, he treats them as if there were only a few: he does not dare to overburden them.
Let there be divisions of tens and hundreds (*shih-po*).	Let the people all have their groups and divisions of tens and hundreds. Then the honored and the despised will not attack and harm one another.
The people's utensils; but they are not used.	"Utensils" refer to the utensils of the farmer. "But not used" means that the ruler does not call the people to service, and rob them of their good (farming) seasons.

The breaking up of the second line from the *Lao-tzu* into two sentences results in an awkward construction. It would appear that Ho-shang Kung recognizes the military background of the term *shih-po*, but, because of his heavy emphasis against the use of military force, he could not see how the term *shih-po* can mean anything other than a general classification of the people according to their status. The world of Ho-shang Kung, we must not forget, is essentially a hierarchical world.

Clearly, Ho-shang Kung and Wang Pi are taking the description of the "small country" as an "example" of quite different things. Yet, the common ground they share also emerges. The *Lao-tzu* continues:

1. Let the people take death seriously,
2. and not migrate far.

Wang Pi	*Ho-shang Kung*
1–2) Let the people not use (their utensils), but only treasure their bodies. Let them not be greedy for goods and gifts, and thus they will be content in their dwellings, take death seriously, and not migrate far.	1) If the ruler can make the beneficial flourish and eliminate the harmful for the people, so that they all have their (proper) place, then the people will take death seriously and be greedy for life.
	2) If government orders are not troublesome, then the people will be content with their work. Thus they will not migrate far and leave their permanent dwellings.

Although the political implications are drawn out more fully in Ho-shang Kung's account, the general emphasis on a simple and secure life is common to both commentaries. The people will "take death seriously" and not risk their lives pursuing change, if they are content with their "place" in life. The task of government, in this sense, is thus to minimize unnecessary change, which disrupts the order inherent in a "Tao-ist" universe. It is interesting that even Wang Pi specifically mentions the importance of valuing one's "body" or physical self. The *Lao-tzu* then goes on to describe this utopian state in greater detail, on which Ho-shang Kung comments:

Text	*Ho-shang Kung*
Although there are boats and carts, no one will ride in them.	Being tranquil and without action, (the ruler) does not engage in elaborate and ceremonial activities, and is not fond of taking journeys for pleasure and entertainment.
Although there are armor and weapons, they will not be displayed.	(The ruler) will not be blamed and disliked by the world.
Let the people again knot cords and use them;	(He) takes away the superficial (written language) and returns to what is of substance; he is trustworthy and without deceit.
relish their food;	(The ruler) relishes his simple food, and does not live off the avails of the people.
find beauty in their clothing;	(He) finds beauty in his coarse garments, and does not value the five colors.
be content with their dwellings;	(He) is content with his humble straw huts, and is not fond of houses with ornaments and decorations.
take delight in their customs.	(He) takes delight in his customs of a simple nature, and does not switch or change them.
Although neighboring states can see one another, and the sound of their cocks and dogs can be heard,	They are near one another.
the people grow old without having visited one another.	They have no desires.

On this long description of the ideal state, Wang Pi simply writes: "They desire nothing."

Both Wang Pi and Ho-shang Kung thus agree that the utopian state is ultimately characterized by the absence of desires; or more precisely by the lack of dissatisfaction, which gives rise to covetousness and engenders conflict. For Wang Pi, chapter 80 of the *Lao-tzu* points to the need of establishing a new society, based on the idea of returning to Tao and on insights discerned from history. The specific practices of government are of secondary importance, so long as the people *are* without desires. Ho-shang Kung, however, sees in this a precise model of government, characterized by the use of "primitive" technology prior to the rise of the written language. In the case of Ho-shang Kung, the process of realizing the ideal society is primarily one of restoration. If one takes the historical context of these two commentaries seriously, it appears that by the time of Wang Pi, after the final collapse of the Han dynasty, the hope of restoring the past has given way to a vision of building a new future. In any case, having superseded the Han house, the ruling Wei power would probably not look kindly on any theory of government centered on an ideal of restoring the past.

Although suggestive, historical speculation of this nature is rarely conclusive. What is beyond dispute is that both Wang Pi and Ho-shang Kung are of the same view in recognizing human desires as the chief cause of political and moral evil. Characteristically, Ho-shang Kung identifies the subject of Lao-tzu's discourse in chapter 80 with the ruler. The assumption here, as we have seen, is that the action of the ruler has a direct bearing on the behavior and attitude of the people. The reason why the people are hungry, according to Ho-shang Kung, is that the ruler imposes heavy taxation on them. On a deeper level, however "the people are all changed by the ruler above and become greedy. They rebel against the Way and oppose virtue, and are therefore hungry" (chap. 75). On this same chapter, Wang Pi writes: "This means that the reason people become perverse and government becomes chaotic stems from the (ruler) above and not the (people) below. The people follow the (ruler) above."[10]

The very possibility of realizing the utopian state of Tao depends on this correspondence between the ruler and the people. In chapter 57, the *Lao-tzu* has the sage saying:

1. I take no action and the people are of themselves transformed.
2. I love tranquility and the people are of themselves rectified.
3. I do not engage in affairs and the people of themselves become rich.
4. I have no desires and the people of themselves become simple.

This is the textual basis that lies behind Wang Pi's and Ho-shang Kung's understanding of the process of self-transformation, which follows from the politics of *wu-wei*. Again, Wang Pi combines the individual details into an integrated discussion:

Wang Pi	*Ho-shang Kung*
What the ruler above desires, the people will follow quickly. If what I desire is only to have no desires, then the people also will have no desires and become simple of their own accord. These four indicate honoring the root and putting to rest the branches.	1) The sage states that I cultivate the Way and obey heaven, without having to change or make anything, and the people are of themselves transformed and made complete.
	2) The sage states that I love tranquility, without speaking and without teaching, and the people of themselves become loyal and rectified.
	3) I do not impose labor on the people or call them to service, then they will be content with their work. Thus they all become rich of themselves.
	4) I am always without desire, discard ornamental words, and place little value on clothes and decorations, then the people will follow me and become simple by nature.[11]

Ho-shang Kung is more specific. But even for Wang Pi, as I have shown, the idea of "honoring the root and putting to rest the branches" is more than a general call to return to Tao. It involves both supporting the people and eliminating corrupt influences that arouse the people. Wang Pi, too, denounces the use of military force and excessive punishment (chaps. 30, 36); he, too, is concerned with the proper appointment and performance of government officials (chap. 3). Wang Pi, in the final analysis, would no doubt underline the notion of "response" (*ying*) in his theory of government. On this point, Ho-shang Kung would readily agree, although he would add that the reciprocal relationship and correspondence between the "Way of heaven" and the "Way of man" should be extended to include the "spiritual body." At one point, the *Lao-tzu* compares the relationship of Tao and the world to that of rivers and streams flowing into the sea (chap. 32). Ho-shang Kung comments:

> This means (by analogy) that the presence of Tao in the world and the people respond to (*ying*) and harmonize with one another, like the rivers and the sea which interpenetrate and flow into one another.[12]

The concept of *ying* is clearly not foreign to the Ho-shang Kung commentary. Ultimately, the ideal ruler accomplishes all things without the people's knowing it; the latter will only think that the way of *tzu-jan* has taken its course. On this, Wang Pi and Ho-shang Kung are in complete agreement (chap. 17).

Up to this point, the discussion of the differences between Wang Pi and Ho-shang Kung has moved from the theoretical to the practical level. A common ground now emerges from a comparison of their political visions. To complete our analysis, the question must be asked whether this similarity extends to their theoretical orientation as well. At first glance, Wang Pi's dialectical reading of "non-being" appears radically different from the cosmological framework of Ho-shang Kung's commentary. A closer reading, however, discloses interesting parallels and raises new questions in a comparative analysis of the two commentaries.

The more obvious fact is that Ho-shang Kung *agrees* with Wang Pi in describing the Tao as *wu*, especially in the sense of what is without form and cannot be named (chaps. 1, 25, 32, 40). Precisely because of the negativity of the Way, Ho-shang Kung's emphasis is shifted to the "One," the essence of Tao, in terms of which the practical implications of a "Tao-ist" view can be brought fully to light. Both Wang Pi and Ho-shang Kung emphasize that Tao is the "beginning" and the "mother" of the cosmos. What is less obvious is that there are indications in Wang Pi's work that it is not entirely free from the same cosmology that dominates Ho-shang Kung's vision.

The correspondence between the "Way of heaven" and the "Way of man" is surely important not only to Ho-shang Kung, but to Wang Pi also. This, again, is presupposed by the latter's emphasis on the notion of "response." According to the *Lao-tzu*, the Way of heaven "does not speak but is good in responding" (chap. 73). Wang Pi's comment brings out the relevance to human life: "To follow it will bring fortune; to act contrary to it will bring harm." The theme of fortune and misfortune, which is central to Ho-shang Kung as well, is repeated in Wang Pi's commentary on chapter 54, while describing the "Tao of the world." As the *Lao-tzu* has it, in the cultivation of Tao, one should "look at the world through the world." Although this difficult passage is interpreted differently in the two commentaries, Ho-shang Kung could hardly object to Wang Pi's conclusion. According to the former, the *Lao-tzu* is saying that "through the ruler who cultivates the Way," whose life will be "preserved," one can discern the opposite that those who oppose the Way will "perish." According to Wang Pi:

> This means to look at the Tao of the world through the minds or hearts of the people in the world. The Tao of the world, adversity or favorable circumstances, fortune or misfortune— all these are like the Tao of man.[13]

This is but another way of expressing the concept of *tzu-jan*; man always "models" himself on earth, which in turn is modeled after heaven (chap. 25). This is why the "Tao of the world," which encompasses both heaven and earth, is in principle (*li*) no different from the "Tao of man." This is why by observing and following (*yin*) the minds of the people and the affairs of the world, one can see the presence of Tao in the cosmos.

Besides this perceived relationship and the effects it has on human affairs, what characterizes the "Tao of the world"? According to Ho-shang Kung, the cosmos is above all regulated by the four seasons and the five phases or elements (*wu-hsing*), integrated with the *yin* and *yang* forces of the "One." Admittedly, this cosmological discussion is largely unique to Ho-shang Kung. But in chapter 9, commenting on the line, "To retire when the task is accomplished, this is the Way of heaven," Wang Pi also writes: "The four seasons take their turns; when the task is completed, they then move on." As Hatano Tarō points out, Wang Pi may have had in mind a similar saying found in the biography of Ts'ai Tse (d. ca. 221 B.C.) in the *Shih-chi*.[14] Ts'ai Tse was the prime minister of Ch'in, before it conquered the other contending states and unified the country. Judging from his discourse preserved in the biography, which emphasizes both longevity and the sovereign power of the ruler, Ts'ai might have been a supporter of the Huang-lao school.[15] I shall come back to this point later.

Chapter 4 of the *Lao-tzu* describes the Way as inexhaustible and born before the "Lord" or "Emperor" (*Ti*). Wang Pi explains:

Text	Commentary
The Way is empty; but use will never exhaust it. Deep, it is like the ancestor of all things. It blunts its sharpness; it unties its tangles; it softens its light; it becomes one with the dusty world. Deep and still, it appears to exist forever. I do not know whose son it is. It seems to have existed before the Lord.[16]	One who relies on the capacity of one family, can never make that family complete. One who relies on the capacity of one state, can never make that state complete. Exhausting one's strength in lifting what is heavy, it cannot be of any use. Thus although a man knows the government of all things, if he does not govern with the Tao of the two modes (*erh-i*), he cannot complete his task. Although the earth has its form and soul (*p'o*), if it does not model on heaven, it cannot maintain its tranquility. Although heaven has its essence and images (*hsiang*), if it does not model on Tao, it cannot preserve its clarity.[17] . . . Heaven and earth cannot be compared to (Tao). Does it not appear to have preceded the Lord? The "Lord" means the Lord of heaven (*T'ien-ti*).

The Tao of the "two modes" (*erh-i*), as the structure of Wang Pi's argument indicates, means the Tao of heaven and earth. According to the *I-ching*, the "Great Ultimate" (*T'ai-chi*) gives rise to the "two modes." Inasmuch as it also states that *yin* and *yang* together constitute Tao, the expression *erh-i* has traditionally been understood in terms of the *yin-yang* theory.[18] It is in this sense that Wang Pi uses the term here, as the reference to the "soul" (*p'o*) of the earth also suggests. Incidentally, Ho-shang Kung also identifies *Ti* with the "Lord of heaven" (*T'ien-ti*).

In Wang Pi's commentary, the Way of heaven is thus understood cosmologically as well, drawing from ideas long established since the early Han dynasty. Of course, as Ho-shang Kung would agree, the Way of heaven is subordinate to Tao itself. Concluding his commentary on chapter 25, where the relationship between human beings, earth, heaven and Tao is set out systematically, Wang Pi writes:

Text	*Commentary*
Man models himself on earth; earth models itself on heaven; heaven models itself on Tao; Tao models itself on *tzu-jan*.	. . . Form and soul (*p'o*) are not as good as essence and images (*hsiang*). Essence and images are not as good as what is without form. What has modes (*i*) is not as good as what does not have modes. Thus they model after one another.

With Tao at the top, like that of Ho-shang Kung, the universe of Wang Pi is also hierarchical.

The term *p'o* is paralleled with "image" (*hsiang*) in both chapters 4 and 25. If *p'o* is the "soul" of the earth, what are the "images" of heaven? According to the *Lao-tzu*, the Way of heaven is not only responsive; it is also "not anxious about things and yet it plans well."[19] Wang Pi's commentary reads:

Heaven hangs out images (*ch'ui-hsiang*) so that fortune and misfortune can be seen. Before things occur, one has to plan for them.[20]

The term *ch'ui-hsiang* is also found in the Ho-shang Kung commentary. When the *Lao-tzu* says, in chapter 39, "Heaven obtained the One and became clear," Ho-shang Kung explains: "This means that heaven obtained the One, and is therefore able to hang out the images (*ch'ui-hsiang*) and to shine clearly." If we turn to Wang Pi's commentary on chapter 4 again, we see that it refers to chapter 39 as well. Although heaven has its images, it will not be "clear" if it does not model itself after Tao. In these instances, the "images" can only be the heavenly constellations.

Both Wang Pi and Ho-shang Kung are here following the tradition of the *I-ching*, in which we read: "Heaven gives birth to spiritual things, after which the sage models himself. Heaven and earth change and transform, and the sage imitates them. Heaven administers the constellations (*ch'ui-hsiang*) . . . for which the sage makes images."[21] In this connection, the "Lord of heaven" (*T'ien-ti*) may even mean the polar star, as the two are sometimes equated in Han literature.[22]

The word *ch'ui* generally signifies the hanging or suspending of something from above, or any action directed from the superior to the inferior; to translate it as "administer" is to render the political implication explicit. Just as the stars naturally respond to the laws of heaven, the people are transformed spontaneously by the ruler. Just as heaven effortlessly "metes out" the placement of the stars, the ruler administers his kingdom without outward action. This calls to mind the concept of *ch'ui-kung*, which expresses the politics of *wu-wei* by depicting the ruler governing with his clothes "hanging down" (*ch'ui*) and his hands "folded" (*kung*).

The *Shu-ching* (Book of History) explicitly defines the concept of *ch'ui-kung* as government by "nonaction".[23] But it is in the *Lun-yü* that the classic expression of this type of government is found. According to Confucius, "a ruler who governs his state by virtue is like the north polar star, which remains in its place while all other stars revolve around (*kung*) it."[24] The word *kung* ("revolve around") is in this context read in the third tone, and is interchangeable with *kung* ("hands folded"). As Wing-tsit Chan has pointed out, beginning from the Han dynasty, this passage has been interpreted in terms of the ideal of *wu-wei*.[25] This reading is supported by the equally famous saying of Confucius:

> By *wu-wei* and the country is well governed—only Shun could have done it! What did he do? All he did was to make himself reverently (*kung*) and correctly face south.[26]

The word *kung*, "reverent," is both phonetically and semantically related to *ch'ui-kung*. Like the north polar star, the royal seat of the ruler faces south.

This is the ideal, the grand vision of order and harmony that Wang Pi and Ho-shang Kung shared. Instead of attributing it to Confucius or even to heaven, it is grounded in Tao. In the "Tao-ist" universe, heaven and humankind interpenetrate one another; everything has its proper place. In the political realm, the sovereign power of the ruler is of course important; but so are the people. Heaven becomes "clear" when the "One" is obtained, but the clarity of heaven is always mediated by the stars. To say that the ruler has secured the "One" is but another way of saying that the people are content and happy. Spiritual contemplation of Tao merges into one with ethical and political concerns. In this sense, what truly characterizes the common ground between Wang Pi and Ho-shang Kung is a profound unity of ethics and spirituality.

Ethics is more than morality, and spirituality cannot be equated with either mysticism or superstition. This applies to both Wang Pi and Ho-shang Kung, for whom ethics and spirituality constitute an *ethos* encompassing the political, religious, and other forms of experience. When raised to the level of thought, this unity of experience gives rise to a form of reflection that does not distinguish between "seeing" and "doing," between *theoria* and *praxis*. The sage, after all, knows all things without having to see, and accomplishes all things without having to act. It is in this sense that I understand the words of Charles A. Moore: "In a very real sense, the ethical and the spiritual are one in China."[27]

The Hermeneutical Turn

When both the similarities and differences are taken into account, the complexities involved in a comparative study of the Wang Pi and Ho-shang Kung commentaries come fully into view. When it is recognized that they are both similar and different, the contrast between "philosophy," and "religion" loses its force. Both commentaries are "philosophical," in that they share the same basic understanding of Tao and its relation to the world. Conversely, neither Wang Pi nor Ho-shang Kung is "philosophical" if it means that their commentaries are divorced from political interests. Both commentaries are "religious," in that they share a fundamental soteriological concern to realize the "Tao-ist" utopia, the reign of "great peace." Conversely, neither one is "religious" if it means that they are exclusively concerned with immortality or spiritual enlightenment.

But the differences between them cannot be left unexplained or, what is worse, explained away. The central discussion of "non-being" and "principle" in Wang Pi's commentary does appear more "philosophical," when compared with Ho-shang Kung's emphasis on the cultivation of the "spiritual body." The question must be raised as to how they come to differ in so many respects, given the common ground that unites them. Can this be explained simply as a matter of emphasis?

The different emphases in the two commentaries are obvious. Emphasis, however, is seldom accidental. In other words, the recognition of the different emphases alone does not answer the question; it merely rephrases it. Stemming from a common worldview, and reacting to the same text, what accounts for their different emphases?

On the basis of the above analysis, there can be little doubt that both commentaries are bound by the same worldview, characterized by a hierarchical universe in which the ethical and the spiritual form a unity. Moreover, as suggested earlier also, both Wang Pi and Ho-shang Kung are careful commentators; neither can be said to have disregarded the *Lao-tzu* so as to force their message across. Bound by the same text, they cannot but adopt a similar vocabulary; yet their interpretations differ significantly. Can the openness of the *Lao-tzu* itself be the sole reason for their divergence? Such concept as the "mysterious female" and the "spirit of the valley" certainly invite different interpretations. But the openness of the *Lao-tzu* only accounts for the possibility of divergence; it does not explain the nature of the divergence. Can the differences between them, then, be attributed to the distinctive Huang-lao flavor of the Ho-shang Kung commentary?

The Huang-lao factor is important, and identifies a key point of divergence between the two commentaries. Nevertheless, our analysis cannot stop here. Although Huang-lao teachings occupy a central place in the Ho-shang Kung commentary, the author did not set out to write an independent treatise on Huang-lao thought. While there is a polemical side to the commentary, it constitutes only one aspect of the work and is derived from a reading of the *Lao-tzu* itself. The author's self-understanding as commentator, in other words, should be recoginzed. What needs to be further explored is how a Huang-lao reading was arrived at in the first place. In the broader context, the Huang-lao dimension signals but the rootedness of the commentary in the accumulative tradition of its time. Wang Pi, too, stood under very much the same tradition as he sought to understand the *Lao-tzu*. Although Wang Pi was not connected with the Huang-lao school, he was not unaware of it. Wang Pi's political orientation, as we have shown, is not totally different from that of Ho-shang Kung. The possible reference to Ts'ai Tse, the prime minister of Ch'in, is also interesting in this regard.

The important point is not whether Wang Pi has actually quoted from anyone, but that he did not hesitate to draw from diverse traditional sources to explain the *Lao-tzu*. In fact, both Wang Pi and Ho-shang Kung have employed older works such as the *I-ching*, *Lun-yü*, and *Chuang-tzu* to serve their interpretive task. Both commentaries are thus bound by a common tradition, the same reservoir of insight and truth in terms of which they relate the *Lao-tzu* to their own unique life-world, and distinguish themselves from other currents of thought. The Huang-lao factor alone does not explain the way in which tradition is reinterpreted in these commentaries, which remains the crucial point in the present discussion. To understand why the two commentaries differ the way they do, our analysis must take what I would call a hermeneutical turn, to see how tacit interpretive principles may have guided their readings of the *Lao-tzu*.

The last two paragraphs set out what may be called the hermeneutical boundaries of the two commentaries. Looking at the text from a common horizon, they chart out new territories as they penetrate the *Lao-tzu*. What makes them different is the way in which the text is read. This is not an argument about the intention of an author. Hermeneutical presuppositions underlie and shape intentions. Moreover, the hermeneutical differences between Wang Pi and Ho-shang Kung are apparent in a comparison of the commentaries themselves.

The most noticeable hermeneutical feature of the Wang Pi commentary is its attention to language. The theme of language, as I have emphasized, is central to Wang Pi's understanding of the *Lao-tzu*. This is true on the "metainterpretive" level as well. Key words in the *Lao-tzu* are interpreted by words of the same phonetic family. "Virtue" (*te*) means "to obtain" (*te*), and *k'ung* means "empty" (*k'ung*), to mention but two examples already discussed. Double meanings are exploited, as in the case of chapters 36 and 57, where the word "sharp" (*li*) is rendered as what is "profitable." Other words such as "ornament" (*wen*) and "opposite" (*fan*), as we have also seen, are treated in a similar way (chaps. 19, 40). When viewed together, these instances point to a hermeneutical pattern largely unique to Wang Pi.

Besides the play on language, Wang Pi's constant reference and cross-reference to the *Lao-tzu* original is also worthy of note, especially when compared with the lack of it in the Ho-shang Kung commentary. What this means is that for Wang Pi, the task of interpretation is to render the meaning of the words of the *Lao-tzu* explicit, in the light of the text as a whole. This seemingly banal observation is itself an indication of the genius of Wang Pi; there is a distinctively modern ring to his way of interpretation.

When we turn to the Ho-shang Kung commentary, we are confronted with a radically different interpretive operation. What is most unique to Ho-shang Kung are the references to Lao-tzu himself. When the first person singular, *wu* or *wo*, appears in the text (chaps. 4, 42, 53, 67, 70), or when the context implies the presence of a speaker (chaps. 54, 57), the commentary identifies Lao-tzu by name. The first line of chapter 70, for example, reads: "My words are very easy to understand, and very easy to put into practice." While Wang Pi quotes from chapter 47 to draw out the meaning of *wu-wei*, Ho-shang Kung is less ambitious:

Wang Pi	*Ho-shang Kung*
It is possible to know without having to set foot outside one's door, or to look through one's window. Thus it is said: "Very easy to understand." Without action and the task is accomplished; thus it is said: "Very easy to put into practice."	Lao-tzu says that what he says is concise and easy to understand, to the point and easy to put into practice.

Interpretation is always concerned with what is "said." But this premise, as opposed to the content of the saying, may itself be interpreted differently. In the case of the Ho-shang Kung commentary, what is said involves the "who" and "why" also. Chapter 53 of the *Lao-tzu* begins with the words, "if I have but little (*chieh*) knowledge, and walk along the great Way":

Wang Pi	*Ho-shang Kung*
This means that if I had but little knowledge, and were to put the great Way into practice in the world. . . .	*Chieh* means great. Lao-tzu was disgusted with the king of his time who did not walk along the great Way. Thus, he made this remark: If I had great (*chieh*) knowledge of government, I would then walk along the great Way and personally take up the transforming work of *wu-wei*.

The word *chieh*, taken by most commentators to mean "little" or "the slightest" in this context, has a wide range of meaning, including that of "great."[28] The important point is that while Wang Pi has taken this to be an introduction to the main message, Ho-shang Kung spells out the "historical" reference and the intent of Lao-tzu's remark. The idea that Lao-tzu was disgusted with the political practices of his day is a recurring theme in Ho-shang Kung's commentary (chaps. 20, 26, 69, 74).

This initial contrast alerts us to the different ways in which our two commentators have interacted with the *Lao-tzu*. In other words, Wang Pi and Ho-shang Kung are expecting and looking out for different things as they read the *Lao-tzu*. The latter's concern with representing and applying Lao-tzu's action and words to a new situation cannot be equated with the former's attempt to integrate the ideas of the text into a coherent whole. To Wang Pi, the identity of the "I" makes little difference to the meaning of what is said; to Ho-shang Kung, however, meaning is mediated by *external* factors, be they autobiographical or historical, to which the text is seen to refer. Simply put, the *Lao-tzu* has a different meaning to them because meaning itself is understood tacitly in different ways.

From this perspective, differences between Wang Pi and Ho-shang Kung take on a new significance. For Ho-shang Kung, the "dark" or "mysterious" refers to heaven—that is, the sky cosmologically conceived. The "spirit of the valley" means real spirits, whom one must carefully nourish. According to Wang Pi, on the other hand, they both signify the negativity of the Way. For Ho-shang Kung, in other words, the meaning of a text is understood when and only when the external referents are identified. Meaning, in this sense, is essentially *referential*. This prior understanding of meaning, conscious or unconscious, is foreign to Wang Pi, for whom meaning resides in the words themselves.

The referentiality of meaning explains the concreteness of Ho-shang Kung's interpretation, which I have already noted. Chapter 2 of the *Lao-tzu* presents a series of paradoxes:

1. The world recognizes beauty as beauty, then there is ugliness.
2. The world recognizes good as good, then there is the bad.

Both Wang Pi and Ho-shang Kung are concerned with resolving the paradox; but guided by their own hermeneutical prerogatives, the results are very different:

Wang Pi	*Ho-shang Kung*
1–2) Beauty is what the human heart enjoys; ugliness is what the human heart dislikes. Beauty and	1) Parading one's beauty to make it widely known, there is danger.

ugliness are like joy and anger;   2) This means that there is merit
good and bad are like right and   and fame; they are what people
wrong. Joy and anger have the   fight for.
same root; right and wrong belong
to the same family. Therefore they
should not be presented onesid-
edly. All these . . . show the way of
tzu-jan.[29]

Beauty and goodness are abstract concepts; as such, they have no
objective referents. For Ho-shang Kung, then, these lines can refer
only to concrete aspects of the human condition, to fame and striving, which bring conflict and danger. This is also why Ho-shang
Kung's commentary is not interested in the concept of "non-
being." It cannot be, because "non-being" does not refer to anything in the phenomenal world; it is meaningful only in a different
frame of reference.

In the case of Wang Pi, the task of the interpreter is to translate
the words of the Lao-tzu into other, more accessible and more comprehensive, concepts. "Beauty and ugliness are like joy and anger,"
and they are all rooted in tzu-jan. In Wang Pi's dialectical framework, none of these can be turned into an absolute. Chapter 3 of
the Lao-tzu states, "therefore in the government of the sage: he
empties the minds (of the people), but fills (their) bellies." According to Ho-shang Kung, as we have seen, this refers to the identity of
self-cultivation and the government of the country, in that the government of the sage begins with the emptying of his own mind.
Since "mind" and "belly" refer to concrete objects, to Ho-shang
Kung, the "emptying of the mind" and the "filling of the belly" can
mean only the sage's interior life—that is, the elimination of desires
and the securing of the spirits of the five viscera. To Wang Pi, however, the internal organs are not the issue at all:

> The mind contains knowledge and the belly contains food.
> This means to empty what has knowledge and to fill what
> does not have knowledge.[30]

According to Wang Pi, what the Lao-tzu means is that the sage realizes the need to "fill," to strengthen and make complete a mode of
being free from the kind of knowledge and cunning that gives rise
to desires. As the rest of chapter 3 confirms, both Wang Pi and Ho-

shang Kung recognize the importance of not having desires; but they are miles apart in bringing the *Lao-tzu* to their audience.

Even more explicit examples can be found; I have chosen the first few chapters to show that this hermeneutical difference pervades the two commentaries. As will be recalled (see p. 165, above), in the commentary to chapter 27, Wang Pi describes the many talents of the sage all in terms of the concept of *tzu-jan*. It is of little significance whether the sage actually "traveled"; the important point is that he always follows the nature of things. Ho-shang Kung, on the other hand, feels compelled to explain that the sage is able to "leave no track or trace" because he does not leave his home at all. On the description of the ideal state in chapter 80, Ho-shang Kung is even more specific, detailing the idyllic way of life that people once enjoyed and could enjoy again. For Wang Pi, inasmuch as meaning does not lie in any external referent, all that is needed to be said is the importance of having few desires. As we have also seen, according to Ho-shang Kung, real "spiritual things" are what the *Lao-tzu* means by the "sacred vessel" of the world (chap. 29). To Wang Pi, this means quite simply that the "Tao-ist" cosmos is "unified" and yet "without form." The implication is that one must not treat it like ordinary objects, characterized precisely by form and names. When the *Lao-tzu* says that "to govern a large country is like cooking a small fish," Ho-shang Kung immediately suggests that the intestines and the scales must not be removed; Wang Pi, of course, does not mention the fish at all (chap. 60).

Wang Pi is most concerned with drawing out the ground and implications of the ideas of *Lao-tzu*. Chapter 16 begins with the famous statement: "Attain utmost emptiness; maintain complete tranquility." As one has come to expect, while Ho-shang Kung comments on the two parts separately, Wang Pi grasps the one central idea at once. The style of the commentary reflects its hermeneutical presuppositions as well:

Wang Pi	*Ho-shang Kung*
This means that "attain emptiness" is the ultimate nature of things; "maintain tranquility" is the true nature of things.	He who has obtained the Way reduces his feelings and gets rid of his desires. His five viscera are clear and tranquil; he attains the ultimate of emptiness.
	He maintains tranquility and acts with seriousness.

The emphasis on the man of Tao testifies succinctly to the referential dimension of Ho-shang Kung's commentary. Precisely because of this hermeneutical framework, Ho-shang Kung is able to employ Huang-lao teachings to explain the *Lao-tzu*, without disregarding the text's meaning. Indeed, this is the full significance of the kind of correspondence that permeates Ho-shangs Kung's universe. It is not only a matter of the perceived correspondence between specific phenomena, but affects the very process of interpretation and thought. It shapes the way in which texts were read and meaning comprehended; it extends, in this case, to the prior hermeneutical structure of the Ho-shang Kung commentary. Wang Pi's work, on the other hand, is shaped by an interpretive framework that is primarily conceptual, and in which the ideas of the *Lao-tzu* are matched, explained, traced to more fundamental principles, and further expanded. It is no accident that the concept of "principle" occupies such a crucial role in Wang Pi's commentary. Compared with Ho-shang Kung's referential mode of understanding, Wang Pi's hermeneutical model is essentially *etiological*.

To conclude this analysis, I suggest that we take a careful look at chapter 50 of the *Lao-tzu*. This is an extremely difficult chapter; but the difficulty itself is instructive. The openness of the original text gives rise to differences in the two commentaries that cannot be satisfactorily explained if their hermeneutical structure remains hidden. The text reads:

1. Coming into life and going into death.
2. The companions of life are ten-three (*shih yu san*); the companions of death are ten-three.
3. Men whose lives move toward the land of death are [also] ten-three.
4. Why is this so?
5. Because of their excessive striving for life.
6. I have heard that one who is good at preserving life,
7. while traveling on land will not encounter wild buffaloes and tigers;
8. while fighting will not [be touched by] avoid weapons of war.
9. The wild buffalo is unable to butt its horns (against him); the tiger is unable to put its claws (on him); weapons of war are unable (to find a place in him) to receive their blades.
10. Why is this so?
11. Because in him there is no place for death.[31]

The textual differences between the two versions are those in lines 3 and 8, where Wang Pi's version is enclosed in square brackets. Because the expression *shih yu san* is interpreted differently by Wang Pi and Ho-shang Kung, a "neutral" reading is adopted here. The commentaries read:

Wang Pi	*Ho-shang Kung*

Wang Pi

1) Coming into the land of life, and going into the land of death.

2–11) "Ten-three" is like saying three out of ten. Those who take the way of life and follow life to the utmost number three out of ten. Those who take the way of death and follow death to the utmost also number three out of ten. And if the people strive excessively for life, they will end up being in the land of no life. One who is good at preserving life, does not take the striving for life as the basis of his life. Thus there is no place for death. There is no instrument more harmful than weapons of war, and there is no animal more harmful than wild buffaloes and tigers. If one can render weapons of war unable (to find a place in him) to receive their blades, and tigers and wild buffaloes unable (to find a place in him) to put their claws and horns, he is indeed one who is not bound by *desires*. How could he have any place for death? Worms (of the sea) find the deep to be shallow, and dig their holes in it. Eagles find the mountain to be low, and build their nests on top of it.[32] Arrows cannot get to them, and nets cannot reach them. Then they can be said to dwell in a place with no death. But in the end, lured by sweet bait,

Ho-shang Kung

1) "Coming into life" means that feelings and desires depart from the five viscera.[34] The *hun* soul is settled and the *p'o* soul is tranquil; therefore one lives. "Going into death" means that feelings and desires enter into the chest. The essence and spirit are burdened and confused; therefore one dies.

2) This means that things of life and death number thirteen each. They are called the nine openings and the four gates. In order to have life: the eyes do not perversely see; the ears do not perversely hear; the nose does not perversely smell; the mouth does not perversely speak; the hands do not perversely touch; the feet do not perversely walk; the essence is not perversely used. With respect to death, it is the opposite.[35]

3) In the quest for life, active striving leads to the opposite: the thirteen will die.

4) This raises the question why striving leads to death.

5) The reason striving leads to death is that too much store is set on matters of seeking life. One goes contrary to the Way and opposes heaven; one acts perversely and loses the thread (of Tao).

they enter into the land of no life. Is this not the case of striving excessively for life? *Therefore* if things are not separated from their root by their longings, and if their true nature is not corrupted by desires, although they walk into battles they will not be hurt, and traveling on land they will not be attacked. The infant can provide a model and should be valued. How true![33]

6) "Preserve" means to nourish.

7) He naturally keeps far away from them, and harm will not reach him.

8) He is not fond of fighting to kill people.

9) He who nourishes life, tigers and wild buffaloes cannot harm, and weapons of war cannot touch.

10) This raises the question why tigers, wild buffaloes, and weapons of war do not harm him.

11) Because he does not violate the thirteen places of death. This means that spirits will protect him, and these things do not dare to harm him.[36]

Ho-shang Kung's commentary on chapter 50 requires little explanation. The expression *shih yu san* was first interpreted by Han Fei-tzu to mean the nine openings (eyes, ears, nostrils, mouth, genitals, and anus) and the four limbs, which make thirteen.[37] The "four gates" probably refer to the four limbs, judging from the commentary on line 2, although according to the Han commentator Kao Yu the term means the ears, eyes, heart, and mouth in the *Huai-nan tzu*.[38] Clearly, for Ho-shang Kung, what is said cannot be understood if the external referents are not identified. In a sense, Ho-shang Kung is also very much a "realist." Although the sage is protected by guardian spirits, the reason he will not meet with wild animals is that he invariably avoids danger. He will not be harmed by weapons of war because he does not engage in battles at all.

Wang Pi and Ho-shang Kung agree that desires, which lead to striving and death, form the antithesis of "Tao-ist" self-cultivation. Yet Wang Pi's interpretation is structured along entirely different lines. Wang Pi's main commentary on chapter 50 begins with a close reading of the text. The reading of *shih yu san* as "thirteen," however, has meaning only in a "referential" hermeneutical universe. As a rough statistical count, the *Lao-tzu* is here seen to be making a general observation about the human condition as a whole. The real argument is introduced with the idea that the man of Tao is not fettered by desires. Considerable care is put into explaining the notion of "deathlessness," by way of analogy, and how it is related to the argument as a whole. The analysis culminates with the "therefore," which concludes that the root or true nature of things must be protected. This is what the *Lao-tzu* "really" means, according to Wang Pi. It is an "etiological" reading in the sense that the meaning of words is traced on a conceptual level to more fundamental "causes." Meaning, as it is reflected in Wang Pi's commentary, is always mediated by language, to be found in relation to other words and ideas.

Conclusion

If this study has made the Wang Pi and the Ho-shang Kung commentaries better understood, its objective will have been achieved. They represent, to me, two comprehensive visions of Tao, similar and yet different. Standing within the same hermeneutical boundaries, they cannot but share fundamental interests and presuppositions. Operating with a different hermeneutical model, they cannot but see different things in the *Lao-tzu*.

The similarity between the two is captured well by the assessment of Tu Kuang-t'ing. Like Ho-shang Kung, Wang Pi too seeks to explain the Way "of governing the family and the country." Because spirituality is never divorced from ethics, both commentaries are not only descriptive, but prescriptive also. There is no disagreement that the *Lao-tzu* describes the origin and profound order of the universe. This order, moreover, has a direct bearing on the nature and destiny of human beings, and for this reason must be carefully preserved. This is why the *Lao-tzu*, and other "classics" also, are so important. The primary text has already pointed to the Way; the task of the commentator is to "re-mind" and "in-form" anew the readers of the wonder of Tao and its implications for human living. The contemplation of Tao is always *purposive*; it describes a mode of being and a way of action that would ideally safeguard the world from falling into chaos and disharmony.[39]

If Wang Pi's commentary appears more "philosophical," it is because of the hermeneutical perspective from which it views the *Lao-tzu*. The play of ideas resembles later conceptions of the nature of philosophic discourse. Looking back several centuries later, Lu Te-ming was no doubt impressed by Wang Pi's understanding of "non-being," unmatched by other commentators up to the T'ang dynasty. Thus, in his words, Wang Pi "alone attained the essential insight of emptiness and nothingness." Thus, Tu Kuang-t'ing also recognized that the Wang Pi commentary is focused on "the Way of ultimate emptiness and nonaction." Indeed, it may even be suggested that Wang Pi has helped to initiate a new mode of intellectual inquiry in the history of Chinese thought.

The Ho-shang Kung commentary, on the other hand, is clearly rooted in the Han ethos. The cosmological framework and the application of Huang-lao thought betray its indebtedness to Han thinking. This is true on the hermeneutical level as well, for interpretation itself is historical; it cannot but be informed by the assumptions, ideas, and aspirations that together constitute the world of the interpreter. From the *Han Fei-tzu* in the pre-Han period to the *Huai-nan tzu* and other Han works, we see how the referentiality of meaning is affirmed and applied to the understanding of the *Lao-tzu* and other classics. The Ho-shang Kung commentary is firmly planted in this tradition. By the time of Wang Pi, however, this mode of understanding was no longer immune to criticism, as questions of meaning were raised by a new generation of interpreters. As I have shown, Wang Pi's criticism of Han scholarship, especially with respect to the interpretation of the *I-ching*, is precisely centered on the referentiality of meaning that earlier commentators took for granted. In this sense, what Wang Pi has helped to initiate can be described as a hermeneutical revolt against traditional interpretations of the classsics. We must not forget that Wang Pi has emphasized the notion of "forgetting the words and images" in his interpretation of the *I-ching*. This presupposes a hermeneutical ideal that seeks to transcend the means of interpretation in an act of understanding that encompasses the subject under investigation as a whole. Wang Pi is always aiming at the ground or "essence" of a given phenomenon, as opposed to other correlated phenomena. It is in this sense that I understand Tu Tao-chien's statement that there were a "Han Lao-tzu" and a "Chin Lao-tzu," both reflecting the spirit of their age. The emergence of the latter, however, did not lead to the demise of the former; rather, both helped to shape the subsequent development of Chinese thought. The implication for *Lao-tzu* studies is that different interpretations can be assessed in terms of their affinity to either one of these alternatives. In this regard, this study may serve to establish the basic groundwork for a history of interpretations of the *Tao-te ching*.

From the hermeneutical perspective, the two commentaries are thus important to our understanding of the development of Chinese intellectual history. At the same time, I am equally convinced that Confucius's dictum—"I transmit but do not innovate" (*Lun-yü*, 7.1)—can be applied to both Wang Pi and Ho-shang Kung. This does not take away the individual genius of the two commentators, or that of Confucius for that matter; and it does not contradict the claim that Wang Pi has contributed to the rise of a new mode of thought. What it shows is that the meaning of the *Lao-tzu* is always primary, for it concerns the meaning of the Way itself. What is new in their commentaries can be understood only in terms of their interaction with the old. The ideal of Tao transcends human "innovation." It would be less than just to disregard their self-understanding as commentators, or to undermine the seriousness of their attempt to revitalize the rule of the Way.

The genius of Ho-shang Kung's commentary, it seems to me, lies in the completeness of its vision. The meaning of the *Lao-tzu* is fully mapped out, objectified, which is then able to serve as a concrete guide for the quest for Tao. The genius of Wang Pi's commentary, on the other hand, lies in the openness of its vision. The meaning of the *Lao-tzu* is gathered, dialectically, into a few all-encompassing concepts, which themselves invite further elaboration and reinterpretation. In this way, Wang Pi's insight has thus laid the foundation of later, including Neo-Confucian, thought. When coupled with the fact that the Ho-shang Kung commentary was later appropriated by the Taoist religion, it is easy to see how the two commentaries have come to represent the locus of "philosophical Taoism" and "religious Taoism."

When the Ho-shang Kung commentary became a part of the Taoist religion, its political ideal was no longer relevant. When Wang Pi's ideas were further developed, the interaction between the commentary and the *Lao-tzu* faded into oblivion. Indeed, it was only when the ideas were lifted from their original context that they were able to form elements of a philosophic system. But this subsequent development cannot be read back into the commentaries themselves. It is, in other words, anachronistic to oppose the two commentaries in terms of a struggle between "philosophical Taoism" and "religious Taoism."

These terms have value only when the Taoist religion was fully established, and cannot be applied to Wang Pi and Ho-shang Kung, or to the *Lao-tzu* itself. As is well known, it was during the Han dynasty that the notion of a "Taoist" school first arose, when such historians as Ssu-ma T'an (d. 110 B.C.) and Liu Hsiang (79–8 B.C.) organized various currents of thought neatly into separate "schools." "Taoism," at that time, was essentially identified with the Huang-lao tradition. In the *Han-shu* we still find "Taoism" (*Tao-chia*) being defined as "the art of 'facing south' for the ruler of men"; that is to say, the art of rulership based on the doctrine of "nonaction."[40] In the Six Dynasties period, with the appearance of new interpretations of the *Lao-tzu*, this definition could no longer do justice to the many facets of Taoism. In the subsequent search for a Taoist identity, one may then speak of two general views that began to rival one another as the "true" heir to the teachings of the *Lao-tzu*. But in the final analysis, it was not until after the Ho-shang Kung, *Hsiang-erh*, and Wang Pi commentaries made their mark that the Taoist tradition fully acquired a dual identity, which led to the development of the two forms of Taoism. Viewed in this light, the early *Lao-tzu* commentaries are indeed crucial to our understanding of the history of Taoism.

No doubt, this is but a suggestion, a possible agenda for another study. In this work, I hope I have shown that the unity of spirituality and ethics that characterizes the Wang Pi and Ho-shang Kung commentaries defies compartmentalization into different "Taoist" schools. For our two commentators, there is only one unified tradition—the tradition of Tao as transmitted by the sages. Ultimately, the vision of Tao in their commentaries is grounded in a reinterpretation of tradition.

Notes

Abbreviations

ch.   *chüan*

HY: *Tao-tsang tzu-mu yin-te.* Harvard-Yenching Institute Sinological Index Series, no. 25

SPPY: *Ssu-pu pei-yao*

SPTK: *Ssu-pu ts'ung-k'an*

TSCC: *Ts'ung-shu chi-ch'eng ch'u-pien*

TT: *Tao-tsang*

WCPC: *Wu-ch'iu pei-chai Lao-tzu chi-ch'eng ch'u-pien*

Preface

1. David Tracy, *The Analogical Imagination: Christian Theology and the Culture of Pluralism* (New York: Crossroad, 1981), p. 108.

2. Ibid.; see also Tracy's more recent work, *Plurality and Ambiguity: Hermeneutics, Religion, Hope* (New York: Harper and Row, 1987), p. 12.

3. "Master Ch'eng" refers to Ch'eng Hao (1032–1085) or Ch'eng I (1033–1107), two of the most important Neo-Confucian thinkers; as cited in

Chu Hsi (1130–1200), *Ssu-shu chi-chu* (Collected Commentaries on the Four Books), SPPY, Preface to the *Lun-yü* commentary, p. 4a.

4. Jonathan Z. Smith, " 'Narratives into Problems': The College Introductory Course and the Study of Religion," *Journal of the American Academy of Religion*, 56 (1988): 728; see also p. 732, n. 6.

Introduction

1. Wing-tsit Chan, trans., *The Way of Lao-Tzu (Tao-te ching)* (Indianapolis: Bobbs-Merrill, 1963; reprint, 1981), p. 77.

2. Wolfgang Bauer, *China and the Search for Happiness*, trans. Michael Shaw (New York: Seabury, 1976), p. xiii.

3. As Shima Kunio has pointed out, while there are a number of sayings that remind us of the *Lao-tzu* in the older, "inner" chapters of the *Chuang-tzu*, direct quotations are found only in the later, "outer" and "miscellaneous" chapters. See Shima Kunio, *Rōshi kōsei* (The *Lao-tzu* Critically Collated) (Tokyo: Kyūkoshoin, 1973), p. 3. The *Chuang-tzu* is a composite work, the earliest parts of which may be dated to the fourth century B.C. See A. C. Graham, trans., *Chuang-tzu: The Seven Inner Chapters* (London: George Allen and Unwin, 1981), pp. 27–29, for a general account of the structure of the work. Also see Graham's more detailed discussion in "How Much of *Chuang Tzu* Did Chuang Tzu Write?," in *Studies in Classical Chinese Thought*, ed. Henry Rosemont, Jr., and Benjamin I. Schwartz, *Journal of the American Academy of Religion Thematic Issue*, 47, 3 (September 1979): 459–501. The *Huai-nan tzu* is traditionally dated to the second century B.C. References to the *Lao-tzu* found in this work are discussed in Shima Kunio, pp. 4–5; on the date and authorship of the *Huai-nan tzu*, see Charles Le Blanc, *Huai-nan tzu: Philosophical Synthesis in Early Han Thought* (Hong Kong: Hong Kong University Press, 1985), pp. 21–52.

4. *Han Fei-tzu*, chaps. 20 and 21. The former is entitled *Chieh-lao* (Explaining the *Lao-tzu*); it comments extensively on chaps. 38, 58, 59, 60, 46, discusses the nature of Tao generally with reference to chaps. 1 and 14, and concludes with a commentary on chaps. 25, 50, 67, 53, and 54. The latter is entitled *Yü-lao* (Illustrating the *Lao-tzu*), and relates selected passages from some 13 chapters to "historical" incidents. It begins, for example, with a discussion of chapter 46 of the *Lao-tzu*. On the phrase, "There is no greater calamity than not being content," the *Han Fei-tzu* explains: "Chih-po (of the state of Chin) annexed the territories of Fan and Chung-hsing, and proceeded to attack Chao. Han and Wei rebelled against Chih-po, whose army thus suffered defeat at Chin-yang. Chih-po himself died to the east of Kao-liang, and his territory was divided (by Chao, Wei, and Han). His skull was even painted (by Chao) and made into a wine vessel. Thus, it is said,

'There is no greater calamity than not being content.' " *Han Fei-tzu* (SPPY; reprinted, Taipei: Chung-hua shu-chü, 1982), 7.1a. See also Shima Kunio, *Rōshi kōsei*, p. 52, nn. 7–8. Cf. Ch'en Ku-ying, *Lao-tzu chin-chu chin-i* (New Annotated Edition of the *Lao-tzu*) (Taipei: Shang-wu, 1960; reprint, 1981), pp. 271–73; and the special study by Chang Su-chen, *Han Fei Chieh-lao Yü-lao yen-chiu* (A Study of the *Chieh-lao* and *Yü-lao* Chapters of the *Han Fei-tzu*) (Taipei, 1976). The various illustrations used by Han Fei-tzu to explain the *Lao-tzu* can usually be found in other sources also; but historicity is of course a much more complex problem.

5. *Han-shu, chüan* 30 (Peking: Chung-hua shu-chü, 1962; reprint, 1983), p. 1729. The four are *Lao-tzu Lin-shih ching-chuan* (The *Lao-tzu* Classic as Transmitted by Master Lin) in four sections (*p'ien*), *Lao-tzu Fu-shih ching-shuo* (by Master Fu) in thirty-seven sections, *Lao-tzu Hsü-shih ching-shuo* (by Master Hsü) in six, and Liu Hsiang, *Shuo Lao-tzu* in four sections. With the exception of Liu Hsiang (79–8 B.C.), nothing is known of the other commentators. All quotations from the dynastic histories are from the Chung-hua edition, and will be identified by their *chüan* and page numbers.

6. This refers to Yen Tsun's (styled Chün-p'ing) *Tao-te chih-kuei lun* (On the Essence of the Way and Virtue) or *Lao-tzu chih-kuei*. Yen Ling-feng has rigorously defended its authenticity; see the Introduction to his edition of this work (WCPC; Taipei: I-wen, 1965). Cf. Wang Chung-min, *Lao-tzu k'ao* (Catalogue of Commentaries on the *Lao-tzu*) (Peking, 1927; reprint, Taipei, 1981), pp. 34–44, in which all the relevant bibliographic records and comments on this work are listed. According to Wang, the current version of the *Lao-tzu chih-kuei* is a forgery made sometime during the Yüan (1260–1368) and Ming (1368–1644) dynasties. For a general discussion of this work, see also Isabelle Robinet, *Les Commentaires du Tao To King jusqu'au VIIe Siècle* (Paris: Presses Universitaires de France, 1977), pp. 11–23. There is also a *Lao-tzu chu* (Commentary on the *Lao-tzu*) in 2 *chüan* attributed to Yen Tsun; but only a number of quotations have survived. These are collected by Yen Ling-feng and included in his massive collection of *Lao-tzu* commentaries (WCPC; Taipei, 1965).

7. On this work, see chapter 3, below, nn. 90–92.

8. See, e.g., Chu Ch'ien-chih, *Lao-tzu chiao-shih* (The *Lao-tzu* Collated and Explained) (Peking: Chung-hua shu-chü, 1963; reprint, 1980), p. 2; Shima Kunio, *Rōshi kōsei*, p. 25.

9. See especially Jao Tsung-i, "Wu Chien-heng erh-nien Su Tan hsieh-pen Tao-te ching ts'an-chüan k'ao-cheng" ("The Su Tan Manuscript Fragment of the *Tao-te ching* (A.D. 270)"), in *Journal of Oriental Studies* (Hong Kong), 2, 1 (January 1955): 1–71. The importance of the Ho-shang Kung commentary is brought out very clearly in this excellent study. According

to Jao, the *Su Tan* manuscript also belongs to the Ho-shang Kung textual family. Further details on the place of the Ho-shang Kung commentary in the Taoist religion will be provided in Chapter 3, pp. 113–16.

10. Eduard Erkes, trans., *Ho-shang-kung's Commentary on Lao-tse* (Ascona, Switzerland: Artibus Asiae, 1950; reprint, 1958). This annotated translation originally appeared in *Artibus Asiae*, 8, 2–4 (1945): 121–96; 9, 1–3 (1946): 197–220; and 12, 3 (1949): 221–51. Although in recent years some scholars have shown signs of interest, there is yet no special study on the Ho-shang Kung commentary available in a Western language. See the general discussion in Wing-tsit Chan, trans., *The Way of Lao Tzu*, pp. 78–81. See also Anna Seidel, *La Divinisation de Lao Tseu dans le Taoisme des Han* (Paris: École Française d'Extrême-Orient, 1969), pp. 32–34, which is especially good on the legend of Ho-shang Kung; Seidel's discussion of the Huang-lao tradition as a whole is also very helpful, and will be discussed later. Isabelle Robinet, *Les Commentaires du Tao To King* (Paris, 1977), pp. 24–39, provides an insightful analysis of the major ideas of the Ho-shang Kung commentary. This is the most comprehensive study of Ho-shang Kung in a Western language to date. Finally, there is also the long footnote by Paul Pelliot, "Autour d'une Traduction Sanscrite du Tao To King," in *T'oung Pao*, 13 (1912): 366–70, n. 1. Pelliot's discussion is particularly helpful in its careful identification and discussion of the main sources.

11. Cheng Ch'eng-hai, *Lao-tzu Ho-shang Kung chu chiao-li* (Collated Edition of the Ho-shang Kung Commentary) (Taipei: Chung-hua shu-chü, 1971). See also Cheng's *Lao-tzu Ho-shang Kung chu su-cheng* (The Ho-shang Kung Commentary Explained) (Taipei: Hua-cheng shu-chü, 1978), which is more concerned with interpreting the text itself. The work of Wang Chung-min, *Lao-tzu k'ao* (Taipei, 1981), pp. 20–32, is again very important for it catalogues most of the traditional comments on the Ho-shang Kung commentary. There is also a short but important discussion on the Ho-shang Kung commentary in Ma Hsü-lun, *Lao-tzu chiao-ku* (Peking, 1956; reprint, Hong Kong, 1965), pp. 1–3. Longer discussions can be found in T'ang Wen-po (1943), Ku Fang (1982), Wang Ming (1984), and Chin Ch'un-feng (1987). These articles are especially concerned with the date and authorship of the commentary.

12. Paul J. Lin, *A Translation of Lao Tzu's Tao Te Ching and Wang Pi's Commentary*, Michigan Papers in Chinese Studies, 30 (Ann Arbor: Center for Chinese Studies, University of Michigan, 1977). See also n. 2 to chap. 1, below. Ariane Rump, trans., in collaboration with Wing-tsit Chan, *Commentary on the Lao-tzu by Wang Pi*, Monographs of the Society for Asian and Comparative Philosophy, 6 (Honolulu: University Press of Hawaii, 1979).

13. Tu Tao-chien, *Hsüan-ching yüan-chih fa-hui* (An Elaboration of the Original Meaning of the Profound Classic) (TT 391; HY 703), B:11.10a. This

is an interpretive work distinct from Tu's commentary on the *Lao-tzu*, entitled *Tao-te hsüan-ching yüan-chih*.

14. A. Rump and W. T. Chan, *Commentary on the Lao Tzu by Wang Pi*, p. xxvi. Cf. Wing-tsit Chan, *The Way of Lao Tzu*, pp. 80–81.

15. Lu Te-ming, *Ching-tien shih-wen* (Explanation of the Classics) (TSCC; Shanghai: Shang-wu 1936), Preface, 1:53.

16. On the meaning of *hsüan* and the "profound learning" movement, see chap. 1, pp. 25ff.

17. As translated in William Hung, "A Bibliographical Controversy at the T'ang Court A.D. 719," in *Harvard Journal of Asiatic Studies*, 20 (1957): 78. The *Han-shu*, as indicated earlier (n. 5, above), has actually listed four titles. Liu Chih-chi probably regarded only the first three to be "commentaries" in the proper sense, for they are identified by their lineage and refer to the *Lao-tzu* as a "classic" (*ching*).

18. The text of the edict is translated in Hung, "Controversy," p. 74. On Hsüan-tsung's own commentary, see the excellent studies by Liu Ts'un-yan, especially "Tao-tsang pen san-sheng chu Tao-te ching chih te-shih" (Strength and Weakness of the Commentaries on the *Tao-te ching* by Three Emperors in the Taoist Canon), in *Chung Chi hsüeh-pao* (Hong Kong), 9, 1 (November 1969): 1–9.

19. Hung, ibid., p. 74.

20. Hung, ibid., p. 81; substantially modified. The Chinese texts are listed in Hung, p. 126, n. 110. The *Wen-yüan ying-hua* version does not have the reference to Ku Huan, who was a major 5th-century A.D. Taoist leader. The terms "bellow-like vacuity" and "mysterious female" refer to chaps. 5 and 6 of the *Lao-tzu*.

21. Major figures and events involved in this response are discussed in Hung, pp. 80, 82, and 126, n. 111.

22. Lu Hsi-sheng, *Tao-te chen-ching chuan* (Commentary on the True Classic of the Way and Virtue), Preface (WCPC; Taipei: I-wen, 1965), 1b.

23. Fan's comments will be discussed later in chap. 1, p. 22.

24. Tu Kuang-t'ing, *Tao-te chen-ching kuang sheng-i* (TT 441; HY 725), 5.12a–12b.

25. Tu Tao-chien, *Hsüan-ching*, p. 10a. It should be noted that the Wang Pi and the Ho-shang Kung commentaries cannot be identified with the first two categories respectively, since the context makes plain that for

Tu the Ho-shang Kung commentary preceded and gave rise to the other types of interpretation. The new categories too are interesting, and point to the proliferation of interpretations beginning perhaps with the T'ang and Sung dynasties.

26. Chiao Hung, *Lao-tzu i* (TSCC; Shanghai: Shang-wu, 1940), pp. 176–78.

27. Tu Kuang-t'ing, *Tao-te*, p. 12b. On the school of *Ch'ung-hsüan*, see especially I. Robinet, *Les Commentaires du Tao To King* (Paris, 1977), part II, pp. 96ff. The entire second part of Robinet's work is devoted to this school of *Lao-tzu* commentators.

28. See especially H. G. Gadamer, *Truth and Method*, 2nd ed., trans. William Glen-Doepel, ed. John Cumming and Garrett Barden (London: Sheed and Ward, 1979). Paul Ricoeur's many studies on hermeneutics have been collected into *Hermeneutics and the Human Sciences*, ed. and trans. John B. Thompson (Cambridge: Cambridge University Press, 1981). For an attempt to apply hermeneutics to Chinese thought, see my "Philosophical Hermeneutics and the *Analects:* The Paradigm of Tradition," *Philosophy East and West*, 34, 4 (October 1984): 421–36.

Chapter One

1. *San-kuo chih, Wei shu* (Records of the Wei Dynasty), ch. 28 (Peking: Chung-hua shu-chü, 1959; reprint, 1982), pp. 795–96. The reason why Wang Pi does not have an "official" biography is significant and will be discussed later.

2. Paul J. Lin, *A Translation of Lao Tzu's Tao Te Ching and Wang Pi's Commentary* (Ann Arbor: Center for Chinese Studies, University of Michigan, 1977), pp. 151–53. As far as the biography is concerned, except for a few mistakes to be noted later, the translation is generally reliable. However, Lin's study as a whole has met with some fairly strong criticism. See the reviews by William G. Boltz and Wing-tsit Chan in *Journal of the American Oriental Society*, 100, 1 (1980): 84–86, and *Philosophy East and West*, 29, 3 (1979): 357–60, respectively. There is also a good discussion of Wang Pi's life and work in Chung-yue Chang, "The Metaphysics of Wang Pi (226–249)," Ph.D. dissertation, University of Pennsylvania, 1979, chap. 1. Unless otherwise stated, all translations from the original Chinese are my own.

3. See Richard B. Mather, trans., *Shih-shuo Hsin-yü: A New Account of Tales of the World*, by Liu I-ch'ing *with Commentary by Liu Chün* (Minneapolis: University of Minnesota Press, 1976), esp. chap. 4. For the Chinese text, I am using the modern critical edition by Yang Yung, *Shih-shuo hsin-yü chiao-chien* (Hong Kong: Ta-chung shu-chü, 1969). See also the helpful index com-

piled by William Hung, Harvard-Yenching Institute Sinological Index Series, 12 (Peking, 1933). All relevant biographical materials can be found in the exhaustive study by Hatano Tarō, *Rōshi dōtokukyō kenkyū* (Studies on the *Lao-tzu*) (Tokyo, 1979), pp. 8–10, 487–96. See n. 80, below, for further detail on this work. Biographical records of Wang Pi are also collected in Lou Yü-lieh, *Wang Pi chi chiao-shih* (Collected Works of Wang Pi, Collated and Annotated) (Peking: Chung-hua, 1980), 2:639–48.

4. *San-kuo chih*, 28:795; cf. Paul Lin, *Translation*, p. 151. The quotation is from the *Lun-yü* (Analects), 9.22. I hesitate to use inclusive language in my translations because the patriarchal structure of traditional Chinese society should be recognized.

5. *Shih-shuo hsin-yü*, chap. 4, no. 6. Richard Mather, trans., p. 95; modified. This passage is also translated in Arthur F. Wright, "Review of A. A. Petrov, *Wang Pi: His Place in the History of Chinese Philosophy*," in *Harvard Journal of Asiatic Studies*, 10 (1947): 81. Cf. *Shih-shuo*, 2.50.

6. Commentary to *Shih-shuo hsin-yü*, 4.6, by Liu Chün (styled, Hsiao-piao, fl. 500 A.D.), citing the now lost *Wen-chang hsü-lu*; cf. Mather, *Shih-shuo*, p. 95. Cf. *Chin-shu* (Peking, 1974), 36:1067, 82:2149.

7. The original reads *pu-chih ming-kao* and is here rendered in the sense of *pu-chih kao-ming*, i.e., not cultivating fame and high office; see also *San-kuo chih*, 27:746, for similar usage. Cf. Lin, *Translation*, p. 151, where the phrase is translated "indifferent, and in great repute."

8. There is also a shorter account of Wang Pi's life in the *Shih-shuo hsin-yü*, preserved by the commentator Liu Chün, entitled the "Separate Biography of Wang Pi" (*Pi pieh-chuan*). It is, however, essentially the same as the account by Ho Shao, and in fact may be a summary of the latter. The "Separate Biography" concludes: "During the Cheng-shih era (249), he [Wang Pi] was dismissed in a public scandal (the fall of Ts'ao Shuang's clique), and in the fall of the same year, falling prey to a pestilence, died in his twenty-fourth year. Ssu-ma Shih sighed over him for days, crying, as Confucius did ⸺t the death of [his favorite disciple] Yen Hui, 'Heaven is destroying me!' [*Lun-yü*, 11.8]. Thus was his loss lamented by the eminent and wise." As translated in Mather, *Shih-shuo*, p. 95. The fact that Wang Pi's death so moved a leading member of the Ssu-ma clan is indeed a telling indication of the high regard his contemporaries had for him. The conflict between Ts'ao Shuang and Ssu-ma I will be discussed shortly.

9. *San-Kuo chih*, 28: 796; *Shih-shuo hsin-yü*, ibid. Mather, p. 95; Lin, p. 153. Mather's translation of the phrase *pu-shih wu-ch'ing*, "insensitive to the feelings of others," is certainly superior to Lin's "did not understand the nature of things," which is both vague and potentially misleading.

10. Mou Tsung-san, *Ts'ai-hsing yü hsüan-li* (Talent, Human Nature, and Transcendental Principles) 3rd ed. (Taipei: Hsüeh-sheng shu-chü, 1974), pp. 79–81.

11. A. F. Wright, "Review of A. A. Petrov," *Harvard Journal of Asiatic Studies*, 10 (1947): 87.

12. Ibid.

13. *Wei Chin hsüan-hsüeh chung ti she-hui cheng-chih ssu-hsiang lüeh-lun* (Brief Discussion of the Social and Political Thought of the Movement of Profound Discourse in the Wei and Chin Dynasties) (Shanghai: Shanghai jen-min ch'u-pan-she, n.d.). According to T'ang, this work is based on one of his pre-1949 lectures, revised and published by Jen Chi-yü. See T'ang Yung-t'ung, *Wei Chin hsüan-hsüeh lun-kao* (Outlines of the Movement of Profound Learning in the Wei-Chin Period) (Peking: Jen-min ch'u-pan-she, 1957), p. 2.

14. T'ang Yung-t'ung and Jen Chi-yü (n. 13, above), pp. 24–25.

15. The conversation between Wang Pi and P'ei Hui at this meeting will be discussed later. For a concise discussion of the government system of the Wei dynasty, see Han Kuo-p'an, *Wei Chin Nan Pei Ch'ao shih-kang* (Outline History of the Wei, Chin, Southern and Northern Dynasties) (Peking: Jen-min ch'u-pan-she, 1983), pp. 39–40.

16. According to Mather (n. 3., above), p. 593, Wang Pi was "executed" in 249 together with Ts'ao Shuang and his followers. No reference, however, is given to support this claim.

17. Noma Kazunori, "Ō Hitsu ni tsuite: rōshi chū o megutte" (On Wang Pi: A Study of His *Lao-tzu* Commentary), in *Tōhō shūkyō*, 59 (May 1982): 66–83. Noma's argument is especially centered around the question of the appointment of officials, i.e., in the context of the so-called nine grade (*chiu-pen*) system.

18. See Sawada Takio, "Rōshi Ō Hitsu chū kōsatsu ichihan" (Study of Wang Pi's Commentary on the *Lao-tzu*), in *Tōyō bunka*, 62 (March 1982): 1–28. Sawada's article is chiefly concerned with Wang Pi's *Lao-tzu chih-lüeh* (Brief Outline of the *Lao-tzu*), long lost but now identified with an anonymous work found in the Taoist Canon (see n. 79, below). Sawada's discussion of the history of this text here is especially helpful.

19. On this whole question, I have especially benefited from the work of T'ang Ch'ang-ju. See his "Chiu-pen chung-cheng chih-tu shih-shih" (Preliminary Discussion of the "Nine Grade" Government System), in his *Wei Chin Nan Pei Ch'ao shih lun-ts'ung* (Collected Essays on the History of the Wei, Chin, Southern and Northern Dynasties) (Peking: San-lien shu-

tien, 1955; reprint, 1978), pp. 85–126; and "Tung Han mo-ch'i ti ta-hsing ming-shih" (Famous Literati from Distinguished Families at the End of the Eastern Han Dynasty), in *Wei Chin Nan Pei Ch'ao shih lun shih-i* (Essays on the History of the Wei Chin Nan Pei Ch'ao, Third Collection) (Peking: Chung-hua shu-chü, 1983), pp. 25–52.

20. Ch'en Yin-k'o, "T'ao Yüan-ming chih ssu-hsiang yü ch'ing-t'an chih kuan-hsi" (The Thought of T'ao Yüan-ming and its Relation to the Movement of Pure Conversation), in *Ch'en Yin-k'o hsien-sheng lun-wen chi* (Collected Essays of Ch'en Yin-k'o) (Taipei, 1974), 2:310–16; and "Shu Shih-shuo hsin-yü wen-hsüeh-lei Chung Hui tsan Ssu-pen lun shih pi t'iao hou" (On the Entry Concerning Chung Hui's *Ssu-pen lun* in the *Shih-shuo hsin-yü*), ibid., 2:601–7. T'ang Yung-t'ung and Jen Chi-yü (n. 13, above), pp. 18–19, 34–35, passim. Also see Lü K'ai, *Wei Chin hsüan-hsüeh hsi-p'ing* (Study of the Movement of Profound Learning in the Wei and Chin Dynasties) (Taipei, 1980), pp. 81–86. The general discussion in Ch'ien Mu, "Lüeh-lun Wei Chin Nan Pei Ch'ao hsüeh-shu wen-fa yü tang-shih men-ti chih kuan-hsi" (Brief Discussion of the Scholarship and Culture in the Wei, Chin, Southern and Northern Dynasties Period and their Relation to the Emphasis on Family Background), in his *Chung-kuo hsüeh-shu ssu-hsiang-shih lun-ts'ung* (Collected Essays on Chinese Intellectual History) (Taipei, 1977), 3:134–99, is also helpful.

21. *Shih-shuo hsin-yü chiao-chien*, ed. Yang Yung (Hong Kong, 1969), p. 210, n. 1. Mather (n. 3, above), p. 140. This reference is again supplied by the early 6th-century commentator Liu Chün. The work of Yüan Hung is no longer extant; for an introductory study of this major Eastern Chin figure, see Ch'ien Mu, "Yüan Hung cheng-lun yü shih-hsüeh" (Yüan Hung's Politics and Historiography), in his *Chung-kuo hsüeh-shu ssu-hsiang-shih lun-ts'ung*, 3:77–96.

22. Yang Yung, p. 205. As trans. in Mather, p. 137; modified. The source here is quoting from a now lost historical treatise, *Hsü Chin yang-ch'iu* (Continuation of the Annals of Chin), by the 5th-century scholar T'an Tao-luan. The original *Chin Yang-ch'iu*, also lost, was written by the famous 4th-century historian Sun Sheng; see n. 51, below. There is a modern reconstructed edition of these two works compiled by T'ang Ch'iu (Shanghai: Shang-wu, 1937). On the question of *ming-shih*, famous men of letters, literati, or gentlemen, see Mou Tsung-san, *Ts'ai-hsing yü hsüan-li* (Taipei, 1974), pp. 67–84. Also see Chou Shao-hsien, *Wei Chin ch'ing-t'an shu-lun* (Study of the Pure Conversation Movement in the Wei-Chin Period) (Taipei: Shang-wu, 1966), pp. 134–56.

23. *Chin-shu*, ch. 43 (Peking: Chung-hua shu-chü, 1974), p. 1236; read *wu* for *wu-wei*, as emended by the Chung-hua editors, p. 1248, n. 9. Cf. Jung Chao-tsu, *Wei Chin ti tzu-jan chu-i* (Naturalism in the Wei and Chin Dynasties) (Shanghai: Shang-wu, 1935), p. 11.

24. 4.18; in *Wen-hsin tiao-lung chu-ting*, ed. Chang li-chai (Taipei: Cheng-chung shu-chü., 1967; reprint, 1979), p. 183. Cf. Vincent Shih, trans., *The Literary Mind and the Carving of Dragons by Liu Hsieh. A Study of Thought and Pattern in Chinese Literature* (New York: Columbia University Press, 1959), p. 102. For a brief introduction to this work, see James J. Y. Liu, *Chinese Theories of Literature* (Chicago: University of Chicago Press, 1975), pp. 21–25, 122–26, passim. The name "Fu Chia" can also be pronounced "Fu Ku," as in Shih, and Lin, *Translation*, p. 151; Mather, however, has opted for "Chia," which I believe to be the older reading, on the basis of the entry in the earliest extant Chinese dictionary *Shuo-wen chieh-tzu* by Hsü Shen (fl. ca. 100 A.D.). In the biography of Fu Chia in the *San-kuo chih*, 21:624, we read that Fu was highly critical of Ho Yen, describing him as a cunning opportunist. In addition to their intellectual differences, there were evidently political differences as well. Cf. n. 32, below.

25. *Chin-shu*, 75:1984; biography of Fan Ning.

26. On these two schools, see Fung Yu-lan, *A History of Chinese Philosophy*, vol. 1, *The Period of the Philosophers*, trans. Derk Bodde (Princeton: Princeton University Press, 1952; reprint, 1983), chaps. 9 and 13. Also see Benjamin I. Schwartz, *The World of Thought in Ancient China* (Cambridge: Harvard University Press, 1985), chap. 8. While the concern with logical analysis is important, it should be recognized that there is a political dimension to *Ming-chia* teachings as well, especially in relation to the "promulgations of laws." See Hsiao-po Wang and Leo Chang, *The Philosophical Foundations of Han Fei's Political Theory* (Honolulu: University of Hawaii Press, 1986), p. 62.

27. Here I am especially indebted to the work of Hsü Fu-kuan; see his *Liang-Han ssu-hsiang-shih* (Intellectual History of the Han Period), vol. 2 (Hong Kong: Chinese University of Hong Kong Press, 1975). The first three chapters of John B. Henderson's recent work, *The Development and Decline of Chinese Cosmology* (New York: Columbia University Press, 1984), are also helpful.

28. See Hsü Fu-kuan, ibid., p. 284; cf. Fung Yu-lan, *A History of Chinese Philosophy*, vol. 2, *The Period of Classical Learning*, trans. Derk Bodde (Princeton: Princeton University Press, 1953; reprint, 1983), p. 47.

29. Wang Fu, *Ch'ien-fu lun*, 2.7 (SPTK; reprint, Shanghai: Shang-wu, 1965), p. 10, bottom; as cited in T'ang Yung-t'ung, *Wei Chin hsüan-hsüeh lun-kao* (Peking, 1957), pp. 13, 18. See also the other references from such major Han thinkers as Chung-ch'ang T'ung (ca. 179–219) and Ts'ui Shih (ca. 103–170) cited by T'ang here. Cf. Mou Tsung-san, *Ts'ai-hsing yü hsüan-li*, pp. 231–38, which is basically a close rehearsing of T'ang's argument. Wang Fu's thesis here is based on the belief that the government of the "sage-

king" (*sheng-wang*) revolves around the "hundred officials," whose whole aim is to conform to "heaven," govern the "earth," and provide for the ordinary people.

30. Robert Henricks, "Hsi K'ang and Argumentation in the Wei," in *Journal of Chinese Philosophy*, 8 (1981): 169–223; see esp. pp. 208–9, n. 10, where a survey of scholarly opinions on the meaning of *ming-li* is provided. On the relationship between *Ming-chia* and *ming-li*, see Mou Tsung-san (n. 29, above), pp. 254–85. Cf. T'ang Chün-i, "Lun Chung-kuo che-hsüeh ssu-hsiang-shih chung 'Li' chih liu-i" (On the Six Meanings of the Concept of "Principle" in the History of Chinese Philosophy), in *Hsin-ya hsüeh-pao* (New Asia Journal), 1, 1 (1955): 65–75, on which Mou's argument is based.

31. As cited in Liu Ta-chieh, *Wei Chin ssu-hsiang lun* (On the Thought of the Wei-Chin Period) (Shanghai, 1939; reprint, Taipei: Chung-hua, 1979), p. 2. This reprint does not mention the name of the author. Cf. *Ts'ao Ts'ao chi* (Collected Works of Ts'ao Ts'ao) (Peking: Chung-hua shu-chü, 1959; reprint, 1962), p. 49; see pp. 32 and 40–41 also for similar statements made by Ts'ao.

32. The question of "talent" and "nature," *ts'ai-hsing*, is a difficult one, and the few details outlined below are meant only to highlight certain aspects of the problem. On this question, see Chu Hsiao-ha, "Ts'ai-hsing Ssu-pen-lun ts'e-i" ("Views on Discussion on Treatise of Talent and Human Nature in Four Standpoints" [author's trans.]), in *Journal of Oriental Studies* (Hong Kong), 18 (1980): 207–24; English ab., 129–30. Also see Chou Shao-hsien, *Wei Chin ch'ing-t'an shu-lun* (Taipei, 1966), pp. 32–48; Lü K'ai, *Wei Chin hsüan-hsüeh hsi-p'ing* (Taipei, 1980), pp. 115–26; and T'ang Ch'ang-ju, "Wei Chin ts'ai-hsing lun ti cheng-chih yi-i" (The Political Dimension of the Discourse on Talent and Nature in the Wei-Chin Period), in his *Wei Chin Nan Pei Ch'ao shih lun-ts'ung* (Peking, 1978), pp. 298–310.

In Wang Pi's biography, we find that P'ei Hui was "immediately amazed" as soon as he saw the young Wang Pi. (See Lin, *Translation*, p. 151.) In the biography of Chung Hui (225–264), to take but one more example, we are told that Chiang Chi (fl. ca. 250) had found the then five-year-old Chung Hui to be "extraordinary" at first sight (*San-kuo chih*, 28:784). These are more than literary embellishments; they presuppose a common understanding that "talent" could be recognized immediately by the expert. Indeed, according to Chiang Chi, to know a person it is enough to look at his eyes (*San-kuo chih*, ibid.).

This is one way of approaching the question of *ts'ai-hsing*; that is, by emphasizing the methods of identifying good talent. Another, more philosophical way, would be to focus on the relation between "talent" and "nature." Is "talent" an inborn quality? Is it different from one's original "nature," to be acquired later in life? These questions were hotly debated during the Wei period; and Wang Pi knew the major participants. From the biography of Chung Hui, who rivaled Wang Pi's reputation as the bright young star of the day, we learn that he was especially noted for his view on this subject. In the biography of Fu Chia, who as we have seen was famous for his discourse on "names and principles," it is said that "Fu Chia often discussed the identity and difference of talent and nature, and Chung Hui had collected these views and examined them" (*San-kuo chih*, 21:627). In the *Shih-shuo hsin-yü*, we are told that Chung Hui wrote a *Ssu-pen lun* (On Four Fundamental Views) in which four main approaches to the question of *ts'ai-hsing* are discussed; namely, (1) that "talent" and "nature" are identical (*t'ung*); (2) that they are different (*i*); (3) that they are integrated or harmonious (*ho*); and (4) that they are separate (*li*) (chap. 4, no. 5, n. 1. In Yang Yung, pp. 149–50; Mather, p. 94). Chung Hui himself has argued for the third view, whereas Fu Chia is said to have championed the first.

Besides Fu Chia and Chung Hui, according to this entry, Li Feng (d. 254) has argued for the second view, and Wang Kuang (ca. 210–251), the fourth. The *Ssu-pen lun* is no longer extant; but judging from other entries in the *Shih-shuo hsin-yü* (for example, chap. 4, nos. 34, 51, and 60), it was a major topic of discussion at the time; see especially Yang Yung's extended note on this point (p. 150, n. 1). As Ch'en Yin-k'o has shown (see n. 20, above), whereas Fu Chia and Chung Hui were followers of the Ssu-ma clan, both Wang Kuang and Li Feng died at the hand of Ssu-ma I; the identity-harmony or difference-separateness of "talent" and "nature" seems indeed to have a political basis. If "nature" is the determining factor, then people from "lesser" families, such as Ts'ao Ts'ao and his clan, surely have no "right" to lay claim to the throne! From this same perspective, we also see more clearly the difference between Fu Chia and Ho Yen mentioned earlier (n. 24).

33. On the relationship between *ch'ing-i* and *ch'ing-t'an*, and the rise of the movement of "pure conversation" in general, see T'ang Ch'ang-ju, "Ch'ing-t'an yü ch'ing-i," in *Wei Chin Nan Pei ch'ao shih lun-ts'ung*, pp. 289–97. According to T'ang, the phenomenon of *ch'ing-i*, from which "pure conversation" sprang, was also concerned with the question of judging human characters, i.e., with the question of *ts'ai-hsing*. See also Ho Ch'ang-ch'ün, *Wei Chin ch'ing-t'an ssu-hsiang ch'u-lun* (Preliminary Study of the Thought of Pure Conversation in the Wei-Chin Period) (Shanghai: Shang-wu, 1947), pp. 25–53; Fan Shou-k'ang, *Wei Chin chih ch'ing-t'an* (The Pure Conversation Movement of the Wei-Chin Period) (Shanghai: Shang-wu, 1936), chap. 1. Fan's work and the study by Liu Ta-chieh cited in n. 31, above, are both very much indebted to the pioneering work of Aoki Masaru, *Seidan* (Tokyo: Iwanami shoten, 1934). In particular, Aoki's classification of three major currents within the *ch'ing-t'an* movement—(1) *ming-li*, (2) *hsi-hsüan*, and (3) *k'ang-ta*—is basically taken over without modification. The first group, as we have seen, refers to those who are interested in the question of "talent" and "nature"; the second has to do with Wang Pi and Ho Yen especially;

and the third, with slightly later figures such as Juan Chi and Hsi K'ang. According to Mou Tsung-san, *hsüan-lun* is a form of discussion on "names and principles" (*ming-li*) as well; but instead of the question of *ts'ai-hsing*, it is focused on the relation between being and non-being, on the "mysterious," "profound" nature of Tao. See his *Ts'ai-hsing yü hsüan-li*, pp. 239–43. In this regard, while *ch'ing-t'an* does represent a shift of intellectual focus in the Cheng-shih period, its rootedness in tradition should not be overlooked. According to Arthur Wright, such terms as *hsüan-lun* and *ch'ing-t'an* refer also to the techniques of argumentation. See his "Review of A. A. Petrov," p. 80; and R. Henricks, "Hsi K'ang and Argumentation," p. 207, n. 4. Both the method and the content of *hsüan-lun* are thus important to an understanding of the "pure conversation" movement.

34. On the origin and development of these cosmological ideas, see esp. Hsü Fu-kuan, *Chung-kuo jen-hsing-lun shih. Hsien-Ch'in p'ien* (History of Chinese Philosophy of Human Nature. The Pre-Ch'in Period) (Taipei: Shang-wu, 1969; reprint, 1984), pp. 509–87. Also see Joseph Needham, *Science and Civilisation in China*, vol. 2, *History of Scientific Thought* (Cambridge: Cambridge University Press, 1956), pp. 232–65; and John Henderson (n. 27, above). Henderson's terms, "correlative cosmology" and "cosmological resonance," derived from Needham's "correlative thinking," are most appropriate in describing the Han cosmological system. The literature on this subject is immense; for a brief introductory study, see my "Metallurgy, Cosmology, Knowledge: The Chinese Experience" (joint author with U. Franklin and J. Berthrong), *Journal of Chinese Philosophy*, 12 (1985): 333–69.

35. In *Han-shu, ch. 30, I-wen chih* (Bibliographical section). The passage begins with a brief description of the "six arts," *liu-i*, i.e., the six classics. Of the six, according to Pan Ku, the *I-ching* reigns supreme. However, by that time the five phases cosmological theory has radically affected the interpretation of the classics. Then Pan Ku goes on to say, the scholars of old "mastered one classic in three years; they aimed at preserving the basic meaning and only read the texts to their own enjoyment. Hence though the time they spent on these texts was not long, the virtue they developed as a result was significant; by thirty they would have completely mastered the five classics. In more recent times, however, not only the transmission of the classics has strayed from the main, learned scholars also have failed to understand the meaning of 'hearing widely' and 'leaving out the doubtful' [the reference is to *Lun-yü*, 2.18; see D. C. Lau, trans., *Confucius. The Analects* (Penguin Classics, 1979), p. 65]. Instead, these latter-day scholars apply themselves to precious details, play on fine words and clever arguments, which destroy the form and substance of the classics; a discussion of a text of five words can take up to twenty or thirty thousand words. And newcomers to the world of learning all seek to outdo their predecessors. Thus even if one began working on one classic from childhood, it would be old

age when one could truly speak about it. These scholars keep to their own field, and criticize what they do not see, ending their lives in ignorance; this indeed is the one big problem with which scholars are confronted." This insightful commentary shows eloquently and forcefully the deteriorating state of Han scholarship. See *Han-shu* 30:1723. Cf. *The Cambridge History of China*, vol. 1, *The Ch'in and Han Empires*, ed. Denis Twitchett and Michael Loewe (Cambridge: Cambridge University Press, 1986), p. 758. Elsewhere, the *Han-shu* (88:3620) explains that this sad development came about when scholarship became the road to office and material rewards. This general assessment was widely accepted by later scholars. The bibliographical section of the *Sui-shu* (History of the Sui Dynasty) (Peking: Chung-hua shu-chü, 1982), 32:947–48, e.g., clearly supports this. See also Ku Shih, *Han-shu i-wen-chih chiang-su* (On the Bibliographical Section of the History of the Former Han Dynasty), 2nd ed. (Shanghai: Shang-wu, 1935), p. 97, for further supporting references.

36. See, e.g., Etienne Balazs. "Nihilistic Revolt or Mystical Escapism: Currents of Thought in China During the Third Century A.D.," in his *Chinese Civilization and Bureaucracy. Variations on a Theme*, trans. Hope M. Wright, ed. A. F. Wright (New Haven and London: Yale University Press, 1964), pp. 226–54.

37. Yü Ying-shih, "Han-Chin chih-chi shih chih hsin-tzu-chüeh yü hsin-ssu-ch'ao" (The New Self-Understanding and New Movement of Thought of the Literati at the Han-Chin Transition), in *Hsin-ya hsüeh-pao*, 4, 1 (August 1959): 25–144. This excellent study of the intellectual history of 3rd-century China moves from the collective consciousness of the literati that emerged toward the end of the Han dynasty, to the deepening self-understanding of the literati, and finally to a consideration of the new current of thought associated with the phenomenon of "pure conversation." In my view, the second section is particularly illuminating. See also Yü's more recent essay, "Individualism and the Neo-Taoist Movement in Wei-Chin China," in Donald Munro, ed., *Individualism and Holism: Studies in Confucian and Taoist Values* (Ann Arbor: Center for Chinese Studies, University of Michigan, 1985), pp. 121–55. Cf. Ho Ch'i-min, *Wei Chin ssu-hsiang yü t'an-feng* (On Wei-Chin Thought and Style) (Taipei: Shang-wu, 1967), which is also comparatively less historically oriented in its approach to the "pure conversation" movement.

38. The earliest extant reference to these three texts collectively as the *san-hsüan* is probably in the 6th-century work *Yen-shih chia-hsün* (Family Instructions of the Yen Clan); as cited in Lü K'ai, *Wei Chin hsüan-hsüeh hsi-p'ing* (Taipei, 1980), p. 113, n. 8. For the original, I have checked the SPPY edition (Taipei: Chung-hua shu-chü, 1979), 3.8, p. 14a; the passage here explicitly links the "three profound treatises" to the movement of "pure conversation." Earlier in this section, the author, Yen Chih-t'ui (531–595), also

provides us with short character assessments of the major Wei figures; e.g., he admonishes his family not to be too proud or overcompetitive, like Wang Pi who because of his tendency to laugh at others died young (p. 12a).

39. See the passing reference to Ho Yen's life and work in the *San-kuo chih*, 9:292. According to the *Shih-shuo hsin-yü*, 4, nos. 7 and 10, Ho Yen was working on (4.10) or had just finished writing (4.7) a full commentary on the *Lao-tzu*, when he went to see Wang Pi and discovered the superiority of the latter's commentary. Thus, he wrote or turned what he had already written into the shorter "Discourse" instead. See Yang Yung (n. 21, above), pp. 152–53; Mather (n. 3, above), pp. 95–97.

40. *San-kuo chih*, 28:786.

41. Ibid., 28:795. I shall discuss the various writings of Wang Pi later in this chapter.

42. Ibid. Cf. Lin (n. 2, above), p. 151. This incident is also recorded in the *Shih-shuo hsin-yü*, 4.8; see Mather (n. 3, above), p. 96. The concluding statement in the *San-kuo chih* is probably corrupt; literally it reads, "Thus [Lao-tzu] constantly spoke of the inadequacies of *wu*," which does not agree with the general context. Most scholars prefer to take the alternate reading in the *Shih-shuo hsin-yü*, which replaces the word *wu* by *ch'i*, i.e., "its," referring to *yu*. See T'ang Yung-t'ung, "Wang Pi chih Chou-i Lun-yü hsin-i," in *Wei Chin hsüan-hsüeh lun-kao* (Peking, 1957), p. 96. This essay is also available in English; see Walter Liebenthal, trans., "Wang Pi's New Interpretation of the *I-ching* and *Lun-yü*," in *Harvard Journal of Asiatic Studies*, 10 (1947): 124–61; the translation of this particular passage, though the accompanying Chinese characters are mismatched, is interesting in its use of the terms "Thingness" and "No-thingness' for *yu* and *wu*, respectively (p. 152). See also Fung Yu-lan, *History*, 2:170, which follows the *Shih-shuo* version; and Rump and Chan, *Commentary on the Lao-tzu by Wang Pi*, p. xiv. For a philosophical discussion of the notion of *wu* in relation to the sage, see Tu Wei-ming, "Wei Chin hsüan-hsüeh chung ti t'i-yen ssu-hsiang: Shih-lun Wang Pi 'Sheng-jen t'i-wu' i kuan-lien ti che-hsüeh yi-i" (The Concept of Experience in the Movement of Profound Discourse during the Wei-Chin Period: Preliminary Discussion of the Philosophical Significance of Wang Pi's Notion of the "Sage's Embodying Non-being"), in *Ming-pao yüeh-k'an*, 18, 9 (1983): 21–26. The emphasis here is on experiential knowledge; cf. Mou Tsung-san, *Ts'ai-hsing yü hsüan-li*, pp. 119–24. I shall return to this issue and the notion of *wu* in the next chapter.

43. As quoted in T'ang Yung-t'ung, *Wei Chin hsüan-hsüeh lun-kao*, p. 96; Liebenthal, trans., p. 151. This reference is taken from a letter by Chou Yung, styled Yen-lun, preserved in the Buddhist collection *Hung-ming chi*.

However, the precise edition is not identified. In both the SPTK and SPPY editions, the text reads "Cheng Ho" instead of "Wang Ho," i.e., Wang Pi and Ho Yen. See Chou Yung (d. 485), "Ch'ung-ta Chang Ch'ang-shih shu" (Second Reply to Chang Jung [444–497]), in *Hung-ming chi*, ch. 6, SPTK (Shanghai: Shang-wu, 1965), p. 82; SPPY (Taipei: Chung-hua shu-chü, 1983), p. 12b. The *Taishō shinshū daizōkyō* (Tripitaka, Taishō Version. Tokyo, 1924, vol. 52, p. 40, bottom) edition likewise has "Cheng," but in the footnote it is emended to "Wang" on the basis of the "Sung" edition and the Japanese Palace edition (= the "Old Sung" edition). Because the two characters look similar, an error in copying could easily have been made; but I have not yet been able to determine the precise reason for this inconsistency. More generally, here, Wang Pi and Ho Yen were merely following the long established tradition of ranking Confucius on the same level as Yao, Shun, and other "sage-kings" of ancient times. In the *Han-shu*, e.g., there is a section entitled "Ku-chin jen-wu piao" (List of Ancient and Contemporary Figures) in which individuals are ranked in a scale of nine. Whereas Confucius occupies the top rank, that of the sage (*sheng-jen*), Lao-tzu is even below Confucius's chief disciples in the fourth rank, *chung-shang*, "above average." And Chuang-tzu fares even worse. Together with Hui Shih, the "logician," and Shen Pu-hai, the "legalist," Chuang-tzu is "below average" in the 6th rank. See *Han-shu*, 20:924, 926, 947.

44. *Lun-yü*, 6.26; in D. C. Lau, trans., *Confucius. The Analects* (Harmondsworth: Penguin Books, 1979), p. 85 (6.28); Lau's system of numbering the text is slightly different from the standard one.

45. This is why, for example, Wing-tsit Chan has added in parenthesis that Confucius's visit to Nan-tzu was made "in an attempt to influence her to persuade the duke to effect political reform." See Chan, *A Source Book in Chinese Philosophy* (Princeton: Princeton University Press, 1963; reprint, 1973), p. 31. More specifically, this interpretation is supported by K'ung An-kuo's (ca. 156–74 B.C.) commentary on this passage of the *Lun-yü*. See Huang K'an's subcommentary on Ho Yen's commentary on the *Analects*, *Lun-yü chi-chieh i-su* (TSCC; Shanghai: Shang-wu, 1937), p. 81. See also James Legge, trans., *The Chinese Classics*, vol. 1, *Confucius. Confucian Analects, the Great Learning, and the Doctrine of the Mean* (Oxford: Clarendon Press, 1893; reprint, New York: Dover, 1971), p. 193, n. 26, for a few of the traditional Confucian attempts to explain this incident. For the *Shih-chi* account, see *ch.* 47, the Biography of Confucius (SPPY; reprint, Taipei: Chung-hua shu-chü, 1970), pp. 9b–10a.

46. Wang Ch'ung, *Lun-heng* (Balanced Inquiries), "Wen K'ung p'ien" (Essay on Questioning Confucius) (Hong Kong: Kuang-chih shu-chü, reprint, n.d.), part 1, p. 95. The term "skeptical" is Needham's; see his *Science and Civilisation in China*, vol. 2, esp. pp. 368–86. Wing-tsit Chan, however, prefers to describe Wang Ch'ung as a "naturalist"; the translation

of the title, "Balanced Inquiries," is also Chan's. See *Source Book*, pp. 292–93. Wang Ch'ung's work is divided into two *chüan*, with a total of 84 essays; the one in question here is essay no. 28. Cf. Alfred Forke, trans., *Lun-heng*, part 1, *Philosophical Essays of Wang Ch'ung*, 2nd ed. (New York: Paragon Book Gallery, 1962), pp. 403–5. Also see the interesting article by S. Englert and R. Ptak, "Nan-tzu, Or Why Heaven Did Not Crush Confucius," in *Journal of the American Oriental Society*, 106 (1986): 679–86, in which the reliability of traditional accounts of Nan-tzu is questioned.

47. Commentary on the *Lun-yü*, in Lou Yü-lieh, ed., *Wang Pi chi chiao-shih* (Collected Works of Wang Pi, Collated and Annotated) (Peking: Chung-hua shu-chü, 1980), 2:623. The original of this passage can be found in the work of Huang K'an, cited in n. 45, above.

48. According to Rudolf Wagner, the T'ang Emperor T'ai-tsung ordered state sacrifices for the 28 "worthies" in 648. See his "Wang Bi: 'The Structure of the Laozi's Pointers' (*Laozi weizhi lilüe*)," in *T'oung Pao*, 72 (1986), p. 92, n. 1. Fan Ning is also among this group of Confucian "worthies"; he would have been surprised, to say the least, to find Wang Pi sharing this honor with him.

49. See Lou Yü-lieh (n. 47, above), 1:11. This story is relatively well known. During the reign of T'ang T'ai-tsung (r. 627–649), the five classics were reedited and standardized. This process began with the establishment of the texts of the five classics by Yen Shih-ku (581–645), completed around 630. A few years later, again under imperial order, K'ung Ying-ta (574–648) and his team established the *Wu-ching cheng-i*, the "official" texts and commentaries of the five classics, completed in 642. Wang Pi's commentary on the *I-ching* was chosen, at the expense of the more traditional and perhaps more "prestigious" commentary by Cheng Hsüan. See, e.g., Lü Ssu-mien, *Sui-T'ang Wu-tai shih* (History of the Sui, T'ang, and Five Dynasties Period) (Shanghai: Chung-hua shu-chü, 1959; reprint, 1961), 2:1260ff. Indeed, according to K'ung Ying-ta, "Transmitters of the *I-ching* have competed with one another to expound their own traditions; only the commentary by Wang Pi of the Wei period surpasses both ancient and contemporary works." As quoted in Jung Chao-tsu, *Wei Chin ti tzu-jan chu-i* (Shanghai, 1935), p. 7. In the bibliographical section of the *Sui-shu*, Wang Pi's commentary on the *I-ching* and that of Wang Su (195–256) are singled out as pivotal works of the Wei period, which led to the supremacy of the school of Pi Chih in *I-ching* studies. Moreover, a Liang dynasty (6th-century) work entitled *Chou-i lan Wang Fu-ssu yi* (Critique of Wang Pi's Understanding of the Book of Changes) is also listed; this may be taken as another indication of the importance of Wang Pi's work on the *I-ching*. See *Sui-shu*, 32:911–13.

50. See *San-kuo chih*, 28:796. Read *wu*, "mistaken," for *wu*, "understand." This emendation is first suggested by T'ang Yung-t'ung, on the ba-

sis of the general context and other versions, in *Wei Chin hsüan-hsüeh lun-kao*, p. 63; cf. Lou Yü-lieh, 2:643, n. 30; Mou Tsung-san, p. 87. Paul Lin, however, is apparently not aware of this, as he retains the corrupt reading (p. 153).

51. Ibid. The original source of Sun Sheng's comment is not clear. However, see the excellent study by Hachiya Kunio, "Son Sei no rekishihyō to rōshi hihan" (Sun Sheng's Historiography and Critique of Lao-tzu), in *Tōyō bunka kenkyūjo kiyō* (Tokyo University: Memoirs of the Institute of Oriental Culture), 81 (March 1980): 19–177, esp. 146–77. This work is not only a technical study on an important 4th-century thinker, but a good contribution to our understanding of Wei-Chin intellectual history in general as well.

52. As translated in Fung Yu-lan, *History*, 2:181–82. Cf. James Legge, trans., *The Sacred Books of China*, vol. 16, *The Texts of Confucianism*, part II, *The Yi King* (Oxford: Oxford University Press, 1882; reprint, 1968), p. 365; and Richard Wilhelm, trans., *The I Ching or Book of Changes*, trans. into English by Cary F. Baynes, Bollingen Series, 19 (Princeton: Princeton University Press, 1979), p. 310. In this latter, the phrase "*ta-yen chih-shu*" is rendered as the "number of the total," which is simpler; however, the word *yen* here is perhaps best taken in the sense of "expand," "extend," or "spread." For the Chinese text, see Lou, (n. 49, above), 2:547.

53. My translation. Cf. Fung, *History*, 2:182; Lou, 2:547–48. This passage, which probably forms a part of Wang Pi's lost work entitled *Ta-yen lun*, is preserved by Han K'ang-po; see my discussion on p. 37. See also Paul Lin, pp. 154–55, n. 7. Lin's translation here, however, is rather poor; the last line, which he translates "Besides, the ultimate of things (49) must be manifested from their source (the One)," is especially weak. The original reads: *ku ch'ang yü yu-wu chih-chi, erh pi-ming ch'i so-yu chih tsung yeh.* On the notion of "One," see the interesting article by Bernard S. Solomon, " 'One is No Number' in China and the West," in *Harvard Journal of Asiatic Studies*, 17 (1954): 253–60. On Wang Pi's understanding of the *I-ching*, see esp. T'ang Yung-t'ung, *Wei Chin hsüan-hsüeh lun-kao*, pp. 84–102. The brief discussion in Jung Chao-tsu, *Wei Chin ti tzu-jan chu-i* (Shanghai, 1935), pp. 15–26, is also good.

54. As quoted by the T'ang commentator K'ung Ying-ta; see *Chou-i chi-chieh* (Collected Commentaries on the Book of Changes), ed. Sun Hsing-yen (1753–1818) (TSCC, 10 vols.; Shanghai: Shang-wu, 1936), 8: 574. According to T'ang Yung-t'ung, ibid., p. 65, the phrase *T'ien chih sheng-ch'i*, which I have translated "heaven produces *ch'i*," is probably a corrupt version of *T'ien-i chu-ch'i*, which is related to the religious worship of the polar star. Cf. Ho Ch'ang-chün, *Wei Chin ch'ing-t'an ssu-hsiang ch'u-lun* (Shanghai, 1947), pp. 9–11, 60–63, 76–78. In English, Ch'i-yün Ch'en's article, "A Confucian

Magnate's Idea of Political Violence: Hsün Shuang's (128–190 A.D.) Interpretation of the Book of Changes," *T'oung Pao*, 54 (1968): 73–115, contains useful information regarding *I-ching* studies in the Han dynasty in general.

55. *Chou-i chi-chieh* (TSCC), 8:574.

56. Ibid., 8:574–75, 577–78. Cf. Legge, trans., *The Yi King*, p. 365, and Wilhelm (n. 52, above), p. 310. I have also consulted the TSCC edition of the *Chou-i Cheng-chu* (The Book of Changes with Cheng Hsüan's Commentary) (Shanghai: Shang-wu, 1936), Supplement, pp. 62–63. The original thesis in the *I-ching* has to do with the idea that 1, 3, 5, 7, 9 form the numbers of heaven, while 2, 4, 6, 8, 10 make up the numbers of the earth. The total amounts to 55. Some scholars would argue that the number of the "Great Expansion" itself should be 55 as well; i.e., 50 being a corrupt version. See for example, Kao Heng, *Chou-i ta-chuan chin-chu* (A New Annotated Edition of the Book of Changes) (Shantung: Ch'i Lu shu-she, 1979), pp. 524–25.

57. See Legge, ibid., p. 368, note on paragraph 51; cf. Wilhelm, p. 311.

58. As cited in Wang Ying-lin (1223–1296), *K'un-hsüeh chi-wen, ch.* 18 (Taipei: Shih-chieh shu-chü, 1963), p. 930. Another T'ang commentator notes that "whereas Cheng (Hsüan) frequently combined heavenly phenomena (in his interpretation of the *I-ching*), Wang (Pi) focused entirely on explaining human affairs." Li Ting-tso, *Chou-i chi-chieh*, in *Chou-i chu-su chi pu-ch'eng* (Taipei: Shih-chieh shu-chü, 1968), Preface, p. 2.

59. Tu Wei-ming, "Ts'ung 'Yi' tao 'Yen' " ("From Implied Meaning to Expressed Form"), in *Chung-hua wen-shih lun-ts'ung*, first series (Shanghai: Ku-chi ch'u-pan-she, 1981), pp. 255–61. In this work, Tu attempts to bring modern hermeneutics, especially the work of Paul Ricoeur, to bear on a discussion of Chinese philosophy.

60. *Chou-i chi-chieh* (TSCC), 8:604–5; cf. Legge, pp. 376–77; Wilhelm, p. 322.

61. Ibid.

62. Lou, *Wang Pi chi chiao-shih*, 2:609; my italics. Cf. Fung Yu-lan, *History*, 2:184, and Hellmut Wilhelm, *Eight Lectures on the I Ching*, trans. C. Baynes, Bollingen Series, 62 (Princeton: Princeton University Press, 1973), p. 87. In the former, the translation is incomplete.

63. Lou, ibid.; cf. Hellmut Wilhelm, ibid. The metaphor is of course from the famous passage in the *Chuang-tzu*, chap. 26; see Burton Watson trans., *The Complete Works of Chuang-tzu* (New York and London: Columbia University Press, 1968), p. 302. The word *t'i*, in this context, does not mean

a "trail," as Wilhelm takes it, but rather a "trap" or "net"; Watson's "rabbit snare" captures the meaning well.

64. Lou, ibid.

65. Ibid. In particular, Wang Pi strongly criticizes the then common reading of the two trigrams *ch'ien* and *k'un* as referring to the "horse" and the "cow," respectively.

66. Ou-yang Chien, *Yen-chin-i lun*, in Yen K'o-chün, ed., *Ch'üan shang-ku san-tai Ch'in-Han san-kuo liu-ch'ao wen*, ch. 109 (reprinted, Kyoto, 1975), p. 2084. A summary of this treatise is also found in the *Shih-shuo hsin-yü*; see Mather (n. 3 above), p. 103; cf. Fung, *History*, 2:185, where the *Shih-shuo* version is translated.

67. *San-kuo chih*, 10:319–20, n. 2, citing a biography of Hsün Ts'an by Ho Shao. This passage is translated in Henricks, "Hsi K'ang and Argumentation," pp. 171–72, although the source is mistakenly said to be the *Chin Yang-ch'iu*. However, as T'ang Yung-t'ung points out, Hsün Ts'an's view cannot be equated with Wang Pi's without qualification; see his essay "Yen-i chih pien," in *Wei Chin hsüan-hsüeh lun-kao*, pp. 36–37; see also pp. 34–35 where Wang Pi's view on "words" and "meaning" is contrasted with that of Ho Yen, by comparing their interpretation of a particular passage in the *Lun-yü*. According to Henricks (p. 211, n. 19), Hsi K'ang also wrote a *Yen pu chin-i lun*, which is now lost.

68. See *Shih-chi* (SPPY), 63.3a–3b.

69. *San-kuo chih*, 28:795; cf. Paul Lin *Translation*, p. 152; Fung Yu-lan *History*, 2:188.

70. See *Shih-shuo hsin-yü*, 4.57, 17.4; in Yang Yung (n. 21, above), pp. 186, 488, and Mather (n. 3, above), pp. 122, 324. This important topic certainly deserves closer attention than it has so far received; it is all the more interesting since "feelings" appear to be a treasured quality among the literati. That is to say, while the sage was generally regarded as beyond human emotions, "genuine" feelings also seem to have become a symbol signifying the nature of the *ming-shih*. It might be that the notion of the sage had become somewhat remote, and was perhaps even displaced by a different ideal—the more accessible model of the *ming-shih*—by Wei-Chin times. Beyond this conjecture, however, we cannot go into a detailed discussion of this question here.

71. See n. 69, above. The "five feelings" are joy, anger, sorrow, delight, and remorse.

72. T'ang Yung-t'ung, "Hsieh Ling-yün Pien-tsung-lun shu-hou" (Postscript to Hsieh Ling-yün's [385–433] "On Identifying the Distinguishing Features of the Buddhist Schools"), in *Wei Chin hsüan-hsüeh lun-kao*, pp.

112–19. T'ang's thesis here is that as opposed to the "indigenous" view, it was the Buddhists who argued that sagehood or buddhahood could be achieved by human effort. In this regard, I disagree with T'ang's conclusion that Wang Pi also subscribed to the view that sagehood was impossible to achieve.

73. "Tu Jen-wu chih" (On the *Study of Human Abilities* by Liu Shao), in *Wei Chin hsüan-hsüeh lun-kao*, pp. 9–10. There is an English translation of Liu Shao's early 3rd-century work by J. K. Shryock, *The Study of Human Abilities: The Jen-wu chih of Liu Shao*, American Oriental Series, vol. 11 (New Haven: American Oriental Society, 1937; reprint, New York, 1966).

74. Chap. 23, "Keng-sang Ch'u." See Ch'en Ku-ying, *Chuang-tzu chin-chu chin-i* (New Annotated Edition of the Chuang-tzu) (Taipei: Shang-wu, 1975; reprint, 1984), 2:674. Cf. Watson trans., *Complete Works of Chuang-tzu*, p. 259. See also Chou Shao-hsien, *Wei Chin ch'ing-t'an shu-lun* (Taipei, 1966), p. 64.

75. The bibliographical section of the *Sui-shu* first records this work, including a *Lu* (Contents or Records) in one *chüan*. It is catalogued in both the *Chiu T'ang-shu* and *Hsin T'ang-shu*, although the "Contents" is no longer listed. In the *Sung-shih* there is no reference to this work altogether. Thus, Wang Pi's *Collected Works* might still be current when the *Hsin T'ang-shu* was compiled (completed around 1060). Relevant data concerning Wang Pi's writings are found in the *Sui-shu*, ch. 32, 34, and 35, pp. 909, 910, 936, 1000, 1060; *Chiu T'ang-shu*, ch. 46 and 47 (Peking: Chung-hua shu-chü, 1975), pp. 1967, 1968, 1981, 2026, 2028, 2057; *Hsin T'ang-shu*, ch. 57, 59, and 60 (Peking: Chung-hua shu-chü, 1975), pp. 1424, 1443, 1514, 1580.

76. Again, the work on the *Lun-yü* is listed in the *Sui-shu*, *Chiu T'ang-shu*, and *Hsin T'ang-shu*, but not in the *Sung-shih*. While the *Sui-shu* indicates a 3-*chüan* work, the two T'ang histories note that it is in 2 *chüan*. Quotations from this work are found in two subcommentaries on Ho Yen's commentary on the *Lun-yü*, esp. in Huang Kan's "Elucidation" (*I-su*) of Ho Yen's *Lun-yü chi-chieh*.

77. Most current texts, the SPTK ed., for example, contain all three. The *Chou-i lüeh-li* ("Brief Discourse") is also printed separately; there is a commentary on it by the T'ang scholar Hsing T'ao.

78. The *Chou-i ta-yen lun* is mentioned in the two T'ang histories, but not in the earlier *Sui-shu*. There is some confusion as to whether it should be identified with the *Chou-i lüeh-li*. However, I see no reason why Wang Pi could not have written two separate treatises on the *I-ching*.

79. How many shorter treatises on the *Lao-tzu* did Wang Pi write? Although this question does not bear directly on my analysis, it may be useful to clarify some of the confusion. In Wang's biography, we read:

"(Wang) Pi commented on the *Lao-tzu*; for it (he) made an outline (*chih-lüeh*), (which is) highly structured and/or systematic. (He) composed (*chu*) the *Tao lüeh-lun*, commented on the *I-ching*, (both of which) often contain splendid sayings." I have translated this passage quite literally here because the original may appear ambiguous, for it is neither punctuated nor does it identify book titles. Paul Lin, for example, has taken this passage to mean: "Pi's commentary on the *Lao-tzu* provides a concise guide, with systematic arrangement which illumines Tao in terse statements (*chu tao lüeh lun*). His commentary on the *I-ching* frequently has excellent statements" (pp. 152–53). Because of the verb *chu*, "compose" or "author," it is not likely that *Tao lüeh lun* (Brief Discussion of Tao) means "terse statements," which "illumine Tao" in this context. Wing-tsit Chan, for example, has identified it as a text; in Ariane Rump and Wing-tsit Chan trans., *Commentary on the Lao-tzu by Wang Pi*, p. xxviii. Indeed, according to Lou Yü-lieh, the passage here actually refers to four titles; i.e., the *Lao-tzu* commentary, the *I-ching* commentary, the *Tao lüeh-lun*, and a *Chih-lüeh* (Brief Outline); see his *Wang Pi chi chiao-shih*, 2:641. Did Wang Pi, then, write two shorter works on the *Tao-te ching*?

There are numerous references to Wang Pi's "Brief Outline" of the *Lao-tzu* in traditional sources. In the bibliographical section of the *Chiu T'ang-shu*, just after Ho Yen's work on the *Lao-tzu*, we find a *Lao-tzu chih-li-lüeh* in two *chüan* to which no author is assigned. In the *Hsin T'ang-shu* this work is ascribed to Wang Pi. Lu Te-ming mentions also, in the Preface to his *Ching-tien shih-wen* (TSCC; Shanghai: Shang-wu, 1936, 1:53), that in addition to his main commentary Wang Pi wrote a *Lao-tzu chih-lüeh* in one *chüan*. This should be the same as the *Chih-lüeh* mentioned in Wang Pi's biography. Did he write another work with the title of *Tao-lüeh-lun*?

In the *Sung-shih* (ch. 205, *I-wen chih*, IV [Peking: Chung-hua shu-chü, 1977], p. 5177), it is reported that Wang Pi wrote a *Tao-te lüeh-kuei*. However, a few pages later (205:5180) the *Sung-shih* mentions as well a *Lao-tzu chih-li-lüeh* in one *chüan* and adds that the author is unknown. In Ch'eng Ch'iao's (1104–1162), *T'ung-chih*, there is a *Lao-tzu chih-lüeh-li* in two *chüan* ascribed to Wang Pi, and right next to it, an unidentified *Lao-tzu chih-lüeh-lun* (ch. 67, in the *Shih T'ung* edition [Shanghai: Shang-wu reprint, 1935, 20 vols.], 4:787.) In another Sung encyclopedia, the *Wen-hsien t'ung-k'ao* by Ma Tuan-lin (ca. 1254–1323), the title of Wang's work is listed as *Lao-tzu lüeh-lun* in one *chüan* (*Shih T'ung* ed., 12:1730). Here Ma Tuan-lin is primarily relying on Ch'ao Kung-wu (fl. 1150), author of the famous annotated bibliography, *Chün-chai tu-shu-chih*, in which the *Lao-tzu lüeh-lun* is attributed to Wang Pi, listed as having 18 sections, and where a certain "Ching-yü" is quoted to have said that Wang Pi was much better on the *Lao-tzu* than on the *I-ching*. Ching-yü is the literary name of Ch'ao Yüeh-chih (1059–1129) who, as we shall see, was very much responsible for the transmission of the current version of Wang Pi's *Lao-tzu* commentary. It is likely that Ch'ao Kung-wu had firsthand knowledge of the work in question. (See the SPTK edition

[Shanghai: Shang-wu reprint, 1935], 8:4a. This passage is actually included in the Supplement to the *Chün-chai tu-shu-chih* by another Sung scholar, Chao Hsi-pien; but since Ma Tuan-lin quotes directly from "Master Ch'ao," I am satisfied to leave this issue unexplored here.) Finally, the monumental encyclopedia *Yü-hai*, compiled by Wang Ying-lin (1223–1296), also identifies the work of Wang Pi as the *Lao-tzu lüeh-lun* (*ch.* 53, p. 11b; vol. 26 of the 1738, 120-vol. reprint of the Yüan block-cut edition).

The easiest way to deal with these different titles is to regard them as variants of one work. Wing-tsit Chan, for example, has suggested that this may even be considered as the general consensus among most modern scholars today (see Rump and Chan, *Commentary*, pp. xxviii–xxix). To support this view, one may point to the case of Ho Yen's work on the *Lao-tzu*. In both the *Sui-shu* (34:1000) and the *Chiu T'ang-shu* (47:2028), Ho's work is recorded as *Tao-te lun* (Discussion of the Way and Virtue) in two *chüan*. In the *Hsin T'ang-shu* (59:1515), however, it becomes the *Tao-te wen* (Questions on the Way and Virtue). Indeed, in the Sung encyclopedia *Tzu-lüeh* by Kao Ssu-sun (fl. 1185), the title is even changed to *Chih-lüeh-lun* (*Mu chüan*, 1.22a; Hsüeh-ching t'ao-yüan, no. 8, Shanghai: Shang-wu, 1922). In other words, it may be argued that such words as *lun*, *lüeh-lun*, *lüeh-li*, and *chih-lüeh* were fluid terms often used interchangeably before modern times. Although this is entirely possible, I would suggest that the other alternative should not be ignored. As Wang Chung-min has also argued, it is possible that there are two separate works involved here. See his *Lao-tzu k'ao*, pp. 54–55; note that Wang's view is mistakenly described in Rump and Chan, *Commentary*, p. xxix. See also Hsieh Fu-ya (= N.Z. Zia), "Hsien-ts'un Lao-tzu Tao-te ching chu-shih shu-mu k'ao-lüeh" (Brief Bibliographical Study of Existing Commentaries on the *Lao-tzu*), in *Ling-nan hsüeh-pao*, 1, 3 (June 1930), pp. 68–69. Hsieh identifies all these titles as variants of one work, and in a footnote (n. 40) indicates that on the basis of structure and style certain passages in the current version of Wang Pi's commentary on the *Lao-tzu* may have belonged originally to this shorter work.

It seems clear that Wang Pi wrote a *Chih-lüeh-li* or *Chih-li-lüeh*, "brief outline by way of examples or selected passages," on the *Lao-tzu*. The two T'ang histories and the *T'ung-chih* all support this. There is also the passing reference to Wang Pi's "two outlines" (*liang-li*) in the *Wen-hsin tiao-lung*, which presumably refer to two shorter works on the *I-ching* and the *Lao-tzu*. (See Chang Li-chai ed., *Wen-hsin tiao-lung chu-ting* [Taipei, 1979], p. 185.) The unauthored work of the same title in the *Sung-shih* may well be this short outline. By the 14th century, Wang Pi's *Lao-tzu chih-li-lüeh* was probably no longer extant or known.

However, as we have seen, the *Sung-shih* also records a *Tao-te lüeh-kuei* by Wang Pi. Can this be the last surviving trace of the *Tao lüeh-lun* ascribed to Wang Pi in his biography, in the *Yü-hai*, in the *Chün-chai tu-shu-chih*, and in the *Wen-hsien t'ung-k'ao*? They are all consistent in listing the work as having one *chüan*, and Ch'ao Kung-wu's comment seems to indicate familiarity with the work. The *T'ung-chih* has a *Lao-tzu chih-lüeh-lun* as well, though listed as having two *chüan* and unidentified. Just as Wang Pi probably wrote an "outline" on the *I-ching* and a separate treatise on the "Number of the Great Expansion," he might have written two separate works on the *Lao-tzu*, in addition to the main commentary.

In 1937 Wang Wei-ch'eng first drew attention to the fact that the Sung Taoist collection *Yün-chi ch'i-ch'ien* (ch. 1.2b-6a; SPTK) contains a long quotation from an unidentified text entitled *Lao-chün chih-kuei lüeh-li*. The quotation is almost identical to the first half of the anonymous work, *Lao-tzu wei-chih li-lüeh*, found in the *Tao-tsang* (TT 998). Wang Wei-ch'eng then identified this work with Wang Pi's shorter work on the *Lao-tzu*. In 1956 Yen Ling-feng made the same case, and since then this identification has been widely accepted. On the identification of this work, see R. Wagner, "Wang Bi: 'The Structure of the Laozi's Pointers,' " *T'oung Pao*, 72 (1986): 92–99. According to Wing-tsit Chan, however, "the work in question was written on the basis of the commentary [by Wang Pi] by someone who did not quite understand Wang Pi's new philosophical ideas" (Rump and Chan, *Commentary*, p. xxx). Although there is no strong reason to reject the identification, arguments based on style and content ultimately remain inconclusive. Suffice it to say that this work is to be used with caution. Wagner's work contains a translation of this treatise, and so does Chung-yue Chang, "The Metaphysics of Wang Pi," Ph.D. dissertation, University of Pennsylvania, 1979.

80. Takeuchi Yoshio, *Rōshi genshi* (Tokyo: Shimizu kōbundō, 1926; reprint, 1967), p. 71. There is a Chinese translation of this work by Chiang Hsia-an, in his *Hsien-Ch'in ching-chi k'ao* (Studies on Pre-Ch'in Classical Texts) (Shanghai, 1933; reprint, 3 vols. in one, Taipei: Ho-lo t'u-shu ch'u-pan-she, 1975), 2:197–324. Cf. Takeuchi, *Rōshi no kenkyū* (Studies on the *Lao-tzu*) (Tokyo: Kaizosha, 1927). This latter study is more comprehensive as far as the *Lao-tzu* itself is concerned; but the discussion on Wang Pi's commentary, and on Ho-shang Kung's as well, is much fuller in the former. More recently these two studies, along with four shorter essays on the *Lao-tzu*, are reprinted together as vol. 5 of the 10-vol. "Collected Works of Takeuchi." See *Takeuchi Yoshio Zenshū*, vol. 5, *Rōshi hen* (Tokyo: Kadokawa shoten, 1978). This work also contains an appreciative appraisal by Kimura Eiichi, and a bibliographical note on these studies by Kanaya Osamu. See also the very important work by Hatano Tarō, *Rōshi dōtokukyō kenkyū* (Studies on the *Lao-tzu Tao-te ching*) (Tokyo: Kokusho kankōkai, 1979). This is a reprint of Hatano's *Rōshi Ō chū kōsei* (Critical Edition of the Wang Pi Commentary on the *Lao-tzu*), first published in the *Yokohama shiritsu daigaku kiyō* (Journal of the Municipal Yokohama University), Series A, nos. 8 (1952), 11 (1953), and 27 (1954), together with other shorter studies on the subject. This work is invaluable especially in that it has collected virtually all relevant scholarly comments, from traditional Chinese and Japanese sources to modern scholarship, bearing on the Wang Pi commentary. The shorter studies include

supplements to the main work, essays on Wang Pi's commentary in Japanese scholarship, and two general articles on the *Lao-tzu*. For the following discussion, see esp. pp. 10–33, 496–519. There is useful review by Kusuyama Haruki, in *Tōhō shūkyō*, 54 (November 1979): 89–98. The following shorter discussions are also useful: Shima Kunio, *Rōshi kōsei* (The *Lao-tzu* Collated) (Tokyo: Kyūkoshoin, 1973), pp. 9–10; Wang Chung-min, *Lao-tzu k'ao*, pp. 48–54; Rump and Chan, *Commentary*, pp. xxiii–xxviii; and Ma Hsü-lun, *Lao-tzu chiao-ku* (The *Lao-tzu* Collated and Explained) (Peking, 1956; reprint, Hong Kong: T'ai-p'ing shu-chü, 1965), pp. 1–3. This work is the revised edition of Ma's *Lao-tzu ho-ku* (Peking, 1924). With respect to the *Lao-tzu* text that accompanies Wang Pi's commentary, see the good discussion in William Boltz, "The *Lao-tzu* Text that Wang Pi and Ho-shang Kung Never Saw," in *Bulletin of the School of Oriental and African Studies*, 48 (1985): 493–501. On the basis of a close reading of chaps. 1 and 39 especially, Boltz argues that the text that Wang Pi and Ho-shang Kung commented on differs from the current version accompanying their commentaries, but is closer to the Ma-wang-tui *Lao-tzu* manuscripts. For the Ma-wang-tui MSS, see n. 111, below.

81. *Sui-shu*, 34:1000.

82. *Chiu T'ang-shu*, 47:2026. In most texts, the loan word *yüan* is used for *hsüan*; now restored. According to Hsieh Fu-ya, some texts have *miao-yen*, which also means roughly "profound words," but with the added connotation of the "marvelous" or "miraculous." See his "Hsien-ts'un Lao-tzu Tao-te ching chu-shih shu-mu k'ao-lüeh," in *Ling-nan hsüeh-pao*, 1, 3 (1930): 68, n. 39.

83. *Hsin T'ang-shu* 59:1514, 1515.

84. *Sung-shih*, 205:5177.

85. See *Ssu-k'u ch'üan-shu tsung-mu t'i-yao* (Annotated Catalogue of the Complete Four Libraries Collection), ed. Chi Yün et al., *ch.* 28 (Wan-yu wen-k'u edition; Shanghai: Shang-wu, 1935), p. 3032. This extremely important annotated bibliography includes not only the 3,000 and more works collected in the *Ssu-k'u ch'üan-shu*, compiled during the Ch'ien-lung era, but also another 6,000 or so titles known to the editors. On the compilation of the *Ssu-k'u* collection, see Kuo Po-kung, *Ssu-k'u ch'üan-shu tsuan-hsiu-k'ao* (Peking: Shang-wu, 1937). The *Ssu-k'u* text of Wang Pi's commentary discussed here belongs to the private collection of Chi Yün, the chief editor, who presumably wrote this article.

86. Takeuchi Yoshio, *Rōshi genshi*, pp. 62–66.

87. Ibid. For a description of this manuscript, see also Ōfuchi Ninji, *Tonkō Dōkyō* (Taoist Manuscripts from Tun-huang), vol. 1, *Mokuroku hen* (Annotated Catalogue) (Tokyo: Hukubu shoten, 1978), section 3, p. 246. Ac-

cording to Takeuchi, when works on the *Tao-te ching* were collected into the T'ang dynasty Taoist canon, they were probably grouped together and assigned this general title.

88. *Sui-shu*, 34:1002.

89. Hsieh Shou-hao, *Hun-yüan sheng-chi, ch*. 3, in TT 551 (HY 769), p. 20a, quoting from the T'ang scholar Fu I (555–639). The "Undifferentiated Ultimate" here refers to Lao-tzu himself; this is basically a hagiographic work. See also Hatano, *Rōshi dōtokukyō kenkyū*, p. 518.

90. P'eng Ssu, *Tao-te chen-ching chi-chu tsa-shuo* (Collected Sayings on the True Classic of the Way and Virtue), TT 403 (HY 709), 2.30b. This is a supplement to P'eng's own commentary on the *Lao-tzu* (TT 398–402), and is composed of general quotations from prefaces and book notes on the *Tao-te ching*. Quoted in Hatano, ibid., p. 502. Cf. Chiao Hung, *Lao-tzu i* (TSCC; Shanghai: Shang-wu, 1940), p. 175.

91. Tung Ssu-ching, *T'ai-shang Lao-tzu Tao-te ching chi-chieh* (The Divine Classic of the Way and Virtue Collated and Explained) (Lu Hsin-yüan, Shih-wan-chüan lou ts'ung-shu edition, 1877), Preface, p. 4b. This text is also collected in the Taoist canon, TT 393 (HY 705). Quoted in Hatano, ibid., pp. 502–3. In this work, the four versions of Wang Pi's *Lao-tzu* text are given as having 5,683, 5,610, 5,355, and 5,590 characters. The last two are listed under the Ho-shang Kung commentary in the works of P'eng Ssu and Chiao Hung, who both cite Hsieh Shou-hao in this instance. In Hsieh's own work, however, the Ho-shang Kung versions are said to have 5,555 and 5,590 characters. Despite the small discrepancy, 5,355 characters vs. 5,555 characters, the context makes it clear that Tung Ssu-ching was borrowing from an earlier source here.

92. Hung I-hsüan, *Tu-shu ts'ung-lu* (Collected Reading Notes), *ch*. 13 (original block-cut edition, 6 *ts'e*, 1822), vol. 4, p. 1b; as quoted in Hatano, p. 506. The main evidence here is that a quotation from chap. 25 of the Wang Pi commentary in the T'ang Buddhist work *Pien-cheng lun* (Arguments Concerning the Orthodox View) by Fa Lin (fl. 625) does not agree with the current versions of Wang Pi's text.

93. Ch'ien Tseng, *Tu-shu min-ch'iu chi* (Insights Gained from Reading), *ch*. 3 (TSCC; Shanghai: Shang-wu, 1936), p. 80. As quoted in the *Ssu-k'u ch'üan-shu tsung-mu t'i-yao*, 28:3032. According to Wang Chung-min, the *Ssu-k'u* chief editor Chi Yün has misinterpreted Ch'ien's comments here. If punctuated differently, Wang argues, the passage does not suggest that the Wang Pi commentary was no longer extant; rather, it would mean that "according to Master Ch'ien, copies of Wang Pi's commentary were very rare in the Sung dynasty, and it was only after Ch'ao Yüeh-chih and Hsiung K'o had published their versions that it became widely available." See Wang

Chung-min, *Lao-tzu k'ao*, p. 54. In my view, however, Wang's reading here is rather forced. The *Ssu-k'u* reading is supported, for example, by Kuan T'ing-fen (b. 1797), in his collated edition of Ch'ien's work. See the revised edition by Chang Yü, *Tu-shu min-ch'iu chi chiao-cheng*, 3a.14b (original block-print edition, 6 *ts'e*, 1926). Moreover, Ch'ien Tseng clearly did not have the Wang Pi commentary in his collection, as this comment is found under the entry on the Ho-shang kung commentary. Ch'ien is well-known as a careful bibliophile—his work is basically an annotated catalogue of his private collection of some 600 works—he would have been more explicit if he had access to the Wang Pi commentary. The work of Ch'ao Yüeh-chih and Hsiung K'o will be discussed shortly.

94. In the long Preface to the *Ching-tien shih-wen*, Lu writes that among the various *Lao-tzu* commentators, "Wang Fu-ssu alone attained the essential insight of emptiness and nothingness (*hsü-wu*); this present study is based on the Wang text." See *Ching-tien shih-wen, hsü-lu* (TSCC; Shanghai, 1936), 1:53; also repeated in *ch*. 25, 16:1403.

95. *Ssu-k'u ch'üan-shu tsung-mu t'i-yao*, 28:3032. Cf. Chou Chung-fu (1768–1831), *Cheng-t'ang tu-shu chi* (Bibliographical Notes from the Cheng Studio), *ch*. 69 (Taipei: Shih-chieh shu-chü reprint, 1960), 2:8; as cited in Wang Chung-min, *Lao-tzu k'ao*, pp. 51–52. Unfortunately the bulk of the *Yung-lo ta-tien* is now lost; of the original 11,095 *ts'e*, only a fraction survives. As far as Wang Pi's commentary on the *Lao-tzu* is concerned, the second half is no longer extant. See Liu Kuo-chün, "Lao-tzu Wang Pi chu chiao-chi," in *T'u-shu-kuan hsüeh chi-k'an* (Library Science Quarterly), 8, 1 (March 1934): 91, and Ariane Rump and Wing-tsit Chan, *Commentary*, p. xxiv.

96. *Ssu-k'u ch'üan-shu tsung-mu t'i-yao*, 28:3032.

97. TT 373 (HY 690). This work can also be found in Yen Ling-feng's WCPC collection of works on the *Lao-tzu*, First Series (Taipei: I-wen, 1965).

98. Usami Shinsui (U Kei), *Ō chū rōshi dōtoku shinkyō*, collected in WCPC. Preface, p. 3b.

99. Detailed biographical information on Ch'ao can be found in the *Sung-Yüan hsüeh-an* (The World of Scholarship in the Sung and Yüan Dynasties), comp. Huang Tsung-hsi (1610–1695) et al., *ch*. 22 (Wan-yu wen-k'u, Kuo-hsüeh chi-pen ts'ung-shu edition; Shanghai: Shang-wu, 1939), 7:67–110.

100. SPPY (Taipei: Chung-hua shu-chü reprint, 1981), p. 25a. According to Hatano, p. 500, there is evidence that in 1128 Ch'ao had obtained another handwritten copy of the *Lao-tzu*, which was also not divided into a *Tao-ching* and a *Te-ching*.

101. For the standard biography of Hsiung K'o, see *Sung-shih, ch.* 445, pp. 13143–44.

102. SPPY, 25b–26a.

103. Ch'en Chen-sun, *Chih-chai shu-lu chieh-t'i* (Annotated Bibliography of the Chih-chai Library), *ch.* 9 (Chiang-su shu-chü, 6 *ts'e*, 1883), vol. 3, p. 14a; as quoted in Wang Chung-min, p. 50.

104. On this point, see Chiang Hsi-ch'ang, *Lao-tzu chiao-ku*, "Annotated Bibliography," pp. 7–8. Cf. Wang Chung-min's comments in *Lao-tzu k'ao*, p. 53.

105. *Ssu-k'u ch'üan-shu tsung-mu t'i-yao*, 28:3033.

106. See Hatano, pp. 501–8. Supporters of this view include such well-known Sung *Lao-tzu* commentators as Shao Jo-yü (fl. 1135), Ch'eng Ta-ch'ang (1123–1195), and Wang Mao-ts'ai (fl. 1174). They include also the poet and scholar Lu Yu (1125–1210), the Ch'ing bibliophiles Chou Chung-fu (1768–1831), Hung I-hsüan (1765–1833), and Ch'ü Yung (fl. 1857). Hatano himself (pp. 11–13) has argued in favor of this view, and that the work of Lu Te-ming has suffered later interpolations.

107. As cited in Hatano, p. 505, and Wang Chung-min, p. 53.

108. Among the supporters of this view are Wu I (1745–1799), Hung Liang-chi (1746–1809), Yü Cheng-hsieh (1775–1840), Liang Chang-chü (1775–1849), Wu Yün (1811–1883), Sun I-jang (1848–1908), Shimada Kan (1879–1915), and in this century, Yü Chia-hsi, Ma Hsü-lun, Wang Chung-min, Chiang Hsi-ch'ang, and Wing-tsit Chan. Without exaggeration, this list reads like a "Who's Who" in contemporary *Lao-tzu* scholarship, if not sinology as a whole. See Hatano, *Rōshi dōtokukyō*, pp. 503–17. And Rump and Chan, *Commentary*, pp. xxvii–xxviii.

109. Hatano, p. 11; that is, not divided into a *Tao-ching* and a *Te-ching*, or into 81 chapters.

110. Rump and Chan, *Commentary*, p. xxviii.

111. There is now a wealth of literature on the Ma-wang-tui corpus, discovered near Ch'ang-sha in 1973. The silk manuscripts of the *Lao-tzu* were found in tomb no. 3, dated 168 B.C. The two manuscripts differ radically from the current versions in one respect: that is, they begin with the *Te* section, chap. 38, of the present *Lao-tzu*. In other words, the traditional order of the text is reversed. For an introduction to the Ma-wang-tui *Lao-tzu*, see D. C. Lau, trans., *Chinese Classics. Tao Te Ching* (Hong Kong: Chinese University Press, 1982). Part 1 of this work is basically a reprint of Lau's 1963 Penguin trans. of the *Lao-tzu*, and part 2 contains an introduc-

tory article and the collated translation of the Ma-wang-tui *Lao-tzu* manuscripts. See also Lau's Chinese article, "Ma-wang-tui Han-mu po-shu *Lao-tzu* ch'u-t'an," I and II, in *Ming-pao yüeh-k'an*, 17, 8 (1982): 11–17; 9 (1982): 35–40. However, see the critical review by William G. Boltz, "Textual Criticism and the Ma-wang-tui *Lao-tzu*," in *Harvard Journal of Asiatic Studies*, 44, 1 (June 1984): 185–224. Boltz is especially critical of Lau's collation of the two manuscripts. See also Jan Yün-hua, "The Silk Manuscripts on Taoism," in *T'oung Pao*, 43, 1 (1977): 65–84. And Paul J. Lin has also made use of this discovery; see esp. Appendix III to his work.

112. Chu Te-chih, *Lao-tzu t'ung-i* (The *Lao-tzu* Explained), *Fan-lieh* (Explanatory Notes) (WCPC; Taipei: I-wen, 1965), pp. 11b-12a. There is an interesting and most thorough study by Robert Henricks on this topic: "On the Chapter Divisions in the *Lao-tzu*," in *Bulletin of the School of Oriental and African Studies*, 45, 3 (1982): 501–24. After a careful review of the sources, including the Ma-wang-tui evidence, Henricks suggests that perhaps the 68-chapter version is closest to the earliest. Henricks has also written extensively on the Ma-wang-tui *Lao-tzu* manuscripts. See, e.g., "The Philosophy of Lao-tzu Based on the Ma-wang-tui Texts: Some Preliminary Observations," in *Society for the Study of Chinese Religions Bulletin* (now renamed *Journal of Chinese Religions*), no. 9 (Fall 1981): 59–78; and "Examining the Ma-wang-tui Silk Texts of the *Lao-tzu*: With Special Note of their Differences from the Wang Pi Text," in *T'oung Pao*, 65 (1979): 166–99.

113. As quoted in Hatano, *Rōshi dōtokukyō*, pp. 507–8.

114. Takeuchi, *Rōshi genshi*, pp. 68–69.

115. According to Shimada Kan, the fourfold division here is the result of editorial effort to conform to the general structure of the Taoist canon. Quoted in Hatano, p. 511; Rump and Chan, p. xxviii. Indeed, on the basis of the TT edition, Shimada has argued that the precise 81-chapter division did not come into being until the Sui-T'ang era, or the late Six Dynasties period at the earliest. See Shimada Kan, *Ku-wen chiu-shu k'ao* (Notes on Some 50 Rare Editions of Ancient Texts), in Chinese (Taipei: Kuang-wen shu-chü fasim. reproduction of the original 1903 edition, 1967), 1:186.

116. The most famous example of this is of course chapters 31 and 75, where in some versions Wang Pi has apparently stated that they are not part of the original *Lao-tzu*. The colophon of Ch'ao Yüeh-chih, for example, points out that Wang Pi was aware that chap. 31 "was not the words of Lao-tzu." Although this is not found in the current versions of the Wang Pi text, chap. 31 remains one of the only two chapters without any commentary. See the exhaustive analysis of these two chapters in Hatano, *Rōshi dōtokukyō*, pp. 211–14, 427–29.

Chapter Two

1. Peter A. Boodberg, "Philological Notes on Chapter One of the *Lao-Tzu*," in *Harvard Journal of Asiatic Studies*, 20 (1957):607.

2. For example, see Derk Bodde, "On Translating Chinese Philosophic Terms," in *Far Eastern Quarterly*, 14, 2 (February 1955):231–32. Wing-tsit Chan, *The Way of Lao Tzu*, p. 100, n. 9. A. C. Graham, " 'Being' in Western Philosophy Compared with *Shih/Fei* and *Yu/Wu* in Chinese Philosophy," *Asia Major*, new series, 7, 1–2 (1959):98–104. And more recently, Chad Hansen, *Language and Logic in Ancient China* (Ann Arbor: University of Michigan Press, 1983), pp. 43–44. Although these scholars agree that *yu* and *wu* are used as nouns, this is not to say that they all understand them in the same way. Briefly, whereas Chan and Bodde would tend to view *wu* as an "abstract" noun, as "nonbeing" in the sense of a fundamental "substance," Graham and Hansen would emphasize the more concrete meaning of *wu* as "lacking" all determination. For Hansen, the term *wu* should also be viewed quite simply as a "term," designating "no-thingness."

3. Graham, ibid., p. 99.

4. Ibid.

5. Ibid., p. 100.

6. In Chinese scholarship, T'ang Yung-t'ung and Ch'ien Mu may be taken as the major spokesmen of this view. See T'ang Yung-t'ung, *Wei Chin hsüan-hsüeh lun-kao* (Peking, 1957), pp. 48–51, 67–70, passim; Ch'ien Mu, *Chuang Lao t'ung-pien* (Essays on the *Chuang-tzu* and *Lao-tzu*) (reprinted, Taipei: San-min shu-chü, 1973), part 3. In the West, this reading is best represented by Fung Yu-lan, *A History of Chinese Philosophy*, vol. 2, *The Period of Classical Learning*, trans. Derk Bodde (Princeton: Princeton University Press, 1953; reprint, 1983), pp. 180–83; and by Wing-tsit Chan. Professor Chan, in particular, has suggested that Boodberg "overlooked" a number of instances in the *Lao-tzu* and *Chuang-tzu* where *yu* and *wu* "do not mean 'having' or 'not having' anything." See his *The Way of Lao Tzu*, p. 100, n. 9. Indeed, for Chan, in Wang Pi's commentary on the *Lao-tzu*, *wu* is identical to "original substance." See A. Rump and W. T. Chan, *Commentary on the Lao-tzu by Wang Pi*, pp. xiii-xiv.

7. Paul J. Lin, trans., *A Translation of Lao Tzu's Tao Te Ching and Wang Pi's Commentary* (Ann Arbor, Center for Chinese Studies, University of Michigan, 1977), pp. xix-xxi.

8. Isabelle Robinet, *Les Commentaries du Tao To King* (Paris, 1977), p. 63.

9. Rump and Chan, *Commentary on the Lao Tzu by Wang Pi*, p. 1; the translation of the *Lao-tzu* original in Rump's work is taken from Chan, *The Way of Lao-tzu*. Cf. Paul J. Lin, *Translation of Tao Te Ching and Wang Pi's Commentary*, p. 3. In the present study, translation of the Wang Pi commentary is generally based on these two works. However, in most cases, I have modified their interpretations on the basis of my own reading of the original text. The *Ssu-pu pei-yao* (SPPY) edition of the Wang Pi commentary will form the main text here, supplemented especially by the critical works of Lou Yü-lieh, *Wang Pi chi chiao-shih*, 2 vols. (Peking, 1980), and Hatano Tarō, *Rōshi dōtokukyō kenkyū* (Tokyo, 1979). Both these works have made use of a large number of editions of Wang Pi's commentary as well as quotations preserved in other commentaries and encyclopedias; see nn. 3 and 80 to chap. 1, above. The SPPY collection was originally compiled in Shanghai by the Chung-hua shu-chü, 1927–1935, in a total of 1,372 *ts'e*. As opposed to the *Ssu-pu ts'ung-k'an* (SPTK), which prefers older and rarer editions, the SPPY simply takes the best edition available. There are also two less comprehensive critical editions of Wang's commentary: Liu Kuo-chün, "Lao-tzu Wang Pi chu chiao-chi" (Textual Notes on Wang Pi's Commentary on *Lao-tzu*), *T'u-shu-kuan hsüeh chi-k'an* (Library Science Quarterly), 8, 1 (March 1934): 91–116. This work is based primarily on the SPPY and the *Tao-tsang* (Taoist canon) edition. And Li Ch'un, "Lao-tzu Wang Pi chu chiao-ting pu-cheng" (Wang Pi's Commentary on the *Lao-tzu* Collated and Explained), M.A. thesis, National Taiwan Normal University, 1979. With respect to the translation of the *Lao-tzu* itself, I am also indebted to D. C. Lau's work, *Lao Tzu Tao Te Ching* (Harmondsworth: Penguin Books, 1963; reprint, 1980). Page references to the works of Rump-Chan and Lin will be given throughout this study for purpose of comparison. On this particular line, see n. 14, below.

10. Cf. Lin, p. 81; Rump-Chan, p. 128. As we shall see, Wang Pi has borrowed from the *Chuang-tzu* in his interpretation of the "Tao-ist" cosmogony here.

11. Cf. Lin, p. 77; Rump-Chan, p. 123.

12. Cf. Lin, p. 3; Rump-Chan, p. 1. On the phrase *chih-shih tsao-hsing* which I have rather generally translated "have to do with things and forms," see discussion in text and the next note. At times, Wang Pi's commentary takes on what may be called a "glossary" style; i.e., the words of the *Lao-tzu* would be quoted or paraphrased first, followed by Wang Pi's comments. The use of the colon is meant to represent this in the translation.

13. As cited in Lou Yü-lieh, *Wang Pi chi chiao-shih*, 1:2, n. 1, and Hatano Tarō, *Rōshi dōtokukyō kenkyū*, p. 37. It is somewhat surprising that this reference has escaped the attention of our two Wang Pi translators. The

Chinese original of Hsü Shen's theory can be located in his famous dictionary *Shuo-wen chieh-tzu* (Hong Kong: Chung-hua shu-chü, Hong Kong Branch, 1972), 15A: 314. Wang Pi's concern with language is also discussed in Chung-yue Chang, "The Metaphysics of Wang Pi," Ph.D. dissertation, University of Pennsylvania, 1979, chap. 2.

14. Cf. Lin, p. 3; Rump-Chan, p. 1. I have put quotation marks around "beginning of the ten thousand things" (*wan-wu chih-shih*) even though the SPPY *Lao-tzu* text has "beginning of heaven and earth" (*t'ien-ti chih-shih*), because the context seems to call for a quotation and also because the two Ma-wang-tui *Lao-tzu* silk manuscripts both have *wan-mu chih-shih*. See D. C. Lau, trans., *Chinese Classics Tao Te Ching* (Hong Kong: Chinese University Press, 1982), pp. 266–67; and William G. Boltz, "The *Lao-tzu* Text that Wang Pi and Ho-shang Kung Never Saw," *Bulletin of the School of Oriental and African Studies*, 48 (1985): 493–94. The second quotation here, "brings them up, nourishes them, makes them secure and stable," is from chap. 51 of the *Lao-tzu*. This phrase has been variously interpreted, but it does not affect the general meaning of this passage; for the different readings, see Hatano, *Rōshi dōtokukyō*, pp. 38–39, and Ch'en Ku-ying, *Lao Tzu: Text, Notes, and Comments*, trans. Rhett Y. W. Young and Roger T. Ames (Chinese Materials Center, 1981), pp. 233–34, n. 3. This latter is a translation of Ch'en's *Lao-tzu chin-chu chin-i* (Taipei, 1960).

15. Cf. Lin, p. 38; Rump-Chan, p. 65. Since almost the exact sentence is used in both chapters 1 and 21, suggesting that all things are created and completed by Tao without their knowing why or how, it is not clear why Rump chooses to render the latter case differently; namely, "we do not know why this is so."

16. The second sentence of this passage is difficult. I have followed the emendation proposed by the late Ch'ing scholar I Shun-ting (1858–1920), taking the phrase *ch'i k'o te chien* to be a mistake for *pu k'o te chien*; as cited in Lou Yü-lieh, 2:55, n. 7, and Hatano, p. 157. This would break up the passage into two parallel statements, both affirming the transcendence of Tao as well as its creative power. This reading agrees better with Wang's understanding of chap. 21 as a whole, and is supported by a quotation found in the *Wen-hsüan*. The current SPPY version may be translated as follows: "The deep and dark cannot be obtained and seen; but the ten thousand things are all derived from it. In this way, it can be obtained and seen, and its true nature can be determined." This would not affect my interpretation; the Tao can be understood only in terms of its relationship with the myriad creatures. The possibility of "obtaining" the Way is thus affirmed here; the next few lines suggest that only by "returning" to the Way can this be accomplished. Cf. Rump-Chan, pp. 65–66; Lin, p. 38.

17. Cf. Lin, pp. 38–39; Rump-Chan, pp. 65–66.

18. Cf. D. C. Lau, *Lao Tzu* (Penguin Books), p. 70; Rump-Chan, p. 43. Some versions of the *Lao-tzu* have "the image that has no image" (*wu-hsiang chih hsiang*) as opposed to *wu-wu chih hsiang*; Paul Lin's translation, for example, has taken this reading. However, since Wang Pi repeats the phrase *wu-wu chih hsiang* in his commentary and since chap. 21 of the *Lao-tzu* parallels *wu* with *hsiang* also, I see no reason to emend the text here. In any case, the meaning of the passage would not be significantly affected.

19. Cf. Lin, p. 25; Rump-Chan, p. 43.

20. Cf. D. C. Lau, *Lao Tzu*, p. 112; for the word *shih*, translated generally as "environment" here, see Ch'en Ku-ying, *Lao Tzu: Text, Notes, and Comments*, pp. 232–33, n. 1.

21. Cf. Lin, p. 95; Rump-Chan, p. 147.

22. See Ch'ien Mu, "Wang Pi Kuo Hsiang chu I Lao Chuang yung li-tzu t'iao-lu" (On Wang Pi's and Kuo Hsiang's Use of the Word *Li* in their Commentaries on the *I-ching*, *Lao-tzu*, and *Chuang-tzu*), in *Hsin-ya hsüeh-pao*, 1, 1 (1955): 137–38; this work is also included in Ch'ien's *Chuang Lao t'ung-pien*, pp. 341–77.

23. Rump-Chan, p. xi.

24. My italics. Cf. Lin, p. 88; Rump-Chan, p. 137. See Lou Yü-lieh, *Wang Pi chi*, 1:126, n. 3 for the *I-ching* original, adapted by Wang Pi here.

25. D. C. Lau, *Lao Tzu*, p. 70.

26. Some versions have "understand" (*ming*) in place of "identify" or "name" (*ming*). According to Ma Hsü-lun, these two words were interchangeable; see his *Lao-tzu chiao-ku* (reprinted, Hong Kong, 1965), p. 137. However, since Wang Pi has used both these words in the same chapter, he might have understood them differently. In addition, one of the Ma-wang-tui *Lao-tzu* silk manuscripts also has *ming* (name). This is why I have retained the SPPY reading and rendered it as "identify," though most commentators seem to prefer the other reading.

27. Cf. Lin, p. 88; Rump-Chan, pp. 137–38.

28. Chap. 2. As translated in B. Watson, *The Complete Works of Chuang Tzu* (New York: Columbia University Press, 1968), p. 43.

29. Cf. Lin, p. 81; Rump-Chan, pp. 128–29. Read *wang-hou te-i che* in place of *te-i che wang-hou*. See Lou Yü-lieh, 1:117. Note also the similar use of the word "master" in the commentary on chap. 47 quoted earlier. The notion of *ch'i*, which is much more important in the Ho-shang Kung commentary, will be discussed later in chap. 4.

30. Cf. Lin, p. 88; Rump-Chan, p. 137.

31. Cf. Lin, p. 76; Rump-Chan, p. 119. The phrase *ke shih i-wu chih sheng*, which I have rendered as "As things are produced by 'One,' " is probably corrupt; cf. Hatano, p. 272, and Lou Yü-lieh, p. 107, n. 1.

32. This is a close paraphrase of the line, "I do not know whose son it [Tao] is," in chapter 4 of the *Lao-tzu*.

33. This passage is also probably corrupt; the translation here is based on Hatano's reading, pp. 174–75. The term "goes round" (*chou-hsing*) may be translated more smoothly as "operates everywhere"; the more literal reading here, however, shows more clearly how Wang Pi has understood the passage. The phrase "produce and preserve the great form" is also difficult, for it may be applied to the Tao itself. Rump-Chan, p. 75, e.g., translates, "That means it can live and preserve its great form." However, since the commentary emphasizes the "formlessness" of Tao, it is perhaps more appropriate to take the "great form" as referring to the created order as a whole.

34. Read *fu* for *ta*; see Hatano, p. 177, and Lou Yü-lieh, p. 66, n. 10.

35. Cf. Lin, pp. 45–46; Rump-Chan, pp. 75–76. The translation of the last ten or so sentences is guided especially by the phrase "what can be expressed" (*k'o-yen*), which is used three times in the commentary, and also by Wang Pi's concluding comments on chap. 25 to be discussed shortly. Instead of taking the word "Tao" as "the greatest of all designations for what can be expressed," it is also possible to see it as "what can be expressed and designated as the greatest." In either case, the distinction between the ineffable Tao in itself and its expressible aspects remains the key to Wang Pi's interpretation.

36. Read *chou-hsing* for *chou*, as the phrase "goes round" is used consistently in this chapter. Cf. Lin, p. 46; Rump-Chan, pp. 76–77. In this instance, it is interesting that Rump's translation suffers because of her emphasis on Wang Pi's metaphysics. Since Rump is concerned to bring out the idea of "substance," the idea that Tao is "unattached" and "stands alone" now becomes "not to hold on to any one great substance," and "because its substance is independent." The "paradox" is clearly foreign to Wang Pi's commentary here.

37. As Wing-tsit Chan has noted, the term *tzu-jan* "appears in the *Lao-tzu* five times but twenty-four times in Wang's commentary, in almost one-third of the eighty-one chapters." See Rump-Chan, p. xvii.

38. Chap. 14; in Watson, *Chuang Tzu*, p. 159.

39. Cf. Lin, p. 11; Rump-Chan, p. 17.

40. Cf. E. Erkes trans., *Ho-shang-kung's Commentary on Lao-tse* (Ascona: Artibus Asiae, 1958), p. 20; Erkes himself, although noting the evidence, argues that this reading is uncertain.

41. Chap. 22. Cf. Lin, pp. 40–41; Rump-Chan, p. 68.

42. Fung Yu-lan, *History*, 2:183.

43. Rump-Chan, p. xii, referring especially to the work of Ch'ien Mu; see n. 22, above.

44. See Lou Yü-lieh, *Wang Pi chi*, 1:195–210, and Yen Ling-feng ed., *Lao-tzu wei-chih li-lüeh* (WCPC; Taipei: I-wen, 1965).

45. Lou, p. 196; Yen, p. 2b.

46. Lou, p. 198; Yen, p. 5b.

47. *Chou-i lüeh-li*, in Lou, *Wang Pi chi*, 2:591–620.

48. See chap. 1, p. 30, above. In this sense, the idea of "One" is applicable to Tao as the principle of unity; it is also the product of Tao, for it remains part of the realm of *tzu-jan*. Within the framework of a dialectic of *wu* and *li*, the apparent inconsistency is thus resolved. In Wang Pi's commentary on the *Lun-yü*, we also read that " 'Tao' is the designation of *wu*, all-encompassing and followed by all. Figuratively called 'Tao,' it is quiet and without shape or body (*t'i*), and cannot be turned into an image." This, too, would seem to confirm my suggestion that Wang Pi was keenly aware of the limitation of ordinary language and that such words as "Tao" and *wu* are not to be taken literally in terms of a "substance." See Lou Yü-lieh, *Wang Pi chi*, 2:624; cf. Graham, " 'Being' in Western Philosophy Compared with *Shih/Fei* and *Yu/Wu* in Chinese Philosophy," pp. 99–100.

49. Cf. Lin, p. 70; Rump-Chan, p. 109.

50. Chap. 16; in Rump-Chan, p. 51. I use Rump's translation here quite deliberately because generally she uses "nonbeing" to render *wu*, to bring out its "being" the "original substance." The idea of *hsü*, however, does not admit such an interpretation.

51. Chap. 32. Cf. Lin, p. 58; Rump-Chan, p. 96.

52. Ironically, the equality of "substance" and "function" is recognized by both Lin and Rump; see Lin, pp. xix, and Rump-Chan, p. xvi. According to the latter, "substance and function involve each other. In the ultimate sense, they are identical." Precisely for this reason, the dialectic of *wu* and *li* must be maintained.

53. Cf. Lin, p. 64; Rump-Chan, pp. 105–6. The last sentence is difficult, although the general meaning is clear.

54. *Han Fei-tzu*, chap. 31 (SPPY; reprinted, Taipei: Chung-hua, 1982), *ch.* 10.2b.

55. *Han Fei-tzu*, chap. 21 (SPPY), 7.2a.

56. Cf. Lin, p. 125; Rump-Chan, pp. 186–87. Wang Pi is here quoting from the *I-ching*; see Lou Yü-lieh, ed., *Wang Pi chi*, 1:171, n. 6; and Lin's and Rump's notes to this chapter.

57. Cf. Lin, p. 52; Rump-Chan, p. 86. The expression "leader of officials" (*kuan-chang*) refers to the ruler in the *Lao-tzu* original. Wang Pi, however, takes this to mean that the ideal ruler appoints all the chief officers for the people. This, no doubt, reflects the different political structure of Wang Pi's time, and his concern with the appointment of able officers as well. This theme is repeated in the commentary on chap. 32.

58. Chap. 23. Cf. Lin, p. 42; Rump-Chan, p. 70. Most scholars have, in light of the commentary on chap. 63, emended *chün* to read *chü* in line 2; i.e., instead of "take nonaction as their master," read "dwell in nonaction." The general meaning, however, is not significantly affected.

59. Chap. 7. As translated in D. C. Lau, *Lao-tzu Tao Te Ching*, p. 63; modified.

60. Chap. 13. Cf. Lin, p. 22; Rump-Chan, p. 40.

61. Cf. Lin, p. 7; Rump-Chan, p. 10. Also see Rump-Chan, p. 12, nn. 2–4, for minor textual problems.

62. Chap. 34. Cf. Lin, p. 61; Rump-Chan, p. 101.

63. According to T'ao Hung-ch'ing, as cited in Hatano, p. 113, this sentence should be emended to read "Attain emptiness and maintain tranquility: this is the true nature of things."

64. Cf. Lin, p. 28; Rump-Chan, p. 49.

65. Lin, p. 131, has emended the word *chü* to read *shih*, "beginning"; but there is no real justification for this. Cf. Rump-Chan, p. 195. On the notion of tranquility, cf. *Lao-tzu*, chaps. 6, 15, 26, 45.

66. Some texts have the negative *pu* instead of *hsia*, "below," which changes the sentence to mean "The highest is not known." But Wang Pi's commentary has *hsia*.

67. The quotation is from the text of chap. 2. Since chap. 2 in the SPPY version differs slightly from Wang Pi's quotation, various changes

have been suggested; but they do not alter the general import of the passage. See Hatano, p. 48, and Chiang Hsi-ch'ang, *Lao-tzu chiao-ku* (The *Lao-tzu* Collated and Explained) (Shanghai, 1937; reprint, Taipei, 1980), pp. 15–16. The translation proposed here is especially concerned to bring out the reason why "the highest" is barely known by the ordinary people.

68. In some versions, this last sentence is found later in the commentary instead. Lin, for example, has followed this (p. 30); cf. Rump-Chan, p. 53, which takes the SPPY reading.

69. The word *fa*, "by law," is considered corrupt by most scholars. See Lou Yü-lieh, 1:42, n. 5; Rump-Chan, p. 55, n. 5.

70. *Han Fei-tzu*, 38 (SPPY), 16.3b.

71. Read *hsing*, "nature"—in parenthesis—for *chih*, "end," because "nature" agrees more with the parallel "feeling" in the same sentence. See Lou Yü-lieh, 1:77, n. 4.; Rump-Chan, p. 89, n. 3. Cf. Lin, p. 53, where the SPPY reading is retained.

72. This reflects Wang Pi's indebtedness to tradition also. According to A. C. Graham, the word *yin* is important to both the *Chuang-tzu* and the Mohist *Canons*, especially as a "logical term"; Graham thus translates *yin* as "go by" and "take as a criterion." See his *Chuang Tzu: The Inner Chapters* (London, 1981), p. 10. Further, the word *yin* was often used in relation to Tao since the Han dynasty. The *Shih-chi*, for example, states that "Emptiness (*hsü*) is the constancy of Tao; *yin* is the guide of the ruler." *Shih-chi* (SPPY), *ch.* 130, p. 5a.

73. The "three" is variously interpreted; cf. Lin, p. 52, and Rump-Chan, p. 86. I also differ from them in taking *te*, "virtue," to mean *te*, "to obtain," as in Wang's commentary on chap. 38. According to most scholars, chap. 28 of the *Lao-tzu* has suffered interpolations; see especially Chiang Hsi-ch'ang, *Lao-tzu chiao-ku*, pp. 187–92. Judging from Wang Pi's commentary, however, whatever mistakes crept into the text must have been early.

74. Read *ch'i-ping* for *ch'i-cheng*, to agree with the text, as Hatano, pp. 359–60, and Lou, 1:150, n. 2, have both suggested. Although not indicated, Lin (p. 107) has also adopted this emended reading. Rump, however, follows the SPPY text and translates, "If one governs the state with correctness, there will be craftiness (*ch'i*) and justice (*cheng*)." It is not clear how "craftiness" is related to "justice" in this context.

75. Chap. 73. Cf. Lin, p. 133; Rump-Chan, p. 198. The first part of this line is missing in Rump. The only other instance in the *Lao-tzu* where the word *ying* is used is in chap. 38: "A man most conversant in the rites

acts, but when no one responds (*ying*) rolls up his sleeves and resorts to persuasion by force." As trans. in Lau, *Lao Tzu*, p. 99.

76. See Wang Pi's commentary on the *I-ching*, in Lou, 1:215. Wang's comment, however, does not deal with the concept of "response" in this instance. Cf. *Chuang-tzu*, chap. 7, in Watson, trans., p. 97.

77. Lou, 2:604. The concept of *ying* is very important in the *Huai-nan tzu* and other Han works also. See especially Charles Le Blanc, *Huai-nan Tzu: Philosophical Synthesis in Early Han Thought* (Hong Kong: Hong Kong University Press, 1985).

78. Cf. Lin, p. 141; Rump-Chan, p. 208.

79. *Lun-yü*, 7.1. Adapted from D. C. Lau, trans., *Confucius: The Analects* (Harmondsworth: Penguin Books, 1979; reprint, 1982), p. 86; and Wing-tsit Chan, trans. and comp., *A Source Book in Chinese Philosophy* (Princeton: Princeton University Press, 1963; reprint, 1973), p. 31.

80. Wang Pi, *Lun-yü shih-i*; in Lou, 2:623–24. P'eng-tsu is a legendary figure who has come to symbolize longevity. The other interpretation established since the Han dynasty is that Lao P'eng was an official of the Shang dynasty (ca. 1520–1030 B.C.), as the name is also found in the *Li chi* (Book of Rites). See Yang Liang-Kung et al., *Ssu-shu chin-chu chin-i* (New Annotated Edition of the Four Books, with Translation into Modern Chinese) (Taipei: Shang-wu, 1979), p. 93. The currency of this interpretation can be seen from the fact that it was maintained by Chu Hsi (1130–1200) in the Sung dynasty. See his *Ssu-shu chi-chu* (Collected Commentaries on the Four Books) (SPPY; reprinted, Taipei: Chung-hua, 1973), 4.1a.

81. See Lou, 2:624. Wang Pi's commentary on the *Lun-yü*, as indicated earlier, survives only in quotations. This and the last reference are both preserved by the Sung scholar Hsing Ping (932–1010), in his *Lun-yü chu-su chieh-ching* (Subcommentary on Ho Yen's Commentary on the Analects) (Taipei: Chung-kuo tzu-hsüeh ming-chu chi-ch'eng, 1977).

82. See the Yü-han shan-fang chi i-shu edition of Wang's *Lun-yü shih-i* (1889), p. 3b. As cited in Lou, 2:635, n. 9.

83. Hsing Ping, *Lun-yü chu-su chieh-ching*, pp. 190–91.

84. Cf. Lin, p. 34; Rump-Chan, p. 58.

85. Cf. Lin, p. 18; Rump-Chan, p. 30. The last verse of the *Lao-tzu* is often emended to read "without action" (*wu-wei*) instead of "without knowledge" (*wu-chih*). But this does not affect the commentary. See the detailed discussion in Chiang Hsi-ch'ang, *Lao-tzu chiao-ku*, pp. 58–62.

Chapter Three

1. See Ch'ao Kung-wu (fl. 1150), *Chün-chai tu-shu chih* (Book Notes from the Chün-chai Studio), ed. Wang Hsien-ch'ien (1842–1917) (Ch'ang-sha, 1884), 11.3a. This reference is not included in the SPTK edition of Ch'ao's work, which is based on the so-called Yüan version; Wang's critical edition is based on the Ch'ü version. Also see Wang Chung-min, *Lao-tzu k'ao* (reprinted, Taipei, 1981), p. 22.

2. As cited in Wang Chung-min, p. 275. These and other critical comments on the Ho-shang Kung commentary are also conveniently collected in Chang Hsin-ch'eng, *Wei-shu t'ung-k'ao* (Critical Study of Forged Books) (Shanghai: Shang-wu, 1939; reprint, 1954), 2:743–45.

3. According to Yen Ling-feng, at present some thirty versions of the Ho-shang Kung commentary are in existence. The earliest of these are two T'ang versions, but they are incomplete. This is also true for the Ho-shang Kung fragments discovered in Tun-huang. See Yen Ling-feng, *Chung-wai Lao-tzu chu-shu mu-lu* (Bibliography of Works on the *Lao-tzu*, East and West) (Taipei: Chung-hua ts'ung-shu wei-yüan-hui, 1957), pp. 373–75. This list, however, does not include the Tun-huang material.

The T'ang versions are included in Ma Tsung (d. 823), comp., *I-lin* (Forest of Ideas), 1.14a–17b (Hsüeh-ching t'ao-yüan edition; Shanghai, 1922), and in Wei Cheng (580–643) et al., ed. *Ch'ün-shu chih-yao* (Study Notes on the World of Books), *ch.* 34 (reprinted SPTK edition; Taipei: Shang-wu, 1965), pp. 440–47. These are basically made up of key passages selected to prepare students for the civil service examinations. Among the fragments of the Ho-shang Kung commentary discovered in Tun-huang, not including several MSS of the Ho-shang Kung version of the *Lao-tzu* text without any commentary, S477, S3926, and P2639 are the most complete. For a detailed description, see Ōfuchi Ninji, ed., *Tonkō Dōkyō* (Taoist Manuscripts from Tun-huang), vol. 1, *Mokuroku hen* (Annotated Catalogue) (Tokyo: Hukubu shoten, 1978), pp. 209–35. On the whole, vis-à-vis the SPTK version, differences are minor. The two Stein manuscripts are now available in a photo-reprinted edition, though the quality of the reprint leaves much to be desired. See Yen Ling-feng, ed., *Tun-huang hsieh-pen Lao-tzu Ho-shang Kung chu* (WCPC; Taipei: I-wen, 1965).

Most commonly known as the *Lao-tzu chang-chü* (*Lao-tzu* Annotated in Sections), the Ho-shang Kung commentatry is collected in the *Ssu-pu ts'ung-k'an* series (first published 1920–1922). The SPTK edition is a facsimile reproduction of the private study-edition of the Yü family of Chien-an, taken from the T'ieh-ch'in t'ung-chien lou collection of Ch'ü Yung (fl. 1857). According to Ch'ü Yung's own catalogue, because of a certain "tabooed" word, this version was probably published after the reign of Sung Hsiao-tsung (r. 1163–1189). See *T'ieh-ch'in t'ung-chien lou tsang-shu mu-lu* (1897),

18.7b. It is in four *chüan*, divided into 81 chapters with chapter titles. Most versions are in either four or two *chüan* with 81 chapters; but the chapter titles appear to be a later addition. The Tun-huang MSS, for example, do not have chapter titles. On the different versions of the Ho-shang Kung *Lao-tzu*, see also the excellent discussion of Naitō Motoharu, "Rōshi kajōkōchū no kōhon ni tsuite" (On the Texts of the Ho-shang Kung Commentary on the *Lao-tzu*), in *Shūkan Tōyōgaku*, 19 (May 1968): 70–81. Naitō's work discusses in turn the *Tao-tsang* version, the Tun-huang versions, the SPTK edition, and three Japanese versions. In this study, I will be using Yen Ling-feng's photo-reprint of the SPTK edition included in his WCPC collection (Taipei: I-wen, 1965).

4. Emperor Wen's wife, the later Empress Dowager Tou, was also a dedicated student of the *Lao-tzu*. The *Shih-chi* relates that "Empress Dowager Tou favored the words of Huang-ti and Lao-tzu. The emperor [i.e., her son, Emperor Ching], the crown prince, and the various members of the Tou family all had to study the *Huang-ti* and *Lao-tzu*, and to revere their art" (*ch.* 49.5b). Also see the discussion in Ma Hsü-lun, *Lao-tzu chiao-ku* (reprinted, Hong Kong, 1965), pp. 7–8; and Hatano Tarō, *Rōshi dōtokukyō kenkyū*, pp. 6–7, 667–70.

5. For a concise analysis of the development of the Taoist religion during the T'ang and Sung dynasties, see Fu Ch'in-chia, *Chung-kuo Tao-chiao shih* (A History of Taoism in China) (Shanghai: Shang-wu, 1937; reprint, Taipei, 1980), chap. 13.

6. Hsüan I, *Chen-cheng lun* (On Distinguishing the Orthodox View), part B, ch. 3, in *Taishō shinshū daizōkyō* (Taishō Tripitaka; abbreviated T), vol. 52, no. 2112, p. 568. For another Buddhist critique, see Fa Lin, *Pien-cheng lun* (Arguments Concerning the Orthodox View), ch. 2, in T 52, no. 2110, pp. 498–99.

7. Takeuchi Yoshio, *Rōshi genshi* (Tokyo, 1926), pp. 35–48.

8. Ōfuchi Ninji, "Rōshi dōtokukyō joketsu no seiritsu" (On the Formation of the *Tao-te ching hsü-chüeh*), parts I and II, in *Tōyō gakuhō*, 42, 1 (June 1959): 1–40; 42, 2 (Sept. 1959): 52–85. Cf. Fukui Kōjun, "Rōshi dōtokukyō joketsu no keisei," in *Nippon Chūgoku gakkaihō*, 11 (1959): 27–37. Fukui's article is primarily aimed at clarifying a number of points in Takeuchi's discussion.

9. The sources Ōfuchi has made use of in reconstructing the text are listed in "Rōshi joketsu," part I, pp. 2–3. Besides Ōfuchi's reconstructed version, there is also the work of Yen Ling-feng, *Chi Ch'eng Hsüan-ying Tao-te ching k'ai-t'i hsü-chüeh i-su* (Reconstructed Version of Ch'eng Hsüan-ying's [fl. 630] Commentary on the *Tao-te ching*) (Taipei: I-wen, 1965). Ch'eng

Hsüan-ying is a major Taoist figure of the T'ang dynasty. His work is composed of three parts, of which the *Hsü-chüeh* forms one. Cf. the description of the Tun-huang fragments S75, P2584—which together give the whole text of the *Hsü-chüeh*—and others in Ōfuchi, ed., *Tonkō Dōkyō*, vol. 1, *Mokuroku hen*, section 3, pp. 246–49.

10. The fivefold division is Ōfuchi's. According to Takeuchi and Fukui, the text is divided into four sections; the third becomes two distinct sections in Ōfuchi's version. Most MSS have the notation "Made by Ko Hsüan, the Great Ultimate Immortal Master of the Left," at the beginning. There is also a detailed discussion of the *Hsü-chüeh* in Shima Kunio, *Rōshi kōsei* (Tokyo, 1973), pp. 12–24.

11. The only major exception is that the name of the official who recommended Ho-shang Kung to Emperor Wen is omitted in the *Hsü-chüeh*. The reference to an official, an undersecretary by the name of P'ei K'ai, in the mature version raises difficulties, because the only known historical personage by that name was a contemporary of Wang Pi. The son of P'ei Hui, P'ei K'ai was well known as a "Neo-Taoist" as well; see his biography in *Chin-shu*, ch. 35 (Peking: Chung-hua, 1974) pp. 1047–50. According to Ma Hsü-lun, P'ei K'ai may be an error for Hsiang K'ai (fl. 166 A.D.), the famous Taoist scholar of the Eastern Han dynasty who was especially important for his connection with the *T'ai-p'ing ching* (Scripture of Great Peace). However, this would still be an anachronism on the part of the author(s) of the Ho-shang Kung legend. See Ma, *Lao-tzu chiao-ku*, p. 2.

12. Takeuchi, *Rōshi genshi*, p. 47; Ōfuchi, "Rōshi dōtokukyō joketsu," I:20–33. Cf. Fukui, "Rōshi dōtokukyō joketsu no keisei," pp. 32–33. The legend of Ho-shang Kung is found in *ch.* 3 of the *Shen-hsien chuan*; see the Han-wei ts'ung-shu edition (1794). I have discussed the reasons why Ko Hsüan's authorship cannot be maintained and other issues concerning the *Hsü-chüeh* in a separate essay, "The Formation of the Ho-shang Kung Legend," forthcoming, in Julia Ching, ed., *Sages and Filial Sons: Studies on Early China* (Hong Kong: Chinese University Press).

13. See James Ware, trans., *Alchemy, Medicine, and Religion in the China of A.D. 320: The Nei P'ien of Ko Hung* (Cambridge: MIT Press, 1966; reprint, 1981), p. 17. Ko Hung, as is well known, is a major figure in the history of Taoism. A grand-nephew of Ko Hsüan, he first received his Taoist training from Cheng Ssu-yüan, who in turn was a disciple of Ko Hsüan himself.

14. Wang Ming, on the other hand, argues that although the *Hsü-chüeh* suffered later interpolations, Ko Hsüan's authorship should be accepted. This means that the *Shen-hsien chuan* account of the Ho-shang Kung legend is modeled on that in the *Hsü-chüeh*. However, I do not see why the author of the *Shen-hsien chuan* account would then omit the name of the

commentary and speak only of a "book of simplicity." In any case, this does not affect the main argument presented here, which seeks to trace the Ho-shang Kung story beyond the Ko family to the Han dynasty. See Wang Ming, "Lao-tzu Ho-shang Kung chang-chü k'ao" (A Study of the Ho-shang Kung Commentary on the *Lao-tzu*), in his *Tao-chia ho Tao-chiao ssu-hsiang yen-chiu* (Essays on Taoist Philosophy and Religion) (Ch'ung-ch'ing: Chung-kuo she-hui k'o-hsüeh ch'u-pan-she, 1984), pp. 293–323. This important essay on Ho-shang Kung was originally published in 1948.

15. See my article, "The Formation of the Ho-shang Kung Legend," for some of the scholarly opinions on this issue.

16. The question of the authenticity of the *Shen-hsien chuan* is impor-tant in this connection. Fukui Kōjun, for example, has argued that the cur-rent version of the *Shen-hsien chuan* may be dated to as late as the Ming dynasty. See his "Shinsenden kō," in *Tōhō shūkyō*, 1 (1951), and "Katsushi-dō no kenkyū" (A Study of the Taoism of the Ko Family), in *Tōyō shisō kenkyū*, 5 (1954), pp. 49–54. The authenticity of the *Shen-hsien chuan* as a whole need not concern us here. What should be pointed out is that its version of the Ho-shang Kung legend is also quoted in a number of T'ang and Sung encyclopedias. This particular part of the *Shen-hsien chuan* at least seems to have escaped the fate of major alteration. Fukui does not mention the Ho-shang Kung legend in his discussion. See also Ōfuchi, "Rōshi dōtokukyō joketsu," pp. 20–26, where the various versions of the *Shen-hsien chuan* account of the Ho-shang Kung legend are compared and discussed.

17. *Shih-chi* (SPPY), *ch.* 80.6b. The reference to Ho-shang Chang-jen is found in the biography of Yüeh I (fl. 284 B.C.). Among Yüeh I's descendants was one Yüeh Chü-kung (or Yüeh Ch'en-kung), who became a follower of the Huang-lao tradition and studied under Ho-shang Chang-jen. The *Shih-chi* then traces the transmission of the school of Ho-shang Chang-jen, be-ginning with the famous 3rd-century B.C. diviner and "immortal," An-ch'i Sheng (Master An-ch'i), through Yüeh Chü-kung and others, to the early Han prime minister Ts'ao Ts'an (d. 190 B.C.). There is an English translation of Yüeh I's biography; see Frank Kierman, Jr., trans., *Ssu-ma Ch'ien's Histo-riographical Attitude as Reflected in Four Late Warring States Biographies* (Wies-baden: Otto Harrassowitz, 1962), pp. 20–25. The family name "Yüeh" is romanized as "Yo" in this and other older studies. See also the excellent discussion of the Ho-shang Chang-jen tradition in Kanaya Osamu, *Shin Kan shisōshi kenkyū* ("A Study of the History of Thought in the Ch'in-Han Pe-riod"), revised edition (Kyoto: Heigakuji shoten, 1981), pp. 151–89.

18. According to Wang Ying-lin (1223–1296), "The figure of Ho-shang Chang-jen is the same as the one who is now called Ho-shang Kung. Since Chin times [265–420 A.D.], it has already been said that he taught Emperor Wen of Han." See Wang, *Han-shu i-wen-chih k'ao-cheng* (Critical Notes on the

Bibliographical Section of the Han History), 6.4a, appended to his *Yü-hai*, *ch.* 204 (1783, 120-vol. reproduction of the Yüan edition), vol. 101. In Hsi K'ang's (233–262 A.D.) *Sheng-hsien kao-shih chuan* (Lives of Sages and Exemplary Men), we likewise read that Ho-shang Kung is also known as Ho-shang Chang-jen (Yü-han shan-fang chi i-shu, 1889 edition, p. 10a).

19. The "mistaken identity" hypothesis is suggested by Anna Seidel; see her *La Divinisation de Lao Tseu dans le Taoisme des Han* (Paris, 1969), p. 33, n.1.

20. As quoted in the Sung encyclopedia, *T'ai-p'ing yü-lan*, 510.5b. There is a reconstructed version of this text by Ch'en Kuo-fu, in his *Tao-tsang yüan-liu k'ao* (A Study of the Origins and Development of the Taoist Canon), revised edition (Peking: Chung-hua, 1963; reprint, Taipei, 1975), pp. 454–504. The story of Master An-ch'iu is found in Hsi K'ang, *Sheng-hsien kao-shih chuan*, p. 11b, and in Huang-fu Mi (215–282 A.D.), *Kao-shih chuan* (Lives of Exemplary Men) (TSCC; Shanghai: Shang-wu, 1937), B:74–75. It is interesting that whereas Ho-shang Chang-jen's disciple is named Master An-ch'i, Ho-shang Kung's is called Master An-ch'iu. The implications of this parallel are addressed in my article on the Ho-shang Kung legend. According to the *Shih-chi* (*ch.* 80), Yüeh Chü-kung was an expert in the teachings of the Huang-lao school, and he was widely known as a saintly teacher in the state of Ch'i. There is a longer version of this story in Huang-fu Mi's *Kao-shih chuan*, B:62–63.

21. Master An-ch'iu was known to Ko Hung, according to a reference preserved in the *T'ai-p'ing yü-lan*, *ch.* 666; as cited in Wang Ming, *Pao-p'u tzu nei-p'ien chiao-shih* (Critical Edition of the Inner Chapters of the *Pao-p'u tzu*) (Peking: Chung-hua shu-chü, 1980), p. 333.

22. Kusuyama Haruki, *Rōshi densetsu no kenkyū* ("Studies in the Commentaries on the *Tao-te ching* and the Legends of Lao-tzu") (Tokyo: Sōbunsha, 1979), part I, chap. 4. This work is invaluable to *Lao-tzu* studies, despite my disagreement with some of its findings. There is a useful review of Kusuyama's work by Sakai Tadao, in *Tōhō shūkyō*, 55 (July 1980): 107–15.

23. Kusuyama, ibid., p. 177. Cf. Kenneth Ch'en, *Buddhism in China: A Historical Survey* (Princeton: Princeton University Press, 1973), pp. 75–77, for a concise discussion of this development.

24. Kusuyama, ibid., p. 192.

25. T'ien Shu was a disciple of Yüeh Chü-kung, according to Ssu-ma Ch'ien and Huang-fu Mi. He was also an important official in the early Han administration. See his biography in *Shih-chi, ch.* 104, and in the *Han-shu, ch.* 37 (Peking, 1983), pp. 1981–85. The *Shih-chi* account is translated in Burton Watson, *Records of the Grand Historian of China* (New York: Columbia

University Press, 1962), 1:556–61. Ts'ao Ts'an first learned the art of Huang-lao while he was in charge of the state of Ch'i. Later, when he became the prime minister of Han, he governed the country by means of "nonaction." See Ts'ao's biography in *Shih-chi*, ch. 54; this chapter is partially translated in Watson, ibid., 1:421–26. For the Empress Dowager Tou, see n. 4, above.

26. *Shih-chi, ch.*, 63 and 74. More precisely, the Huang-lao movement was in full force during the early decades of the Han dynasty, and it is generally accepted that its root can be traced to the late Warring States period. Although the Huang-lao school may have originated as an independent movement, since the Han dynasty it has been identified as a branch of "Taoism." For a general discussion of this school, see Anna Seidel, *La Divinisation de Lao Tseu dans le Taoisme des Han* (Paris, 1969), pp. 18–42, 48–53. Ku Chieh-kang, *Ch'in Han ti fang-shih yü ju-sheng* (Magicians-Diviners and Confucian Scholars in the Ch'in and Han Dynasties) (reprinted, Hong Kong: I-hsin shu-tien, 1976; original, Shanghai, 1936, under the title *Han-tai hsüeh-shu-shih lüeh*), pp. 9–42. Wang Shu-min, "Huang-lao k'ao," *Journal of Oriental Studies* (Hong Kong), 13, 2 (July 1975): 146–53. Akizuki Kan'ei, "Kōrō kannen no keifu" ("The Genealogy of the Huang-lao Concept"), *Tōhōgaku*, 10 (1955): 69–81.

27. Kuo Mo-jo, *Shih p'i-p'an shu* (Ten Critical Essays), revised edition (Peking: jen-min ch'u-pan-she, 1954), pp. 152–54. According to Kuo, three "schools" may be distinguished within this form of "Taoism," which emerged from the Chi-hsia academy. In this connection, I should add that I am certainly aware of the claim that the word "Huang" in the compound "Huang-lao" may refer to the Han thinker Huang Sheng, who was the teacher of the Grand Historian Ssu-ma T'an. However, I do not see much merit in this view; the Ma-wang-tui discovery confirms quite clearly that "Huang-lao" refers to the Yellow Emperor and Lao-tzu.

28. Kanaya Osamu, *Shin Kan shisōshi kenkyū*, revised edition (Kyoto: Heigakuji shoten, 1981), pp. 181–85.

29. On the relationship between Taoism and Legalism, see Fung Yu-lan, *A History of Chinese Philosophy*, trans. Derk Bodde (Princeton: Princeton University Press, 1952; reprint, 1983), 1:330–335. Also see Léon Vandermeersch, *La Formation du Légisme* (Paris: École Française d'Extrême-Orient, 1965), chap. 11. In this regard, H. G. Creel stands alone in maintaining that to Shen Pu-hai at least, no Taoist influence can be attributed. Creel's argument is primarily based on the assumption that both the *Lao-tzu* and *Chuang-tzu* are late. See Creel, *Shen Pu-hai: A Chinese Political Philosopher of the Fourth Century B.C.* (Chicago and London: University of Chicago Press, 1974), pp. 193–94.

30. *Shih-chi*, 74.4a. The other figures included in this passage are T'ien P'ien and Chieh-tzu of Ch'i, and Huan Yüan of Ch'u. See Fung Yu-lan, *History*, 1:132–33, 153–59, for a brief description of their thought.

31. *Shih-chi*, 63.4b.

32. Ibid., 63.5a.

33. *Han-shu*, 30:1730–31. They are: the *Huang-ti ssu-ching* in four sections (*p'ien*), *Huang-ti ming* in six, and *Huang-ti chün-ch'en* in ten, the last of which is particularly said to be "similar to the *Lao-tzu*." There is also a *Tsa Huang-ti* (Miscellaneous Works of the Yellow Emperor) in 58 *p'ien*, which is ascribed to the "saintly men" of the Warring States period. The four works listed above are included in the Taoist section. There are also some twenty others ascribed to the school of the Yellow Emperor, including those attributed to his chief ministers, in other sections as well, notably in those on the schools of military strategy, medicine, and "immortals." See the *Han-shu*, 30:1729–80. As I shall argue, the Huang-lao tradition seems to involve both ethico-political concerns and a religious dimension centering on the idea of immortality.

34. See the excellent discussion in Creel, "The Meaning of *Hsing-ming*," in his *What is Taoism?* (Chicago and London: University of Chicago Press, 1970; reprint, 1977), pp. 79–91. Cf. Creel, *Shen Pu-hai* (see n. 29, above), pp. 119–24. Creel is particularly concerned to bring out the political aspects of this concept. However, also see Fung Yu-lan, *History*, 1:192, where the relationship of *hsing-ming* and the "School of Names" is discussed; and Hsiao-po Wang and Leo Chang, *The Philosophical Foundations of Han Fei's Political Theory* (Honolulu: University of Hawaii Press, 1986), pp. 57–78. The meaning of *hsing-ming* is often ambiguous especially because the character *hsing*, "punishment," is generally used where the cognate *hsing*, "form," seems to be meant.

35. Léon Vandermeersch, *La Formation du Légisme* (Paris, 1965), pp. 264–65; cf. p. 226, where the relationship with the Mohists and the Dialecticians is discussed.

36. See n. 34, above.

37. *Han Fei-tzu*, 2.12a (SPPY); as trans. in Creel, *Shen Pu-hai*, pp. 120–21.

38. *Han-shu*, 9:278, n. 4, as quoted by the T'ang commentator Yen Shih-ku; as trans. in Creel, "The Meaning of *Hsing-ming*," *What is Taoism?*, p. 86.

39. Creel, *What is Taoism?*, p. 82.

40. *Han-shu*, 9:277. This is the passage on which Yen Shih-ku commented by quoting Liu Hsiang (see n. 38, above). Cf. Creel, *Shen Pu-hai*, p. 120; *What is Taoism?*, p. 87.

41. *Han Fei-tzu*, chap. 8 (SPPY), 2.10b. See also Ch'en Ch'i-yu ed., *Han Fei-tzu chi-shih* (The *Han Fei-tzu* Collated and Explained) (Shanghai: Shanghai jen-min ch'u-pan-she, 1974), 1:122.

42. See, e.g., Kao Heng and Ch'ih Hsi-chao, "Shih-t'an Ma-wang-tui Han-mu chung-ti po-shu Lao-tzu" (Preliminary Discussion of the Ma-wang-tui *Lao tzu* Silk Manuscripts), in *Wen-wu*, no. 11 (1974): 1–2. And Michael Loewe, "Manuscripts Found Recently in China: A Preliminary Survey," *T'oung Pao*, 63, 2–3 (1977): 118. Cf. n. 111 to chap. 1, above.

43. The translations of these titles are from Tu Wei-ming, "The 'Thought of Huang-Lao': A Reflection on the Lao Tzu and Huang Ti Texts in the Silk Manuscripts of Ma-wang-tui," *Journal of Asian Studies*, 39, 1 (November 1979): 97; compare, however, the earlier work of Jan Yün-hua, "The Silk Manuscripts on Taoism," in *T'oung Pao*, 63, 1 (1977): 65–84. The second of these four texts was originally entitled *Shih-ta ching* (Ten Great Scriptures); see *Ma-wang-tui Han-mu po-shu: Ching-fa* (abbreviated *Ching-fa*), ed. Ma-wang-tui Han-mu po-shu cheng-li hsiao-tsu (Study Group of the Ma-wang-tui Silk Manuscripts) (Peking: Wen-wu ch'u-pan-she, 1976). It was later changed to *Shih-liu ching* in the 1980 edition of the *Ma-wang-tui Han-mu po-shu* (abbreviated MWT), vol. 1, ed. Kuo-chia wen-wu chü ku-wen-hsien yen-chiu-shih (National Bureau of Cultural Relics, Division of Ancient Literary Documents) (Peking: Wen-wu ch'u-pan-she, 1980). As far as the internal division of the text is concerned, both editions are the same in dividing it into fifteen sections. According to the MWT editors, the change was made on the basis of a comparison of the writing or calligraphic style of the various Ma-wang-tui silk manuscripts; see MWT, p. 80, n. 163. The 1976 edition, *Ching-fa*, also contains a number of important articles on these four texts.

44. Jan Yün-hua, "*Tao Yüan* or Tao: The Origin," in *Journal of Chinese Philosophy*, 7, 3 (September 1980): 195–204.

45. T'ang Lan, "Ma-wang-tui ch'u-t'u Lao-tzu i-pen chüan-ch'ien ku-i-shu ti yen-chiu, chien-lun ch'i yü Han-ch'u Ju-Fa tou-cheng ti kuan-hsi" (On the Ancient Lost Texts Preceding the B Version of the Ma-wang-tui *Lao-tzu*: With a Discussion of their Relation to the Struggle between Confucianism and Legalism during the Early Han Dynasty), in *Ching-fa* (Peking, 1976): 149–66. This study first appeared in *K'ao-ku hsüeh-pao*, no. 1 (1975): 7–38. Also see T'ang's shorter study, "Huang-ti ssu-ching ch'u-t'an," in *Wen-wu*, no. 10 (1974): 48–52.

46. *Ching-fa*, p. 153. See *Sui-shu*, 34:1093. Again, while it is possible that the Huang-lao school originated as an independent movement, it was soon regarded as a branch of "Taoism," as the *Sui-shu* clearly suggests. T'ang's thesis is also briefly summarized in Michael Loewe, "Manuscripts Found Recently In China," p. 120.

47. See T'ang, "Huang-ti ssu-ching ch'u-t'an," p. 49, where all the works attributed to the Yellow Emperor in the *Han-shu* are listed.

48. For example, some may disagree with T'ang's dating of the texts to about 400 B.C. or with his tracing them to the State of Cheng. According to Lung Hui, on linguistic grounds, the texts may be traced to the State of Ch'u. According to K'ang Li, the *Shih-liu ching* should perhaps be dated to the early Han period. To take but one more example, according to Kao Heng and Tung Chih-an, the *Shih-liu ching* or *Shih-ta ching* may be the *Huang-ti chün-ch'en* (Discourses between the Yellow Emperor and his Ministers) also listed in the *Han-shu*. However, on the whole, the connection with the Huang-lao tradition is seldom challenged. See Lung Hui, "Ma-wang-tui ch'u-t'u Lao-tzu i-pen ch'ien ku-i-shu t'an-yüan," in *K'ao-ku hsüeh-pao*, no. 2 (1975): 23–32. K'ang Li, "Shih-ta ching ti ssu-hsiang ho shih-tai," in *Ching-fa*, pp. 105–11; originally in *Li-shih yen-chiu*, no. 3 (1975): 81–85. Kao Heng and Tung Chih-an, "Shih-ta ching ch'u-lun," in *Ching-fa*, pp. 112–27; originally in *Li-shih yen-shiu*, no. 1 (1975): 89–97.

49. As far as I know, the only critic who does not acknowledge the close relation between the Ma-wang-tui Huang-ti texts and the Huang-lao school is Saiki Tetsurō, who argues that the Ma-wang-tui texts are strictly Taoist works of the late Warring States period. According to Saiki, the Huang-lao tradition remains essentially a Han phenomenon. See Saiki Tetsurō, "Maōtai hakusho yori mita dōka shisō no ichi sokumen" (One Aspect of Taoist Thought as Reflected in the Ma-wang-tui Silk Manuscripts), in *Tōhōgaku*, 69 (January 1985): 44–58. In an earlier work, Saiki has suggested that Huang-lao thought may be seen as an elaboration of the philosophy of the *Lao-tzu*. See Saiki, "Kōrō shisō no sai-kentō" (A Reexamination of Huang-lao Thought), in *Tōhō shūkyō*, 62 (1983): 19–36.

50. Jan Yün-hua, "The Silk Manuscripts on Taoism," *T'oung Pao*, 63, 1 (1977): 74.

51. As trans. in Jan Yün-hua, "*Tao Yüan* or Tao: the Origin," *Journal of Chinese Philosophy*, 7 (1980): 198, lines 11–12.

52. Jan, "Silk Manuscripts," pp. 74–75; modified.

53. MWT (see n. 43, above), p. 72; *Ching-fa*, p. 73. The section title is partly supplied by the editors; the manuscript is slightly damaged here and only the character *fa* is left intact. Since the term *Ch'eng-fa* is found in the text, the editors thus entitled this section "Complete Law." In the Ma-wang-tui texts, Li Mu is given as Li Hei.

54. MWT, Ibid. On the relationship between Tao and "One," the text literally reads: "The One: Tao is its root."

55. MWT, p. 67; *Ching-fa*, p. 62.

56. MWT, p. 79; *Ching-fa*, p. 88. The two readings here differ slightly, but the basic meaning is clear.

57. MWT, p. 43; *Ching-fa,* p. 1.

58. Ibid.

59. MWT, p. 43; *Ching-fa,* p. 2.

60. Ibid. Here I am relying on the editors of the *Ching-fa* for the meaning of these terms, though I have also added the more common interpretation of two of these; see p. 5, n. 14. On the idea of *wu-wei* as "nonaggressive" action, see Holmes Welch, *Taoism: The Parting of the Way,* revised edition (Boston: Beacon Press, 1965), pp. 18–34.

61. MWT, p. 43; *Ching-fa,* p. 2.

62. MWT, p. 44; *Ching-fa,* p. 3.

63. MWT, p. 57; *Ching-fa,* p. 39.

64. In this regard, Tu Wei-ming's conclusion is most judicious: "Huang-Lao is definitely not a haphazard, eclectic compromise. The interplay of the Taoist and Legalist symbols is so salient a feature of this mode of thinking that I am tempted to interpret it as a conscious attempt at a new fusion." See Tu, "The 'Thought of Huang-Lao' " (see n. 43, above), p. 108. Both the theoretical and practical aspects of the Huang-lao tradition are brought out very clearly in Tu's analysis. However, I am more inclined to see that the Huang-lao tradition has perhaps deeper roots, as Tu (ibid., p. 109) also recognizes the possibility. My analysis here is also indebted to Jan Yün-hua's excellent discussion in "Tao, Principle, and Law: The Three Key Concepts in the Yellow Emperor Taoism," *Journal of Chinese Philosophy,* 7, 3 (September 1980): 205–28.

65. The legend of Master An-ch'i is itself worthy of serious attention. He was sought by Ch'in Shih-huang-ti for the secret to immortality. Despite the treasures and riches given to him by the emperor, Master An-ch'i retired to the land of the immortals, the fabulous island of P'eng-lai. See Huang-fu Mi, *Kao-shih chuan* (TSCC), B:61. According to this account, Master An-ch'i was also sought by Hsiang Yü, archrival of the founder of the Han dynasty, Liu Pang. There is a similar account in the *Lieh-hsien chuan* (Biographies of Various Immortals), traditionally ascribed to Liu Hsiang (79–8 B.C.); see the Ku-chin i-shu edition (reprinted, Shanghai: Shang-wu, 1937), part A, pp. 13b–14a. Master An-ch'i reappears later in the context of Han Wu-ti's (r. 140–87 B.C.) attempt to acquire the secret of immortality. See, e.g., *Shih-chi,* ch. 28; translated in Burton Watson, *Records of the Grand Historian* (New York, 1962), 2:13–69.

66. See Huang-fu Mi, *Kao-shih chuan,* B:63–64, where Ko Kung is identified as a disciple of Yüeh Chü-kung. See also Ts'ao Ts'an's biography in *Shih-chi,* ch. 54, in which Ko Kung is quoted to have told the minister,

"Value tranquility and quietude, and the people will be naturally well governed," which calls to mind chap. 57 of the *Lao-tzu*.

67. MWT, p. 57; *Ching-fa*, p. 39. The term *ming-li* is also used to describe the knowledge of the sage. This shows that *ming-li* indeed served a political purpose; see chap. 1, above, pp. 23–24.

68. *Sui-shu*, 34:1003.

69. See Hsi K'ang, *Sheng-hsien kao-shih chuan*, p. 11b, and Huang-fu Mi, *Kao-shih chuan*, B:74–75. According to the latter, Master An-ch'iu also wrote a commentary on the *Lao-tzu*. We shall come back to this point later.

70. T'ang Lan, "Ma-wang-tui ch'u-t'u Lao-tzu i-pen chüan-ch'ien ku-i-shu ti yen-chiu," in *Ching-fa*, p. 163. Some may perhaps object to the identification of the *fang-shih* tradition with the *shen-hsien chia*. Admittedly the latter is a later phenomenon; but it seems clear that it has grown out of the *fang-shih* tradition. By "immortality" I have in mind especially what Yü Ying-shih has called "worldly immortality," though I think it is important to recognize the metaphysical or cosmological basis behind this conception as well; this is why I have tried to present both the theoretical and practical dimensions of the Huang-lao tradition. See Yü Ying-shih, "Life and Immortality in the Mind of Han China," in *Harvard Journal of Asiatic Studies*, 25 (1964–1965): 80–122. Indeed, according to Yü, this "worldly immortality" has much to do with the *fang-shih* tradition: "And the keen political interest of the *fang-shih* or Taoist immortalists also makes it more likely that they were in some way related to the so-called Huang-lao Taoism of the Former Han period." Ibid., p. 120. It is precisely this that I am trying to explicate here. Also see A. Seidel, *La Divinisation*, pp. 50–58; and Ngo Van Xuyet, *Divination, Magie, et Politique dans la Chine Ancienne* (Paris, 1976).

71. As described in Huang-fu Mi, *Kao-shih chuan*, B:62. The "biography" of Ho-shang Chang-jen is translated in my article, "The Formation of the Ho-shang Kung Legend."

72. A second burial shroud, in poor condition, was also found in tomb 1. See especially Michael Loewe, *Ways to Paradise: The Chinese Quest for Immortality* (London: Allen and Unwin, 1979); part 1 is devoted to the Ma-wang-tui find. There is a detailed review of this work by Anna Seidel, "Tokens of Immortality in Han Graves, with an Appendix by Marc Kalinowski," in *Numen*, 29, 1 (July 1982): 79–122. Also see Yü Ying-shih, "New Evidence on the Early Chinese Conception of Afterlife—A Review Article," in *Journal of Asian Studies*, 41, 1 (November 1981): 81–85. In a more recent study, Yü has convincingly argued that the silk painting probably served as a burial shroud, as distinguished from a banner used in funeral processions. See Yü Ying-shih, " 'O Soul, Come Back!' A Study in the Changing Conceptions of the Soul and Afterlife in Pre-Buddhist China," *Harvard Journal of Asiatic Studies*, 47 (1987): 365–69.

73. See Michael Loewe, ibid., and his more general study, *Chinese Ideas of Life and Death: Faith, Myth, and Reason in the Han Period (202 B.C.–220 A.D.)* (London: Allen and Unwin, 1982). Also see the studies by Yü Ying-shih, cited in nn. 70 and 72, above, and his article "Chung-kuo ku-tai ssu-hou shih-chieh-kuan ti yen-pien" (The Development of the Idea of the Afterworld in Ancient China), in *Ming-pao yüeh-k'an*, 18, no. 9 (1983): 12–20. Also Joseph Needham, *Science and Civilisation in China*, vol. 5, part 2 (Cambridge: Cambridge University Press, 1974), pp. 77–113. These works have contributed greatly to our understanding of Chinese religion; earlier studies tended to overemphasize the intellectual aspects and to relegate the religious dimension to the background. For example, see Hu Shih, "The Concept of Immortality in Chinese Thought," in *Harvard Divinity School Bulletin*, 43, 3 (March 1946): 23–42; and Ch'ien Mu, "Chung-kuo ssu-hsiang-shih chung ti kuei-shen kuan" ("The Conception of Spirits and Deities in the History of Chinese Thought"), in *Hsin-ya hsüeh-pao*, 1, 1 (1955): 1–43.

74. On Wu Kuang, who is said to have refused the throne when the founder of the Shang dynasty offered it to him, and killed himself to show his distaste for politics, see *Shih-chi*, 61.1b; Liu Hsiang, *Lieh-hsien chuan* (Shanghai, 1937), A:7a–7b; and especially the *Chuang-tzu*, chap. 28; see Burton Watson trans., *The Complete Works of Chuang Tzu* (New York: Columbia University Press, 1968), pp. 320–21. But this picture of a "true" recluse must be balanced by the account in the *Han Fei-tzu*, in which Wu Kuang's death is traced to the emperor's own careful scheming. See *Han Fei-tzu*, chap. 22 (SPPY), ch. 7.6a. Hsien-men Tzu-kao was an "immortal" much sought after by Ch'in Shih-huang-ti, and there was also a *fang-shih* by the name of Hsien-men Kao; see the *Han-shu*, 25A:1202–3. The last figure in this line of transmission is rather obscure. I suspect Ch'iu-tzu is the same as the diviner Ch'iu Tzu-ming mentioned in the *Shih-chi*, 128.2a, who is said to have acquired powerful influence and much wealth because of his art in the early Han dynasty. These figures are, according to the Taoist master Tu Kuang-t'ing (850–933), identified as Ho-shang Kung's special pupils by Ch'eng Hsüan-ying, the famous Taoist of the 7th century. See *Tao-te chen-ching kuang sheng-i*, TT 441, 5.10b. See also Akizuki Kan'ei, "Kōrō kannen no keifu," *Tōhōgaku* 10 (1955): 69–81, which is especially good on the relationship between the immortalist tradition and the Huang-lao school.

75. *Shih-chi*, 49.5b; cf. B. Watson trans., *Records*, 1:386. It is interesting that the reference to the work of Huang-ti is omitted in the biography of the empress dowager in the *Han-shu* (97A:3945). It seems that the figure of the Yellow Emperor declined in importance as the tradition developed.

76. See n. 20, above.

77. Seidel, *La Divinisation*, pp. 51–52.

78. Ibid., p. 52. This theme is elaborated in Seidel's "Imperial Treasures and Taoist Sacraments: Taoist Roots in the Apocrypha," in M. Strickmann ed., *Tantric and Taoist Studies in Honour of R. A. Stein*, vol. 2 (Brussels, 1983), esp. pp. 345–48.

79. Kimura Eiichi, "Kōrō kara rōsō oyobi dōkyō e: ryōkan jidai ni okeru rōshi no gaku" (From Huang-lao to Lao-chuang and the Taoist Religion: Interpretations of the *Lao-tzu* in the Two Han Dynasties), in *Kyōto daigaku jinbun kagaku kenkyujō sōritsu 25 shūnen kinen ronbunshū* (Silver Jubilee Volume of the Research Institute of the Humanities, Kyoto University) (Kyoto, 1954), pp. 97–98.

80. Anna Seidel, *La Divinisation*, p. 26.

81. Yü Ying-shih, "Chung-kuo ku-tai ssu-hou shih-chieh-kuan ti yen-pien" (see n. 73, above), p. 18. This does not necessarily mean that the Ho-shang Kung legend "originated" as a "folk" tradition; the political interest, it seems to me, is too strong for such an interpretation.

82. Naitō Motoharu, "Kajōkō chū rōshi no yōjōsetsu ni tsuite" (On the View of Self-Cultivation in the Ho-shang Kung Commentary on the *Lao-tzu*), in *Yoshioka hakushi kanreki kinen dōkyō kenkyū ronshū* (Tokyo: Kokusho kankōkai, 1977), pp. 319–39. Naitō's work, however, is excellent in bringing out this aspect of the commentary.

83. As preserved in Li Shan's (fl. 660) commentary on the *Wen-hsüan*, compiled by Hsiao T'ung (501–531). Anna Seidel and her teacher, Maxime Kaltenmark, were apparently the first to call attention to this passage. See Seidel, *La Divinisation de Lao Tseu dans le Taoisme des Han* (Paris, 1969), p. 32, n. 4. The *Tung-ching fu* is now available in English in David Knechtges trans., *Wen xuan or Selections of Refined Literature*, vol. 1 (Princeton: Princeton University Press, 1982), from which the title "Eastern Metropolis Rhapsody" is taken. The quotation from Ho-shang Kung, however, is not reproduced in the translation. For the original, I have checked the *Liu ch'en chu Wen-hsüan*, ch. 3 (reprinted, SPTK edition; Taipei: Shang-wu, 1965), 1:79.

84. Besides an extra particle, the only difference is that instead of the verb *chih*, "to govern, cultivate," in the SPTK edition, the Hsüeh Tsung reference has *wu*, "to work, cultivate," which does not alter the meaning of the passage.

85. Yü Ho's *Lun shu piao* is found in a number of T'ang and Sung sources; for example, in Chang Yen-yüan (fl. 847–874), *Fa-shu yao-lu* (Extracts from Essential Calligraphic Works), ch. 2 (TSCC; Shanghai: Shang-wu, 1936), p. 17; Ch'en Ssu (fl. 1235), *Yü-lan shu-yüan ch'ing-hua* (Essential Calligraphic Works), 14.11b–12a (Ts'ang-hsiu t'ang ts'ung-shu, 1890); and Chang Hao (fl. 1216), *Yün-ku tsa-chi* (Miscellaneous Notes from the Valley of

Clouds), 1.20a–22b (Ssu-k'u ch'üan-shu chen-pen pieh-chi, no. 209, photo-reprint of the Wen-yüan-ko edition; Taipei: Shang-wu, 1975). This last has the most detailed account of this incident, and contains a discussion of the question whether Wang Hsi-chih copied the *Lao-tzu* or the *Huang-t'ing ching*, as he is also quoted to have done. From a different source, the same story is also quoted in the Sung encyclopedia *T'ai-p'ing kuang-chi*, 207.2a. See Ma Hsü-lun, *Lao-tzu chiao-ku*, p. 2, where some of these are first cited. For a more detailed account, see Yen Ling-feng, *Wu-ch'iu pei-chai hsüeh-shu lun-chi* (Taipei: Chung-hua, 1969), pp. 288–97. I have listed all these sources here because this reference has often been doubted, owing to the slightly different account in the *Chin-shu*; see text and n. 87, below. "Quantity" can-not of course be equated with authenticity, but it does indicate that the story was widely known from an early time.

86. The passage reads: "the Taoist geese keeper said to Wang Hsi-chih, 'I have always wanted to have the Ho-shang Kung *Lao-tzu* written; the silk has been ready for a long time, but nobody was able to do it. If you Sir do not object to writing two sections (*chang*) from each (part) of the *Tao-te ching*, I would respectfully offer you my entire herd (of geese)." *Fa-shu yao-lu*, 2.17. It seems that Wang Hsi-chih was not asked to write the entire text; this is not unimportant, because a copy of this is said to have survived. See Yen Ling-feng, ibid.

87. *Chin-shu*, 80:2100.

88. For instance, the commentary on the *Lun-yü* by Huang K'an (ca. 488–545) has quoted from chap. 4 of the Ho-shang Kung commentary. Most of these early references are first identified in Ma Hsü-lun, *Lao-tzu chiao-ku*, pp. 1–3. For a more detailed discussion, see Kusuyama Haruki, *Rōshi densetsu no kenkyū*, pp. 125–33.

89. Ma Hsü-lun, ibid., and Takeuchi Yoshio, *Rōshi genshi*, pp. 35–48. According to the former, the Ho-shang Kung commentary has inadvert-ently incorporated some of the mistakes in Wang Pi's commentary. For ex-ample, Ma argues that in chap. 31, Wang Pi's commentary was mistakenly made part of the *Lao-tzu* text itself. And since the Ho-shang Kung text is the same in this instance, it is therefore later than the Wang Pi version. This argument, however, is now proven incorrect by the Ma-wang-tui *Lao-tzu*, which has basically the same reading. Takeuchi, on the basis of a study of the *Hsü-chüeh*, which I have already discussed, even more specifically traces the Ho-shang Kung commentary to the Ko family or school in the 4th century A.D.

90. Jao Tsung-i, *Lao-tzu Hsiang-erh chu chiao-chien* ("A Study on Chang Tao-ling's Hsiang-er Commentary of Tao Te Ching") (Hong Kong: Tung-nan ch'u-pan-she, 1956). Also see his "Lao-tzu Hsiang-erh chu hsü-lun" (Fur-

ther Discussion on the Hsiang-erh), in *Fukui hakushi shōju kinen tōyō bunka ronshū* (Festschrift for Dr. Fukui on the Occasion of his 70th Birthday) (Tokyo: Waseda University Press, 1969), pp. 1155–71. The *Hsiang-erh* commentary (S6825, or 6798 in the new Giles catalogue), unfortunately, is incomplete. The fragment now in the British Museum contains only the first part, i.e., the *Tao-ching* of the *Lao-tzu*; more precisely, beginning with the middle of the chap. 3 to the end of chap. 37, since the beginning is also damaged.

91. Jao has at first adhered to tradition and ascribed the *Hsiang-erh* commentary to Chang Ling, or Chang Tao-ling, the founder of the Celestial Master tradition; see *Hsiang-erh chu chiao-chien*, p. 5. Later, after further examination and in agreement with others, Jao concludes that the work can be traced to Chang Lu and was subsequently attributed to Chang Ling; see "Hsiang-erh chu hsü-lun," p. 1168. Two other important studies on the *Hsiang-erh* are Ch'en Shih-hsiang, "Hsiang-erh Lao-tzu Tao-ching Tun-huang ts'an-chüan lun-cheng" ("On the Historical and Religious Significance of the Tun-huang MS of *Lao-tzu, Book I, With Commentaries by 'Hsiang Erh'* "), in *Tsing-hua Journal of Chinese Studies*, new series, 1, 2 (April 1957): 41–62; and Ōfuchi Ninji, "Rōshi sōjichū no seiritsu" (The Formation of the *Hsiang-erh* Commentary), in *Okayama shigaku*, 19 (1967): 9–31. Ōfuchi's view is also contained in his "Gotobeidō no kyōhō ni tsuite: rōshi sōjichū o chūshin toshite, Parts I and II" (On the Teaching of the Five Pecks of Rice Taoism: The Core of the *Hsiang-erh* Commentary on the *Lao-tzu*), *Tōyō gakuhō*, 49, 3 (Dec. 1966): 40–68; 49, 4 (March 1967): 97–129. Ōfuchi has written a short article especially on the relationship between the *Hsiang-erh* and the Ho-shang Kung commentary as well; see the next note. All these studies are in fundamental agreement with regard to their assessment of the *Hsiang-erh* commentary.

92. See Ōfuchi Ninji, ibid., and "Rōshi sōjichū to kajōkōchū to no kankei ni tsuite" (On the Relationship between the Hsiang-erh and Ho-shang Kung Commentaries), in *Yamazaki sensei taikan kinen tōyō shigaku ronshū* (Essays on East Asian History in Commemoration of the Retirement of Dr. Yamazaki) (Tokyo, 1967), pp. 103–8. Yoshioka Yoshitoyo, "Rōshi kajōkō hon to dōkyō" (The Ho-shang Kung Version of the *Lao-tzu* and Religious Taoism), in *Dōkyō no sōgōteki kenkyū* (Proceedings of the Second International Conference on Taoist Studies, Chino, Japan, 1972), ed. Sakai Tadao (Tokyo: Kokusho kankōkai, 1977), pp. 291–332. Anna Seidel, *La Divinisation de Lao Tseu dans le Taoisme des Han* (Paris, 1969), pp. 75–76, n. 3. Yü Ying-shih, "Chung-kuo ku-tai ssu-hou shih-chieh-kuan ti yen-pien," *Ming-pao yüan-k'an*, 18, 9 (1983): 12–20. Naitō Motoharu, "Kajōkō chū rōshi no yōjōsetsu ni tsuite," in *Yoshioka hakushi kanreki kinen dōkyō kenkyū ronshū* (Tokyo, 1977), pp. 319–39. Kobayashi Masayoshi, "Kajō shinjin shōku no shisō to seiritsu," *Tōhō shūkyō*, 65 (May 1985): 20–43. Kusuyama's study has al-

ready been mentioned on a number of occasions; for the work of Shima Kunio, see the next note.

93. Shima has argued his thesis in a number of places. See his *Rōshi kōsei* (Tokyo: Kyūkoshoin, 1973), pp. 25–34; "Rōshi kajōkō hon no seiritsu" (The Formation of the Ho-shang Kung Text), in *Uno Tetsuto sensei hakuju shukuga kinen tōyōgaku ronsō* (Essays on East Asian Studies: Festschrift for Dr. Uno Tetsuto) (Tokyo, 1974), pp. 529–49; and "Maōtai rōshi kara mita kajōkō hon" (The Ho-shang Kung Version from the Perspective of the Ma-wang-tui *Lao-tzu*), in *Shūkan tōyōgaku*, 36 (November 1976): 1–26.

94. For example, *Rōshi kōsei*, p. 27. As we shall see more clearly, Shima's argument is primarily based on a quotation attributed to the T'ang scholar Fu I (555–639) found in a number of Sung sources.

95. Yoshioka, "Rōshi kajōkō hon to dōkyō" (see n. 92, above). Besides pointing out that Shima's reading of the quotation ascribed to Fu I is problematic, Yoshioka has also surveyed a number of Taoist texts that attest to the priority and antiquity of the Ho-shang Kung commentary. Some of these are identified by Jao Tsung-i as well, and will be discussed shortly.

96. Jao Tsung-i, *Lao-tzu Hsiang-erh chu chiao-chien*, pp. 87–92. Jao's second example reads chap. 20, which is a misprint for chap. 28.

97. Jao, ibid., p. 89. The *Hsiang-erh* commentary actually does not mention the word *hsüan* here, though it does take *hsüan* to mean "heaven," e.g., in chaps. 10 and 15; see Jao, pp. 14 and 19.

98. E. Erkes, *Ho-shang-kung's Commentary on Lao-tse* (Ascona: Artibus Asiae, 1958), pp. 9–11. According to Erkes, the priority of Ho-shang Kung "follows from Kao Yu's only casually mentioning this conception of *hsüan*, whereas Ho-shang-kung makes a complete system of it" (p. 10). See, however, Wing-tsit Chan's critique, in *The Way of Lao Tzu* (Indianapolis: Bobbs-Merrill, 1981), pp. 79–80; and A. Rump and W. T. Chan, *Commentary on the Lao-tzu by Wang Pi* (Honolulu: University Press of Hawaii, 1979), pp. xxvi–xxvii. In this connection, Chu Ch'ien-chih also maintains that the Ho-shang Kung commentary precedes that of Wang Pi; see his *Lao-tzu chiao-shih* (Shanghai, 1958; reprint, Peking: Chung-hua, 1980), pp. 1–2. See also the two essays on the Ho-shang Kung commentary by Chin Ch'un-feng, in his *Han-tai ssu-hsiang shih* (Han Intellectual History) (Peking: Chung-kuo she-hui k'o-hsüeh ch'u-pan-she, 1987). Chin is among the few who would date the Ho-shang Kung commentary to the Former Han period, before the commentary by Yen Tsun (1st century B.C.). Chin's argument is basically that both the language and thought of the Ho-shang Kung commentary point to its rootedness in the Hans ethos. I would agree that the Ho-shang Kung commentary reflects earlier ideas and interests; but it is difficult to

establish a precise date on the basis of a general comparison with other Han texts alone.

99. Jao, *Hsiang-erh chu chiao-chien*, p. 88.

100. Most scholars have identified the subject of the phrase *erh pu-tz'u* with Tao, but they disagree on the meaning of the verb in question. Among the various translations, the following may be noted: "disown" (A. Waley), "turn away" (W. T. Chan), "claim no authority" (D. C. Lau), "does not attempt to be their master" (Ch'en Ku-ying); J. Legge has rendered it as "refusing obedience," identifying the subject with the "ten thousand things." On this difficult expression, see esp. the discussion in Ch'en Ku-ying, *Lao-tzu: Text, Notes, and Comments*, pp. 61–62, n. 8.

101. Erkes, *Ho-shang Kung's Commentary*, p. 67.

102. Jao, *Hsiang-erh chu chiao-chien*, p. 46.

103. See *Ku Huan Tao-te ching chu-su*, ed. Yen Ling-feng (WCPC; Taipei, 1965), 3.33b. The authenticity of this commentary is a question I cannot go into here. For a general discussion of this text, see Isabelle Robinet, *Les Commentaires du Tao To King* (Paris, 1977), pp. 77–89. Also see Fujiwara Takao, "Ko Kan rōshichū kō," (Study of Ku Huan's *Lao-tzu* Commentary), in *Uchino hakushi kanreki kinen tōyōgaku ronshū* (Essays on East Asian Studies: Festschrift for Dr. Uchino) (Tokyo: Kangibunka kenkyūkai, 1964), pp. 163–84. Both Robinet and Fujiwara have pointed out that the Ku Huan commentary was indebted to Buddhist influence. According to Liu Ts'un-yan, the current text of the commentary may be dated to the Sung dynasty; but it seems to have carefully preserved earlier material. See Liu, "Lun Tao-tsang pen Ku Huan chu Lao-tzu chih hsing-chih" (On the Characteristics of the Taoist Canon Version of the Ku Huan Commentary on the *Lao-tzu*), in *Lien-ho shu-yüan hsüeh-pao* (United College Journal), 8 (1970–71): 15–28.

104. See, e.g., the commentaries on chaps. 3, 5, 14, 21, and 22.

105. Jao, *Hsiang-erh chu chiao-chien*, p. 88.

106. See William G. Boltz, "The Religious and Philosophical Significance of the 'Hsiang Erh' *Lao Tzu* in the Light of the *Ma-wang-tui* Silk Manuscripts," in *Bulletin of the School of Oriental and African Studies*, 45 (1982): 105.

107. Ibid., p. 109, n. 26.

108. As Boltz himself has pointed out, though the Ma-wang-tui MSS and the *Hsiang-erh* are sometimes in agreement against the "received" text of Wang Pi and Ho-shang Kung, the reverse is true as well. In some in-

stances, the *Hsiang-erh* reading is unique. For Boltz, if the cases where the *Hsiang-erh* differs from the Ma-wang-tui and the "received" text can be explained in terms of the former's "deliberate" attempt to alter the text because of its distinctive religious orientation, then the apparent contradiction is resolved. For example, Boltz has argued that chap. 4 is a good example of what he calls the *Hsiang-erh*'s "deliberate and conscious deviations from the established *Lao tzu* text arising within an identifiable religious milieu" (p. 109). In this instance, the Ma-wang-tui and Wang Pi texts agree in describing the Tao, to use Boltz's translation, as "suffusive-so, seemingly *at times* present (*huo ts'un*)." The *Hsiang-erh*, however, has "suffusive, seemingly *perpetually* present (*ch'ang ts'un*)." According to Boltz, then, the *Hsiang-erh* has deliberately changed the text to bring out its preoccupation with "matters eternal" (p. 110). Moreover, in the same chapter the Ho-shang Kung commentary explains that the word *huo* means *ch'ang*. This has led Boltz to conclude that the Ho-shang Kung commentary is probably influenced by the *Hsiang-erh* here; i.e., the rather unique reading of *huo* as *ch'ang* is indebted to the *Hsiang-erh* text (p. 111). Incidentally, Shima Kunio has also proposed the same argument in his *Rōshi kōsei* (Tokyo, 1973), p. 61. Despite Boltz's arguments, I am more inclined to agree with Ma Hsü-lun that those versions that have the word *ch'ang*, including the *Hsiang-erh*, were influenced by the Ho-shang Kung commentary; see Ma, *Lao-tzu chiao-ku* (reprinted, Hong Kong, 1965), pp. 39–40. At least, the question of "textual priority" cannot be easily settled, and will no doubt continue to attract diverse opinions. I am also uncomfortable with the assumption that the Ma-wang-tui MSS represent a kind of "pure" text by which the trustworthiness of other versions can be measured. Although the Ma-wang-tui MSS are important and remain the oldest in existence, it cannot be assumed that they were in fact the "original," or closest to the "pristine" *Lao-tzu*. Robert Henricks's forthcoming study of the Ma-wang-tui *Lao-tzu* (New York: Random House) may shed more light on this question.

109. This same conclusion is reached by Ōfuchi Ninji, though he is favorable to Jao's thesis. See his "Rōshi sōjichū to kajōkōchū to no kankei ni tsuite" (cited in n. 92, above), pp. 107–8.

110. Jao, *Hsiang-erh chu chiao-chien*, p. 87. Jao has discussed this and other supporting evidence in greater detail in a separate article; see his "Wu Chien-heng erh-nien Su Tan hsieh-pen Tao-te ching ts'an-chüan k'ao-cheng" ("The Su Tan Manuscript Fragment of the *Tao-te ching* [A.D. 270]"), in *Journal of Oriental Studies* (Hong Kong), 2, 1 (January 1955): 1–71. This quotation from Ch'eng Hsüan-ying's *Lao-tzu k'ai-t'i* (Introduction to the *Lao-tzu*), discovered in Tun-huang, is discussed on p. 10.

111. A number of Tun-huang manuscripts of the *Lao-tzu*, for example, have 4,999 characters. See Ōfuchi Ninji, *Tonkō dōkyō*, vol. 1 (Tokyo, 1978), pp. 187–200. Ch'eng Hsüan-ying's work is also included in Yen Ling-feng's

WCPC collection, first series (Taipei, 1965); see *ch.* 1.12b. A French translation of the *Lao-tzu k'ai-t'i* can be found in I. Robinet, *Les Commentaires du Tao To King* (Paris, 1977), pp. 227–60.

112. See Jao, *Hsiang-erh chu chiao-chien*, p. 90; "Su Tan hsieh-pen Tao-te ching," pp. 7–8. This manuscript (P 2417) is dated to the tenth year of the T'ien-pao reign era, or 751 A.D.; at the end of the manuscript, a contract with the name of the recipient is recorded. This shows that the "5,000-character" version of the *Lao-tzu* was widely used during the T'ang dynasty. See Ōfuchi, *Tonkō dōkyō*, p. 192.

113. Jao, *Hsiang-erh chu*, p. 90; "Hsiang-erh chu hsü-lun" (see n. 90, above), p. 1162. See esp. Yoshioka, "Rōshi kajōkō hon to dōkyō," pp. 297–303, where the view of Ōfuchi is cited with approval. Both Shima Kunio and Kusuyama Haruki, however, have dated this text to the T'ang dynasty. See Shima, "Rōshi kajōkō hon no seiritsu" (see n. 93, above), p. 18, and Kusuyama, *Rōshi densetsu*, p. 140. The text itself (TT 989, HY 1228) goes into some detail explaining in mythological terms why the Ho-shang Kung commentary is ranked after the *Lao-tzu* "large character" version but ahead of the *Hsiang-erh*; see esp. pp. 2a–4b.

114. Yoshioka, ibid., pp. 314–19. The text in question is "The Precious Book of the Most High Supreme Heaven, a Tung-chen Scripture" (*Tung-chen t'ai-shang t'ai-hsiao lang-shu*, TT 1034–35, HY 1341). The same order is mentioned in 4.15b–16a. According to Yoshioka, this text may be dated to between A.D. 450 and 500.

115. see n. 110, above.

116. Jao, "Su Tan hsieh-pen Tao-te ching," p. 71.

117. Yen Ling-feng, *Wu-ch'iu pei-chai hsüeh-shu lun-chi* (Taipei, 1969), pp. 285–88. Yen was able to look at the manuscript himself; but his criticism is largely a matter of conjecture. For example, he has based one of his arguments on the *Lao-tzu Tao-te ching hsü-chüeh*, assuming that it was in fact the work of Ko Hsüan. The criticism that the title of the manuscript, *T'ai-shang hsüan-yüan Tao-te ching*, seems to reflect a later date is explained very well by Jao (pp. 4–6), by tracing it to the *T'ien-shih tao*. Although the title "Profound Origin of the Most High" (*T'ai-shang hsüan-yüan*) did not become popular until the T'ang dynasty, it had a long history. The point that the MS uses a reign era of the Wu Kingdom may, however, pose a problem. As both Jao himself and Yen Ling-feng point out, by 270 A.D. the Tun-huang area was already part of the Chin domain; it would seem strange that Su Tan, who was not known to have any connection with the Wu Kingdom, did not use a Chin date. Jao suggests that perhaps when Su Tan was a student in the capital, his patron might have been a senior person who had connection with the Taoist school of Wu (p. 2), which does not sound

convincing. It is surprising that this manuscript has not attracted much attention even in Chinese and Japanese sources. Kusuyama, for example, has merely alluded to it and accepted Jao's finding; in *Rōshi densetsu*, pp. 155–56.

118. Kusuyama, *Rōshi densetsu*, pp. 17–18, 125–69.

119. Ibid., pp. 157–63. For a similar, though more complex, argument, see Kobayashi Masayoshi, "Kajō shinjin shōku no shisō to seiritsu," *Tōhō shūkyō*, 65 (1985): 20–43.

120. Huang-fu Mi, *Kao-shih chuan* (TSCC; Shanghai, 1937), B:62.

121. *Sui-shu*, 34:1000.

122. Kusuyama, *Rōshi densetsu*, pp. 158, 162.

123. Ibid., pp. 126–27. Kusuyama has argued this point in greater detail in a special article; see his "Ri Zen shoin no Setsu Sō chū ni tsuite" (Study on the Hsüeh Tsung Commentary as Quoted by Li Shan), in *Fukui hakushi shōju kinen tōyō bunka ronshū* (Tokyo: Waseda University Press, 1969), pp. 339–54. In fact, according to Kusuyama, all quotations ascribed to Hsüeh Tsung are probably penned by a later forger.

124. With regard to the *Hsiang-erh*, see Kusuyama, *Rōshi densetsu*, pp. 239–69, esp. pp. 259–60. The Ho-shang Kung legend in the *Shen-hsien chuan* would also have to be late; ibid., p. 172.

125. Master An-ch'iu (An-ch'iu Hsien-sheng) is also known as An-ch'iu Chang-jen and An-ch'iu Wang-chih. See Huang-fu Mi, *Kao-shih chuan*, B:74–75.

126. Lu Te-ming, *Ching-tien shih-wen* (TSCC; Shanghai, 1936), Preface, p. 53. The name of the author is given as Wu-ch'iu Wang-chih, a variant for An-ch'iu Wang-chih.

127. *Sui-shu*, 34:1000, also under Wu-ch'iu Wang-chih.

128. See n. 136, below, and discussion in text.

129. Anna Seidel, *La Divinisation de Lao Tseu dans le Taoisme des Han* (Paris, 1969), p. 33, n. 1.

130. *Hou Han-shu*, 19:703. Here Master An-ch'iu is said to have taught Keng Huang and Wang Chi the *Lao-tzu*; the latter is a cousin of Wang Meng. Similarly, Hsi K'ang's *Sheng-hsien kao-shih chuan*, p. 11b, identifies Master An-ch'iu as an expert on the *Lao-tzu*, but does not mention a commentary.

131. The connection between the Huang-lao school and "Celestial Master" Taoism may perhaps be traced to the figure of T'ien Shu, the disciple of Yüeh Chü-Kung (see n. 25, above), who for over ten years served as the governor of Han-chung (southern Shensi and northern Szechuan), where the "Celestial Master" tradition later developed. Perhaps the deification of Lao-tzu and the recognition of the *Tao-te ching* as revealed literature, as reflected in the legend of Ho-shang Kung, may help to explain the transition from Huang-lao Taoism to the "Way of the Celestial Masters."

132. *Sui-shu*, 33:992.

133. See *Sui-shu*, 33:903–9. This is one of the most important accounts of the development of early bibliographic catalogues in traditional Chinese sources.

134. Lu Te-ming, *Ching-tien shih-wen* (TSCC), Preface, p. 9. As far as I can determine, of these two works, only the Preface and the Table of Contents to the work of Juan Hsiao-hsü have survived. I have consulted a 1934 edition entitled *Ch'i-lu hsü-mu* published by Yao Wei-tsu (Chin shih-han ts'ung-shu Series), which is based on the T'ieh-ch'in t'ung-chien lou edition of Ch'ü Yung. No information, however, can be gleaned from this with regard to the Ho-shang Chang-jen and the An-ch'iu commentaries.

135. According to Takeuchi Yoshio and Naitō Motoharu, only 13 commentaries are cited in Lu Te-ming's "phonological explanation" of key passages of the *Lao-tzu* (*Lao-tzu yin-i*) in his *Ching-tien shih-wen*. See Takeuchi, *Rōshi genshi*, p. 35; Naitō Motoharu, "Kajōkō chū rōshi no yōjōsetsu ni tsuite," p. 319. There are, as I count them, a few other unidentified sources not included in their list; but the point remains that of the total 32 commentaries listed in the Preface, not half are cited in the main commentary. Interestingly, Lu Te-ming has made references to two versions of the Ho-shang Kung *Lao-tzu*; see n. 138, below.

136. Hsieh Shou-hao, *Hun-yüan sheng-chi* (TT 551, HY 769), 3.20a. This passage is also recorded in, e.g., P'eng Ssu, *Tao-te chen-ching chi-chu tsa-shuo* (TT 403, HY 709), 2.30b; cf. nn. 89–91 in chap. 1, above. The discussion in Yoshioka Yoshitoyo, "Rōshi kajōkō hon to dōkyō," pp. 292–97, is especially helpful. With respect to the version transmitted by Ch'iu Yüeh, the context seems to imply that it was the work of Ch'iu himself; see Ma Hsü-lun, *Lao-tzu chiao-ku*, p. 3.

137. Yoshioka, ibid., p. 296.

138. Lu Te-ming, *Ching-tien shih-wen*, ch. 25, *Lao-tzu yin-i* (TSCC; Shanghai, 1936), 16:1403–16. Whereas the Ho-shang Kung text is cited 48 times, in my rough estimate, the "old version" is referred to only twice, or four times at the most.

139. On this question, see esp. Richard Mather, "K'ou Ch'ien-chih and the Taoist Theocracy at the Northern Wei Court, 425–451," in *Facets of Taoism*, ed. Holmes Welch and Anna Seidel (New Haven: Yale University Press, 1979), pp. 103–22.

140. See Rolf A. Stein, "Religious Taoism and Popular Religion from the Second to Seventh Centuries," in *Facets of Taoism*, pp. 53–81; and Michel Strickmann, "On the Alchemy of T'ao Hung-ching," ibid., pp. 123–92. Stein's work is especially important in this connection because it details the interaction between the "Celestial Master" sect and popular local traditions, which led to reforms and caused tension within the Taoist community.

141. As cited in Ch'en Kuo-fu, *Tao-tsang yüan-liu k'ao* (reprinted, Taipei, 1975), pp. 44–45, 478. Admittedly, this remains merely a conjecture; there is little evidence to support this identification. The context seems to call for a "famous" 5th-century southern Taoist master, to correspond to K'ou Ch'ien-chih in the north, and Sun Yu-yüeh immediately comes to mind.

Chapter Four

1. Chap. 19. Cf. Eduard Erkes trans., *Ho-shang-kung's Commentary on Lao-tse* (Ascona: Artibus Asiae, 1958), p. 41. All translations from the Ho-shang Kung commentary are my own; references to Erkes's work will be provided for purpose of comparison.

2. The "Five Emperors" have been variously identified. See especially Ku Chieh-kang and Yang Hsiang-k'uei, "San Huang k'ao" (A Study of the Three Sovereigns), in *Ku-shih pien* (Essays on Ancient Chinese History), vol. 7B, ed. Lü Ssu-mien and T'ung Shu-yeh (Peking, 1941; reprint, Hong Kong: T'ai-p'ing shu-chü, 1963), pp. 20–275. Ho-shang Kung's interpretation is based on the "Appended Remarks" (*Hsi-tz'u*) of the *I-ching*: "In the heavens hang images that reveal good fortune and misfortune." As translated by Richard Wilhelm, *I Ching or Book of Changes*, trans. Cary F. Baynes, 3rd edition, Bollingen Series, 19 (Princeton: Princeton University Press, 1967; reprint, 1979), p. 320. For the Chinese text, see Kao Heng, *Chou-i ta-chuan chin-chu* (New Annotated Edition of the Great Appendixes to the Book of Changes) (Shantung: Ch'i-lu shu-she, 1979), p. 540.

3. Like the "Five Emperors," there are several traditions with respect to the identity of "Three Sovereigns." See Ku Chieh-Kang and Yang Hsiang-k'uei, ibid. Vol. 7B of the *Ku-shih pien* is devoted to this topic. The *Hsi-tz'u* also says: "In the highest antiquity people knotted cords in order to govern. The sages of a later age introduced written documents instead, as a

means of governing the various officials and supervising the people."
Wilhelm, ibid., p. 335; modified. Kao Heng, ibid., p. 567.

4. The *Shih-chi* begins with the genealogy of the "Five Emperors"; the
other two are Chuan-hsü, identified as the grandson of the Yellow Emperor, and Ti-k'u, a great grandson. *Shih-chi, ch.* 1 (SPPY).

5. Cheng Hsüan, commentary on the Book of History; as cited in Ku
Chieh-kang and Yang Hsiang-k'uei, ibid., p. 129.

6. Following Shun, Yü founded the Hsia dynasty, traditionally dated
to the second millennium B.C. Hou Chi was the legendary ancestor of the
Chou clan, and was credited with the "invention" of agriculture. Cf. Erkes,
p. 76, where the term "lowly house" (*po-wu*) is mistaken for a person.

7. Cf. Erkes, p. 108. The Ku Huan version, which Erkes followed,
alone has "the time of the Three Sovereigns" (*san-huang chih-shih*) as opposed to *san-huang chih-ch'ien*. There is no reason to emend the SPTK text
here. See Cheng Ch'eng-hai, *Lao-tzu Ho-shang Kung chu chiao-li* (Critical Edition of the Ho-shang Kung Commentary on *Lao-tzu*) (Taipei, 1971), p. 376.
This work will be cited as *Chiao-li*.

8. The *Lao-tzu* original is adapted from Wing-tsit Chan trans., *The Way
of Lao-tzu* (Indianapolis: Bobbs-Merrill, 1981), p. 131. Note that the translation of the *Lao-tzu* in this chapter does not always agree with that adopted
in chap. 2, as the SPTK and SPPY versions at times differ. The differences
are generally minor; on this question, see esp. Shima Kunio, *Rōshi kōsei*
(Tokyo, 1973), and Ma Hsü-lun, *Lao-tzu chiao-ku* (reprinted, Hong Kong,
1965).

9. Cf. Erkes, p. 40. See Cheng, *Chiao-li*, p. 118, where the phrase
"there were loyalty and trust in the household" (*hu yu chung-hsin*) is
emended to read "there were loyal ministers in the state" (*kuo yu chung-
ch'en*). While the emended reading makes better sense in this context, it is
supported by only two versions.

10. Read *liu chi chüeh* in place of *liu chüeh chüeh*, which is clearly a
mistake; emended according to six other versions in Cheng, *Chiao-li*, p. 119.
While Wang Pi understands the "six relations" to mean those of father and
son, brother and brother, and husband and wife, Ho-shang Kung equates
them with the "six threads" of family relation. This latter is traditionally
identified as the various elders, brothers, clansmen, maternal uncles, teachers, and friends. In the Confucian tradition, each of these corresponds to a
specific virtue. See Cheng Ch'eng-hai, *Lao-tzu Ho-shang Kung chu su-cheng*
(Explanation of the Ho-shang Kung Commentary) (Taipei: Hua-cheng shu-
chü, 1978), p. 128; this work will be cited as *Su-cheng* hereon.

11. Read "in the world of the great Way" (*Ta-tao chih-shih*) for "the ruler of the great Way" (*Ta-tao chih-chün*), as in six other versions. Cheng, *Chiao-li*, p. 121.

12. On this theme, see esp. Norman J. Girardot, *Myth and Meaning in Early Taoism* (Berkeley: University of California Press, 1983); and Roger T. Ames, *The Art of Rulership: A Study in Ancient Chinese Political Thought* (Honolulu: University of Hawaii Press, 1983), chap. 1. The view of history presupposed here comes closest to that of the *Chuang-tzu*, chap. 16. See Burton Watson trans., *The Complete Works of Chuang-tzu* (New York: Columbia University Press, 1968), pp. 171–74. See also the discussion of "Primitivist" thought in the *Chuang-tzu* in A. C. Graham, "How Much of *Chuang Tzu* did Chuang Tzu Write?," in *Studies in Classical Chinese Thought*, ed. Henry Rosemont, Jr., and Benjamin I. Schwartz (Chico: American Academy of Religion, 1980), pp. 459–501.

13. Cf. Erkes, (n. 1, above), p. 13.

14. Cf. Erkes, pp. 29–30. The first sentence is difficult and is translated in light of the chapter as a whole.

15. Cf. Erkes, p. 78.

16. Benjamin I. Schwartz, *The World of Thought in Ancient China* (Cambridge: Harvard University Press, 1985), p. 181.

17. "The One" is missing in the SPTK version; emended in the light of eight other versions. See Cheng, *Chiao-li*, p. 271. Cf. Erkes, p. 80.

18. Read *ho ch'ing cho* for *ho ch'i cho*, as in six other versions. Cheng, *Chiao-li*, p. 271. Cheng himself prefers the reading *ho-ch'i ch'ing-cho*, as in the *Tao-tsang* and one Japanese version, emphasizing the act of harmonizing or blending of the "clear" and "turbid" breaths. I think the context implies three types of *ch'i*; but the difference is not great.

19. Add *jen*; see Cheng, *Chiao-li*, p. 272.

20. *Huai-nan tzu* (SPPY), 3.1a; as translated in Wing-tsit Chan, *A Source Book in Chinese Philosophy* (Princeton: Princeton University Press, 1963; reprints, 1973), p. 307; modified.

21. Hsü Shen (fl. 100 A.D.), *Shuo-wen chieh-tzu* (reprinted, Hong Kong: Chung-hua shu-chü, 1979), p. 286. As cited in Cheng, *Su-cheng*, p. 291.

22. Ch. 1, in *Lieh-tzu chi-shih* (The *Lieh-tzu* Collated and Explained), ed. Yang Po-chün (Hong Kong: T'ai-p'ing shu-chü, 1965), p. 5. Cf. A. C. Graham trans., *The Book of Lieh-tzu* (London: John Murray, 1960), p. 19.

23. See Hsü Fu-kuan, *Chung-kuo jen-hsing-lun shih. Hsien-Ch'in p'ien* (History of Chinese Philosophy of Human Nature. The Pre-Ch'in Period) (Taipei, 1969; reprint, 1984), pp. 510–11. Cf. note 34 to chap. 1, above.

24. Cf. Erkes, p. 80.

25. Read *Shih che Tao yeh* or *Shih Tao yeh* in place of *Shih yu Tao yeh*, "The beginning has the Way"; see Cheng, *Chiao-li*, p. 315.

26. The Wang Pi text has "Having obtained *(te)* the mother," as opposed to "Having known *(chih)* the mother." According to Chiang Hsi-ch'ang, *Lao-tzu chiao-ku*, p. 320, the latter seems to be the original reading.

27. Cf. Erkes, p. 33.

28. See Cheng, *Chiao-li*, p. 248; variants are minor, mostly involving particles. The reading of the last line of the *Lao-tzu* text is uncertain; but this does not affect our discussion.

29. Yü Ying-shih, "Chung-kuo ku-tai ssu-hou shih-chieh-kuan ti yen pien," in *Ming-pao yüeh-k'an*, 18, no. 9 (1983), pp. 14–16; " 'O Soul, Come Back!' A Study in the Changing Conceptions of the Soul and Afterlife in Pre-Buddhist China," *Harvard Journal of Asiatic Studies*, 47 (1987): 369–78. According to Yü, the notion of *p'o* seems to be the older of the two, and might have been related to the worship of the moon. *Hun*, on the other hand, seems to have been introduced from the south.

30. This is a large topic; see note 34 to chap. 1, above. On the five phases or elements theory, the best collection of essays remains that of *Ku shih pien*, vol. 5 part 2, ed. Ku Chieh-kang (1935). In addition, see the important work by Shima Kunio, *Gogyō shisō to Raiki Getsurei no kenkyū* (A Study of Five Phases Thought and the "Monthly Commands" Chapter of the Book of Rites) (Tokyo: Kyūkoshoin, 1971). On the correspondence of various phenomena generated by this theory, see "Table 12" in Joseph Needham, *Science and Civilisation in China*, vol. 2 (Cambridge: Cambridge University Press, 1956), 2: 262–63.

31. Chap. 6. Cf. Erkes, p. 21. As is well known, this was later elaborated in the Taoist religion to form a complex system of "internal alchemy." For this development and the practice of nourishing the spirits, see Henri Maspero, *Taoism and Chinese Religion*, trans. Frank A. Kierman, Jr. (Amherst: University of Massachusetts Press, 1981), esp. books 5, 7, and 9. Also see the excellent studies by Isabelle Robinet, "Metamorphorsis and Deliverance from the Corpse in Taoism," in *History of Religions*, 19, 1 (August 1979): 37–70; and *Méditation taoiste* (Paris: Dervy Livres, 1979). See also nn. 49 and 51, below.

32. See Chiang Hsi-ch'ang, *Lao-tzu chiao-ku*, pp. 38–39, for a discussion of the various interpretations of the first line of chap. 6.

33. I have in mind especially the work of Girardot cited in n. 12, above. However, it should be noted that Girardot is concerned mainly with "early Taoism," i.e., the *Lao-tzu, Chuang-tzu*, and *Huai-nan tzu*. The only place in the Ho-shang Kung commentary that may be taken to suggest a return to "chaos" is chap. 1, where the "constant name" is described as like an unborn chick. As this is paralleled with the infant who does not yet talk, the pearl that is still within the shell, and the precious stone that is within the rock, the emphasis remains that of ideal order—what is fully formed, as opposed to formlessness.

34. Kristofer Schipper, "The Taoist Body," in *History of Religions*, 17, 3–4 (1978): 355. See also Schipper's book, *Le corps taoiste* (Paris: Fayard, 1982). This theme is also emphasized by I. Robinet, *Les Commentaires du Tao To King* (Paris, 1977), pp. 30–39.

35. As cited in Cheng, *Su-cheng*, p. 25.

36. Of the 28 versions consulted by Shima Kunio, 22 do not have the word *min*; see *Rōshi kōsei* (Tokyo, 1973), p. 58. According to Wing-tsit Chan, the word *min* "does not appear in the Ho-shang Kung and 47 other texts," though "its presence is necessary to maintain the parallelism of the three sentences"; *The Way of Lao Tzu*, p. 104, n. 4. Both Ma Hsü-lun and Chiang Hsi-ch'ang favor the Ho-shang Kung reading, and agree that the Wang Pi commentary itself suggests the absence of the word *min*. See Ma, *Lao-tzu chiao-ku*, pp. 35–36; Chiang, *Lao-tzu chiao-ku*, pp. 21–22. However, in the commentary on chap. 27, Wang Pi quotes from chap. 3, again with the word *min*.

37. Erkes translates: "Within the empire nobody risks to be a servant serving Tao." Although "nobody" is too strong, Erkes also senses the nominal construction involved here (p. 65).

38. The phrase "model themselves (after them)" may also be interpreted in the sense of "model after themselves," in which case the idea of self-transformation would be emphasized. The word *hsiao* has the basic meaning of "to model" or "to follow"; two other versions employ the variant *hsiao*, which has the same meaning and that of "to serve"; i.e., if the ruler could secure Tao, everything would be transformed of its own accord and serve him.

39. Read *tao* for *yu*, which is clearly a mistake; see Cheng, *Chiao-li*, p. 40.

40. The "five breaths" (*wu-ch'i*) are variously identified; they are also correlated with the five cardinal points. According to Cheng Hsüan, the

breath of the lungs is "hot," while that of the kidneys is "cold"; the rest lies somewhere in between. As cited in Cheng Ch'eng-hai, *Su-cheng*, pp. 51–52.

41. The "five natures" can also refer to the five musical tones; i.e., modifying the "voice and sound." As "natures" of the five viscera, they are again variously identified. According to one tradition, whereas the liver is "tranquil," the heart is "impetuous."

42. The word *kuei* is perhaps more accurately translated "ghost." According to Yü Ying-shih, the pairing of both *hun* and *p'o* with *kuei*—as opposed to the common parallelism of *hun/shen*, "spirit," and *p'o/kuei*—suggests that Ho-shang Kung's commentary reflects the beliefs of the popular culture. See Yü, "Chung-kuo ku-tai ssu-hou shih-chieh-kuan ti yen-pien," p. 18.

43. The "five tastes" (*wu-wei*) are sour, bitter, acrid, salt, and sweet, corresponding to the spleen, liver, kidneys, lungs, and heart, respectively.

44. Read *wei*, "taste," for *hsing*, "nature," as in four other versions, and in line with the preceding sentence; see Cheng, *Chiao-li*, p. 41.

45. The "six feelings" are identified since the Han dynasty as joy, anger, sorrow, delight, likes, and dislikes. Interestingly, Wang Pi speaks only of "five feelings." As Chin Ch'un-feng points out, numerological considerations in the service of politics were responsible for this change. The use of "six feelings," according to Chin, thus testifies to the early Han date of the Ho-shang Kung commentary. See his "Yeh t'an Lao-tzu Ho-shang Kung chang-chü chih shih-tai," in his *Han-tai ssu-hsiang-shih* (Peking, 1987), p. 671; this essay first appeared in *Chung-kuo che-hsüeh*, 9 (1983).

46. The SPTK has "connected with heaven and earth"; "heaven" disrupts the symmetry of the parallelism, and is deleted on the basis of seven other versions. See Cheng, *Chiao-li*, p. 41.

47. The translation of this sentence is tentative; the meaning of the last clause is not entirely clear. Cf. Erkes, p. 22.

48. This sentence is missing in eight other versions, and reads like a later subcommentary. See Cheng, *Chiao-li*, p. 60.

49. *Chuang-tzu* (SPPY), 6.1a. B. Watson trans., *The Complete Works of Chuang-tzu* (New York: Columbia University Press, 1968), pp. 167–68; substantially modified. Cf. Ngo Van Xuyet's discussion of the various techniques of self-cultivation current in the Han dynasty, in his *Divination, Magie, et Politique dans la Chine Ancienne* (Paris, 1976), Appendice.

50. M. Kaltenmark, "The Ideology of the T'ai-p'ing ching," in *Facets of Taoism*, ed. Holmes Welch and A. Seidel (New Haven: Yale University Press, 1979), p. 42. The *T'ai-p'ing ching* is one of the earliest and most im-

portant scriptures of the Taoist religion. The term *shou-i* is also found in it. Although the discussion here involves details not found in the Ho-shang Kung commentary, it seems clear that the *T'ai-p'ing ching* understands the practice of *shou-i* generally in a similar way, as related to both self-cultivation and government, and centered on the notion of *ch'i*. See Wang Ming ed., *T'ai-p'ing ching ho-chiao* (Peking: Chung-hua shu-chü, 1979), pp. 16, 409–22, 728, 739–43; cf. Kaltenmark, pp. 41–42, which does not address the political dimension. However, beyond these general observations, it is difficult to relate the Ho-shang Kung commentary to the *T'ai-p'ing ching*. While it is traditionally dated to the Han dynasty, the current *T'ai-p'ing ching* has gone through a long process of redaction. The current text thus also refers to methods of self-cultivation that are closer to later Taoist practices. For example, at one point the text speaks of the "superior adept" as one who "would not eat what has form [i.e., all ordinary food] but would eat only *ch'i.*" See Wang Ming ed., *T'ai-p'ing ching ho-chiao*, p. 90; and I. Robinet, *Méditation taoiste* (Paris, 1979), pp. 100–102, where a few of the more specific techniques of meditation are discussed. For a general study of the *T'ai-p'ing ching*, see Wang Ming, "Lun T'ai-p'ing ching ti ssu-hsiang," in his *Tao-chia ho Tao-chiao ssu-hsiang yen-chiu* (Peking, 1984), pp. 108–38; and Chin Ch'un-feng, *Han-tai ssu-hsiang shih* (1987), pp. 526–58. As is well known, the practice of "avoiding the five grains" is already mentioned in the *Chuang-tzu* (chap. 1; Watson trans., *Complete Works*, p. 33). But this does not mean that there was only one method of self-cultivation followed by all adepts from an early time. Thus, in Ko Hung's *Pao-p'u tzu* (*ch.* 18), we still read that the art of *shou-i*, among other things, hinges on "having few desires and a restricted diet." See Wang Ming ed., *Pao-p'u tzu nei-p'ien chiao-shih* (Peking, 1980), p. 297.

51. On *shou-i* in Taoism, see esp. the following: Poul Andersen, *The Method of Holding the Three Ones: A Taoist Manual of Meditation of the Fourth Century A.D.* (London: Curzon Press, 1980); I. Robinet, *Méditation taoiste*, chap. 4; K. Schipper, *Le corps taoiste* (Paris, 1982), chap. 8; and esp. Livia Kohn, "Guarding the One: Concentrative Meditation in Taoism" in *Taoist Meditation and Longevity Techniques*, ed. Livia Kohn, in cooperation with Yoshinobu Sakade (Ann Arbor: Center for Chinese Studies, University of Michigan, 1989), pp. 125–58. Two other essays in this excellent volume are also relevant to the present discussion: H. Ishida, "Body and Mind: The Chinese Perspective," pp. 41–71; and Catherine Despeux, "Gymnastics: The Ancient Tradition," pp. 225–61. On the practice of avoidance of the "five grains," Despeux explains that it "must be understood as referring in a general way to the common diet of the people of the day. . . . The texts specify quite clearly that the practice of abstention [from cereals] is not a total fasting, but rather a replacement of ordinary food with more refined and subtle materials, usually concoctions or drugs with vegetable or mineral bases" (pp. 247–48). Cf. Schipper, *Le corps taoiste*, pp. 216–21, which is

also devoted to this topic. This and related practices are also linked to the idea that within the human body there are harmful spirits, which delight in rich food, cause death, and against which the "One" must be guarded.

52. Cf. Erkes, p. 35. The meaning of the final sentence is uncertain.

53. Cf. Erkes, p. 93. Some versions specify that the "essence and spirit" must not be discharged "outside," which makes the meaning more complete. See Cheng, *Chiao-li*, p. 319.

54. *Shih-chi* (SPPY), 68.5a, the biography of Shang Yang. The context makes it clear that they are employed here to show the importance of self-knowledge in general, and of humility in particular; i.e., not "showing off" what one sees and hears. The term *nei-shih* is also used in the *Huai-nan tzu* (SPPY, 16.1a) as a means to reach the formless Tao; but as in the Ho-shang Kung commentary, the term is left unexplained. Cf. *Chin-shu*, 75:1988.

55. *Chuang-tzu*, chap. 4 (SPPY), 2.7a. Cf. Watson trans., *Complete Works*, pp. 57–58; A. C. Graham trans., *Chuang-tzu: The Seven Inner Chapters* (London: George Allen and Unwin, 1981), p. 68. Again, the later development of meditation techniques, often under the name of "inner observation" (*nei-kuan*), is important; but it does not bear directly on the present discussion. On the mature Taoist practice, see esp. Livia Kohn, "Taoist Insight Meditation: The Tang Practice of *Neiguan*," in *Taoist Meditation and Longevity Techniques*, pp. 193–224. What should be emphasized is that the use of such terms as "inward vision" does not mean that the Ho-shang Kung commentary must therefore be dated to the post-Han period. The *Chuang-tzu*, in the same chapter, goes on to say that "if the ears and eyes could be directed to penetrate inwardly . . . then even ghosts and spirits will come to dwell (in you)." Whether this involves a specific method or methods remains unclear. What is clear is that the development of meditative techniques has a long history, and what is suggested here is that the Ho-shang Kung commentary stands very much at the early stages of this history.

56. For a general account of the various rebellions that plagued the dying Han house, see Lü Ssu-mien, *Ch'in Han shih* (A History of the Ch'in and Han Dynasties) (reprinted, Hong Kong: T'ai-p'ing shu-chü, 1962), 1:334–41. According to Howard Levy, immense suffering caused by floods, drought, and epidemics were reported in the dynastic histories in the years A.D. 173, 175, 176, 177, 179, 182, 183, which precipitated the Yellow Turban rebellion of A.D. 184. See Howard S. Levy, "Yellow Turban Religion and Rebellion at the End of Han," in *Journal of the American Oriental Society*, 76, 4 (1956): 219. Incidentally, as both Schipper (*Le corps taoiste*, p. 219) and Despeux ("Gymnastics," p. 248) have pointed out, the practice of "abstention from cereals" was especially common in times of economic hardship

and famine. In other words, the socio-political background of "religious" practices should not be overlooked.

57. Cf. Erkes, p. 88. The first part can also be translated to mean that the ruler should not "overwork" himself, in which case the parallel between self-cultivation and government will be emphasized. The action of "burdening" is more likely directed toward the people, especially since one Japanese version has the extra word "people" (*min*). See Cheng, *Chiao-li*, p. 297.

58. Read "hungry and cold" (*chi-han*) in place of "very hungry" (*chi-shen*), as in nine other versions. See Cheng, *Chiao-li*, p. 443.

59. Read *t'an*, "greedy," in the first sentence for the particle *i*, which makes no sense in this context. Twelve other versions have *t'an*; see Cheng, ibid.

60. As translated in Wing-tsit Chan, *The Way of Lao Tzu*, p. 230.

61. For example, in D. C. Lau's translation, the first sentence reads: "Were the people always afraid of death, and were I able to arrest and put to death those who innovate, then who would dare?" Lau, *Lao Tzu Tao Te Ching*, p. 136. Translators are evenly divided on this. Whereas A. Waley agrees with Chan, for instance, Legge also writes: "Who would dare to do wrong?"

62. See Wing-tsit Chan, *The Way of Lao Tzu*, p. 220, n. 3. The term "deep love" is also Chan's.

63. The *Lao-tzu* passage may also mean that the sage "stays ahead of the people, and they are not harmed," in which case the last sentence of the commentary should be rendered as "the sage does not have any thought of harming the people." Cf. Erkes, p. 115, which takes this reading.

64. This translates the term *tzu-chien*, which means literally "self-seeing." It also appears in chap. 24. According to Ho-shang Kung, it refers to those who look at themselves and think that they are good looking, and look at their own conduct and believe that it corresponds to the teaching of Tao. Cf. Erkes, p. 51.

65. Chap. 47. Read *t'ien* for *ta*; see Cheng, *Chiao-li*, p. 292.

66. See Cheng, *Chiao-li*, pp. 393–96 for minor emendations. Cf. Erkes, pp. 113–14. The *Shih-liu ching* (MWT. p. 72) uses the term *shou-i* precisely to describe the special knowledge of the sage.

67. Read *ch'iu* for *jung*, as in six other versions; *Chiao-li*, p. 44.

68. Chap. 13. As translated in W. T. Chan, *The Way of Lao Tzu*, p. 122; modified. There are many variants to this particular line; see Chan, p. 123, n. 5, and Chiang Hsi-ch'ang, *Lao-tzu chiao-ku*, pp. 71–75. The general meaning is not affected.

69. I. Robinet, *Les Commentaires du Tao To King*, pp. 31–32. On this topic in general, see also the concise analysis of Cho-yun Hsu, "The Concept of Predetermination and Fate in the Han," in *Early China*, 1 (1975): 51–56.

Chapter Five

1. Some versions have "non-being" (*wu*) instead of "mother" (*mu*); see Paul J. Lin trans., *Translation of Tao Te Ching and Wang Pi's Commentary*, p. 4, n. 2. "Beginning" and "mother" are two other key concepts in chap. 1.

2. See, e.g., Isabelle Robinet, *Les Commentaires du Tao To King* (Paris, 1977), pp. 6–7. According to Robinet, Chinese commentaries "ne se soucient guère de fidélité et visent au système. Car le commentaire s'avère en fait une veritable forme littéraire . . . forme particulièrement apte à permettre à un penseur de présenter ses propres idées, ou celles de son école, en se reclamant de l'autorité d'un ancien, ce qui convenait tout spécialement aux exigences de l'esprit chinois." While it is important to recognize the uniqueness of commentary as a literary form in Chinese intellectual history, and that it is much more than paraphrases of the original, one must not go to the other extreme and disregard its rootedness in the tradition of the text.

3. On this verse, see also the interesting exchanges between E. Erkes and H. H. Dubs, in *Asia Major*, New Series, 3 (1952): 156–59, 159–61; 4 (1954): 149–50. As Erkes concludes, "The expression *sz erh pu wang* [*sic*] thus seems to point to Taoist practices which tried to secure a kind of perpetual life after death by preserving the body" (p. 158). Dubs responds by saying that the expression means "that genuine long life is to be found only in the immortality of fame and influence" (p. 160).

4. The text of chap. 55 is also found in chap. 30, which has led Ma Hsü-lun to suspect the integrity of the former. See Ma, *Lao-tzu chiao-ku*, p. 155. Wang Pi's commentary on chap. 30, however, also sidesteps the issue of longevity by saying that men of violence would die early. Cf. chaps. 7 and 50.

5. It should be noted that according to a few versions, Wang Pi doubted the authenticity of chap. 75: appended to the end of the commentary are the words, "I suspect that this was not written by Lao-tzu." See Hatano, *Rōshi dōtokukyō kenkyū*, p. 428.

6. Adapted from D. C. Lau, *Lao Tzu*, p. 84, and Wing-tsit Chan, *The Way of Lao Tzu*, p. 147. The numbers correspond to the commentaries.

7. Cf. Lin, pp. 49–50; Rump-Chan, pp. 82–83.

8. Because of this difficulty—i.e., how the "small country" can serve as an "example" for a "large country"—one Japanese scholar at least has suspected the textual integrity of Wang Pi's commentary on this chapter. See Hatano, p. 438.

9. On the military background, see esp. the detailed discussion in Chiang Hsi-ch'ang, *Lao-tzu chiao-ku*, pp. 460–61, and Rump-Chan, p. 209, n. 1. The possessive *chih* also seems to suggest a type and not a quantity, of utensils. The Ho-shang Kung and Ma-wang-tui texts, however, have the extra word "people" (*jen*) after *shih-po*, which would render the latter an expression of quantity. In this sense, the phrase may also be translated "Let there be ten times and a hundred times as many utensils" (Rump-Chan, p. 208). Thus, in light of the Ma-wang-tui evidence, D. C. Lau changes his earlier translation—"Ensure that even though the people have tools of war . . . "—to read, "Ensure that even though there are tools ten times or a hundred times better than those of other people." See Lau trans., *Chinese Classics. Tao Te Ching* (Hong Kong: Chinese University Press, 1982), pp. 115, 239. In the Ma-wang-tui manuscripts, chap. 80 is found immediately after chap. 66.

10. Rump has taken the first clause to mean "The reason people will avoid him," which is also possible. See Rump-Chan, p. 201; cf. Lin, p. 136.

11. Read *wei* for *cheng*, which is clearly a scribal error; as emended in Cheng Cheng-hai, *Chiao-li*, p. 350, in line with six other versions. The final clause is also translated in the light of Cheng's reading.

12. The SPTK edition has duplicated the word *yen* at the beginning, which is superfluous. See Cheng, *Chiao-li*, p. 219.

13. Chap. 54. Cf. Lin, p. 102; Rump-Chan, p. 155.

14. Hatano, p. 81; cf. Rump-Chan, p. 28, n. 2, where the rough date is provided.

15. *Shih-chi* (SPPY), 79.13a–17b. Ts'ai is said to be from the state of Yen, to which, together with Ch'i, the *fang-shih* tradition is generally traced. At one point in his discourse (p. 14a), Ts'ai seems to be elaborating on chap. 18 of the *Lao-tzu*.

16. As translated in Wing-tsit Chan, *The Way of Lao Tzu*, p. 105; modified. Since the four lines beginning with "It blunts its sharpness" appear also in chap. 56, various emendations have been suggested. But both the

Wang Pi commentary and the Ma-wang-tui manuscripts support the SPPY reading. Wang Pi's comments on these four lines, not reproduced here, focus on the idea that the Way would not be affected by these actions; e.g., while Tao "becomes one with the dusty world," its true nature is not thereby "corrupted" or "polluted."

17. Read "clarity" (*ch'ing*) for "essence" (*ching*). See Lou Yü-lieh, *Wang Pi chi chiao-shih* (Peking, Chung-hua, 1980), 1:12, n. 7; cf. Rump-Chan, p. 16, n. 4.

18. See the discussion in Fung Yu-lan, *History*, 1:384, where the relevant texts are translated.

19. Chap. 73. As translated in Rump-Chan, p. 198.

20. Ibid.

21. Adapted from R. Wilhelm, *I Ching* (Princeton: Princeton University Press, 1979), p. 320. As cited in Lou Yü-lieh, *Wang Pi chi*, 1:183, n. 8.

22. On this topic, see, e.g., Joseph Needham, *Science and Civilisation in China*, vol. 3, *Mathematics and the Sciences of the Heavens and the Earth* (Cambridge: Cambridge University Press, 1959), pp. 259–62.

23. See James Legge trans., *The Chinese Classics*, vol. 3, *The Shoo King* (reprinted, Hong Kong: Hong Kong University Press, 1960), 5:3:10, p. 316.

24. *Lun-yü*, 2.1; as translated in Wing-tsit Chan, *A Source Book in Chinese Philosophy* (1973), p. 22.

25. W. T. Chan, ibid.

26. *Lun-yü*, 15.4; W. T. Chan, ibid., p. 43; modified.

27. In Charles A. Moore ed., *The Chinese Mind: Essentials of Chinese Philosophy and Culture* (Honolulu: University Press of Hawaii, 1967; reprint, 1977), p. 5.

28. See W. T. Chan, *The Way of Lao Tzu*, p. 194, n. 1.

29. Adapted from Rump-Chan, p. 7; and Lin, p. 5.

30. There is much controversy surrounding the second part of this passage, which reads: *hsü yu-chih erh shih wu-chih yeh*. See Hatano, p. 53, and Lou, 1:9–10, n. 6, for the various scholarly opinions. The difficulty here lies in the fact that most scholars have taken *hsü* ("empty") and *shih* ("full"/ "solid") as nouns, in which case the statement would mean "what is empty is what has wisdom." This is, for example, how Lin (p. 7) and Rump (p. 11) have understood it. Although grammatically correct, it seems to contradict

Wang Pi's understanding of "emptiness" as precisely without "wisdom" (*chih*). The problem is resolved, it seems to me, if the two words are taken as verbs.

31. Cf. Wing-tsit Chan, *The Way of Lao Tzu*, p. 188; D. C. Lau, *Lao Tzu*, p. 111.

32. According to Lou Yü-lieh, this analogy is taken from the *Ta Tai Li-chi* (The Elder Tai's Version of the Book of Rites); see Lou, 1:136, n. 8. A number of similar sayings in Han literature are listed in Hatano, p. 334. "Worms (of the sea)" and "eagles" are rough translations; the SPPY version speaks of "lizards and earthworms," and "eagles and (?) sparrow hawks." The first pair may also be interpreted as serpentine or "dragonlike" creatures; see Hatano, p. 333.

33. Cf. Lin, pp. 93–94; Rump-Chan, pp. 144–45. The "infant" refers to chap. 55 of the *Lao-tzu*.

34. Read *wu-nei* for *wu-nei*(*), which does not make sense; as emended in Cheng, *Chiao-li*, p. 304, on the basis of nine other versions.

35. See Cheng, *Chiao-li*, p. 305, for minor textual problems.

36. Cf. Erkes, pp. 89–91.

37. As cited in W. T. Chan, *The Way of Lao Tzu*, p. 188, n. 1.

38. *Huai-nan tzu* (SPPY), 8.8b.

39. I have in mind, of course, the distinction made by H. G. Creel between "contemplative" and "purposive" Taoism. See his "On Two Aspects in Early Taoism" and "What is Taoism?," both in *What is Taoism? And Other Studies in Chinese Cultural History* (Chicago: University of Chicago Press, 1970; reprint, 1977) pp. 37–47, 1–24, respectively. Though heuristically useful, this distinction does not fully reflect the nature of the *Lao-tzu* and our two commentaries, where the "contemplative" and "purposive" merge into a unified whole.

40. *Han-shu*, 30:1732. Three relevant studies appeared too late to be included in my discussion. I mention them here: Charles Holcombe, "The Exemplar State: Ideology, Self-Cultivation, and Power in Fourth-Century China," in *Harvard Journal of Asiatic Studies*, 49, 1 (June 1989): 93–139; Rudolf G. Wagner, "The Wang Bi Recension of the *Laozi*," in *Early China*, 14 (1989): 27–54; and Karen Turner, "The Theory of Law in the *Ching-fa*," in *Early China*, 14 (1989): 55–76. Holcombe's analysis details the central role played by Confucianism in politics and thought throughout the Six Dynasties Period. "In general," he writes, "throughout this period the classics of Confucianism remained the foundation of a gentleman's education, and

favorite subjects for the writing of commentaries. Six Dynasties philosophers thus did not turn their backs on Confucianism, but rather advanced
to what they considered to be a deeper understanding of Confucian truth"
(p. 120). This can certainly be applied to Wang Pi, although my argument
envisages a higher "Tao-ist" truth that encompasses both the Confucian
and Taoist schools. Karen Turner's article is especially important for its discussion of the nature and sources of law in the *Ching-fa*. What I did not
realize is that the term *shen-ming*, used by Wang Pi to distinguish the sage
from ordinary human beings, is specifically understood in the early literature as "the essential factor for understanding how to rule in accord with
the *tao*" (p. 70, n. 51). This would strengthen the argument that Wang Pi
was motivated by political interests, for it shows that his conception of the
sage is rooted in a long tradition that aims to establish the ideal utopian
state. With respect to the analysis of the *Ching-fa*, however, one suggestion
may be made. The role of the sage as teacher of rulers is too important in
the Huang-lao school to be neglected. When the *Ching-fa* states that "One
who holds fast to the *tao* is viewed by the world as not . . . selfish" (as
trans. in Turner, p. 60), it is more likely referring to the sage and not "the
behavior of the ruler" (p. 60). The passage goes on to say that only the
person "who holds fast to the *tao*" can realize the way of heaven and discern the fundamental distinction between the ruler and the ministers. Because of his special knowledge and power, as the *Ching-fa* (1980 edition, p.
57) pushes the argument one step futher, the person "who holds fast to the
tao" can therefore "establish the son of heaven and appoint the three chief
ministers." Wagner's study argues that the modern *Lao-tzu* text accompanying Wang Pi's commentary is not the "original" text that Wang Pi actually
saw and commented on. On the whole, it does not affect the conclusions
reached in the present study. Wagner believes that the *Lao-tzu* text at Wang
Pi's disposal was divided into many untitled units or chapters (*chang*), but
not into a *Tao-ching* and a *Te-ching*. He is careful to add, however, that "this
is not to say that it did not have two *pian*" (p. 49). Although I am still not
entirely convinced that Wang Pi's *Lao-tzu* text was originally divided into
chapters, my findings also suggest that it was probably divided into two
untitled sections. I note in passing that there are a few minor difficulties in
Wagner's otherwise careful discussion: there seems to be some confusion
regarding the figure of Master An-ch'iu (pp. 35–36, identified as "Wang
An Qiu"); also, Hsüeh Tsung (Xue Zong, in the *pinyin* system) is identified
as Xie Zong (p. 39), and the first six *chüan*, not "chapters," are missing
from Yen Tsun's work on the *Lao-tzu* (p. 37). Finally, I regret that Howard
Goodman's work, "Exegetes and Exegeses of the Book of Changes in the
Third Century A.D.: Historical and Scholastic Contexts for Wang Pi" (Ph.D.
Dissertation, Princeton University, 1985) did not come to my attention until
recently; also, reference should have been made to Itano Chōhachi's study,
"Ka An Ō Hitsu no shisō," in *Tōhō gakuhō*, 14 (1943): 43–111.

Glossary

an 安
An-ch'i Sheng 安期生
An-ch'iu Hsien-sheng / Chang-jen 安丘先生，丈人
An-ch'iu Wang-chih 安丘望之
chang 章
ch'ang (constant) 常
Chang Chih-hsiang 張之象
Chang Heng 張衡
Chang Hui-ch'ao 張惠超
Chang Jung 張融
Chang Ling (Chang Tao-ling) 張陵，張道陵
Chang Lu 張魯
Chang Ssu 張嗣
ch'ang-ts'un 常存
Chao Hsi-pien 趙希弁
Ch'ao Kung-wu 晁公武
Chao Shih-hsiu 趙師秀
Ch'ao Yüeh-chih (I-tao, Ching-yü) 晁說之，以道，景迂
ch'en 臣
Ch'en Chen-sun 陳振孫
cheng 徵
Ch'eng 稱
Ch'eng Ch'iao 鄭樵

Ch'eng-fa 成法
Cheng Ho 正何
Cheng Hsüan 鄭玄
Ch'eng Hsüan-ying 成玄英
Cheng-shih 正始
Cheng Ssu-yüan 鄭思遠
Ch'eng Ta-ch'ang 程大昌
ch'i (its) 其
ch'i (breath) 氣
ch'i (vessel) 器
ch'i-cheng 奇正
Ch'i-chih 七志
chi-han 飢寒
Chi-hsia 稷下
ch'i k'o te-chien 其可得見
Ch'i-lu 七錄
Ch'i-lüeh 七略
ch'i-ping 奇兵
chi-shen 飢深
Chiang Chi 蔣濟
Chiao Hung 焦竑
chieh (little) 介
Chieh 桀
Chieh-lao 解老
Chieh-tzu 接子
ch'ien 乾
Ch'ien Ta-hsi 錢大昕
Ch'ien Tseng 錢曾
chih (will, intention) 志
chih (wisdom) 知, 智
chih (reach, "end") 至
chih (govern, cultivate) 治
ch'ih 持
chih-kuo 治國
chih-lüeh 指略
chih-lüeh lun 指略論
Chih-po 智伯
chih-shen 治身
chih-shih tsao-hsing 指事造形
chih-wei 知為
Chin-yang 晉陽

Chin Yang-ch'iu 晉陽秋
ching (essence) 精
ching (tranquility) 靜
ching (classic) 經
ch'ing (feeling) 情
ch'ing (clarity) 清
ching-ch'i 精氣
ch'ing-ching 清靜
Ching-fa 經法
Ching Fang 京房
ch'ing-i 清議
ch'ing-t'an 清談
ch'iu 求
chiu-pen 九品
Ch'iu Yüeh 仇嶽
Ch'iu-tzu 丘子
Ch'iu Tzu-ming 丘子明
Chou 紂
Chou Chung-fu 周中孚
chou-hsing 周行
Chou-i lan Wang Fu-ssu yi 周易難王輔嗣義
Chou-i lüeh-li 周易略例
Chou-i ta-yen lun 周易大衍論
Chou Yung (Yen-lun) 周顒，彥倫
chu (compose) 著
chü (dwell) 居
Chü-chen 聚珍
Chü Hsüan-pi 車玄弼
Chu Yu 諸樑
Ch'ü Yung 瞿鏞
chüan 卷
ch'üan 權
Chuan-hsü 顓頊
Ch'uan-shou ching-chieh i-chu-chüeh 傳授經戒儀注訣
ch'üan-tao 權道
Chuang-tzu yin-i 莊子音義
ch'ui-hsiang 垂象
ch'ui-kung 垂拱
chün 君
Chün-chai tu-shu-chih 郡齋讀書志
ch'ung 聰

Chung-ch'ang T'ung 仲長統
Chung-hsing 中行
ch'ung-ho 沖和
Ch'ung-hsüan 重玄
Chung Hui 鍾會
ch'ung-ju 寵辱
ch'ung-pen hsi-mo 崇本息末
chung-shang 中上
Ch'ung-ta Chang Ch'ang-shih shu 重答張長史書
erh-i 二儀
fa 法
Fa-chia 法家
Fan 范
fan (return) 返
fan (reversal) 反
fan (troublesome) 煩
Fan Ning 范甯
fan-t'ing 反聽
fang-shih 方士
fen 分
fen-san 分散
Fo T'u-teng 佛圖澄
fu 夫
Fu Chia 傅嘏
Fu Chien 符堅
Fu-hsi 伏羲
Fu I 傅奕
han 含
Han Fei-tzu 韓非子
Han K'ang-po 韓康伯
ho (harmony) 和
ho (integrated) 合
ho ch'i cho 和氣濁
ho-ch'i ch'ing-cho 和氣清濁
ho ch'ing cho 和清濁
Ho-shang Chang-jen 河上丈人
Ho-shang Kung 河上公
Ho Shao 何劭
Ho Yen 何晏
Hou Chi 后稷
hsi 希

hsi-hsüan 析玄
Hsi K'ang 嵇康
Hsi-shih t'ing Ho-shang chen-jen chang-chü 係師定河上真人章句
Hsi-tz'u 繫辭
hsia 下
Hsia-hou Hsüan 夏侯玄
hsiang 象
Hsiang-erh 想爾
hsiang-hsing 象形
Hsiang K'ai 襄楷
hsiao (model) 效
hsiao (model, serve) 効
Hsieh Shou-hao 謝守灝
hsien (worthies) 賢
hsien (immortals) 仙
Hsien-men Tzu-kao 羨門子高
hsin 心
hsin-chai 心齋
Hsin-chi hsüan-yen tao-te 新記玄言道德
Hsin-yü 新語
hsing (nature) 性
hsing (form) 形
hsing (punishment) 刑
hsing-ming 形名
Hsing Ping 邢昺
Hsing T'ao 邢璹
hsiu 宿
Hsiung K'o 熊克
hsü 虛
Hsü Chin-yang-ch'iu 續晉陽秋
Hsü Shen 許慎
hsü-wu 虛無
hsü yu-chih erh shih wu-chih yeh 虛有智而實無知也
hsüan 玄
hsüan-chih-yu-hsüan 玄之又玄
hsüan-hsüeh 玄學
hsüan-lun 玄論
hsüan-p'in 玄牝
hsüan-t'an 玄談
hsüan-yen 玄言
Hsüan-yen hsin-chi ming-Chuang-pu 玄言新記明莊部

Hsüan-yen hsin-chi tao-te 玄言新記道德
Hsüeh Tsung 薛綜
Hsün Ts'an 荀粲
hu yu chung-hsin 戶有忠信
hua-ts'un 或存
hua yu ch'ang 化有常
Huai-nan tzu 淮南子
Huan Yüan 環淵
Huang-fu Mi 皇甫謐
Huang Hsüan-tse 黃玄順
Huang K'an 皇侃
Huang-lao 黃老
Huang Sheng 黃生
Huang-ti 黃帝
Huang-ti chün-ch'en 黃帝君臣
Huang-ti ming 黃帝銘
Huang-ti ssu-ching 黃帝四經
hun 魂
Hun-yüan sheng-chi 混元聖紀
Hung I-hsüan 洪頤煊
Hung Liang-chi 洪亮吉
Hung-ming chi 弘明集
i (invisible) 夷
i (as, for) 以
i (different) 異
i (particle) 矣
I-chih t'ai-chi 易之太極
I Shun-ting 易順鼎
i Tao tso jen-chu che 以道佐人主者
jen 人
Juan Chi 阮籍
Juan Hsiao-hsü 阮孝緒
jung 榮
k'ang-ta 曠達
Kao-liang 高梁
Kao Ssu-sun 高似孫
Kao Yu 高誘
ke shih i-wu chih sheng 各是一物之生
Keng Huang 耿況
Ko Hsüan 葛玄
Ko Hung 葛洪

Ko Kung 蓋公

k'o-yen 可言

K'ou Ch'ien-chih 寇謙之

ku (valley) 谷

ku (grain) 穀

ku ch'ang yü yu-wu chih-chi, erh pi-ming ch'i so-yu
    chih tsung yeh 故常於有物之極而必明其所由之宗也

Ku-chin jen-wu piao 古今人物表

Ku Huan 顧歡

ku-pen 古本

kuan-chang 官長

Kuan T'ing-fen 管庭芬

kuei 鬼

k'un 坤

K'un-hsüeh chi-wen 困學紀聞

kung (revolve around) 共

kung (hands folded) 拱

kung (reverent) 恭

k'ung (empty) 空

k'ung (great, empty) 孔

K'ung An-kuo 孔安國

k'ung-hsü 空虛

K'ung Ying-ta 孔穎達

kuo yu chung-ch'en 國有忠臣

Lao P'eng 老彭

Lao-tzu chang-chü 老子章句

Lao-tzu chih-kuei lun 老子指歸論

Lao-tzu chih-kuei lüeh-li 老子指歸略例

Lao-tzu chih-li-lüeh 老子指例略

Lao-tzu chih-lüeh 老子指略

Lao-tzu chih-lüeh-li 老子指略例

Lao-tzu chih-lüeh-lun 老子指略論

Lao-tzu Fu-shih ching-shuo 老子傅氏經說

Lao-tzu Hsü-shih ching-shuo 老子徐氏經說

Lao-tzu Lin-shih ching-chuan 老子鄰氏經傳

Lao-tzu lüeh-lun 老子略論

Lao-tzu Tao-te ching hsü-chüeh 老子道德經序訣

Lao-tzu wei-chih li-lüeh 老子微指例略

Lao-tzu yin-i 老子音義

lei 累

li (principle, reason) 理

li (profit, sharp) 利
li (separate) 離
li-ch'i 利器
Li Feng 李豐
Li Hei 力黑
Li Jung 李榮
Li Mu 力牧
Li Shan 李善
li-shu 隸書
Li Yüan-hsing 黎元興
Liang Chang-chü 梁章鉅
liang-li 兩例
Lieh-tzu 列子
liu chi chüeh 六紀絶
Liu Chih-chi 劉知幾
Liu Chin-hsi 劉進喜
liu chüeh chüeh 六絶絶
Liu Chün (Hsiao-piao) 劉峻, 孝標
Liu Hsiang 劉向
Liu Hsin 劉歆
Liu Jen-hui 劉仁會
Liu Shao 劉邵
lu (contents) 錄
Lu Chia 陸賈
Lu Hsi-sheng 陸希聲
Lu Hsiu-ching 陸修靜
Lu Te-ming 陸德明
Lu Yu 陸游
luan 亂
Lun-shu piao 論書表
Lun-yü shih-i 論語釋疑
Ma Jung 馬融
Ma Tuan-lin 馬端臨
Ma-wang-tui 馬王堆
Meng Chih-chou 孟智周
miao-yen 妙言
min 民
ming (name, identify) 名
ming (understanding, bright) 明
ming (destiny) 命
Ming-chia 名家

Ming-hsiang 明象
ming-li 名理
ming-shih (name and actuality) 名實
ming-shih (men of letters) 名士
Ming-shih chuan 名士傳
mu 母
Nan-tzu 南子
Nao Yai 姚鼐
nei-kuan 內觀
nei-shih 內視
ning-jen 佞人
Nü-kua 女媧
Ou-yang Chien 歐陽建
pan 版
Pan Ku 班固
pang 邦
pao-i 抱一
P'ei Hui 裴徽
P'ei K'ai 裴楷
P'ei Sung-chih 裴松之
pen 本
P'eng-lai 蓬萊
P'eng Ssu 彭耜
P'eng-tsu 彭祖
Pi pieh-chuan 弼別傳
Pieh-lu 別錄
p'ien 篇
p'ien-mu 篇目
p'o 魄
po-wu 白屋
pu 不
p'u 樸
pu k'o te-chien 不可得見
pu-chih ming-kao 不治名高
pu-neng she-wu i wei-t'i 不能捨無以為體
pu-shih wu-ch'ing 不識物情
pu tz'u-hsieh en, Tao pu tse yeh 不辭謝恩道不責也
san 散
San-ching Chin-chu 三經晉註
san-hsüan 三玄
san-huang chih-ch'ien 三皇之前

san-huang chih-shih 三皇之時
san-shih 三事
san-yen 三言
se 嗇
Shao Jo-yü 邵若愚
shen (spirit) 神
shen (body) 身
shen-ch'i 神器
Shen-hsien chuan 神仙傳
shen-jen 神人
shen-ming 神明
Shen-nung 神農
Shen Pu-hai 申不害
Shen Tao 慎到
sheng 聖
Sheng-hsien kao-shih chuan 聖賢高士傳
sheng-jen 聖人
sheng-wang 聖王
shih (beginning) 始
shih (loss) 失
shih (actuality) 實
shih (power, "environment") 勢
shih ("proceed") 逝
shih che Tao yeh 始者道也
Shih-liu ching 十六經
shih-po chih-ch'i 什伯之器
Shih-ta ching 十大經
shih Tao pu-k'o wei t'i 是道不可為體
shih yu san 十有三
shih yu Tao yeh 始有道也
shou-i 守一
shu 數
shuai 衰
Shun 舜
shun (follow) 順
Shuo Lao-tzu 說老子
Shuo-wen chieh-tzu 說文解字
ssu 司
Ssu-k'u ch'üan-shu 四庫全書
Ssu-ma Chen 司馬貞
Ssu-ma Ch'ien 司馬遷

Ssu-ma I 司馬懿
Ssu-ma Kuang 司馬光
Ssu-ma T'an 司馬談
Ssu-ma Yen 司馬炎
Ssu-pu pei-yao 四部備要
Ssu-pu ts'ung-k'an 四部叢刊
su-shu 素書
Su Tan 素紞
Sun I-jang 孫詒讓
Sun Sheng 孫盛
Sun Teng 孫登
Sun Yu-yüeh 孫遊嶽
Sun Yüeh 孫嶽
Sung-ling 松靈
ta 大
ta-tao chih-chün 大道之君
ta-tao chih-shih 大道之世
Ta-yen 大衍
Ta-yen chih-shu 大衍之數
T'ai-chi 太極
T'ai-chi tso-hsien-kung 太極左仙公
t'ai-p'ing 太平
T'ai-shang hsüan-yüan 太上玄元
T'ai-shang hun-yüan huang-ti 太上混元皇帝
T'ai-shang Tao-chün 太上道君
t'an 貪
T'an Tao-luan 檀道鸞
Tao ch'ang wu-wei 道常無為
Tao-fa 道法
Tao-hsüeh chuan 道學傳
T'ao Hung-ching 陶弘景
T'ao Hung-ch'ing 陶鴻慶
Tao lüeh-lun 道略論
Tao pu tz'u-hsieh erh ni-chih yeh 道不辭謝而逆止也
Tao sheng fa 道生法
Tao-te chen-ching kuang sheng-i 道德真經廣聖義
Tao-te lüeh-kuei 道德略歸
Tao-te lun 道德論
Tao-te wen 道德問
Tao-tsang 道藏
Tao-tsang tzu-mu yin-te 道藏子目引得

tao-yin 導引|
Tao-yüan 道原
te (virtue) 德
te (obtain) 得
ti (emperor) 帝
ti (earth) 地
t'i (body, substance) 體
t'i (trap) 蹄
Ti-k'u 帝嚳
T'ieh-ch'in t'ung-chien lou 鐵琴銅劍樓
t'ien 天
t'ien-chih sheng-ch'i 天之生氣
t'ien-hsia 天下
t'ien-hsia pu-kan yu ch'en shih Tao che yeh 天下不敢有臣使道者也
t'ien-i chu-ch'i 天一主氣
T'ien P'ien 田駢
T'ien-shih tao 天師道
T'ien Shu 田叔
T'ien-ti 天帝
t'ien-ti chih-shih 天地之始
ting 定
Tōjō Ichitō 東條一堂
Tou 竇
Tou Lüeh 竇略
Tsa Huang-ti 雜黃帝
ts'ai-hsing 才性
Ts'ai Tse 蔡澤
Ts'ai Tzu-huang 蔡子晃
Ts'ang Chieh 倉頡
Tsang Hsüan-ching 臧玄靜
Ts'ao Fang 曹芳
Ts'ao P'ei 曹丕
Ts'ao Shuang 曹爽
Ts'ao Ts'an 曹參
Ts'ao Ts'ao 曹操
Ts'ui Shih 崔寔
Ts'ung-shu chi-ch'eng ch'u-pien 叢書集成初編
t'u 吐
Tu Kuang-t'ing 杜光庭
Tu Tao-chien 杜道堅
Tu Yüan-k'ai 杜元凱

t'ung 同
t'ung-chih 同志
Tung-ching fu 東京賦
Tung Chung-shu 董仲舒
Tung Ssu-ching 董思靖
tz'u (deep love) 慈
tz'u (turn away) 辭
tzu-chien 自見
tzu-jan 自然
Tzu-lu 子路
Tzu-lüeh 子略
tz'u-hsieh 辭謝
Usami Shinsui (U Kei) 宇佐美灊水，宇惠
wan-wu chih-shih 萬物之始
wan-wu shih-chih erh sheng erh pu-tz'u 萬物恃之而生而不辭
wang (king) 王
Wang Chi (critic of Wang Pi) 王濟
Wang Chi (student of Master An-ch'iu) 王汲
Wang Chien 王儉
Wang Ch'ung 王充
Wang Fu 王符
Wang Ho 王何
wang-hou te-i che 王侯得一者
Wang Hsi-chih 王羲之
Wang Kuang 王廣
Wang Li 王黎
Wang Mao-ts'ai 王茂材
Wang Pi (Fu-ssu) 王弼，輔嗣
Wang Su 王肅
Wang Ts'an 王粲
Wang Wei-ch'eng 王維誠
Wang Ying-lin 王應麟
wei (action) 為
wei (falsehood, hypocrisy) 偽
wei (oppose) 違
wei (force) 威
wei (subtle) 微
wei (taste) 味
wen (culture, letters) 文
Wen-chang hsü-lu 文章敘錄
Wen-hsien t'ung-k'ao 文獻通考

Wen-hsin tiao-lung 文心雕龍
Wen-hsüan 文選
Wen K'ung p'ien 問孔篇
wo 我
wu (non-being) 無
wu (things) 物
wu (first person pronoun) 吾
wu (mistaken) 誤
wu (understand) 悟
wu (work, cultivate) 務
Wu Ch'eng 吳澄
wu-ch'i 五氣
wu-chih (without knowledge) 無知
wu-chih 無執
Wu-ching cheng-i 五經正義
Wu-ch'iu pei-chai Lao-tzu chi-ch'eng ch'u-pien 無求備齋老子集成初編
wu-ch'u 無處
wu-hsiang chih hsiang 無象之象
wu-hsing (five phases or elements) 五行
wu-hsing (five natures) 五性
wu-hsing (formless) 無形
wu-hsing wu-ming che 無形無名者
Wu I 武億
Wu Kuang 務光
wu-nei 五內
wu-nei (*) 无內
wu-shih 無事
wu-ssu 無私
wu-t'i 無體
wu-wei (nonaction) 無為
wu-wei (five tastes) 五味
wu-wu 無物
wu-wu chih hsiang 無物之象
Wu-ying (palace) 武英
wu-yü 無欲
Wu Yün 吳雲
Yang Hu 羊祜
yao (key, kernel) 要
Yao 堯
yen (words) 言
yen (expand) 衍

Yen Chih-t'ui 顏之推
yen-chin-i lun 言盡意論
yen pu chin-i 言不盡意
Yen-shih chia-hsün 顏氏家訓
Yen Shih-ku 顏師古
Yen Tsun (Chün-p'ing) 嚴遵，君平
yi 意
yin (follow) 因
yin-yang 陰陽
ying (response) 應
ying (name of Emperor Hui) 盈
yu (being, having) 有
Yü (sage, founder of Hsia) 禹
Yü (family name) 虞
Yü Chia-hsi 余嘉錫
Yü Cheng-hsieh 俞正燮
Yü-hai 玉海
Yü Ho 虞龢
Yü-lao 喻老
yü Tao t'ung-t'i 與道同體
yüan 元
Yüan Hung 袁宏
Yüan Shao 袁紹
Yüeh Chü-kung (Ch'en-kung) 樂巨公，臣公
Yüeh I 樂毅
yung (function) 用
Yung-lo ta-tien 永樂大典

Selected Bibliography

Chinese and Japanese Sources

Akizuki Kan'ei 秋月觀暎. "Kōrō kannen no keifu" 黃老觀念の糸譜. *Tōhōgaku* 東方學, 10 (1955): 69–81.

Aoki Masaru 青木正兒. *Seidan* 清談. Tokyo: Iwanami shoten, 1934.

Chang Hsin-ch'eng 張心澂. *Wei-shu t'ung-k'ao* 偽書通考. Shanghai: Shang-wu yin-shu-kuan, 1939; reprint, 1954. 2 vols.

Chang Li-chai 張立齋, ed. *Wen-hsin tiao-lung chu-ting* 文心雕龍註訂. Taipei: Cheng-chung shu-chü, 1967; reprint, 1979.

Chang Su-chen 張素貞. *Han Fei Chieh-Lao Yü-Lao yen-chiu* 韓非解老喻老研究. Taipei: Ch'ang-ko ch'u-pan-she, 1976.

Chao I 趙翼. *Nien-erh shih cha-chi* 廿二史劄記. Annotated by Tu Wei-yün 杜維運. Taipei: Ting-wen shu-chü, 1975.

Ch'en Ch'i-yu 陳奇猶. *Han Fei-tzu chi-shih* 韓非子集釋. 2 vols. Reprinted, Shanghai: Shanghai jen-min ch'u-pan-she, 1974.

Ch'en Ku-ying 陳鼓應. *Lao-tzu chin-chu chin-i* 老子今註今譯. Taipei: Shang-wu yin-shu-kuan, 1960; reprint, 1981.

————, ed. *Chuang-tzu chin-chu chin-i* 莊子今註今譯. 2 vols. Taipei: Shang-wu yin-shu-kuan, 1975; reprint, 1984.

Ch'en Kuo-fu 陳國符. *Tao-tsang yüan-liu k'ao* 道藏源流考. Enlarged edition. Peking: Chung-hua shu-chü, 1963; reprint, Taipei: Ku-t'ing shu-wu, 1975.

Ch'en Shih-hsiang 陳世驤. " 'Hsiang-erh' Lao-tzu Tao-ching Tun-huang ts'an-chüan lun-cheng" 想爾老子道經燉煌殘卷論證. *Tsing Hua Journal of Chinese Studies*, new series, 1, 2 (April 1967): 41–62.

Ch'en Yin-k'o 陳寅恪. "T'ao Yüan-ming chih ssu-hsiang yü ch'ing-t'an chih kuan-hsi" 陶淵明之思想與清談之關係. *Ch'en Yin-k'o hsien-sheng lun-wen chi* 陳寅恪先生論文集. Vol. 2. Taipei: San-jen-hsing ch'u-pan-she, 1974. Pp. 309–33.

————. "Shu Shih-shuo hsin-yü Wen-hsüeh-lei 'Chung Hui tsan Ssu-pen lun shih-pi' t'iao hou" 書世說新語文學類鍾會撰四本論始畢條後. Ibid., pp. 601–7.

Cheng Ch'eng-hai 鄭成海. *Lao-tzu Ho-shang Kung chu chiao-li* 老子河上公注斠理. Taipei: Chung-hua shu-chü, 1971.

————. *Lao-tzu Ho-shang Kung chu su-cheng* 老子河上公注疏證. Taipei: Hua-cheng shu-chü, 1978.

Ch'eng Yi-shan 程宜山. "Wang Pi che-hsüeh ssu-hsiang pien-wei" 王弼哲學思想辨微. *Che-hsüeh yen-chiu*, no. 5 (1984): 54–60.

Chi Ch'eng Hsüan-ying Tao-te ching k'ai-t'i hsü-chüeh i-su 輯成玄英道德經開題序訣義疏. Ed. Yen Ling-feng 嚴靈峰. WCPC. Taipei: I-wen yin-shu-kuan, 1965.

Chiang Hsi-ch'ang 蔣錫昌. *Lao-tzu chiao-ku* 老子校詁. Shanghai: Shang-wu yin-shu-kuan, 1937; reprint, Taipei: Tung-hsing ch'u-pan shih-yeh kung-ssu, 1980.

Chiang Hsia-an 江俠庵. *Hsien-Ch'in ching-chi k'ao* 先秦經籍考. Shanghai, 1933; reprint, Taipei: Ho-lo t'u-shu ch'u-pan-she, 1975.

Chiao Hung 焦竑. *Lao-tzu i* 老子翼. TSCC. Shanghai: Shang-wu yin-shu-kuan, 1940.

Ch'ien Mu 錢穆. "Chung-kuo ssu-hsiang-shih chung chih kuei-shen kuan" 中國思想史中之鬼神觀. *Hsin-ya hsüeh-pao*, 1, 1 (1955): 1–43.

——. "Wang Pi Kuo Hsiang chu I-Lao-Chuang yung Li-tzu t'iao-lu" 王弼郭象注易老莊用理字條錄. *Hsin-ya hsüeh-pao*, 1, 1 (1955): 135–56.

——. *Shih-chi ti-ming k'ao* 史記地名考. Hong Kong: Lung-men shu-tien, 1968.

——. *Chuang Lao t'ung-pien* 莊老通辨. Reprinted, Taipei: San-min shu-chü, 1973.

——. *Chung-kuo hsüeh-shu ssu-hsiang shih lun-ts'ung* 中國學術思想史論叢. Vol. 3. Taipei: Tung-ta T'u-shu, 1977.

Ch'ien Ta-hsi 錢大昕. *Nien-erh shih k'ao-i* 廿二史考異. TSCC. 15 *ts'e*. Shanghai: Shang-wu yin-shu-kuan, 1937.

Chin Ch'un-feng 金春峰. "Yeh t'an Lao-tzu Ho-shang Kung chang-chü chih shih-tai chi ch'i yü Pao-p'u tzu chih kuan-hsi" 也談老子河上公章句之時代及其與抱樸子之關係. *Chung-kuo che-hsüeh* 中國哲學, 9 (1983): 137–68.

——. *Han-tai ssu-hsiang shih* 漢代思想史. Peking: Chung-kuo she-hui k'o-hsüeh ch'u-pan-she, 1987.

Chin-shu 晉書. Peking: Chung-hua shu-chü, 1974; reprint, 1982. 10 vols.

Ch'ing Hsi-t'ai 卿希泰. *Chung-kuo tao-chiao ssu-hsiang shih-kang* 中國道教思想史綱. Vol. 1, *Han Wei liang-Chin Nan-Pei Ch'ao shih-ch'i* 漢魏兩晉南北朝時期. Ch'eng-tu: Szechuan jen-min ch'u-pan-she, 1980.

Chiu T'ang-shu 舊唐書. Peking: Chung-hua shu-chü, 1975. 16 vols.

Chou Chi-chih 周繼旨. "Wei-Chin wen-lun ti hsing-ch'i yü hsüan-hsüeh chung 'T'ien-jen hsin-yi' ti hsing-ch'eng" 魏晉文論的興起與玄學中天人新義的形成 *Che-hsüeh yen-chiu* 哲學研究, no. 5 (1984): 45–53.

Chou-i Cheng-chu 周易鄭注. TSCC. Shanghai: Shang-wu yin-shu-kuan, 1936.

Chou-i chi-chieh 周易集解. Ed. Sun Hsing-yen 孫星衍. TSCC. 10 vols. Shanghai: Shang-wu yin-shu-kuan, 1936.

Chou Shao-hsien 周紹賢. *Wei Chin ch'ing-t'an shu-lun* 魏晉清談述論. Taipei: Shang-wu yin-shu-kuan, 1966.

——. *Tao-chia yü shen-hsien* 道家與神仙. 2nd ed. Taipei: Chung-hua shu-chü, 1974.

Chu Ch'ien-chih 朱謙之. *Lao-tzu chiao-shih* 老子校釋. Shanghai, 1958; reprint, Peking: Chung-hua shu-chü, 1980.

Chu Hsiao-ha 朱曉海. "Ts'ai-hsing Ssu-pen-lun ts'e-i" 才性四本論測義. *Journal of Oriental Studies* (Hong Kong), 18 (1980): 207–24; English abstract, 129–30.

Chu Te-chih 朱得之. *Lao-tzu t'ung-i* 老子通義. WCPC. Taipei: I-wen yin-shu-kuan, 1965.

Chu T'ien-shun 朱天順. *Chung-kuo ku-tai tsung-chiao ch'u-t'an* 中國古代宗教初探. Shanghai: Jen-min ch'u-pan-she, 1982.

Chung Chao-p'eng 鍾肇鵬. "Huang-lao po-shu ti che-hsüeh ssu-hsiang" 黃老帛書的哲學思想. *Wen-wu*, 文物, no. 2 (1978): 63–68.

Fa Lin 法琳. *Pien-cheng lun* 辯正論. Taishō Tripitaka (1927; reprinted, 1960). Vol. 52, no. 2110.

Fan Shou-k'ang 范壽康. *Wei Chin chih ch'ing-t'an* 魏晉之清談. Shanghai: Shang-wu yin-shu-kuan, 1936.

Fu Ch'in-chia 傅勤家. *Chung-kuo Tao-chiao shih* 中國道教史. Shanghai: Shang-wu yin-shu-kuan, 1937; reprint, Taipei: Shang-wu yin-shu-kuan, 1980.

Fujiwara Takao 藤原高男. "Ko Kan rōshichū kō" 顧歡老子注考 *Uchino hakushi kanreki kinen tōyōgaku ronshū* 內野博士還暦記念東洋學論集. Tokyo: Kangibunka kenkyūkai, 1964. Pp. 163–84.

Fukui Kōjun 福井康順. "Katsu-shi-dō no kenkyū" 葛氏道の研究. *Tōyō shisō kenkyū* 東洋思想研究 Ed. Tsuda Saukichi, no. 5. Tokyo: Iwanami shoten, 1954. Pp. 43–86.

————. "Rōshi dōtokukyō joketsu no keisei" 老子道德經序訣の形成.
Nippon-Chūgoku gakkaihō 日本中國學會報, 11 (1959): 27–37.

Hachiya Kunio 蜂屋邦夫. "Son Sei no rekishihyō to rōshi hihan" 孫盛の歷史評と老子批判. *Tōyō bunka kenkyūjo kiyō* 東洋文
化研究所紀要 (Tokyo University), 81 (March 1980): 19–177.

Han Fei-tzu 韓非子. SPPY. Reprinted, Taipei: Chung-hua shu-chü,
1982.

Han Kuo-p'an 韓國磐. *Wei Chin Nan Pei Ch'ao shih-kang* 魏晉南
北朝史綱. Peking: Jen-min ch'u-pan-she, 1983.

Han-shu 漢書. Peking: Chung-hua shu-chü, 1962; reprint, 1983. 12
vols.

Hatano Tarō 波多野太郎. *Rōshi dōtokukyō kenkyū* 老子道德經研究. Tokyo: Kokusho kankōkai, 1979.

Ho Ch'ang-chün 賀昌群. *Wei Chin ch'ing-t'an ssu-hsiang ch'u-lun*
魏晉清談思想初論. Shanghai: Shang-wu yin-shu-kuan, 1947.

Ho Ch'i-min 何啓民. *Wei Chin ssu-hsiang yü t'an-feng* 魏晉思想與談風.
Taipei: Shang-wu yin-shu-kuan, 1967.

Ho-shang Kung 河上公. *Ho-shang Kung chu Lao-tzu Tao-te ching*
河上公注老子道德經. Ku Ch'un Shih-te t'ang 顧春世德堂 edition,
1530. Reprinted, WCPC. Taipei, 1965.

————. *Sung-k'an Ho-shang Kung chu Lao-tzu Tao-te ching* 宋刊河上公
注老子道德經. SPTK. Reprinted, WCPC. Ed. Yen Ling-feng.
Taipei: I-wen yin-shu-kuan, 1965.

————. *Tun-huang hsieh-pen Lao-tzu Ho-shang Kung chu* 敦煌寫本
老子河上公注. WCPC. Taipei, 1965.

Hou Han-shu 後漢書. Peking: Chung-hua shu-chü, 1965. 12 vols.

Hsi K'ang 嵇康. *Sheng-hsien kao-shih chuan* 聖賢高士傳. Yü-han shan-
fang chi i-shu 玉函山房輯佚書, 1889.

Hsieh Fu-ya 謝扶雅. "Hsien-ts'un *Lao-tzu Tao-te ching* chu-shih shu-
mu k'ao-lüeh" 現在老子道德經注釋書目考略. *Ling-nan hsüeh-
pao* 嶺南學報, 1, 3 (June 1930): 59–99.

Hsieh Shou-hao 謝守灝. *Hun-yüan sheng-chi* 混元聖紀. TT 551–553. HY 769.

Hsin T'ang-shu 新唐書. Peking: Chung-hua shu-chü, 1975. 20 vols.

Hsü Fu-kuan 徐復觀. *Chung-kuo jen-hsing-lun shih. Hsien-Ch'in p'ien* 中國人性論史，先秦篇. Taipei: Shang-wu yin-shu-kuan, 1969; reprint, 1984.

———. *Liang Han ssu-hsiang shih* 兩漢思想史. Vol. 2. Hong Kong: Chinese University of Hong Kong Press, 1975.

Hsüan I 玄嶷. *Chen-cheng lun* 甄正論. Taishō Tripitaka (1960). Vol. 52, no. 2112.

Huai-nan tzu 淮南子. SPPY. Reprinted, Taipei: Chung-hua, 1974.

Huang-fu Mi 皇甫謐. *Kao-shih chuan* 高士傳 TSCC. Shanghai: Shang-wu yin-shu-kuan, 1937.

Jao Tsung-i 饒宗頤. "Wu Chien-heng erh-nien Su Tan hsieh-pen Tao-te ching ts'an-chüan k'ao-cheng" 吳建衡二年索紞寫本道德經殘卷考證. *Journal of Oriental Studies* (Hong Kong), 2, 1 (January 1955): 1–71.

———. *Lao-tzu Hsiang-erh chu chiao-chien* 老子想爾注校箋. Hong Kong: Tung-nan ch'u-pan-she, 1956.

———. "Lao-tzu Hsiang-erh chu hsü-lun" 老子想爾注續論. *Fukui hakushi shōju kinen tōyōbunka ronshū* 福井博士頌壽記念東洋文化論集. Tokyo: Waseda University Press, 1969. Pp. 1155–71.

Jung Chao-tsu 容肇祖. *Wei Chin ti tzu-jan chu-i* 魏晉的自然主義. Shanghai: Shang-wu yin-shu-kuan, 1935.

Kanaya Osamu 金谷治. *Shin Kan shisōshi kenkyū* 秦漢思想史研究. Revised edition. Kyoto: Heigakuji shoten, 1981.

Kao Heng 高亨. *Chou-i ta-chuan chin-chu* 周易大傳今註. Shantung: Ch'i Lu shu-she, 1979.

Kao Heng, and Ch'ih Hsi-chao 池曦朝. "Shih-t'an Ma-wang-tui Han-mu chung ti po-shu Lao-tzu" 試談馬王堆漢墓中的帛書老子. *Wen-wu*, no. 11 (1974): 1–7.

Kimura Eiichi 木村英一. "Kōrō kara rōsō oyobi dōkyō e: ryōkan jidai ni okeru rōshi no gaku" 黄老から老荘及び道教へ：兩漢時代における老子の學. *Kyōto daigaku jinbun kagaku kenkyūjo sōritsu 25 shūnen kinen ronbunshū* 京都大學人文科學研究所創立廿五周年記念論文集. Kyoto: Kyoto University, 1954. Pp. 85–144.

Ko Hung 葛洪. *Shen-hsien chuan* 神仙傳. Han-Wei ts'ung-shu, Lung-wei pi-shu, 1794.

Kobayashi Masayoshi 小林正美. "Kajō shinjin shōku no shisō to seiritsu" 河上真人章句の思想と成立. *Tōhō shūkyō*, 65 (1985): 20–43.

Ku Chieh-kang 顧頡剛. *Ch'in Han ti fang-shih yü ju-sheng* 秦漢的方士與儒生. Reprinted, Hong Kong: I-hsin shu-chü, 1976.

Ku Chieh-kang et al., ed. *Ku Shih-pien* 古史辨. 7 vols. Reprinted, Hong Kong: T'ai-p'ing shu-chü, 1962–1963.

Ku Fang 谷方. "Ho-shang Kung Lao-tzu chang-chü k'ao-cheng" 河上公老子章句考證. *Chung-kuo che-hsüeh* (Peking), 7 (1982): 41–57.

Ku Huan Tao-te ching chu-su 顧歡道德經注疏 WCPC. Taipei, 1965.

Ku Shih 顧實. *Han-shu i-wen-chih chiang-su* 漢書藝文志講疏. 2nd edition. Shanghai: Shang-wu yin-shu-kuan, 1935.

Kuo Mo-jo 郭沫若. *Shih p'i-p'an shu* 十批判書. Revised edition. Peking: Jen-min ch'u-pan-she, 1954.

Kuo Po-kung 郭伯恭. *Ssu-k'u ch'üan-shu tsuan-hsiu k'ao* 四庫全書纂修考. National Peking Research Institute, Society for the Study of History Publication. Peking: Shang-wu yin-shu-kuan, 1937.

Kusuyama Haruki 楠山春樹. "Ri Zen shoin no Setsu Sō chū ni tsuite: rōshi kajōkōchū no seiritsu ni chinamu" 李善所引の薛綜注について：老子河上公注の成立に因む. *Fukui hakushi shōju kinen tōyōbunka ronshū* 福井博士頌壽記念東洋文化論集. Tokyo: Waseda University Press, 1969. Pp. 339–54.

————. "Review of Hatano Tarō, *Rōshi dōtokukyō kenkyū*." *Tōhō shūkyō* 東方宗教, 54 (November 1979): 89–98.

————. *Rōshi densetsu no kenkyū* 老子傳說の研究. Tokyo: Sōbunsha, 1979.

Lau, D.C. "Ma-wang-tui Han-mu po-shu Lao-tzu ch'u-t'an" 馬王堆漢墓帛書老子初探. Parts I and II. *Ming-pao yüeh-k'an* 明報月刊, 17, 8 (1982): 11–17; 9 (1982): 35–40.

Li Ch'un 李春. "Lao-tzu Wang Pi chu chiao-ting pu-cheng" 老子王弼注校訂補正. M.A. thesis. Taipei: National Taiwan Normal University, Chinese Studies, 1979.

Liu Hsiang 劉向. *Lieh-hsien chuan* 列仙傳. Ku-chin i-shih edition. Shanghai: Shang-wu yin-shu-kuan, 1937.

Liu Kuo-chün 劉國鈞. "Lao-tzu Wang Pi chu chiao-chi" 老子王弼注校記. *T'u-shu-kuan hsüeh chi-k'an* 圖書館學季刊. (Peking), 8, 1 (March 1934): 91–116.

————. "Lao-tzu shen-hua k'ao-lüeh" 老子神化玫略. *Chin-ling hsüeh-pao* 金陵學報 4, 2 (1934): 61–87.

Liu Ta-chieh 劉大杰. *Wei Chin ssu-hsiang lun* 魏晉思想論. Shanghai: Chung-hua shu-chü, 1939; reprint, Taipei, 1979.

Liu Ts'un-yan 柳存仁. "Tao-tsang pen san-sheng chu Tao-te ching chih te-shih" 道藏本三聖注道德經之得失. *Chung Chi hsüeh-pao* 崇基學報 9, 1 (November 1969): 1–9.

————. "Lun Tao-tsang pen Ku Huan chu Lao-tzu chih hsing-chih" 論道藏本顧歡注老子之性質. *Lien-ho shu-yüan hsüeh-pao* 聯合書院學報 (United College Journal) (Hong Kong), 8 (1970–1971): 15–28.

————. "Tao-tsang pen san-sheng chu Tao-te ching hui-chien" 道藏本三聖注道德經會箋. Parts I-III. *Chung-kuo wen-hua yen-chiu-so hsüeh-pao* 中國文化研究所學報 (Chinese University of Hong Kong), 4, 2 (1971): 287–343; 5, 1 (1972): 9–75; 6, 1 (1973): 1–43.

Lou Yü-lieh 樓宇烈. *Wang Pi chi chiao-shih* 王弼集校釋. 2 vols. Peking: Chung-hua shu-chü, 1980.

Lu Hsi-sheng 陸希聲. *Tao-te chen-ching chuan* 道德真經傳. WCPC. Taipei: I-wen yin-shu-kuan, 1965.

Lü K'ai 呂凱. *Wei Chin hsüan-hsüeh hsi-p'ing* 魏晉玄學析評. Taipei: Shih-chi shu-chü, 1980.

Lü Ssu-mien 呂思勉. *Sui T'ang Wu-tai shih* 隋唐五代史. 2 vols. Shanghai: Chung-hua shu-chü, 1959; reprint, 1961.

────. *Ch'in Han Shih* 秦漢史. 2 vols. Hong Kong: T'ai-p'ing shu-chü, 1962.

Lu Te-ming 陸德明. *Ching-tien shih-wen* 經典釋文. Ch. 1, *Hsü-lu* 序錄 and 25, *Lao-tzu yin-i* 老子音義. TSCC. Shanghai: Shang-wu yin-shu-kuan, 1936. Vols. 1 and 16.

Lun-yü chi-chieh i-su 論語集解義疏. Commentary by Ho Yen 何晏. Explanation by Huang K'an 皇侃. TSCC. 4 vols. Shanghai: Shang-wu yin-shu-kuan, 1937.

Lun-yü chu-su chieh-ching 論語注疏解經. Commentary by Ho Yen. Explanation by Hsing Ping 邢昺. Taipei: Chung-kuo tzu-hsüeh ming-chu chi-ch'eng, 1977.

Lung Hui 龍晦. "Ma-wang-tui ch'u-t'u Lao-tzu i-pen ch'ien ku-i-shu t'an-yüan" 馬王堆出土老子乙本前古佚書探原. *K'ao-ku hsüeh-pao* 考古學報, no. 2 (1975): 23–32.

Ma Hsü-lun 馬敘倫. *Lao-tzu chiao-ku* 老子校詁. Revised edition. Peking, 1956; reprint, Hong Kong: T'ai-p'ing shu-chü, 1965.

Ma-wang-tui Han-mu po-shu 馬王堆漢墓帛書. Vol. 1. Ed. Kuo-chia wen-wu chü ku-wen-hsien yen-chiu-shih 國家文物局古文獻研究室. Peking: Wen-wu ch'u-pan-she, 1980.

Ma-wang-tui Han-mu po-shu: Ching-fa 馬王堆漢墓帛書：經法. Ed. Ma-wang-tui Han-mu po-shu cheng-li hsiao-tsu 馬王堆漢墓帛書整理小組. Peking: Wen-wu ch'u-pan-she, 1976.

Mou Jun-sun 牟潤孫. *Lun Wei Chin i-lai chih ch'ung-shang t'an-pien chi ch'i yin-hsiang* 論魏晉以來之崇尚談辯及其影響. Hong Kong: Chinese University of Hong Kong Press, 1966.

Mou Tsung-san 牟宗三. *Ts'ai-hsing yü hsüan-li* 才性與玄理. 3rd edition. Taipei: Hsüeh-sheng shu-chü, 1974.

Naitō Motoharu 内藤幹治. "Rōshi kajōkōchū no kōhon ni tsuite" 老子河上公注の校本について. *Shūkan tōyōgaku* 集刊東洋學, 19 (May 1968): 70–81.

———. "Kajōkō chū rōshi no yōjōsetsu ni tsuite" 河上公注老子の養生説について. *Yoshioka hakushi kanreki kinen dōkyō kenkyū ronshū* 吉岡博士還暦記念道教研究論集 Tokyo: Kokusho kankōkai, 1977. Pp. 319–39.

Noma Kazunori 野間和則. "Ō Hitsu ni tsuite: rōshichū o megutte" 王弼について：老子注をめぐって. *Tōhō shūkyō*, 59 (May 1982): 66–83.

Ōfuchi Ninji 大淵忍爾. "Rōshi dōtokukyō joketsu no seiritsu" 老子道德經序訣の成立. Parts I-II. *Tōyō gakuhō* 東洋學報, 42, 1 (1959): 1–40; 42, 2 (1959): 52–85.

———. "Gotobeidō no kyōhō ni tsuite: rōshi sōjichū o chūshin to shite" 五斗米道の教法について：老子想爾注を中心として. Parts I-II. *Tōyō gakuhō*, 49, 3 (December 1966): 40–68; 49, 4 (March 1967): 97–129.

———. "Rōshi sōjichū to kajōkōchū to no kankei ni tsuite" 老子想爾注と河上公注との關係について. *Yamazaki sensei taikan kinen tōyōshigaku ronshū* 山崎先生退官記念東洋史學論集. Tokyo, 1967. Pp. 103–8.

———. *Tonkō dōkyō* 敦煌道經. Vol. 1. *Mokuroku hen* 目錄篇. Tokyo: Hukubu shoten, 1978. Section 3, *Dōtokukyō rui* 道德經類. Pp. 187–250.

P'eng Ssu 彭耜. *Tao-te chen-ching chi-chu tsa-shuo* 道德真經集註雜説. TT 403. HY 709.

Saiki Tetsurō 齋木哲郎 "Kōrō shisō no saikentō" 黄老思想の再檢討. *Tōhō shūkyō* 東方宗教, 62 (October 1983): 19–36.

———. "Maōtai hakusho yori mita dōka shisō no ichi sokumen" 馬王堆帛書より見た道家思想の一側面. *Tōhōgaku* 東方學, 69 (January 1985): 44–58.

Sakai Tadao 酒井忠夫. "Review of Kusuyama Haruki's *Rōshi densetsu no kenkyū.*" *Tōhō shūkyō*, 55 (July 1980): 107–15.

San-kuo chih 三國志. Peking: Chung-hua shu-chü, 1959; reprint, 1982. 5 vols.

Sawada Takio 澤田多喜男. "Rōshi Ō Hitsu chū kōsatsu ichihan" 老子王弼注考察一斑. *Tōyō bunka* 東洋文化, 62 (March 1982): 1–28.

Shih-chi 史記. SPPY edition. Taipei: Chung-hua shu-chü, 1970.

Shih Tao-shih 釋道世. *Fa-yüan chu-lin* 法苑珠林. SPTK edition. Reprinted, Taipei: Shang-wu yin-shu-kuan, 1965.

Shima Kunio 島邦男. *Rōshi kōsei* 老子校正. Tokyo: Kyūkoshoin, 1973.

———. "Rōshi kajōkō hon no seiritsu" 老子河上公本の成立 *Uno Tetsuto sensei hakuju shukuga kinen tōyōgaku ronsō* 宇野哲人先生白壽祝賀記念東洋學論叢. Tokyo, 1974. Pp. 529–49.

———. "Maōtai rōshi kara mita kajōkō hon" 馬王堆老子から見た河上公本. *Shūkan tōyōgaku*, 36 (November 1976): 1–26.

———. *Gogyō shisō to Raiki Getsurei no kenkyū* 五行思想と禮記月令の研究. Tokyo: Kyūkoshoin, 1971.

Ssu-k'u ch'üan-shu tsung-mu t'i-yao 四庫全書總目提要. *Tao-chia lei* 道家類 (Taoist Section). Ed. Chi Yün 紀昀 et al. Wan-yu wen-k'u. Shanghai: Shang-wu yin-shu-kuan, 1935. Vol. 28.

Sui-shu 隋書. Peking: Chung-hua shu-chü, 1973. 6 vols.

Sun K'o-huan 孫克寬. "T'ang i-ch'ien Lao-tzu ti shen-hua" 唐以前老子的神話. *Ta-lu tsa-chih* 大陸雜誌, no. 1 (1974): 1–12.

Sung-shih 宋史. Peking: Chung-hua shu-chü, 1977. 20 vols.

Takeuchi Yoshio 武内義雄. *Rōshi genshi* 老子原始. Tokyo: Shimizu Kōbundō, 1926; reprint, 1967.

———. *Rōshi no kenkyū* 老子之研究. Tokyo: Kaizosha, 1927.

———. *Takeuchi Yoshio zenshū* 武内義雄全集. Vol. 5. *Rōshi hen* 老子篇. Tokyo: Kadokawa shoten, 1978.

T'ang Ch'ang-ju 唐長孺. *Wei Chin Nan Pei Ch'ao shih lun-ts'ung* 魏晉南北朝史論叢. Peking: San-lien shu-tien, 1955; reprint, 1978.

————. *Wei Chin Nan Pei Ch'ao shih lun shih-i* 魏晉南北朝史拾遺. Peking: Chung-hua shu-chü, 1983.

T'ang Chün-i 唐君毅. "Lun Chung-kuo che-hsüeh ssu-hsiang-shih chung 'Li' chih liu-i" 論中國哲學思想史中理之六義. *Hsin-ya hsüeh-pao* 新亞學報, 1, 1 (1955): 45–98.

T'ang Lan 唐蘭. "Huang-ti ssu-ching ch'u-t'an" 黃帝四經初探. *Wen-wu* 文物, no. 10 (1974): 48–52.

T'ang Wen-po 唐文播. "Ho-shang Kung Lao-tzu chang-chü tso-che k'ao" 河上公老子章句作者考. *Tung-fang tsa-chih* 東方雜誌, 39, 9 (July 1943): 44–50.

T'ang Yung-t'ung 湯用彤. *Wei Chin hsüan-hsüeh lun-kao* 魏晉玄學論稿. Peking: Jen-min ch'u-pan-she, 1957.

T'ang Yung-t'ung and Jen Chi-yü 任繼愈. *Wei Chin hsüan-hsüeh chung ti she-hui cheng-chih ssu-hsiang lüeh-lun* 魏晉玄學中的社會政治思想略論. Shanghai: Jen-min ch'u-pan-she, n.d.

Ts'ao Ts'ao chi 曹操集. Peking: Chung-hua shu-chü, 1959; reprint, 1962.

Tu Kuang-t'ing 杜光庭. *Tao-te chen-ching kuang sheng-i* 道德真經廣聖義. TT 440–448. HY 725.

Tu Tao-chien 杜道堅. *Hsüan-ching yüan-chih fa-hui* 玄經原旨發揮. TT 391. HY 703.

Tu Wei-ming 杜維明. "Ts'ung 'Yi' tao 'Yen'" 從意到言. *Chung-hua wen-shih lun-ts'ung* 中華文史論叢. First Series. Shanghai: Ku-chi ch'u-pan-she, 1981. Pp. 255–61.

————. "Wei Chin hsüan-hsüeh chung ti t'i-yen ssu-hsiang: Shih-lun Wang Pi 'Sheng-jen t'i-wu' i kuan-lien ti che-hsüeh yi-i" 魏晉玄學中的體驗思想：試論王弼聖人體無一觀念的哲學意義. *Ming-pao yüeh-k'an*, 18, 9 (1983): 21–26.

Tung Ssu-ching 董思靖. *T'ai-shang Lao-tzu tao-te ching chi-chieh* 太上老子道德經集解. Shih-wan-chüan lou edition, 1877.

Usami Shinsui 宇佐美灊水, revised and ed. *Ō chū rōshi dōtoku shinkyō* 王注老子道德真經. WCPC. Taipei: I-wen, 1965.

Wang Chih-ming 王志銘, ed. *Lao-tzu wei-chih li-lüeh, Wang Pi chu tsung-chi* 老子微指例略王弼注總輯. Taipei: Tung-hsing ch'u-pan shih-yeh, 1980.

Wang Ch'ung 王充. *Lun Heng* 論衡. Hong Kong: Kuang-chih shu-chü, n.d.

Wang Chung-lo 王仲犖. *Wei Chin Nan Pei Ch'ao shih* 魏晉南北朝史. 2 vols. Shanghai: Jen-min ch'u-pan-she, 1979; reprint, 1981.

Wang Chung-min 王重民. *Lao-tzu k'ao* 老子考. Peking, 1927; reprint, Taipei: Tung-hsing ch'u-pan shih-yeh, 1981.

Wang Fu 王符. *Ch'ien-fu lun* 潛夫論. SPTK edition; reprint, Taipei: Shang-wu yin-shu-kuan, 1965.

Wang Hui 王恢. *Shui Ching chu Han hou-kuo chi-shih* 水經注漢侯國集釋. Taipei: Chung-kuo Wen-hua ta-hsüeh ch'u-pan-pu, 1981.

Wang Ming 王明. *T'ai-p'ing ching ho-chiao* 太平經合校. Peking: Chung-hua shu-chü, 1979; first published, 1960.

——— . *Pao-p'u tzu nei-p'ien chiao-shih* 抱朴子內篇校釋. Peking: Chung-hua shu-chü, 1980.

——— . *Tao-chia ho Tao-chiao ssu-hsiang yen-chiu* 道家和道教思想研究. Ch'ung-ch'ing: Chung-kuo she-hui k'o-hsüeh ch'u-pan-she, 1984.

Wang Pi 王弼. *Chou-i lüeh-li* 周易略例. With Commentary by Hsing T'ao 邢璹. Hsüeh-ching t'ao-yüan edition, First series, 12. Shanghai: Shang-wu yin-shu-kuan, 1922.

——— . *Lao-tzu wei-chih li-lüeh* 老子微指例略. Ed. Yen Ling-feng 嚴靈峰. WCPC. Taipei: I-wen yin-shu-kuan, 1965.

——— . *Tao-te chen-ching chu* 道德真經注. TT 373. HY 690. WCPC. Taipei: I-wen, 1965.

——— . *Lao-tzu* 老子. SPPY edition. Taipei: Chung-hua shu-chü, 1981.

Wang Shu-min 王叔岷. "Huang-lao k'ao" 黃老考. *Journal of Oriental Studies* (Hong Kong), 13, 2 (July 1975): 146–53.

Yang Po-chün 楊伯峻, ed. *Lieh-tzu chi-shih* 列子集釋. Hong Kong: T'ai-p'ing shu-chü, 1965; original, Shanghai, 1958.

Yang Yung 楊勇, ed. *Shih-shuo hsin-yü chiao-chien* 世說新語校箋. Hong Kong: Ta-chung shu-chü, 1969.

Yen Ling-feng 嚴靈峰. *Chung-wai Lao-tzu chu-shu mu-lu* 中外老子著述目錄. Taipei: Chung-hua ts'ung-shu wei-yüan-hui, 1957.

———. *Wu-ch'iu pei-chai hsüeh-shu lun-chi* 無求備齋學術論集. Taipei: Chung-hua shu-chü, 1969.

———. *Lao Chuang yen-chiu* 老莊研究. 2nd edition. Taipei: Chung-hua shu-chü, 1979.

Yen Tsun 嚴遵. *Tao-te chih-kuei lun* 道德指歸論. WCPC. Taipei, 1965.

Yoshioka Yoshitoyo 吉岡義豐. "Rōshi kajōkō hon to dōkyō" 老子河上公本と道教. *Dōkyō no sōgōteki kenkyū* 道教の總合的研究. Proceedings of the 2nd International Conference on Taoist Studies. Ed. Sakai Tadao 酒井忠夫. Tokyo: Kokusho kankōkai, 1977. Pp. 291–332.

Yü Ying-shih 余英時. "Han Chin chih-chi shih chih hsin-tzu-chüeh yü hsin-ssu-ch'ao" 漢晉之際士之新自覺與新思潮. *Hsin-ya hsüeh-pao*, 4, 1 (1959): 25–144.

———. *Chung-kuo chih-shih chieh-ts'eng shih-lun (ku-tai p'ien)* 中國知識階層史論，古代篇. Taipei: Lien-ching, 1980.

———. "Chung-kuo ku-tai ssu-hou shih-chieh kuan ti yen-pien" 中國古代死後世界觀的演變. *Ming-pao yüeh-k'an*, 18, 9 (1983): 12–20.

Western Sources

Ames, Roger T. *The Art of Rulership: A Study in Ancient Chinese Political Thought*. Honolulu: University of Hawaii Press, 1983.

Andersen, Poul. *The Method of Holding the Three Ones: A Taoist Manual of Meditation of the Fourth Century A.D.* London: Curzon Press, 1980.

Balazs, Etienne. *Chinese Civilization and Bureaucracy: Variations on a Theme*. Trans. Hope M. Wright. Ed. A. F. Wright. New Haven and London: Yale University Press, 1964.

Bauer, Wolfgang. *China and the Search for Happiness: Recurring Themes in Four Thousand Years of Chinese Cultural History*. Trans. Michael Shaw. New York: Seabury Press, 1976.

Bodde, Derk. "On Translating Chinese Philosophic Terms." *Far Eastern Quarterly*, 14, 2 (February 1955): 231–44.

Boltz, William G. "Review of *A Translation of Lao-tzu's Tao-te ching and Wang Pi's Commentary* by Paul J. Lin." In *Journal of the American Oriental Society*, 100, 1 (1980): 84–86.

————. "The Religious and Philosophical Significance of the 'Hsiang Erh' *Lao-tzu* in the Light of the *Ma-wang-tui* Silk Manuscripts." *Bulletin of the School of Oriental and African Studies*, 45, 1 (1982): 95–117.

————. "Textual Criticism and the Ma Wang Tui *Lao-tzu*." *Harvard Journal of Asiatic Studies*, 44, 1 (1984): 185–224.

————. "The *Lao-tzu* Text that Wang Pi and Ho-shang Kung Never Saw." *Bulletin of the School of Oriental and African Studies*, 48 (1985): 493–501.

Boodberg, Peter A. "Philological Notes on Chapter One of the *Lao Tzu*." *Harvard Journal of Asiatic Studies*, 20 (1957): 598–618.

Chan, Alan K. L. "Philosophical Hermeneutics and the *Analects*: The Paradigm of Tradition." *Philosophy East and West*, 34 (1984): 421–36.

————. "The Formation of the Ho-shang Kung Legend." *Sages and Filial Sons: Studies on Early China*. Ed. Julia Ching. Hong Kong: Chinese University Press.

Chan, Wing-tsit. "Review of *A Translation of Lao-tzu's Tao-te ching and Wang Pi's Commentary* by Paul J. Lin." *Philosophy East and West*, 29, 3 (1979): 357–60.

————, comp. *A Source Book in Chinese Philosophy*. Princeton: Princeton University Press, 1963; reprint, 1973.

————, trans. *The Way of Lao Tzu*. Indianapolis: Bobbs-Merrill, 1963; reprint, 1981.

Chang, Chung-yue. "The Metaphysics of Wang Pi (226–249)." Ph.D. dissertation. University of Pennsylvania, 1979.

Ch'en, Ch'i-yün. "A Confucian Magnate's Idea of Political Violence: Hsün Shuang's (128–190 A.D.) Interpretation of the Book of Changes." *T'oung Pao*, 54 (1968): 73–115.

——— . *Hsün Yüeh (A.D. 148–209): The Life and Reflections of an Early Medieval Confucian*. Cambridge: Cambridge University Press, 1975.

——— . *Hsün Yüeh and the Mind of Late Han China*. Princeton: Princeton University Press, 1980.

Ch'en, Kenneth K. S. *Buddhism in China: A Historical Survey*. Princeton: Princeton University Press, 1964; reprint, 1973.

Ch'en, Ku-ying. *Lao Tzu: Text, Notes, and Comments*. Trans. Rhett Y. W. Young and R. T. Ames. San Francisco: Chinese Materials Center, 1981.

Ching, Julia. "The Mirror Symbol Revisited: Confucian and Taoist Mysticism." *Mysticism and Religious Traditions*. Ed. Steven T. Katz. Oxford: Oxford University Press, 1983. Pp. 226–46.

Creel, Herrlee G. *What is Taoism? And Other Studies in Chinese Cultural History*. Chicago and London: University of Chicago Press, 1970; reprint, 1977.

——— . *Shen Pu-hai: A Chinese Political Philosopher of the Fourth Century B.C.* Chicago and London: University of Chicago Press, 1974.

de Crespigny, Rafe. *Portents of Protest in the Later Han Dynasty: The Memorials of Hsiang K'ai to Emperor Huan*. Oriental Monograph Series, 19. Canberra: Faculty of Asian Studies, Australian National University, 1976.

DeWoskin, Kenneth J., trans. *Doctors, Diviners, and Magicians of Ancient China: Biographies of Fang-shih*. New York: Columbia University Press, 1983.

Erkes, Eduard, trans. *Ho-shang Kung's Commentary on Lao-tse*. Ascona, Switzerland: Artibus Asiae, 1958.

Forke, Alfred, trans. *Lun-heng*. Part 1. *Philosophical Essays of Wang*

Ch'ung. 2nd edition. New York: Paragon Book Gallery, 1962; original, 1907.

Fung, Yu-lan. *A History of Chinese Philosophy.* Trans. Derk Bodde. 2 vols. Princeton: Princeton University Press, 1952, 1953; reprint, 1983.

Girardot, Norman J. *Myth and Meaning in Early Taoism.* Berkeley: University of California Press, 1983.

Graham, A. C. " 'Being' in Western Philosophy Compared With *Shih/Fei* and *Yu/Wu* in Chinese Philosophy." *Asia Major,* new series, 7, 1–2 (1959): 79–112.

————. "How Much of *Chuang Tzu* Did Chuang Tzu Write?" *Studies in Classical Chinese Thought.* Ed. Henry Rosemont, Jr., and Benjamin I. Schwartz. *Journal of the American Academy of Religion Thematic Issue* (1979). Chico: American Academy of Religion, 1980. Pp. 459–501.

————, trans. *Chuang-tzu: The Seven Inner Chapters and Other Writings from the Book Chuang-tzu.* London: George Allen and Unwin, 1981.

Hansen, Chad. *Language and Logic in Ancient China.* Ann Arbor: University of Michigan Press, 1983.

Henderson, John B. *The Development and Decline of Chinese Cosmology.* New York: Columbia University Press, 1984.

Henricks, Robert G. "Examining the Ma-wang-tui Silk Texts of the *Lao-tzu:* With Special Note of their Differences from the Wang Pi Text." In *T'oung Pao,* 65, 4–5 (1979): 166–99.

————. "The Philosophy of Lao-tzu Based on the Ma-wang-tui Texts: Some Preliminary Observations." *Society for the Study of Chinese Religions Bulletin* (now renamed *Journal of Chinese Religions*), no. 9 (fall 1981): 59–78.

————. "Hsi K'ang and Argumentation in the Wei." *Journal of Chinese Philosophy,* 8 (1981): 169–223.

————. "On the Chapter Divisions in the *Lao-tzu.*" *Bulletin of the School of Oriental and African Studies,* 45, 3 (1982): 501–24.

————, trans. *Philosophy and Argumentation in Third-Century China:*

The Essays of Hsi K'ang. Princeton: Princeton University Press, 1983.

Hsu, Cho-yun. "The Concept of Pre-Determination and Fate in the Han." *Early China*, 1 (fall 1975): 51–56.

Hu, Shih. "The Concept of Immortality in Chinese Thought." *Harvard Divinity School Bulletin*, 43, 3 (March 1946): 23–42.

Hung, William. "A Bibliographical Controversy at the T'ang Court A.D. 719." *Harvard Journal of Asiatic Studies*, 20 (1957): 74–134.

Jan, Yün-hua. "The Silk Manuscripts on Taoism." *T'oung Pao*, 43, 1 (1977): 65–84.

————. "Tao, Principle, and Law: The Three Key Concepts in the Yellow Emperor Taoism." *Journal of Chinese Philosophy*, 7, 3 (September 1980): 205–28.

————, trans. "*Tao Yüan* or Tao: The Origin." *Journal of Chinese Philosophy*, 7, 3 (September 1980): 195–204.

Kierman, Frank A., Jr. *Ssu-ma Ch'ien's Historiographical Attitude as Reflected in Four Late Warring States Biographies.* Wiesbaden: Otto Harrassowitz, 1962.

Kohn, Livia, ed., in cooperation with Yoshinobu Sakade. *Taoist Meditation and Longevity Techniques.* Ann Arbor: Center for Chinese Studies, University of Michigan, 1989.

Lau, D. C. *Chinese Classics. Tao Te Ching.* Hong Kong: Chinese University Press, 1982.

————, trans. *Lao Tzu Tao Te Ching.* Harmondsworth: Penguin Books, 1963; reprint, 1980.

————, trans. *Confucius. The Analects.* Harmondsworth: Penguin Books, 1979.

Le Blanc, Charles. *Huai-nan Tzu: Philosophical Synthesis in Early Han Thought.* Hong Kong: Hong Kong University Press, 1985.

Legge, James. *The Sacred Books of the East.* Vol. 16. *The Texts of Confucianism.* Part 2. *The Yi King.* Oxford: Oxford University Press, 1882; reprint, Delhi: Motilal Banarsidass, 1968.

————, trans. *The Chinese Classics.* Vol. 1. *Confucius. Confucian Analects, the Great Learning and the Doctrine of the Mean.* 2nd revised edition. Oxford: Clarendon Press, 1893; reprint, New York: Dover, 1971.

Levy, Howard S. "Yellow Turban Religion and Rebellion at the End of Han." *Journal of the American Oriental Society*, 76, 4 (1956): 214–27.

Lin, Paul J., trans. *A Translation of Lao-tzu's Tao-te ching and Wang Pi's Commentary.* Michigan Papers in Chinese Studies, 30. Ann Arbor: Center for Chinese Studies, University of Michigan, 1977.

Liu, James J. Y. *Chinese Theories of Literature.* Chicago and London: University of Chicago Press, 1975.

Loewe, Michael. "Manuscripts Found Recently in China: A Preliminary Survey." *T'oung Pao*, 63, 2–3 (1977): 99–136.

——— . *Ways to Paradise: The Chinese Quest for Immortality.* London: George Allen and Unwin, 1979.

——— . *Chinese Ideas of Life and Death: Faith, Myth, and Reason in the Han Period (202 B.C.–220 A.D.).* London: George Allen and Unwin, 1982.

Maspero, Henri. *Taoism and Chinese Religion.* Trans. Frank A. Kierman, Jr. Amherst: University of Massachusetts Press, 1981.

Mather, Richard B. "The Controversy over Conformity and Naturalness during the Six Dynasties." *History of Religions*, 9, 2–3 (1969–1970): 160–80.

——— , trans. *Shih-shuo Hsin-yü: A New Account of Tales of the World, by Liu I-ch'ing.* Minneapolis: University of Minnesota Press, 1976.

Moore, Charles A., ed. *The Chinese Mind: Essentials of Chinese Philosophy and Culture.* Honolulu: University of Hawaii Press, 1967; reprint, 1977.

Needham, Joseph. *Science and Civilisation in China.* Vol. 2. *History of Scientific Thought.* Cambridge: Cambridge University Press, 1956; reprint, 1972.

——— . *Science and Civilisation in China.* Vol. 5, part 2. *Chemistry and Chemical Technology. Spagyrical Discovery and Invention: Magisteries of Gold and Immortality.* Cambridge: Cambridge University Press, 1974; reprint, 1975.

Ngo, Van Xuyet. *Divination, magie, et politique dans la Chine ancienne.* Bibliothèque de l'École des Hautes Études, section des sciences religieuses, vol. 73. Paris: Presses Universitaires de France, 1976.

Pelliot, Paul. "Autour d'une Traduction Sanscrite du Tao To King." *T'oung Pao,* 13 (1912): 351–430.

Robinet, Isabelle. *Les Commentaires du Tao To King jusqu'au VIIe siècle.* Mémoires de l'Institut des Hautes Études Chinoises, vol. 5. Paris: Presses Universitaires de France, 1977.

———. *Méditation taoiste.* Paris: Dervy Livres, 1979.

———. "Metamorphosis and Deliverance from the Corpse in Taoism." *History of Religions,* 19, 1 (August 1979): 37–70.

Rubin, Vitaly A. "The Concepts of *wu-hsing* and *yin-yang.*" *Journal of Chinese Philosophy,* 9, 2 (June 1982): 131–57.

Rump, Ariane, and Wing-tsit Chan, trans. *Commentary on the Lao-tzu by Wang Pi.* Monographs of the Society for Asian and Comparative Philosophy, no. 6. Honolulu: University Press of Hawaii, 1979.

Schipper, Kristofer. "The Taoist Body." *History of Religions,* 17, 3–4 (1978): 355–86.

———. *Le corps taoiste.* Paris: Fayard, 1982.

Schwartz, Benjamin I. *The World of Thought in Ancient China.* Cambridge: Harvard University Press, 1985.

Seidel, Anna K. *La Divinisation de Lao Tseu dans le Taoisme des Han.* Publications de l'École Française d'Extrême-Orient, vol. 71. Paris: École Française d'Extrême-Orient, 1969.

———. "The Image of the Perfect Ruler in Early Taoist Messianism: Lao-tzu and Li Hung." *History of Religions,* 9, 2–3 (1969–1970): 216–47.

———. "Tokens of Immortality in Han Graves," with an Appendix by Marc Kalinowski. *Numen,* 29, 1 (July 1982): 79–122.

———. "Imperial Treasures and Taoist Sacraments: Taoist Roots in the Apocrypha." *Tantric and Taoist Studies in Honour of R. A. Stein.* Ed. M. Strickmann. Vol. 2. Brussels, Institut Belge des Hautes Études Chinoises, 1983. Pp. 291–371.

Shih, Vincent Y. C., trans. *The Literary Mind and the Carving of Drag-ons by Liu Hsieh: A Study of Thought and Pattern in Chinese Liter-ature*. Records of Civilization: Sources and Studies, no. 58. New York: Columbia University Press, 1959.

Shryock, J. K., trans. *The Study of Human Abilities: The Jen Wu Chih of Liu Shao*. American Oriental Series, vol. 11. New Haven: American Oriental Society, 1937; reprint, New York, 1966.

Sivin, Nathan. "On the Word 'Taoist' as a Source of Perplexity. With Special Reference to the Relations of Science and Religion in Traditional China." *History of Religions*, 17, 3–4 (1978): 303–30.

Solomon, Bernard S. " 'One is No Number' in China and the West." *Harvard Journal of Asiatic Studies*, 17 (1954): 253–60.

Stein, Rolf A. "Remarques sur les Mouvements du Taoisme politico-religieux au IIe siècle AP J.-C." *T'oung Pao*, 50, 1–3 (1963): 1–78.

Strickmann, Michel. "History, Anthropology, and Chinese Reli-gion." *Harvard Journal of Asiatic Studies*, 40, 1 (June 1980): 201–48.

T'ang, Yung-t'ung. "Wang Pi's New Interpretation of the *I Ching* and the *Lun-yü*." Trans. Walter Liebenthal. *Harvard Journal of Asiatic Studies*, 10, 2 (1947): 124–61.

Tu, Wei-ming. "The 'Thought of Huang-Lao': A Reflection on the Lao Tzu and Huang Ti Texts in the Silk Manuscripts of Ma-wang-tui." *Journal of Asian Studies*, 39, 1 (1979): 95–110.

Twitchett, Denis, and Michael Loewe, eds. *The Cambridge History of China*. Vol. 1. *The Ch'in and Han Empires, 221 B.C.–A.D. 220*. Cambridge: Cambridge University Press, 1986.

Vandermeersch, Léon. *La Formation du Légisme*. Paris: École Française d'Extrême-Orient, 1965.

Wagner, Rudolf G. "Wang Pi: 'The Structure of the Laozi's Pointers' (*Laozi weizhi lilüe*)." *T'oung Pao*, 72 (1986): 92–129.

Waley, Arthur. *The Way and Its Power: A Study of the Tao Te Ching and Its Place in Chinese Thought*. New York: Grove Press, 1958; re-print, 1980.

Wang, Hsiao-po, and Leo S. Chang. *The Philosophical Foundations of*

Han Fei's Political Theory. Honolulu: University of Hawaii Press, 1986.

Ware, James R. "The *Wei Shu* and the *Sui Shu* on Taoism." *Journal of the American Oriental Society,* 53, 3 (1933): 215–50.

————, trans. and ed. *Alchemy, Medicine, and Religion in the China of A.D. 320: The Nei P'ien of Ko Hung.* Cambridge: MIT Press, 1966; reprint, New York: Dover, 1981.

Watson, Burton, trans. *Records of the Grand Historian of China Translated from the Shih Chi of Ssu-ma Ch'ien.* 2 vols. New York and London: Columbia University Press, 1961.

————, trans. *The Complete Works of Chuang Tzu.* New York and London: Columbia University Press, 1968.

Welch, Holmes. *Taoism: The Parting of the Way.* Revised edition. Boston: Beacon Press, 1965.

————, and Anna Seidel, eds. *Facets of Taoism: Essays in Chinese Religion.* New Haven and London: Yale University Press, 1979.

Wilhelm, Hellmut. *Eight Lectures on the I Ching.* Trans. Cary F. Baynes. Bollingen Series, 62. Princeton: Princeton University Press, 1960; reprint, 1973.

Wilhelm, Richard, trans. *The I Ching or Book of Changes.* Trans. C. F. Baynes. Bollingen Series, 19. Princeton: Princeton University Press, 1950; reprint, 1979.

Wright, A. F. "Review of A. A. Petrov, *Wang Pi: His Place in the History of Chinese Philosophy.*" *Harvard Journal of Asiatic Studies,* 10 (1947): 75–88.

Yu, David C. "Present-day Taoist Studies." *Religious Studies Review,* 3,4 (October 1977): 220–39.

Yü, Ying-shih. "Life and Immortality in the Mind of Han China." *Harvard Journal of Asiatic Studies,* 25 (1964–65): 80–122.

————. "New Evidence on the Early Chinese Conception of Afterlife—A Review Article." *Journal of Asian Studies,* 41, 1 (November 1981): 81–85.

————. "Individualism and the Neo-Taoist Movement in Wei-Chin China." *Individualism and Holism: Studies in Confucian and Taoist*

Values. Ed. Donald Munro. Ann Arbor: Center for Chinese Studies, University of Michigan, 1985. Pp. 121–55.

————. " 'O Soul, Come Back!' A Study in the Changing Conceptions of the Soul and Afterlife in Pre-Buddhist China." *Harvard Journal of Asiatic Studies*, 47 (1987): 363–95.

Zürcher, Erik. "Buddhist Influence on Early Taoism: A Survey of Scriptural Evidence." *T'oung Pao*, 66, 1–3 (1980): 84–147.

Index